THE TWO TARÍACURIS
and the Early Colonial and
Prehispanic Past of Michoacán

THE TWO TARÍACURIS

and the Early Colonial and Prehispanic Past of Michoacán

David L. Haskell

UNIVERSITY PRESS OF COLORADO

Louisville

© 2018 by University Press of Colorado

Published by University Press of Colorado
245 Century Circle, Suite 202
Louisville, Colorado 80027

 The University Press of Colorado is a proud member of
the Association of University Presses.

The University Press of Colorado is a cooperative publishing enterprise supported, in part, by Adams State University, Colorado State University, Fort Lewis College, Metropolitan State University of Denver, Regis University, University of Colorado, University of Northern Colorado, Utah State University, and Western State Colorado University.

∞ This paper meets the requirements of the ANSI/NISO Z39.48-1992 (Permanence of Paper).

ISBN: 978-1-60732-820-9 (cloth)
ISBN: 978-1-60732-748-6 (paper)
ISBN: 978-1-60732-749-3 (ebook)
DOI: https://doi.org/10.5876/9781607327493

Library of Congress Cataloging-in-Publication Data

Names: Haskell, David L. (David Louis), author.
Title: The two Taríacuris and the early colonial and pre-hispanic past of Michoacán / by David L. Haskell.
Description: Boulder : University Press of Colorado, 2018. | Includes bibliographical references and index.
Identifiers: LCCN 2017054092| ISBN 9781607328209 (cloth) | ISBN 9781607327486 (pbk.) | ISBN 9781607327493 (ebook)
Subjects: LCSH: Relación de Michoacán—Criticism, Textual. | Indians of Mexico—Mexico—Michoacán de Ocampo—History—Sources. | Tarasco Indians—History—Sources. | Tarasco Indians—Social life and customs. | Michoacán de Ocampo (Mexico)—History—Sources.
Classification: LCC F1219.1.M55 H37 2018 | DDC 972/.37—dc23
LC record available at https://lccn.loc.gov/2017054092

Cover photograph of Bascilica de Nuestra Señora de la Salud in Patzcuaro, Michoacan, by Helen Pollard, 1976

For my son, Siler, so that one day he might understand what all of the fuss and all of the time spent was about.

May he also understand the importance of stories from all corners of the world, and the power of a story well told.

Contents

Acknowledgments

An appropriate place to begin my acknowledgments seems to be an acknowledgment that this is book is in certain respects the result of an unusual undertaking. Concerned with history and historical production, this work is not the result of innumerable hours spent in archives, making friends with fellow historians, archivists, art historians, and so on. This is, rather, a work that is the result of a lengthy and often lonely engagement with the document known as the *Relación de Michoacán* and specifically the narrative of an indigenous priest that comprises most of the second part of that document. Because that document exists in print, I was able to analyze that narrative working at home, without visiting archives. Due to these facts, the acknowledgments will perhaps seem brief, with a paucity of names. Any resulting perception of ingratitude could not be further from the truth. The present work was most prominently enabled by two scholars and mentors, to whom words cannot express my appreciation and gratitude. The first is Susan Gillespie, who was my master's and doctoral committee chair at the University of Florida. My engagement with the *Relación de Michoacán* became my master's thesis, and was incorporated into my doctoral dissertation. To the extent that this book is a valuable contribution to narrative analysis and studies of Mesoamerican historicity, Susan deserves the lion's share of the credit, having worked tirelessly to train me, to guide me toward readings and help me understand them, to correct my misperceptions, and offer insights and answer my questions. Following my dissertation, Susan continued to be a tireless colleague and supporter. The other person whom I cannot thank enough is Helen Pollard, who introduced me to Michoacán archaeology and has, ever since, always made herself available to answer my questions and provide feedback and corrections. I always got the feeling that I saw the documentary sources in a different light than she did, and yet to her tremendous credit she not only tolerated my approach but was indefatigable in providing whatever I might need to bring my ideas to fruition. In that sense she is the very definition of a scholar—one who not only produces knowledge herself but also assists others in projects such that others might find some value in their products.

I would also like to thank the people of Erongarícuaro, Michoacán, Mexico, where I got my start in Michoacán archaeology (thanks to Helen) and to which I returned to carry out my dissertation fieldwork. Without falling in love with the town, the area, the people, and their history, I would not have had the desire to carry this project through to fruition.

As I said above, this has been a largely solo project and I do not have a lengthy list of people that I consider myself friends and colleagues with. Nevertheless there were a handful of scholars and colleagues who deserve thanks. Claudia Espejel of the Colegio de Michoacán has been very kind in sharing up-to-date scholarship via email, which has been of great assistance. At various times I have met a few scholars of Michoacán history and prehistory, who could not have been nicer; their kindness and collegiality even in our brief encounters has made me feel like a welcome colleague, and for that I am grateful. Such people include Angélica Afanador-Pujol, Ben and Patty Warren, Eduardo Williams, and Aida Castilleja (who was particularly helpful in assisting my and Helen's fieldwork in Erongarícuaro). Not only their kindness but the quality of their scholarship has been essential to the present work. The same indebtedness on account of their scholarship must be said of Rodrigo Martínez Baracs, Hans Roskamp, Cristina Monzón, and Roberto Martínez González. I have only engaged these scholars through their publications, but that engagement has been productive and essential. Particularly without the work of Drs. Martínez Baracs and Roskamp, the present work either would not have existed or would have been laughably short on information concerning the historical context of the production of the *Relación de Michoacán* and therefore the Priest's Speech. Although we might disagree over how best to interpret that narrative, I recognize that I owe these first-rate historians, along with Ben Warren and Angélica Afanador-Pujol, a tremendous debt, particularly since for various reasons I did not and could not sift through archives for contextual and comparative information.

The same could be said of the immense intellectual debts I owe to the various anthropologists investigating and theorizing historicity. Too many to name here, I'll leave those debts to the obvious citations and references. But I would be remiss if I did not mention Michael Heckenberger, who also sat on my master's and doctoral committees. Mike was instrumental, along with Susan, in introducing me to the literature from Amazonia; Mike's combined archaeological and ethnographic work impressed an interest in me, necessarily from a distance, in the complexities in Amazonia that to some extent I have applied and grappled with in this work. It could be said that in certain ways this book is what happens when a Mesoamericanist is influenced by that Amazonian literature.

I would also like to thank the various institutions that I have been affiliated with at the many stages of this project: the University of Florida, Franklin University, the Ohio State University, Shawnee State University, and Ohio University. My affiliations with these institutions have allowed me to have critical library access, particularly at Ohio State. For that affiliation I thank Clark Larsen. They have also offered workspace. At Shawnee State I had the opportunity to teach non-Western civilization and literature, in which I taught my understanding of the Priest's Speech, and doing so helped me develop further insights into the details of that narrative. For that opportunity I thank Amr al-Azm and Roberta Milliken.

I would like to thank the staff of the University Press of Colorado, including prominently Jessica d'Arbonne, Laura Furney, Daniel Pratt, Darrin Pratt, Kelly Lenkevich, the board, and the editors and reviewers. They helped me tremendously throughout the entire process of bringing this book to fruition. I also thank the anonymous reviewers for their suggestions as to how to improve the original manuscript.

Finally I would like to thank my wife, Emmy, for her love and support. My time spent laboring through graduate school, and then spent laboring on this book while also having an erratic teaching schedule, was enabled and encouraged by that love and support. Without her this book would not have been possible.

THE TWO TARÍACURIS

and the Early Colonial and
Prehispanic Past of Michoacán

1

Introduction

The Two Tariacuris

Look how you promised a great thing: that you would make the seedbeds for our god Curicaueri and you promised the cinch and the axe, so that you would carry firewood for his temples, and that you would be at the backs of his battalions, so that you could aid in the battles . . . Now Curicaueri has pity for you in this year in which we find ourselves. (Alcalá 2000:528)

And they garroted him [the King] and like that he died. And they put a lot of firewood around him and burned him. And his servants went around collecting his ashes, and so Guzmán had them thrown in the river. And the people fled because of his death, out of fear, although some servants carried those ashes and buried them in two places: in Pátzcuaro and in another place. (Alcalá 2000:689–690)

The two quotes above both come from an Early Colonial (ca. 1540) document commonly known as the *Relación de Michoacán*.[1] The quotations generally sum up the state of indigenous society at the time in what had been, before the arrival of the Spaniards twenty years earlier, the second most powerful empire in Mesoamerica—the Tarascan kingdom of West-Central Mexico (see map 1.1). The second quote is a remembrance of the death of the last fully autonomous indigenous king of the Tarascan kingdom. That king, Tzintzicha Tangáxoan, had been killed as a result of a politically motivated trial in 1530 that was orchestrated by Beltrán Núño de Guzmán, the highest-ranking Spanish official in New Spain (the president of the First Royal Audiencia of New Spain).[2] His death occurred roughly eight years

DOI: 10.5876/9781607327493.c001

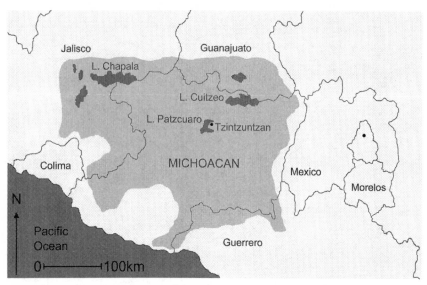

MAP 1.1. The location and extent of the Tarascan kingdom at its height ca. 1520, with the names and borders of modern Mexican states included for context. The extent of the kingdom is indicated by the light-gray shading. Reproduced with permission from School for Advanced Research Press from Haskell 2015.

after the entrance of Spanish forces into Tarascan territory. The first quote is commonly attributed to the indigenous chief priest, though who actually spoke and/or wrote these words is unclear (as I address below). What is more certain, however, is that the author of these words was speaking to either an actual audience or at the very least the audience constituted by the readers of the document. He is speaking roughly ten years after Tzintzicha Tangáxoan's death and during the early years of the imposition of a Spanish colonial system that was contentious and multifaceted. Here the priest mourns the fate and treatment of the primary deity of the state ideology, Curicaueri, due to the fact that the lords in particular and the people more generally are not willing to fight for the old gods, and perhaps by extension the old ways. In the earliest years of the colonial encounter, everything was in flux and open for negotiation: the status of the gods, the nature of ultimate authority and who would wield it and why, and the relative statuses of nearly everyone involved in this encounter. Various individuals jockeyed for position while indigenous peoples were simultaneously trying to pick up the pieces, just as the kings' servants and followers picked up the last kings' ashes, and do what they could do to adjust to the new order and work to preserve and weave into the new order what they could of the old, indigenous order.

The document from which these quotes are drawn, the *Relación de Michoacán*, is of paramount importance for understanding these historical processes in the earliest years of the Spanish Colonial era. The *Relación de Michoacán* is critical for understanding the prehispanic Tarascan kingdom for two reasons. The first is the extent of its content. This document is the closest thing modern scholars have to an encyclopedic account of Tarascan culture, the prehispanic past, and the functioning of the Tarascan state. This is true even if it falls short of, for example, Bernardino de Sahagún's *Florentine Codex*, which describes Aztec culture and society in the Basin of Mexico in the first few decades of the colonial experience. The second reason why the *Relación de Michoacán* is so important is that the corpus of other documents pertaining to the prehispanic Tarascan state or indigenous lives during the late prehispanic and Early Colonial Periods is quite small compared to the Central Mexican corpus. While some excellent historians are doing their best to search out and investigate documentary sources pertaining to Tarascan state and culture, the number of documentary sources available to scholars studying Tarascan culture, society, and history will likely never catch up to the state of affairs in Central Mexico. Understanding the *Relación de Michoacán* and the goals and intentions behind it and reflected within it is therefore of utmost importance; not only does no document approach its wealth of information but precious few documents exist that can variably corroborate or contest it. In short, it is the best single source for modern scholars who want to understand the prehispanic past—both in terms of social processes as they played out over roughly the last few centuries before Spanish contact as well as the culture of the Tarascans and functioning of the Tarascan kingdom in the recently passed "ethnographic present" on the "eve" of Spanish contact.

The main problem in properly contextualizing and understanding the document and in particular its second section, which purports to describe the history of the Tarascan state, is that this legendary history of the Tarascan royal dynasty, the Uacúsecha, has not been analyzed in a way that fully problematizes how and why it represented the past as it does. This book engages the legendary history of the Uacúsecha from an explicitly anthropological point of view by drawing on the theoretical literature concerning "historicity." Historicity is the theoretical view that other cultures have different reasons for and ways of organizing representations of the past compared to Western historiography. These differences go beyond simply casting the representations of other cultures, and particularly their elites, as exemplars of Western conceptions of "propaganda," or simply a "biased" and "one-sided" account, or reductive analytic categories such as "myth" and "history." A similar problematic term is "legend"; while the priest's narrative is often used as a stand-in for history, this use is accompanied by the caveat that it is "legendary history," a term that is nevertheless rarely examined or its implications not carried to their fullest extent (these issues are discussed below). This study is thus situated within the wider and ongoing debate over the meaning and mission of the field of ethnohistory. The work of ethnohistory has always been a dual one (Krech 1991; Sturtevant 1966). According to one mode, ethnohistorians write the unwritten past of non-Western peoples. Where representations of the past are available, ethnohistorians sort through these representations to discover "what really happened" in the past. In the other mode, present at the outset of ethnohistory as an academic and practical field though given less importance, ethnohistorians concern themselves with understanding the non-Western ways in which the past and time more generally are understood and represented. The basic question becomes how culture influences temporal representation. In this formulation, "Ethnohistory," as the endeavor with which the present work is engaged as applied to Tarascan representations of the past, must "also practice the ethnography of historical consciousness" (Whitehead 2003:x).

The main goal of this book, then, is to investigate the guiding principles or logic behind the narrative concerning the ancestors of the king that the priest told in the context of the production of the *Relación de Michoacán*. These principles and logics are understood in reference to two contexts. The first is his personal and historically situated motivations. The second is the place of his actions and formulation of his narrative within wider but culturally influenced understandings of how the past relates to the present. The relationship between these two contexts is investigated as a recursive one; therefore I also examine how his production of his narrative was intended to shape the course of history moving forward by shaping how the past should be understood. The priest sought to influence the course of history by shaping how the past was represented, essentially reformulating the past for this novel opportunity offered by the production of the *Relación de Michoacán*. The priest reformulated the past to make one character, Taríacuri, the focal point of the entire narrative and the point of reference around which revolved both the processes of state formation and the ideologically formulated paradigmatic category of "kingship." I argue that he did this in order to advocate for Don Francisco Taríacuri to assume the position of highest indigenous authority in colonial Michoacán at the time of the document's production. The end result is that the priest actively constructed the past in order to shape the present and future. At the same time as he was embarking on producing the effect of Taríacuri's centrality and novel significatory power, he was also doing so in fairly conservative Mesoamerican ways by embracing the culturally constructed cyclicity of time and events. In order to examine the logics that went into the priest's novel representation of the past— what I call a "concretization" (see chapter 3)—I analyze in depth the structure of the narrative in terms of the selection and sequential arrangement of its elements. The understanding of the narrative resulting from this investigation of its processual

structure is then understood in relation to the social structural factors and the institutionalization of remembrances of the past from which the priest drew on as he
formulated his narrative. I argue that the narrative was composed of what might
have been actual historical events, and/or possibly somewhat fabricated events, but
that the recollection of "the real past" was *not* the priest's aim. Rather, events from
the past were selectively chosen and ordered by the chief priest so that he could
communicate overt messages to the Spaniards and both overt and covert messages
to the indigenous people who he felt should still consider themselves subjects of
the Uacúsecha royal dynasty. Essentially, the surface content of the narrative—its
plot—as well as its logical ordering comprise an eloquent explication of the nature
of kingship in the Tarascan kingdom, its place as an organizing principle of indigenous society, and finally its function as a full-throated call for the people to rally
around Don Francisco Taríacuri in the chaotic time of the Early Colonial Period.

In this way the approach in this book rejects investigating the representation of
the prehispanic past as something that was static; such an approach is exemplified in
the old practice of viewing the priest's narrative as simply a retelling of a fixed "text"
(Kirchhoff 1956). Engaging the past, as the priest was doing, was an agentive action
in which the past and its potential to both make sense of the present and impact
the present were all skillfully woven together, and this process of weaving leaves
evidence of its processual logic and skill in its final form. I also reject interpreting
the priest's narrative as somehow emblematic of the historical and rhetorical skills
of an entire culture. The priest drew on cultural knowledge, ideologies and philoso-
phies of time and the past, and structurally constituted knowledges of the past, but
he must be understood as a single and incredibly skillful agent responding to the
events swirling around him. With his narrative, the priest entered that swirling fray
and became a part of it—this was definitely not some traditional or stereotypical
act of cultural conservatism. The priest's interests and motivation should not be
viewed as isomorphic with other members of indigenous society in the early years
of the colonial encounter—it must be recognized that his position and role led him
to formulate not only a historically unique concretization of the past but perhaps
also a uniquely ideologically oriented and loyalist narrative. This research follows
other recent detailed understanding of the agencies recoverable through detailed
analysis of the *Relación de Michoacán* and other colonial documents (Afanador-
Pujol 2010, 2015; Espejel Carbajal 2008; Fernández 2011; Monzón, Roskamp, and
Warren 2009; Roskamp 2003, 2010a, 2010b, 2012, 2015; Roskamp and César-Villa
2003; Stone 2004). This book is necessary in large measure because "our record
of histories has expanded much farther than our understanding of the historicities that create them, and this disjuncture in our understanding has produced a
rather defective framework of analysis in anthropology" (Whitehead 2003:xi). As

I stated above, this is certainly the case for the priest's narrative in the *Relación de Michoacán*. Simply put, this narrative presents problems for modern scholars who seek to understand it, and this lack of understanding in turn entails that what we think we know about the prehispanic past of the Tarascan kingdom is inherently flawed. In order to address this shortcoming in how historicities are investigated and analyzed, I apply a method of narrative analysis that has been described as "an important and indispensable tool" (Willis 1982:xiii; see below and chapter 3). This method of analysis enables an understanding of how and why the priest composed his narrative of the history in the form that he did—in other words the underlying logic of his composition.

THE CONTENTS OF THE *RELACIÓN DE MICHOACÁN* AND THE PRIEST'S SPEECH

The *Relación de Michoacán* was written by an anonymous friar and presented to Antonio de Mendoza, viceroy of New Spain, in 1541. Cynthia Stone (2004:7) believes the largest time frame in which the *Relación de Michoacán* could have been in production was between the years 1538 and 1541 (other research and views on the timeline of the document's production can be found in León 1984:265–271; Warren 1977: 439–457; see also Oviedo [1537–1548] 1959, 4:252–253). The identity of the anonymous friar has been the source of some debate, though J. Benedict's Warren's (1971) suggestion that Jerónimo de Alcalá produced the document has gained general acceptance to the extent that a recent publication of the *Relación de Michoacán* cites him as the author (Alcalá 2000). The document was produced with the aid and testimony of numerous indigenous informants, scribes, and artists, leading Stone (2004) to eschew referring to Alcalá as the "author," instead choosing to refer to him more appropriately as the "friar-compiler" (and the role of "editor" and planner must also not be overlooked; see discussions in Stone's [2004] own work as well as in Espejel Carbajal [2008] and Fernández [2011]).

The friar-compiler's prologue explains that the *Relación de Michoacán* originally consisted of three parts (not including the prologue) (Alcalá 2000:330). Each part is then divided into chapters that contain related information or, in the case of the priest's narrative, related "events." The first part, which according to the prologue, told of the gods that the people of Michoacán worshipped and other religious practices, has since been lost, save for one folio. The third and final section of the *Relación de Michoacán* describes the responsibilities of state officials and members of the priesthood; recorded certain ethnographic facts such as marriage practices, mortuary rites, and military tactics; and tells the story of the Spanish "conquest" up until the death of the last indigenous king in 1530. The picture of the Tarascan king-dom that emerges from this third section concerning the "ethnographic present" of the Tarascan kingdom on the eve of the Spaniards' intrusion into Michoacán and into the earliest years of the colonial encounter is one of a highly centralized king-dom in which the ruler's authority was unquestioned.[3]

The second part, the part that this book focuses on more than any other, is described in its first chapter as the story of "how the ancestors of the king came to this land and conquered it" (Alcalá 2000:330; all translations from Spanish are mine, except where otherwise noted). This section of the document is comprised of seventy-eight folios, the majority of these folios possessing writing on the front and back. In addition, it contains painted illustrations, just as the rest of the docu-ment, that depict some of the events described in the narrative. The story of the ancestors of the king was, the document tells us, recited once a year at a religious festival as a preamble to the punishment of wrongdoers (see figures 1.1a and 1.1b). During that festival it was the job of the high priest, the Petámuti, to tell this story, and other members of the priesthood would travel throughout the kingdom and recite the story in the towns of the kingdom. Essentially, the story relates how the Uacúsecha lineage began with a character named Hireticatame who arrived at Zacapu. Through the generations, his direct descendants moved into the Lake Pátzcuaro Basin, settling first at Uayameo, then Pátzcuaro, and eventually Ihuatzio and Tzintzuntzan. The story details their relations with the peoples of central Michoacán and in particular the Lake Pátzcuaro Basin and its immediate surround-ings; such relations focused on skirmishes and disputes but also intermarriage with certain groups. Throughout the story, the Uacúsecha are destined for greatness, and eventually they manage to subjugate these peoples and institute a unified kingdom with capitals at Pátzcuaro, Ihuatzio, and Tzintzuntzan, where apparently coreign-ing factions of the Uacúsecha lineage resided.

In this second part of the document, there are also sections that are not part of the priest's narrative. Two sections help frame this narrative in its cultural con-text by describing the religious festival at which it was told and then the "summa-tion,"[4] as it could be described, in which the priest speaks directly to his audience and relates the point of telling the story to the context of the here and now. As Stone (2004:127–132, 135) points out, this part of the priest's speech likely is in ref-erence to the Early Colonial context in which the people and the king (or gover-nor who had been acting in his place) had been subjugated by the Spaniards. The priest shames the audience because they have not been diligent and vigilant in their defense of the king and of the deity Curicaueri, the patron deity of the Uacúsecha royal dynasty and therefore the state as a whole. This could be similar to whatever form such a summary took in the prehispanic era (and the Tarascan kingdom

A

B

FIGURE 1.1. Depictions of Priest giving speech. (A) Depiction in the *Relación de Michoacán* by indigenous artists of the festival Equata cónsquaro. At this festival, wrongdoers were called before secular and religious authorities, and punishment was meted out. As part of this festival, the chief priest, the Petámuti, recited the "history" of the king's ancestors. The chief priest is shown wearing his characteristic garb, including his metal "tweezers" on his chest supported by a necklace, and holding his sacred staff. It is a version of this "history" that comprises almost all of the second part of the document, the analysis of which is the subject of this book. This image follows the "chapter" heading that introduces the narrative and precedes any of the text that tells that narrative or relates details concerning the festival. Gathered nobles, marked by the blue dots representing their turquoise lip plugs and their smoking pipes, appear to watch both the chief priest and the actual punishments. (B) Depiction in the *Relación de Michoacán* by indigenous artists of the chief priest relating his speech in front of a group of gathered people. At least some—the front row—are nobles of the Tarascan kingdom. They are marked as nobles by their lip plugs and their stools. This depiction comes at the end of the lengthy, multiple-chapters-long narration of the history of the Uacúsecha in the second part of the document. The illustration follows the chapter heading that introduces the text as essentially a "summation" of the point of telling the story and reminding those in attendance of the sad state of the god Curicaueri and precedes any of the actual text of that chapter of the document. Compositionally, it depicts largely the same thing as the illustration of figure 1a, except that here nothing else except the chief priest and the audience is shown; the narration appears abstracted out of its cultural context.

appears to have been engaged in frequent enough warfare that such rhetoric would not have seemed out of place), but in light of the subjugation and humiliation the royal dynasty had suffered, it certainly relates well to the Early Colonial Period. In both the prehispanic and Early Colonial contexts, the clear purpose is to legitimize the state and the royal dynasty. The fact that in the two illustrations of the Petámuti speaking (Alcalá 2000:333, 525), he is doing so in front of the assembled lords of the realm in one illustration and in the other is accompanied by scenes of the punishment of criminals makes it clear that this speech is about the possession of power and the right to rule.

It is essential to note in regard to this discussion that we lack important information concerning the actual audience of the priest's testimony/narrative. The text of the *Relación de Michoacán* itself simply slides into the priest's narrative, saying that the chief priest used to begin thusly" (Alcalá 2000:340). The narrative then follows this brief introduction. This construction of the context and subsequent narration omits who the narrator of the actual account recorded in the document was. It could have been the chief priest himself or it could have been another, lesser priest. The idea that a "pure" version told by "a" or "the" chief priest within the folios of the *Relación de Michoacán* lives on in the very common practice of referring to the narrative contained within the *Relación de Michoacán* as "the chief priest's narrative" (e.g., Kirchhoff 1956; Martínez Baracs 2005; Michelet 1989; Stone 2004),[5] even though there is precious little information as to whether the chief priest actually narrated the version contained in the *Relación de Michoacán* or even if such an individual was alive at the time of the production of the document. We also have no idea if any Spaniards witnessed this narration in its original (at least as described) cultural context and the larger ceremony of the punishment of wrongdoers of which it was a part, nor how the friar-compiler found or asked a priest to recount or retell (or recreate) the narration for the purposes of producing the *Relación de Michoacán* itself. The context of the production of this narrative could have included a rather small audience composed only of the friar-compiler and other indigenous informants and scribes involved in the document's production.

On the other hand, whoever narrated the story contained in the *Relación de Michoacán* likely had a wider audience in mind. The document was presented to Viceroy Mendoza in 1541 (an event depicted in the frontispiece of the document itself), and judging by the friar-compiler's own prologue, the presentation of the document to the viceroy as a means of further converting the indigenes of Michoacán to Catholicism and pacifying them under Spanish rule was a goal at the outset of the production of the document. It could therefore be reasonably surmised that the indigenous persons who aided in its production and served as informants knew at least this proximate destination of the manuscript in the hands of Viceroy Mendoza. This could have led to their taking advantage of having such a powerful audience as the viceroy, in effect taking the opportunity to advocate certain positions to the viceroy in the context of this document (how this unique opportunity to speak directly to the viceroy was taken advantage of by the artists that painted the illustrations is examined by Afanador-Pujol [2014, 2015]). It is also not rare in the context of the production of documents in colonial Mexico that information would be tailored to audiences that the document might be expected to encounter. In this regard, Stone (2004:14, 128–132) believes the narrator of the story contained in the *Relación de Michoacán* to have been speaking directly to the indigenous nobility in his prelude and summation, in effect chastising them for their lack of support of the king and the god Curicaueri. I agree that these passages take on a certain tone of admonishment and firmly ground the narration within the present context of the production of the document as a whole; it is worth noting again, however, that we have no evidence for whether or not these spoken words met directly with a public audience composed of the native nobility.

It is interesting to note, however, that Stone's investigation of the physical document and comparison with another Early Colonial document that contains passages almost identical to the *Relación de Michoacán* led her to conclude that "of the several drafts of the *Relación de Michoacán* produced from about 1538 to 1541, it is likely that at least one remained in the possession of the indigenous nobility" (Stone 2004:35). She also notes that a figure standing behind Viceroy Mendoza was subsequently painted over (see figure 1.2), and that "what makes this individual particularly compelling is his similarity in terms of size, clothing, and hairstyle to the sons of the Cazonci—Don Francisco Taríacuri and Don Antonio Huitziméngari— pictured in plate 27 [the illustration of the family tree within the document]" (Stone 2004:61) (see figure 1.3 for the illustration of the Uacúsecha royal dynasty / family tree as depicted in the *Relación de Michoacán*). While Stone (2004:62) hedges somewhat in her suggestion that this painted-over individual was a son of Tzintzicha Tangáxoan, Rodrigo Martínez Baracs (2005:299) states more assertively his opinion that this figure must have been Don Francisco Taríacuri. In his interpretation of the "double significance" of the frontispiece in its original form, Martínez Baracs suggests that on one level, the more apparent and official (due to the erasure of the individual from view) level, the illustration depicts the transfer of the book, and the information it contains, from a Spanish friar to the Spanish viceroy. On the second level, however: "the governor [Don Pedro] and the three Indian priests . . . delivered to the future governor, Irecha or Cazonci, a manuscript that contained, for the first time in written form, the complete history of the gods of Michoacán, the festivals, the conquest of the territory and the formation of the kingdom, as the Petámuti had narrated it" (Martínez Baracs 2005:299).

The fact that the individual next to Mendoza was eliminated from the picture censored this aspect of Indian-to-Indian communication visible in the document but which nonetheless was likely a goal of indigenous informants who participated in the document's very production.

FIGURE 1.2. Line drawing of the frontispiece of the *Relación de Michoacán*. The illustration depicts the anonymous friar, Don Pedro Cuinierángari, and indigenous elders presenting the document to Viceroy Mendoza. A fish in Don Pedro's hat has been interpreted as an iconic indicator of his namesake (Saint Peter) but also his Islander identity. The hair and parts of the garments of the figure standing behind/above Viceroy Mendoza, the majority of this figure having been erased from the image, are emphasized in this drawing.

In addition to these framing chapters, the second part contains three additional chapters that relay "historical" information. Two tales follow the priest's summation. The first (Alcalá 2000:533–534) tells the story of one of the great hero Taríacuri's

FIGURE 1.3. Depiction in the *Relación de Michoacán* of the ancestors of the last indigenous Tarascan king, Tzintzicha Tangáxoan, in the form of a family tree. Tzintzicha Tangáxoan is pictured at the top in the center of the figure, flanked by his sons Don Francisco Taríacuri (to the right of Tzintzicha Tangáxoan) and Don Antonio Huitziméngari (to the left). At the base is Hireticatame; a red line or string established something of a line of succession as given in the narrative of the *Relación de Michoacán*. Most of the members of the Uacúsecha are depicted according to the manner in which they were killed. Note the position of Taríacuri, at the midpoint of the tree but off-center on the right; he is below Don Francisco Taríacuri.

sons, Tamapucheca, who is barely mentioned in the priest's larger narrative, but is related in an ancillary way to the initiation of the conquests that created a unified kingdom. The second story, that of how a daughter of Taríacuri killed a nobleman from a rival town (Alcalá 2000:537–540), is introduced within the document as a story that a priest of Curicaueri had learned from a "grandfather." This could mean a literal grandfather or, more likely, an elder and more knowledgeable person, as kinship terms are frequently used metaphorically in the document. The priest relays this tale upon a trip to Corínguaro, and has now told the friar (presumably) so that the friar could include it within the document. Finally, following these two tales is a chapter that names the Uacúsecha members who had ruled in the capitals following the initial establishment of the kingdom down through the years until the arrival of the Spaniards (Alcalá 2000:541–543). The fact that these episodes were remembered by the indigenous priesthood and perhaps nobility more generally and yet were purposefully left out of the priest's narrative as contained in the majority of the second part of the document is essential to my argument in this book. It demonstrates that the priest selected from a wide array of known or remembered events; I contend that there was a consistent underlying logic behind that process of selection and arrangement, and that this logic which points to Don Francisco Taríacuri succeeding his father as both the preservation of indigenous social and ideological structure and as the outcome of a coherent vision of a historical-looking chain of events is what the priest's narrative is really all about.

THE HISTORICAL CONTEXT OF THE PRODUCTION OF THE *RELACIÓN DE MICHOACÁN*

The production and presentation of the document took place less than twenty years after the submission of the last native king, Tzintzicha Tangáxoan, to the presence and supremacy of the Spaniards in his territory. As explained by Warren (1985), it is nearly impossible to speak of the "conquest" of Michoacán, or of the lands ruled over by Tzintzicha Tangáxoan, as a single event. There was no war, no battle, and no official surrender between the Spaniards and the indigenous government. Rather, Tzintzicha Tangáxoan acquiesced to the Spaniards' presence and actions in his capital of Tzintzuntzan and in time throughout his kingdom. Importantly, however, he also continued to exercise his own authority over his subjects, and this authority included receiving tribute and requiring the lords of his realm to attend court frequently and for long stretches of time (Warren 1985). Such practices, and the inherent instability of what was more or less an arrangement of two different authorities (the Spanish and the indigenous) that could not help but clash over certain issues, was brought to a tragic end when Beltrán Nuño de Guzmán, president of the First

Audiencia of New Spain, tried and then executed Tzintzicha Tangáxoan in 1530 (see Krippner-Martinez 2001; Scholes and Adams 1952; Warren 1985).

Don Pedro Cuinierángari had married a woman from the king's palace,[6] and therefore because an adopted "brother" at least partially due to this status as an affine. Following Tzintzicha Tangáxoan's execution, Cuinierángari was made indigenous governor of the province after being supported by Spanish authorities.[7] Don Pedro later became one of the primary informants in the production of the *Relación de Michoacán*, but it is important to emphasize that he was not properly of the king's lineage. Instead, Don Pedro was regarded as an "Islander" (this term, and the evidence for such a characterization will be explained through the course of the narrative and the analysis thereof; Stone [2004:157, 160] and Afanador-Pujol [2015] also discuss some of the evidence for Don Pedro's characterization as such and how this is represented in the document). Don Pedro was chosen because none of Tzintzicha Tangáxoan's sons were old enough to assume the office of leadership. Nonetheless, the rupture in kingly succession and the social inversion of having a formerly subordinate "Islander" assume the preeminent position of indigenous leadership was a point of contention in indigenous society, one that seemingly only grew in importance as the king's sons grew old enough to replace their father (see also Afanador-Pujol 2015).

Vasco de Quiroga, who first came to Michoacán as *oidor* of the First Audiencia of New Spain (1530–1538) (Martínez Baracs 2005:164) and would later become the first bishop of Michoacán (1538–1565), was also radically transforming the religious and political landscape at the time of the production of the *Relación de Michoacán* (Martínez Baracs 2005). One of his first acts was founding a *pueblo-hospital* at the site of the indigenous town of Uayameo, or Santa Fe as it would become known. Apparently this action was met with some enthusiasm by many indigenous nobles (Stone 2004:148–149). Don Pedro also played a major role in this event by giving Quiroga the land for the construction of the pueblo-hospital—land that could very well have come under his administration thanks to his marriage to numerous members of the royal family upon the arrival of the Spaniards in the first place. In this particular case, Afanador-Pujol (2015:137) notes that Don Pedro's wife, Doña Inés, complained in the contemporaneous legal dispute involving Juan de Infante (see below on this figure's importance) that some of the lands in question she had brought with her as part of her dowry in her marriage to Don Pedro, and that some of these lands had in turn been given to Quiroga. The largest upheaval occurred when Quiroga moved the seat of the diocese of Michoacán from Tzintzuntzan, capital of the Tarascan kingdom, to Pátzcuaro in 1538–1539 (Martínez Baracs 2005:chap. 6). Pátzcuaro had been an important place in the prehispanic era, and possibly was the most sacred site in the kingdom even at the time of the Spaniards' arrival (Alcalá 2000:363–365). Quiroga had his own motivations for the transfer, and his role in the (re)founding of Pátzcuaro saw the development of a mythology of its own (which are beyond the scope of the current book). Among the indigenous nobility the transfer either created or exposed large fissures. Some nobles favored the move, while others, presumably more loyal (or more closely related) to Tzintzicha's lineage in Tzintzuntzan strongly opposed the move, and members of both sides lined up to offer their testimony on the issue. The Spaniards themselves were hardly monolithic, as the Franciscans (as well as Mendoza himself) opposed Quiroga. In the end, Quiroga won, and the seat of the diocese was moved.

Another legal issue of great magnitude—the status of a large and possibly fraudulent *encomienda* (a colonial grant of land and native inhabitants to provide labor service on or related to that land) claim by Juan de Infante—was being fought over at the time of the production of the *Relación de Michoacán*. This fight endured for many years and involves a significant number of back-and-forth judgments and reversals; here I will briefly summarize its salience for understanding the priest's narrative. First and foremost, this case was likely the most pressing issue for Viceroy Mendoza, and it was a significant motivation in his many visits to Michoacán and was related to the impetus for the production of the document. Its resolution was in many ways going to set important precedents for the colony of New Spain and how it would be run and by whom. At issue was essentially whether Juan de Infante had the right to claim numerous towns within the Lake Pátzcuaro Basin as parts of his encomienda or alternatively if all of the towns of that lake basin essentially constituted *barrios*, or segments of the capital (see Warren 1963, 1985; see also Afanador-Pujol 2015:12). Indigenous nobles contended that the entire lake basin was one unit and could not be split apart; from their point of view, especially from the point of view of the descendants of the king and his closest allies, Tzintzicha Tangáxoan had peacefully acquiesced to the presence of the Spaniards and their imposition of authority in what had been provincial areas of the kingdom were tolerable so long as the lake basin remained in his and his family's possession (Afanador-Pujol 2015:102–104). The integrity of the lake basin was also imagined by Hernán Cortés, who took the basin as his own personal encomienda (and later the lake basin had become a possession of the Spanish Crown directly after Cortés had fallen out of favor for various reasons that are tangential to the production of the *Relación de Michoacán*). While the final results are not specifically consequential to the production of the *Relación de Michoacán* and in fact this legal struggle extended past its production, the combined effect of this fight and the fight over the move of the diocese to Pátzcuaro created a highly complex colonial situation in which various groups were simultaneously at odds with and allied with other groups, depending on which issue in particular is being considered and how each of those struggles was going at any particular moment. For example, Quiroga had gotten in the good graces of some members of the indigenous nobility by fighting against Juan de Infante, even threatening or perhaps actually taking up arms against the *encomendero*, even as they resisted his proposal to move the diocese (Afanador-Pujol 2015:102; Martínez Baracs 2005; Warren 1963, 1985; Warren and Monzón 2004). Quiroga and Franciscan friars, who were the most significant agents of religious conversion in the earliest years of the colonial encounter, demonstrated rifts among the colonizers themselves; the Franciscans advocated for the diocese to remain in Tzintzuntzan, where they had established their first chapel. Among indigenous peoples, those loyal to Tzintzicha Tangáxoan, or more precisely his heirs, were forced to simultaneously work with Don Pedro in the production of the *Relación de Michoacán* in order to present a united front that would preserve the integrity of the Pátzcuaro Basin as a single political unit even as they fought against Don Pedro and strongly implicated that due to his "Islander" and therefore subordinate status he was essentially unfit to hold the office of governor, a point made by Afanador-Pujol (2015:13, 22, also 93).

The legal fights and status of possessions and questions of leadership were also taking place at the same time that the heirs of Tzintzicha Tangáxoan were reaching an age when they could fight for what many viewed as their birthright. The eldest son of the last king was named Don Francisco Taríacuri, and along with his brother Don Antonio Huitziméngari he had served as a page in the court of Viceroy Antonio de Mendoza since 1535 (Afanador-Pujol 2010; 2015:25). As the eldest son of the last king, Don Francisco had already begun to become a player in local and regional politics, returning to Tzintzuntzan from Viceroy Mendoza's court to protest Quiroga's proposed movement of the seat of the diocese to Pátzcuaro in person in 1538 (López Sarrelangue 1965:170). He and his brother Don Antonio are shown apart from, and smaller than, a group of indigenous noblemen in an illustration (painting 9) of deliberations over the move contained in Pablo Beaumont's *Crónica de Michoacán* (1932 [1778–1780], written in the eighteenth century but based on earlier sources (see Roskamp 1997).

Documentary evidence indicates that Don Francisco Taríacuri was treated as a *ladino*, a term that was applied to indigenous peoples, mostly descendants of the prehispanic aristocracies who could take advantage of their position and ancestry, who had learned Castilian and furthermore gained rights otherwise restricted to Spaniards through the Spanish colonial legal system. Afanador-Pujol (2010:301; translations those of Afanador-Pujol) writes that "Don Francisco knew Spanish legal traditions and used them effectively" and discusses the testimony of Viceroy Mendoza in support of Don Francisco Taríacuri's *probanza* (a legal document that is a collection of evidence in support of, or as a petition for, a legal status or privileges), in which the viceroy states that Don Francisco "always 'dressed in Spanish clothes'" and "'dealt like a Spaniard.'" In this way, Don Francisco Taríacuri was largely in step with most members of the indigenous nobility in pursuing the best possible arrangements for themselves under the imposed Spanish colonial system. The strategy of these elites was essentially one of accommodation and acquiescence to that system and its new rules. Members of the indigenous nobility engaged in such a strategy in order to keep what wealth they still had and could reasonably hope to maintain against various encroachments and the effects of new legal and economic realities, as well as distinguish themselves from the commoners by seeking privileges that Spaniards enjoyed (just as Don Francisco had done; see also Kuthy 1996, 2003; López Sarrelangue 1965). Tarascan elites were thus not significantly different from elites throughout Mesoamerica, who similarly seemed to have sought wealth and privileges based on their lineage, whether real or fabricated, as well as the extent to which they embraced the arrival of the Spaniards as a chance to remake their place in society.[8] Part of the aim was to prevent the collapse of the distinction between nobles and commoners, a collapse which the K'iche' Maya author or authors of the *Popol Vuh* (see Christensen 2007), for example, explicitly mourned roughly a decade and a half after the production of the *Relación de Michoacán*. Oftentimes Tarascan nobles, again like members of the indigenous nobilities of societies throughout Mesoamerica, sought those privileges through the Spanish court system and as such had to present themselves as deserving subjects of the Crown's justice—and therefore in the process represent themselves as willingly subservient and loyal subjects of that Crown. In other words, these nobles, including Don Francisco Taríacuri, had no reserve about maximizing their position and status in the developing colonial order by petitioning and taking on the Spanish legal system and at times the Crown itself, but did so according to the Crown's rules of engagement.

On some level the priest's narrative constitutes an act of covert resistance, or at least by calling for Don Francisco Taríacuri to accede to the governorship he is hoping that indigenous society and its political structure can be conserved if not restored in some form. Surely this would have been against the Spaniards' goals, and so it is important to consider among the large amount of evidence for indigenous accommodation among the political elites and nobility of the Spanish colonial system, instances in which actions by indigenous peoples contested the encroaching Spanish hegemony. There are a few instances of engagement and resistance in Michoacán that fall outside of the realm of the Crown's preferred battlefield, the imposed legal and official system the rules of which it could ostensibly control. One example is the backdrop to the trial spearheaded by Nuño Beltrán de Guzmán that ended in Tzintzicha Tangáxoan's death. Guzmán was at the time leading a military expedition into what is today Jalisco to conquer the peoples of the region (see recent discussions of the efforts to "pacify" that region in Weigand 2015a, 2015b). Success in this endeavor was reliant on indigenous allies, just as indigenous allies had played a significant role in earlier Spanish conquests throughout Mesoamerica (Restall 2004; Matthew and Oudijk 2007; Yannakakis 2011). Some of the questions put to Tzintzicha Tangáxoan and other members of the Tarascan nobility concerned the possibility of an ambush of Tarascan soldiers based on rumors that Guzmán had heard; his mission could ill afford dissension among the ranks of indigenous allies, let alone open rebellion. Other questions put to the Tarascan king and other nobles also concerned whether or not he or his subordinates were responsible for the deaths of a few Spaniards in his kingdom during that uneasy period when both power structures vied for their existence and for supremacy. We will likely never know what role if any Tzintzicha Tangáxoan played in such deaths, nor whether there ever was an actual threat of ambush on the road into present-day Jalisco, but the fact that these events existed in the realm of possibility for Guzmán and at least some of his fellow Spaniards could indicate that in certain regards or at certain times, acts of open rebellion by the Tarascan elites were at least not unthinkable. Even the act of gathering up the ashes of the dead king from the Lerma River, carried out by numerous indigenous peoples following his trial and execution (as in the second quote that opens this book), was from a juridical point of view a rebellious one—it violated Guzmán's explicit desire that there be nothing left of the king that could serve as a rallying point or foment rebellion among the indigenous populace (Alcalá 2000:689–690; Scholes and Adams 1952; Warren 1985)—if not also a symbolic one.[9]

The *Relación de Michoacán* itself states that after the death of Tzintzicha Tangáxoan, the people had to be put in prisons to keep them from fleeing (Alcalá 2000:690). Later, chroniclers of the region in the eighteenth century would claim that due to the death of Tzintzicha Tangáxoan indigenous peoples "renounced the Spanish government and Michoacán was temporarily lost 'to God and to the King'" (Afanador-Pujol 2015:163; the quote is from Moreno 1989). Guzmán is a dichotomous figure in Mexican history and has been ever since his ouster (Afanador-Pujol 2010; Martínez Baracs 2005; Warren 1985), in large part because of actions such as the trial and execution of Tzintzicha Tangáxoan, and so political motivations to reflect poorly on the man cannot be ruled out in these after-the-fact reports of the consequences of Guzmán's actions. If such reports are true (and political motivations do not necessarily indicate that they are not), there is a sense that certain drastic actions could be and in some respects were met with indigenous defiance of the process of imposing a colonial order.

In addition, the supposed presence of armed indigenous warriors that accompanied Quiroga's actions in forestalling an act of possession by Juan de Infante should not be minimized; whether or not such a force existed, Infante apparently believed that it was within the realm of possibility. While such an armed force of indigenous warriors (if it existed) was acting in concert with a Spaniard, and a powerful one at that in Quiroga, and perhaps those warriors might not have been willing to take up arms against Infante without Quiroga playing a role in the affair, I suggest that at certain times and in regards to certain issues, extrajudicial (or legally highly ambiguous) actions and the threat of violence were believed to be possible.

In sum, the context of the production of the *Relación de Michoacán* was a highly contentious one in which numerous individual agendas and the presence of multiple factions with competing interests renders a simple dichotomy between "conquerors" and "conquered" misleading. Furthermore, the individuals and factions allied themselves with one another in a manner that was quite transitory and limited to specific goals—not only were these alliances liable to shift at a moment's notice but they crosscut one another at any single point in time. For any particular individual or faction, delineating goals and priorities was itself a culturally and historically mediated process, such as the desire of the indigenous nobility to preserve not merely a gap in wealth between themselves and former subordinates, but a social gap marked by different privileges and bodily adornment and modes of being (e.g., wearing Spanish-style clothing and hairstyles and obtaining the right to own and ride a horse). Kuthy's (1996; see also 2003) study demonstrates that one strategy employed by Tarascan elites for preserving their privileges and offices in the Colonial era was to rotate offices among themselves and thereby keep lower elites from assuming them. These were not merely social concerns but also reflected ideological beliefs in the nature of hierarchy and the interrelationship between sociopolitical position and the spiritual essence of personhood—rulers had the right to rule because spiritually or ideologically they were different kinds of people (see especially López Austin 1973, 1988 for Mesoamerica in general and Martínez González 2010, 2011 for Michoacán in particular). For them, preserving a social system was about economics and privilege, but it also had significant undertones that related to very basic understandings of how the cosmos worked and how the social world of humans fit into and reflected more totalizing ideas concerning how that larger cosmos worked.

Turning toward the issue of ideology and religion, little is explicitly known concerning the impacts of the imposition of the colonial order on the indigenous people relied upon to mediate or interpolate between the human world and the cosmos, namely, the indigenous priesthood. Priests in indigenous society clearly held respected positions above the commoners, but they were not members of the aristocratic class strictly speaking for the simple fact that they had no claims to land in the same manner as the native nobility. They appear in the *Relación de*

Michoacán to have been essentially members of the state bureaucratic field and to have lived off of the state's largesse in the form of "temple lands," though of course differentiated from the lay bureaucracy (Alcalá 2000:568–569). They tended to the temples and the idols of the gods and their accouterments, performed rites and ceremonies of a purely religious nature, officiated politically motivated rites of passage such as marriages that cemented alliances between the king and subordinate lords, spoke on behalf of the king, and made speeches in preparation for war and even fought in war as both warriors and bearers of flags or standards as well as the god idols themselves (Alcalá 2000:568, 584). The subject matter of those occupations—namely, theological and philosophical understandings of the cosmos—was of course the target of intense efforts at eradication on the part of both secular and religious Spanish officials in the new colonial order. Without anything resembling an indigenous state apparatus, moreover, the priesthood must have lost its primary source of patronage. The at least nominal conversion of Tzintzicha Tangáxoan to Christianity and his baptism into the new faith, along with the baptism of the other members of the nobility including the king's sons, was likely also problematic for the indigenous priests. These different but interrelated processes could only have brought into stark clarity the reality that their role was severely threatened. In this way, while the priesthood was officially the keepers of tradition and history in the Tarascan kingdom, and it is important to remember that in Mesoamerica as in many societies "tradition" and "history" are bound up with ideological ideas concerning how human history *should* work as it must fit with larger cosmological precepts (Boone 2000, 2007; Gillespie 1989; see chapter 2), their experiences and viewpoint with respect to the encroaching colonial order was unique and different in significant respects from any other class or faction of indigenous peoples. This fact only underscores the necessity to examine the ways in which "historicity" is multiple and unavoidably operates with respect to social position and the differential outlooks on various modes of social action in the flow of time (see chapter 3).

LITERALIST ASSUMPTIONS AND THE PROBLEM OF TARÍACURI

In this respect, it is essential to provide background regarding how native historical traditions have been treated in Mesoamerican studies. Investigations of the ethnohistoric record of Michoacán have been part and parcel of these larger trends, and below I detail specifically how understandings of the priest's speech in the *Relación de Michoacán* in particular have been grounded in the same implicit predispositions and biases. The search for and claims of having found unproblematic, historical information that characterized early studies of the *Relación de Michoacán* and ethnohistoric documents throughout Mesoamerica were aided in large part by the nature of Mesoamerican societies themselves. Mesoamerica as a culture area was home to complex societies that produced and kept records concerned with the past, in contrast to other areas encountered by European colonialists. As such, indigenous informants drew upon a rich tradition of relating the past within the present in their responses to Spanish colonial authorities, often using, interpreting, and reinterpreting existing documents. The fact that Mesoamerica was composed of cultures that possessed such a rich written and literary tradition when it came to their past—and additionally that this tradition was produced within entirely different assumptions of meaning, temporality, and evidence—makes it an important anthropological site for different case studies. Tarascan society has at times been seen as having a problematic relationship to the rest of Mesoamerica and by extension its literary traditions (Anawalt 1992; Pollard 1993a; Roskamp 1998; Stone 2004), but this is changing in favor of accepting more of a cultural literacy that produced written (or painted—see chapter 2) documents than was previously acknowledged. At the very least we can say that Tarascan society possessed a rich tradition of oral history and oratory, codified particularly within the indigenous priesthood, which was likely buttressed to some extent by physical documents (see below). Such variation and particularities of practice only add, furthermore, to the complex but rewarding task of attempting to understand how Tarascan practitioners regarded and engaged their histories in the task of making, remaking, and relating their past to the present, and thus how they relate to the larger Mesoamerican tradition.

Past scholarship on Mesoamerican societies' relations with their pasts has typically had its own agenda of taking indigenous testimonies and historical representations and distilling out the "real" historical past from indigenous sources. In this regard Tarascan culture and history, and the *Relación de Michoacán* in particular, have been examined very much within this mainstream. Investigating some "true" prehispanic past has entailed dividing such representations into presumably or "demonstrably" (using historical methods such as source criticism and confirmation in multiple sources) historical parts and mythical parts. In some instances, whole documents were classified as "mythic" or "historical" in orientation (see discussion in Gillespie 1989), and the priest's narrative in the *Relación de Michoacán* has for a long time been implicitly treated as a historical source. Isolated characterizations of the "deeper past" in the narrative as "mythic" and other episodes in the more recent past as allegory aside (such characterizations are footnoted along with the presentation and analysis of the narrative in chapter 4), this narrative has for many reasons been treated as a reasonable approximation of the real prehispanic past (Haskell 2013, 2015; Kirchhoff 1956; López Austin 1981; Martínez Baracs 2005; Roskamp 2010a, 2011). At the very least it is often presented as the past and the historical events that produced the Tarascan kingdom, with little to no mention of the assumptions behind its use as such.

This interpretive framework has been increasingly recognized as a deeply flawed one. By dichotomizing between myth and history, scholars do a severe disservice to the creative products of highly skilled indigenous scholars in literature and history. In the hands of Western scholars, "historical" sources are contaminated by "mythic" material or alternatively historical events become "garbled" mythological ideas or concepts. "Mythic" sources are purely, or nearly so, the products of an indigenous mentality in which events are subordinated to ideology and indigenous scholars thereby reproduce their culture, boiled down to an ideology that cosmological structure perpetuates itself at the expense of historical events. Implicitly, the dichotomy robs indigenous scholars of their own agency, and their own *kinds* of agency. On the one hand they are seen as embodiments of Levi-Strauss's oft-criticized "cold" societies in which history's events barely enter the equation and ideology reproduces itself even without agency on the part of these scholars.[10] On the other hand indigenous scholars could be categorized as "historically minded," in the same sense as modern Western historians, scholars who unimaginatively recite events from the past in the same order that they happened. In the most extreme form of such "historicism" as applied to the priest's narrative, some modern scholars presume that the priest was merely a vehicle for tradition, reciting a fixed and unalterable narrative that had been passed down to him over generations of fellow priests (as in Kirchhoff's view, discussed below). Either way, there is no room for indigenous agency, and this is a result of a lack of anthropological imagination, a "defective framework of analysis in anthropology" (Whitehead 2003:xi), rather than a reflection of the actual abilities of past practitioners of what we have come to call "historicity"—the active production of the relation between the past, present, and future.

Literalist or historicist readings of the priest's speech in the *Relación de Michoacán* can be traced back to at least the turn of the twentieth century, and indeed they might be implicit in the understandings and goal of the friar that guided the production of the document. Due to the human-centric (rather than deity-centric[11]) nature of the priest's narrative and the admittedly immense level of detail it contains, in coordination with the rise and dominance of "literal-mindedness" (Burke 1990) among historians, the priest's narrative was interpreted at the outset of serious scholarly inquiry as "historical." More recent investigations of the narrative and the document as a whole have undertaken a more nuanced approach to the document, detailing how the specific words and phrases used reveal biases and struggles for power between the many factions involved in its production. In addition, the instrumental nature of the narrative as the priest who told it used the occasion to have his telling recorded in such an important document is being increasingly recognized and made the focus of scrutiny. In spite of these advances, however, there remains a bias toward regarding the narrative as "historical."

An early "father" of the modern study of the prehispanic Tarascan kingdom and its history was Nicolás León. Writing in the late nineteenth century and early twentieth century, León leaned heavily on the *Relación de Michoacán* in order to write his "Tarascan Kings" (Reyes tarascos [1903]). By doing so, León effectively assumed that the document was authoritative and accurate in terms of its representation of the prehispanic past. A half-century later, in his "preliminary study" of the *Relación de Michoacán*, which accompanied its 1956 publication, Paul Kirchhoff codified and defended the logic behind this assumption. Kirchhoff (1956: xx) states that we are dealing with a text whose parts "have the character of words fixed by tradition. Observe, in the first place, the great historical narration of the chief priest that, it seems, is reproduced word for word." If these tales and narrations are "fixed by tradition," then what is being reproduced "word for word" is not simply what the chief priest is telling the friar, but what that priest had learned from his predecessors as part of that fixing. This is all to say that Kirchhoff interpreted the enormous amount of detail in the priest's version of the history recorded in the *Relación de Michoacán* as evidence that the narrative was memorized and passed down from generation to generation, as an unalterable text.[12]

León's basic assumption, codified by Kirchhoff, that the priest's narrative was a fairly faithful representation of the prehispanic past went mostly unchallenged for decades. More recently, however, the *Relación de Michoacán* as a whole and the priest's narrative specifically have been the subject of interrogation. One vein of this examination has been the investigation of the mismatch of word choice and rhetoric in the document in contrast to what was going on in the larger context of the document's production. Thus a "bias" toward the Tzintzuntzan faction of the Uacúsecha (the Uanacaze) has been identified due to the fact that the document refers to Tzintzuntzan as "Michoacán," implying the title of "Ciudad de Michoacán." This title was, however, one that Tzintzuntzan could no longer claim, due to the fact that Bishop Quiroga moved the seat of the diocese in 1538, thereby also moving the colonial and indigenous governments to Pátzcuaro. As part of this move, Pátzcuaro now claimed the title "Ciudad de Michoacán." To refer to Tzintzuntzan as such was to make a point concerning this transfer and its propriety or lack thereof (Bravo Ugarte 1962b; Martínez Baracs 1989, 2005; Roskamp 1998; see also summary in Stone 2004:123–124). The appreciation that, at least in such minutiae, the *Relación de Michoacán* was produced to reflect certain positions is thus a departure from Kirchhoff's (1956) earlier analysis in which speeches were passed down and related to the friar "word for word." Like Kirchhoff, however, the advocates of this "Tzintzuntzanist" position still adopt a historicist view of the narrative, that is, that it does describe some version of the "real" past, just from a biased viewpoint with an axe to grind.

Roskamp has done much work to advance the state of research into representations of the Tarascan past in recent years and generally takes the view that Tarascan narratives of the past constitute what he calls "sacred history" (Roskamp 2012:124).[13] His work has shone an essential light on the presence of a distinct historical tradition among a community of noble Nahua speakers in Tzintzuntzan who present themselves in one document as essential to the transition of power to Tzintzuntzan and the ascendancy of King Tzitzispandáquare, the grandfather of Tzintzicha Tangáxoan, there (Monzón, Roskamp, and Warren 2009; Roskamp 2010a, 2012, 2015; see also Haskell 2013). More recently he has compared the version of the past presented in the *Relación de Michoacán* by the priest with this Nahua tradition concerning Tzintzuntzan, another Nahua tradition from the southern copper-mining area of Michoacán in the form of the *Lienzo de Jicalán*,[14] and other Purhépecha (Tarascan) language or Purhépecha community primordial land titles (*Títulos Primordiales*) (Roskamp 2010b, 2015; see table 1.1 for a listing of the documents and the Uacúsecha members mentioned in each). He notes the differences between these land titles and the priest's "official" version recorded in the *Relación de Michoacán* but focuses more on the similarities that they all possess. In contrast, I believe that the differences manifested in these documents are salient to an understanding of how historicity was practiced by various communities in Michoacán, particularly insofar as they list Uacúsecha characters (some of whom reportedly functioned as kings) out of order, introduce names not found in the *Relación de Michoacán*, delete names found in that document, at times discuss Uacúsecha members as ruling at the same time or being brothers in ways that differ from the *Relación de Michoacán*, and finally attribute greatness or critically important events (such as founding towns) to different Uacúsecha members. Note in table 1.1 that Taríacuri's status as the main Uacúsecha character is far from universal, and in many documents he is completely absent. In almost all of the documents any genealogical relationships between members that are mentioned in the *Relación de Michoacán* are different in the other sources.

It is furthermore crucial to note that in spite of the proclamations of caveats that the priest's narrative is problematically "legendary history," "biased," and contains "mythical" or "allegorical" elements, when it comes down to "writing" or "describing" the prehistory of Michoacán, such caveats are forgotten and the version of "history" presented in the *Relación de Michoacán* is re-presented *as the prehispanic past*, as if the priest's narrative is good enough as a historical source to use it as the main, or sole, basis of reconstructions of that past. Most commonly this process of *re*-presenting the priest's narrative as a stand-in for "the" prehispanic past is straightforward and presented in a style of history familiar to Westerners as a sequence of events or actions. Frequently the characters of the deep past, beginning with

TABLE 1.1. List of ethnohistoric documents from Purhépecha communities and the *Uacúsecha* leaders/kings that they mention, along with sources that discuss and in some cases reproduce the documents.

Ethnohistoric Document	Uacúsecha Kings	Source(s)
Relación de Michoacán	Hireticatame, Sicuirancha, Paucume, Uapeani, Curátame, Uapeani, Pauacume, Aramen, Cetaco, Taríacuri,[†] Tangáxoan,* Hiripan,* Curátame, Hiquíngaxe,* Tzitzispandáquare, Ticatame, Hiquíngaxe, Zuangua, Tzintzicha Tangáxoan	Alcalá 2000
Códice Plancarte (Carapan)	Rey Harame,* Rey Vacusticatame,* Rey Tzitzispandáquare,* Rey Tziuanqua, Rey Taríacuri, Rey Sicuirhancha, Rey Carapu, Rey Thagajoan tzintzicha	*Códice Plancarte* 1959; see also Roskamp 2003, 2015
Genealogía de los Caciques de Carapan	Calapu, Uacusticatame, Sicuirancha, Tzitzispandáquare, Zuangua, Don Francisco Tsitsicha Dag	León 1903; Roskamp 2003
Lienzo de Pátzcuaro, Lienzo de Carapan	Harame, Uacusticatame, Carapu, Tzintzicha Tangáxoan, Pauacupe	Roskamp 2003
Coats of Arms of Tzintzuntzan, 1593	Harame, Uacusticatame	Roskamp 1997, 2002
Coat of Arms of Tzintzuntzan, early eighteenth century	Sinsicha, Chiguangua (Zuangua), Chiguacua	Beaumont 1932; Roskamp 2011
Lienzo de Nahuatzen	Yrecha Tsintsicha	Roskamp 2004
Lienzo de Aranza	Possible depiction of Yrecha Tzintzicha, only visible in a drawing by Pablo García Abarca in the late nineteenth century and the location of which in the original is unclear	Roskamp and César Villa 2003 (on the possible doubt surrounding the depiction of Tzintzicha see pg. 235)
Primordial Title from Jarácuaro, version 1	Chupitante,* Cacua,* Vipinchuan,* Hareme,* Gusman,* Tsintsichan,* Tsipetaqua,*[†] Phanguarequa,* Quitsique, Sinderindi	Roskamp 2010b; see also discussion in Roskamp 2012; León 1906
Primordial Title from Jarácuaro, version 2	Ziuangua,[†] who has three sons, (from oldest to youngest) Tzintzicha, Tzitzispandáquare, Taríacuri	Roskamp 2010b; see also discussion in Roskamp 2012; León 1906

* Kings who are said to have existed at the same time / ruled jointly within each respective document.

† Importance/greatness in cases in which one king or character is clearly more important than others. I point out this inescapable fact not to cast aspersions on Tarascan historicity, as to our Western eye these data appear to be a jumbled mess. On this point I would simply say that this would be a result of expecting Tarascan historicity to conform to Western historicity, which it does not seem to do; this basic

continued on next page

Table 1.1 continued

statement is part of the point of this book. More specifically to the point, moreover, we must recognize that Taríacuri's prominence in the *Relación de Michoacán* becomes something to be investigated rather than assumed as historical fact for the actual prehispanic past. Seeing Taríacuri's prominence in the assumed prehispanic past is, I argue, largely the result of interpreting the priest's narrative in the *Relación de Michoacán* as the "official" state history and as (therefore) good enough for the "real past." The guiding assumption is that because it is the "official" state history, the priest that told the narrative must have been in the best position to draw on the institutionalization of education and memory, and therefore that the narrative constitutes the "best" and/or "fullest" account of the real past. Concomitant with this implicit view is the belief that it is likely to be the closest approximation of both the real past and a prehispanic version of a narrative of the Uacúsecha's origins and exploits in the formation of a unified kingdom that we will likely never have available to us. Roskamp (2015:125–126) displays such historicist assumptions concerning the Priest's Speech by holding it as a benchmark against which to evaluate these other documents: "Whereas some documents include accurate and extensive references that coincide with elements from the official history of the lineage (recorded in the petámuti's discourse), others include information that is less certain." Note here how Roskamp *assumes* that the priest's narrative is the most factual, but that this contention is not demonstrated nor explicitly defended on theoretical grounds. I take the point of view that the priest's narrative and the Priest that formulated it had the most at stake—the future of the royal dynasty and what overarching political organization it still symbolized and headed—and therefore might be the *most* unconventional or the most significant departure from the prehispanic and Early Colonial representations of the past that had existed up until that time.

the founder of the Uacúsecha, Hireticatame, are called "mythical" or "legendary." Martínez Baracs (2005:96–98), for example, calls this founding character "mythic" but proceeds to give dates ("ca. 1340–1360") to his son Sicuirancha and for every Uacúsecha member that follows. This basic approach, of finding some dividing line between a past that is presumably too far gone to have been represented faithfully and a recent past as represented in narrative in a way that is believed to be close enough to the real past is universal across discussions of the prehispanic past of the Tarascan state. Only the particular boundary line between "legendary" and "historical" shifts, and even then it only shifts slightly, insofar as interpretations only vary by a generation or two in terms of when they see "history" as beginning in the *Relación de Michoacán*. Furthermore, Kirchhoff (1956) and Alfredo López Austin (1981) go beyond mere representation and base their interpretations of the rise of the state as the result of the economic and military bases and capacities of the feuding factions/polities as described in the priest's narrative.

THE RISKS OF RECENT EMPHASES ON HYBRIDITY IN THE *RELACIÓN DE MICHOACÁN*

Contemporary ethnohistorians, influenced by developments in postcolonial theory and studies of the relationship between colonial-era ethnohistoric documents and the context in which they were produced, have recently begun to emphasize the inescapably colonial nature of the document and the priest's role in its production.

This is a productive line of inquiry, and there is much to be said for approaching the *Relación de Michoacán* as an inescapably hybrid document (Afanador-Pujol 2010, 2015; Espejel Carbajal 2008; Fernández 2011; Stone 2004). It is the product of a number of agencies, as reflected in the difference of the sources for the two quotes—one (the narrator of the history of the Uacúsecha) a priest and likely a frustrated advocate of the old order and the other (Don Pedro Cuinierángari) an individual whose newfound status was entirely due to the fluidity of the colonial encounter itself. It is undoubtedly a predominantly Spanish document, as a Franciscan friar was asked by the viceroy of New Spain to produce such a document, this friar appears to have chosen those who participated in its production, he exercised editorial control over its contents, and most obviously of all the document was written in Spanish. More than this, the *Relación de Michoacán* was a complex amalgamation of goals, intentions, viewpoints, and collaborations. It was furthermore likely influenced by a much wider cultural dialog and interchange that is now being investigated in its many manifestations and implications by a number of scholars working from various disciplines.[15] I do not deny that the priest who told his story for its production was a historically and politically situated actor; in fact this point is a central part of my argumentation. The manner in which he was brought into the project shaped the ultimate form of the *Relación de Michoacán* and so too must this opportunity to tell "a" or even "*the* story of the royal dynasty" (as it would come to be, given the prominence of the document, a fact the priest very well might have appreciated) shaped his narrative as he sought to influence, in an authoritative way, the historical moment in which he found himself. His allegiances and alliances with the indigenous nobility, his relationship with the indigenous gods, and perhaps certain Spaniards all likely shaped his narrative as well. Those shaping processes thus makes the narrative hybrid in many complex and interwoven ways.

The fact that the priest's exhortation to his people in the quote that opens this book is an agentic act has been recognized (Stone 2004). Similarly, certain disparate passages of the priest's narrative and other passages based on indigenous testimony have recently been viewed as agentic acts on the part of these indigenous persons in the face of attempts to impose Spanish hegemony; the same can be said for the illustrations of the document (Afanador-Pujol 2015). However, it is something of a tragic irony that contemporary investigations of the subtleties of cultural dialog in the Early Colonial dialog between cultures, interpretations of collaboration and tension evident in such projects (Afanador-Pujol 2010, 2015; Stone 2004), and hybridity or even the modeling of the priest's words on European forms of rhetoric and argumentation (Espejel Carbajal 2008; Fernández 2011), run the risk of downplaying or detracting from the voices of the indigenous people.[16] Such voices are complex, as are their relations to such projects, and I do not wish to minimize this complexity (nor return to a naive indigeneity that it is intended to correct; see Quiroa 2011). However, as anthropologists and historians have sought to investigate agency and alternative and even complementary processes of accommodation and resistance in the imposition of a colonial order, an admirable goal, such efforts have been undercut in part due to this new emphasis in which everything is hybrid and novel, and nothing can be called "authentically" indigenous. Such a viewpoint fails to incorporate advancements in anthropological theory ever since the "historical turn" that view culture as always in flux. "Authenticity" is problematic in such a theoretical view so long as "authentic" is used to mean "static" (Ohnuki-Tierney 2001, 2005). Simply because the context of production is ineluctably tied up in colonialist power relations and historical contingencies does not necessarily imply that individual and agentic protestations and responses to such processes are not "indigenous" so long as "indigenous" incorporates some theoretical room for culturally influenced agency, praxis, and improvisation (e.g., in the manner of Bourdieu 1977; see chapter 3 in this book).

Such an emphasis on hybridity in its many manifestations also fails to engage the hierarchical nature of culture and particularly of the symbolic forms that exist in a recursive relationship with it. For this particular study of narrative, Terence Turner's work is the explicit literature of reference concerning the hierarchical nature of culture (Turner 1969, 1977, 1985; this oeuvre on narrative draws on Piaget's structuralism, which is thoroughly hierarchical—see Turner [1973] on the adaptation of Piaget's work in anthropology). In such an understanding of culture, hybridity can and does exist, but it can exist at various levels. A Spanish or European element can be used but at the level of "surface content," while the deeper-level structure can remain much as it had before. Of course, one of Marshall Sahlins's (1981, 1985, 2004) main points is that in time the substitution at the surficial level has deeper-level consequences, but his other point is that this is precisely the object of analysis—how culture changes over time but now with the recognition that changes in different phenomena happen at various levels at various times (see also, e.g., Fausto and Heckenberger, 2007; Gillespie 1989; Hill 1988; Ohnuki-Tierney 1990a, 1990b; Ohnuki-Tierney 2005; Parmentier 1987; Rosaldo 1980a, 1980b).[17] Bringing this argument to the realm of the concrete and the case at hand, it is inescapably true that in many ways the *Relación de Michoacán* and the priest's narrative within it are hybrid products. The document, and presumably the friar who interjects in the midst of the priest's narrative, is explicit on this point: the narrative from the point of the friar's own early interjection onward is going to be different than the priest would have told it, indeed as he began to tell it before that interjection (Alcalá 2000:341). This is the clearest and most explicit influence, but there are undoubtedly others up to and including the facts that the narrative would have been told to indigenous lords as opposed to a Spanish friar and that it would have served to legitimate the rule of the indigenous king rather than (as I contend) advocate for a new king. These indications of hybridity are clear and self-evident. It would also be a mistake, however, to presume that such hybridity—the infiltration of Spanish influence and the contingent facts of history—left its mark and did so to the same extent at all levels of cultural/symbolic production on the part of the indigenous participants in the document's production. Searching for "pure" and/or prehispanic indigeneity as manifested in symbolic forms is the wrong analytic tack. Instead, we can investigate the opposite end of the equation—how far away is a given representation from what we know of the Spanish cultural matrix at that point in time, and just as important, at what cultural level or depth are these departures from those Spanish and contextual impingements. By investigating in this direction and at various/deeper levels I contend that indigenous voices—not unchanged or unaffected to be sure, but indigenous in some way such as intent, larger level structures of meaning, and a cognizance of formulating histories and futures explicitly at odds with Spanish visions of both[18]—can and should be identified and analyzed. In this way the present study is similar in its approach to the *Relación de Michoacán* and "hybridity" to Afanador-Pujol's (2015) analysis of the paintings of the document. Her approach engaged in very detailed analyses of the hands and painting styles (including appropriation of Spanish and European artistic conventions and innovations) to identify specific agents and their relation to this larger hybrid project and the even larger cultural interchange in which both indigenous peoples and Spaniards were engaged. The difference is one not of goals but of subject matter. She paid close attention to the details of the artistry and composition of the paintings. I pay close attention to the composition and structure employed by the priest to produce his narrative's many episodes and the logic of the transformations of the nature and sequences of actions in which the characters engage themselves and in which one figure, Taríacuri, produces his own transformation into the embodiment of supreme authority.

Outside of Michoacán and among the more literarily productive cultures of Mesoamerica—namely, the Aztecs (Nahua), Maya, and peoples of Oaxaca—contemporary scholars have made and continue to make significant advances in appreciating the decidedly non-Western and typically pictographic, cartographic, and/or mixed textual and image-based approaches to producing and representing the past and its temporal flow of cultural events.[19] In this way they are using "hybridity" in a productive manner. Their work for the most part escapes the potential risks of such a focus on a naive indigeneity by using sophisticated methodologies to identify and investigate particular and specific practices and agencies and the extent to which they interrelate with the goals and nature of the projects in which they are incorporated and even the colonial contexts writ large. Such studies bring us closer to an indigenous approach by bypassing or importantly contextualizing and situating documents produced using the media of representation imposed by the Spaniards, namely, lengthy written testimonies. This development is to be applauded, but we should also not completely leave behind such lengthy testimonies, due largely to epistemological issues. Camilla Townsend (2012) notes that these studies frequently involve the glosses in some way and contends that such alphabetic documents are the epistemologically most secure way of appreciating and understanding what the indigenous and/or mestizo persons of the Early Colonial Period were saying (even as they were interpreting nonnarrative forms of record keeping). In this way written documents "let[ting] historical subjects speak for themselves" (Townsend 2012:184). She writes, furthermore, that "we need to hear words—long, intricate strings of words with subordinate clauses and ranging notions of predicativity—to know others deeply."[20] In much the same vein, Tedlock (2010:1) complains that when it comes to the rich and lengthy Maya writing tradition, much "decipherment" of Maya texts has taken place, but much "translation" of such texts, particularly in terms of understanding their literary qualities in ways that get us closer to the original and intended meanings, has yet to be achieved.

I fully acknowledge that in working with the priest's narrative, much information concerning indigenous conceptions of time and historical processes has been lost because it exists only as it has been translated to Spanish within the context of the *Relación de Michoacán*.[21] In the best of scenarios, listening to the priest and understanding him "deeply" would mean listening and understanding his narrative in its original language. However, I contend that the fact this narrative is translated into Spanish should not preclude an appreciation of at least some of the skill in its crafting as well as its overarching meaning. The method of narrative analysis that I utilize was developed by the anthropologist Terence Turner (1969, 1977, 1985), and as noted above has been called "an important and indispensable tool" (Willis 1982:xiii).[22] Within his discussion of this method, Turner (1977:123) has pointed out that narrative possesses qualities above the level of other aspects of language, such as phonology and syntax, that are amenable to analysis and particularly to investigating the indigenous construction of temporality and human agency through time. Therefore I make no claim to know the priest and the full range of culturally grounded knowledge and skill made manifest in his narrative completely and authoritatively, but I do believe that the appreciation of the artistry and meaning uncovered in the present work is an improvement over previous works. Therefore while the original indigenous language and therefore complexity of the priest's narrative as recorded in the *Relación de Michoacán*, and therefore in Spanish, can never be recovered, I examine the ways that larger-order linguistic structures are also constitutive of meaning and therefore help us better understand what the priest is doing in his narrative.

THE MEANING OF TARÍACURI IN THE *RELACIÓN DE MICHOACÁN*

The political chaos in both the indigenous world and the Spanish one, and of course the difficulty of merging the two into a single colonial society, spurred those involved to make sense of the new arrangements and evaluate the intense social posturing occurring based on any and all available conceptualizations of how society and the cosmos ought to work. More than this, new leaders were required that could evaluate the possible avenues for action and transform or help set the terms on which the various factions vying for power would engage one another. Clearly in the indigenous political system, as it had been transformed into a subordinate colonized administrative system, there was likely a crisis of leadership. Indigenous peoples, and the nobles in particular, had to adjust to a new system of governance in which the office of governor (as were the other offices in the indigenous system as it had been established by the Spaniards) was not only an elected one but one for which elections were held regularly. Thus not only was the primary indigenous authority in the new system divorced from the prehispanic power structure in terms of the personages that filled it, but the nature of the office was a far cry from the prehispanic power structure predicated upon a king who ruled for life and an office of kingship that was hereditary or at the very least confined to a candidate within the Uacúsecha.[23] Kuthy (1996, 2003) has demonstrated that in the Early Colonial Period the indigenous upper nobility in Michoacán managed to maintain a hold on these offices such that possession of the offices was in effect rotated among the more powerful families that comprised the upper nobility. This arrangement was, however, only in its infancy, if it had begun to be formulated at all by those involved in 1538–1541, when the *Relación de Michoacán* was being produced—remember that rotating the officeholder of the supreme indigenous authority was only necessary beginning in 1530 upon the death of Tzintzicha Tangáxoan. It is also important to remember that as far as we know, Don Pedro Cuinierángari, an "Islander" or traditionally subservient member of the king's royal house, had served as governor for most of the time since Tzintzicha's death until the production of the document. I suggest that rather than adapt to the imposed colonial structure of governance, the priest who related his narrative for inclusion in the *Relación de Michoacán* envisioned a novel, transformative figure who could effectively reset the terms of the colonial arrangement, if not separate the indigenous society from the Spanish colonial system and reconstitute it as an autonomous one. In this respect I agree with Stone (2004:135) that the priest's narrative is concerned primarily with pointing out who this individual is. "When the petámuti asks where more Chichimecs [lords/ warriors; see below] are to come from . . . [t]he unspoken corollaries are: Who is destined to follow in the footsteps of Taríacuri? Who will serve to unite the powers of the solar god Curicaueri in his various manifestations, with those of the goddess Xarátanga and other lunar deities? Who will have the power to symbolically reconstitute the iréchequa [the indigenous word for kingdom], to bring order out of chaos?"

Stone (2004:148) suggests that the priest believes Quiroga to be that person, and the evidence she cites does have some merit, which I discuss in detail in chapter 5 because it involves specific episodes of the priest's narrative and other sections contained in the *Relación de Michoacán*.

I argue, however, that the structure and content of the narrative indicate Don Francisco Taríacuri to be that figure who can reconstitute indigenous society and the grounds on which it relates to Spanish society. Don Francisco Taríacuri was, I suggest, the same kind of dual figure who the original Taríacuri is said to be in the priest's narrative, a figure who could inhabit two different social worlds and work to stitch those worlds together.[24] As early as 1525, Tzintzicha Tangáxoan, who had been baptized and taken the name "Don Francisco" as his Christian name himself, agreed that some of the sons of the indigenous nobility should be educated in the Christian faith, though this apparently involved children other than his own going to Mexico City to learn from the Franciscans there (Warren 1985:82–83). Don Francisco Taríacuri himself had begun to learn the Christian doctrine early in his life at the Monastery of Saint Francis of the Province of Michoacán, constructed in Tzintzuntzan (Jiménez 2002:137; López Sarrelangue 1965:170). However, Nora Jiménez (2002:137) believes that such efforts at missionization by the earliest Franciscans should not be exaggerated because they were not very successful in converting the indigenous peoples of Michoacán prior to 1535. As noted above, Don Francisco became a page in Viceroy Mendoza's court, in Mexico City. He had been taken there by Don Pedro Cuinierángari and other nobles in 1535, and the express reason for Don Francisco and his brother Don Antonio being removed from Tzintzuntzan to Mexico City was as hostages to help guarantee the loyalty and compliance of the leaders of indigenous society in Michoacán (López Sarrelangue 1965:170). However, the experience was also an exercise in "intense cultural acculturation" (Jiménez 2002:137) to Spanish and Catholic practices and beliefs. While in Mexico City, he learned Castilian and Latin grammar. Documents from this period state that Don Francisco dressed as a Spaniard and was always treated as such (López Sarrelangue 1965:171). He also married a Spanish woman in 1542 (López Sarrelangue 1965:171), though it is important to note that this union occurred after the production of the *Relación de Michoacán* and its presentation to Viceroy Mendoza.

Therefore I suggest that Don Francisco was "the best of both worlds," perhaps quite literally. He was the oldest son of the previous king and therefore the legitimate heir to the kingship, or whatever version of the indigenous kinship existed or which he could fashion for himself in the Early Colonial Period. His birthright to the kingship is likely reflected in his not-so-subtle use of the title Caltzontzin, the Nahua-cum-Spanish name of choice for the king of Michoacán (see discussions of the etymology of Cazonci/Caltzontzin in Martínez Baracs [1997, 2003]), as a surname. He also would have been comfortable within the Spanish colonial world, having been educated within it and to some extent being regarded as a Spaniard himself. In these regards he was an indigenous Spaniard; he united two contrary and antagonistic worlds and societies within his person.

These qualities, along with his name, he shared with the character Taríacuri as related in the priest's narrative. While Stone has certain reasons for believing that Quiroga is the person being indicated through allusions within the priest's narrative as the one who will reconstitute and lead indigenous society forward (which I note in the course of chapter 5 as they appear in the narrative), it is interesting to ask why she, or any other commentator for that matter, has not seen parallels between the two Taríacuris.[25] I suggest it is because Don Francisco Taríacuri is, in our modern understandings of the priest's narrative and its relation to the political chaos of the time at which it was produced, hiding in plain sight. He remains hidden because of the underlying assumption that the priest's narrative was a fixed oration, or that it is at least a faithful enough representation of the past that we should believe that a real Taríacuri existed in the past and performed the deeds that are attributed to him. Even in the recognition of the *Relación de Michoacán* as a "hybrid" and "biased" document, the reigning (though implicit) assumption is that the story written down in the *Relación de Michoacán* is largely the same as it existed in the prehispanic except for changes in wording and minor details intended to make points in favor of certain factions. At any rate, if Taríacuri really existed in the manner in which he is described in the priest's narrative (which almost if not all interpretations either implicitly assume or fail to question), the relation between him and his namesake five generations later has been regarded as an unproblematic matter of history—simply the way things actually happened. This relationship becomes quite interesting and a problem to be investigated if we do not assume historical veracity and instead allow for the active construction of the narrative and Taríacuri within it to suit the times. This is reflected in the differences among Purhépecha documents such as land titles (see above; Roskamp 2010b, 2015) as well as in the results of the analysis presented here.

Taríacuri is obviously an important character throughout much of the narrative, and his actions, more than the actions of any other character, result in the formation of the Tarascan kingdom. Taríacuri emerges as the cause and embodiment of the kingdom not only through the plot (events) of the narrative, however, but also through its structure. Taríacuri constructs but also embodies the kingship according to the indigenous cultural logic of hierarchy and legitimate authority. This cultural logic is dependent upon constructing two "elementary categories" (Haskell 2008a; Sahlins 1985), the "Islanders" and "Chichimecs." These categories have certain structural similarities to the categories at play in other Mesoamerican narratives, namely, the "autochthons" and "foreigners" in general and as they are specifically manifested in the Mexica and other Central Mexican narratives, the "Culhua" and the "Mexica" (and other "Chichimec" groups) (Gillespie 1989; Graulich 1997; López Austin and López Luján 2000; Martínez González 2010; see chapter 6 for a more in-depth discussion). This complementary dualism is also a widespread and deep-rooted construction of cosmology and kingship in Mesoamerica. For example, the "Feathered Serpent," an obvious conflation of opposed but complementary categories, was an important symbol at the Classic Period metropolis of Teotihuacán and from that time forward throughout much of Mesoamerica. If it wasn't at the very beginning at Teotihuacán, Feathered Serpent imagery quickly came to embody the cosmos writ large, the totality of power within that cosmos, and in a synecdochic relation, came to stand for the paradigmatic category of kingship as a microcosm of that power that simultaneously drew on that power but also helped ensure its ordering and preservation (Gillespie 1989; this draws on analyses of "sacred kingship," e.g., Feeley-Harnik 1978).

Narratives such as the priest's narrative construct the kingship as a production of symbolic hierarchy based on a cultural logic of encompassment (Haskell 2008a, 2008b, 2012; Sahlins 1985). The construction of hierarchy as the novel third term that encompasses or incorporates two complementary but opposed elementary categories is common to those constructions of authority that fall under Sahlins's term "Stranger King" (see chapter 4; Haskell 2008a). In such a "cultural logic" (Haskell 2008a) of kingship, the novel encompassing term combines and thus can stand for both original terms; therefore it also simultaneously subordinates those terms while elevating itself above them. Taríacuri's pivoting—his reversal from a stereotypically "Chichimec" character to an "Islander" character that works out sequentially his dual ambiguity that has always been latent in the symbolic content of his nature (see chapters 3 and 4)—constructs him as one who can embody both the Chichimec and Islander categories. This ability is only achieved by the personage of Taríacuri strictly speaking, and it is only made manifest in the action of the narrative (i.e., in contrast to his lineage and foretold greatness) sequentially. He can only be one status or quality at a time, even if through the course of the narrative, he can and does take on both Chichimec and Islander identities. After Taríacuri's pivoting and sequentially demonstrated ability to be both Islander and Chichimec, as well as his acquisition and incorporation of the wives and feminine wealth of the Islander category (i.e., the land and lake) in addition to his Chichimec nature, Taríacuri is enabled to reproduce that ability to embody both categories as a paradigmatic arrangement embodied by multiple characters simultaneously. The first such transformation takes place when he searches for and finds his nephews, Hiripan and Tangáxoan, followed by the transformation of Zapiuatame from a sacrificial victim to a productive ally, and ending with the addition of Hiquíngaxe to his two nephews. Taríacuri is instrumental in all of these events. In this way he stands for the encompassing duality achieved within the Uacúsecha not merely because he is the character that achieves it but also because he reproduces that duality in the succeeding generation.

The analysis presented here thereby demonstrates that the process of construction is more complex than a simple dualism in such "Stranger King" narrative structures, including the story of Taríacuri. This is the case because the novel encompassing term originates as one of the original two complementary but opposed elementary categories. In the priest's narrative it is the "Chichimec" category embodied by Taríacuri and the Uacúsecha as a whole that encompasses and appropriates, through the nature of Taríacuri's character and his actions—namely, his pivoting—that thereby becomes the novel third term, the term of kingship or sovereignty. In other words "Chichimec" means something very different at the end of the priest's narrative from what it does at the beginning, in concordance with Marshall Sahlins's (1985) insistence that structure is dynamic and processual. Taríacuri is simultaneously the result of that process of construction but was also its motivating factor; it was his own actions by which he came to be both Islander and Chichimec. He is thus a paradigmatic category, but a category that has as its semantic content an operational/transformative capacity. In this key aspect, he is not a static or simple symbol but fits into Terence Turner's (1985:52–53) discussion of "symbols [that] have an internal structure, not only of static oppositions but of coordinated transformations of the relations among their constituent meaningful features." This character of operational transformation is manifested most strikingly by his Chichimec ability to shoot the hummingbird at the urging of Zurumban, the act which sets his pivoting in motion. He, just like the narrative that relates his deeds, is an autopoietic (self-producing; see chapter 3) character and symbol of the poiesis by which society around him takes shape as a result of his actions.

In this vein, the priest's narrative does more than simply relate variations on the composition of the Uacúsecha as a set of imperfect, but increasingly correct, arrangements of Uacúsecha characters until the ascendancy of Hiripan, Tangáxoan, and Hiquíngaxe. As a set viewed synchronically, the multiple variations and the relations among them demonstrate the essential characteristics in terms of the elementary categories necessary in what ultimately is the proper arrangement for the establishment of the kingdom and the kingship. This understanding, however, shortchanges the character of Taríacuri and his meaning as not merely a symbol but an operational symbol. "The temporal or sequential form of narrative cannot therefore be dismissed . . . merely as a convenient device for the serial presentation of a complex paradigmatic structure" (Turner 1969:34). It is essential that, particularly in the latter half of the narrative, Taríacuri is the one who determines the composition of the Uacúsecha through the actions enumerated above. Concomitantly, the first half of the narrative can also be read in this fashion as the sequentially organized *production* of Taríacuri (a production in which he himself takes part, when possible) as a dually composed—both Chichimec and Islander—figure who would possess such agency. Having been thus properly constructed, Taríacuri goes on to actively produce the correct combination of Uacúsecha leaders, partly out of his own self-referential actions (his self-production), out of his own person in the case of his son Hiquíngaxe (Hiquíngaxe is presented as a reproduction of Taríacuri's Islander nature), and to his decisions and actions with regard to his nephews and whom he pairs with them. He is the operative principle by which the correct arrangement of characters and categories is recognized and subsequently is made manifest. This paradigmatic quality of the past Taríacuri is precisely what was needed in the context of the present Taríacuri, Don Francisco, as indigenous society sought to resynthesize itself in the face of, and probably by partly appropriating aspects of, Spanish society.

The symbolic content of Taríacuri and his sequentially manifested agency has yet further ramifications as revealed by the syntagmatic relations within the priest's narrative. Taríacuri's act of pivoting becomes the axis upon which the narrative folds back upon itself in terms of its syntagmatic arrangement and concomitant paradigmatic relations (as demonstrated and discussed in chapter 4). This is much more significant than simply saying that Taríacuri is the focal point of the action of the narrative. Through the merger of the pivoting of Taríacuri with the pivoting of the total sequence of the narrative, the person of Taríacuri and the "surface" meaning of the narrative (the story of the creation of the Tarascan kingdom) are fused into one. This equivalency of Taríacuri with kingship and the kingdom established through both the plot and the structural arrangement of paradigmatically related episodes is even manifested at the small scale within the last episode of the narrative in which the Uacúsecha triumvirate conquers the towns of the region thereby establishing the kingdom. In a telling syntagmatic juxtapositioning, Taríacuri dies in the midst of the conquests, and specifically after the towns Zacapu and Tariaran are named in separate lists of conquests. Zacapu, as the town where the Uacúsecha are said to have originated, and Tariaran, as the longtime seat of the goddess Xarátanga (a prominent female fertility goddess who complements the Uacúsecha patron deity Curicaueri) in the narrative, together signify the two complementary categories upon which the kingdom would be founded and the two categories that the narrative has taken pains to join together. Once these two places are conquered, the kingdom itself is a dually composed entity, and Taríacuri as the personification of the duality that had existed before it and worked so hard to bring it to fruition can meet his end. One form of the combination of the elementary categories (Taríacuri) is transformed into the other (the kingdom). Taríacuri is both the state and the process of state formation personified, which is to say he is the manifestation of a supreme transformational capacity within a single character.[26] The autopoietic nature of Taríacuri and the autopoietic nature of the narrative itself are produced as metaphors for one another, and merged through the identity of Taríacuri's pivoting as *both* a reversal of the content of his character and his relations with other groups of the Pátzcuaro Basin (particularly the Islanders) *and* the pivoting of the story in its mirror-imaging of salient paradigmatic themes and transformations. Again this makes complete sense as, particularly before the mention of Taríacuri and his birth, the story has its own autopoietic qualities in its system of logical reversals, but this autopoietic quality is precisely in the service of producing Taríacuri. After Taríacuri's arrival in narrative time, of course, his autopoietic construction and the narrative's autopoietic construction are actually identical as he drives the sequence and nature of the interactions. In this way, even casting Taríacuri as state formation personified is insufficient. If Taríacuri and the actions of the narrative, which are in the end the actions of a range of characters interacting with one another, are fused into one through the structure of the narrative, then Taríacuri becomes the manifestation of all transformations, and therefore all agency. If he is *all* agency, then he is also the *only true agent*. I believe, once more, that the surface events of the narrative also serve to establish this characterization of Taríacuri, as he is everywhere in the narrative. He is always a factor, even if a latent one, as he advises other characters, carries out negotiations "off-stage" through the course of the narrative, and has his greatness foretold before his birth (i.e., before he exists as a character).

In this way the priest's narrative shares much in common with more widespread conceptualizations of rulership in Mesoamerica. It is common in Mesoamerican political ideologies, as manifested in artworks throughout the culture area, to represent the king as the central axis that constructs the cosmos around him. A common motif in Maya art is to merge kings with sacred trees that define the center (Freidel 1992:120; Schele and Freidel 1990:67; Schele and Miller 1986:108–109), and in chapter 4 I note how Taríacuri is represented at the midpoint of the oak upon which the Uacúsecha family tree in the *Relación de Michoacán*, effectively producing the same merger and centering function. Another example closer in time and space to the Late Postclassic / Early Colonial Tarascan context illustrates this conflation of rulership with time and the temporal process. Echoing a proposal by Emily Umberger (1988), David Stuart (n.d.), identifies the central face on the famous Aztec Sun Stone as having certain features that identify it as an Aztec (Mexica) ruler, likely Moteuczoma II. This face constitutes the majority of the *Olin* ("movement"/"earthquake") glyph that is the central element of the entire monument, and which represents the fifth sun/age that follows and is the culmination of the previous suns, the glyphs of which are themselves embedded in the *Olin* glyph as its protruding box elements. Viewed together, what visual art in Mesoamerica often does through visual or compositional juxtapositions of "costumes," names, depictions of enactments, roles in sacrifices, and so on, to conflate rulers with totalities of time (and/or the sacred forces that control or compose it), narrative does in the relationship of the paradigmatic character with the syntagmatic unfolding of the action (Turner's [1977: see chap. 3] relativization of the paradigmatic axis with the syntagmatic axis in which the former takes on properties of and becomes synonymous with the properties of the latter).

Taríacuri's agency, manifested as his characteristic "Chichimecness" and the semantic load of coordinated transformations it carries, is in stark opposition to the Islanders through much of the narrative, particularly the second half. While the Islanders as a category play an ennobling role in relation to the Chichimecs in the first half, part of the significance of Taríacuri's pivoting at the midpoint of the narrative is to paradigmatically invert the dimensions and categories (and who will occupy those categories) of the narrative in its second half, and from this point onward the Chichimecs no longer need the ennobling actions, wealth, and larger ennobling role of the Islanders. In fact, the action of the second half largely revolves around relations within the Uacúsecha, and we see that when they are included, Islander characters are the subjects of decisions made by the Uacúsecha, such as the inclusion of Zapiuatame with Taríacuri's nephews, and the acquisition of sacrificial victims from Pacandan, and that they are epitomized finally by the subordinate role as either allies or victims in the conquests that create the unified kingdom.

In terms of the context in which the priest formulated and told his narrative, furthermore, the colonial-era version of the Tarascan kingdom had been governed by Don Pedro Cuinierángari for almost a decade following Tzintzicha Tangáxoan's death in 1530. Recall from above that Don Pedro was an "adopted" brother, having married a woman of the last king's lineage. He and his own brother, Huitzitziltzi, had played an increasingly important role in negotiating relations between the king and the Spaniards as the latter encroached into Tarascan territory and subsequently sought to establish suzerainty over it. The problem was, particularly following the death of Tzintzicha Tangáxoan and from the point of view of the established ruling class, the Uacúsecha, and (their) history, that Don Pedro was an "Islander." As an obvious contrast to Don Pedro and his governorship, Don Francisco Taríacuri was not only a Uacúsecha Chichimec but the rightful heir to his father's position of supremacy. Thus he should assume the position of indigenous governor due to his parentage as well as his class and the social distinction that went with it. In addition, however, is the specific relation to his namesake as a transformative character that had the power to bridge cultures by means of the ability to transform himself and therefore transform the social landscape. As an Islander, so the indigenous priest's case stated, Don Pedro had no such ability. He was dictated to; he was a passive agent. In contrast, Don Francisco Taríacuri's Chichimec and Spanish nature gave him the capacity to transform the chaos and subjugation of the indigenous people occurring up to that point into an order more favorable for indigenous society. The origins of that dual character must be recognized—that Spanish nature had been realized by way of that Chichimec nature, as Don Francisco Taríacuri had been chosen by Viceroy Mendoza due to his parentage and therefore his inherently Chichimec birthright and character, and he had subsequently impressed the viceroy due to those same Chichimec qualities.

Don Francisco Taríacuri's presence in the present as the best hope for some kind of negotiation and possible reconstitution of an indigenous kingdom makes him the touch point around which a past Taríacuri is constructed, and just as important the advocacy of this present Taríacuri necessitates the concretization of this past Taríacuri as not simply a great leader but as the literal and symbolic embodiment of the kingdom. There is not enough evidence to suggest that Don Francisco Taríacuri was named after the past Taríacuri—that is, that a notion of a past Taríacuri was completely unheard of. I am also not suggesting that the idea of a Taríacuri was a completely novel idea. The symbolic content of Taríacuri as a centering figure and a dually composed character, judging by the likely rich symbolism of the name as well as other forms of evidence such as the name of the mountain that borders Tzintzuntzan and which exists in the center of the Lake Pátzcuaro Basin, is likely to be a prehispanic concept in some form. I consider "Taríacuri" as an idea or a bundle of symbolic relations constitutive of kingship or of some cosmic import in Tarascan culture to have a prehispanic origin. The fact that Taríacuri's various locations and markedly different importance in other representations of the prehispanic past, however, indicates that "Taríacuri" occupied no fixed point and no fixed importance within remembrances and concretizations of the past (see in this chapter, explicitly as demonstrated in table 1.1). The narrative and the context of its production imply that it is the past Taríacuri that is the symbolic projection of the present Taríacuri (Don Francisco). At the very least, drawing on established and temporally

persistent ideas about kingship in Mesoamerica as composed of dual figures or entities, there was in Michoacán this idea of kings as dual figures who were microcosms
of cosmic powers writ large, that such figures were powerful because they could
negotiate various "social worlds" and that in the context of the colonial encounter,
the fact that such a dual figure is not only necessary but sitting right there (after
having been forced to sit on the sidelines as a "pretender" to how his father's authority had run things for the majority of the time) worked in tandem to produce in
essence both Taríacuris, past and present. In other words a Taríacuri in the past that
likely was a broadly held cosmological ideal of what Tarascan kings were supposed
to be was adapted and pinned down in the past and pinned to a figure who shared
Don Francisco Taríacuri's name at precisely the time that Don Francisco himself
was emerging as a potential and potentially powerful player in the ongoing development of the colonial encounter/power struggle. The priest manages to mythologize, so to speak, Don Francisco in the present not directly but by mythologizing
a past Taríacuri. The indirect nature of this process reveals the power of narrative
to resignify and produce coherent arguments for future-oriented action surrepti-
tiously. Furthermore, the results of the analysis and this approach to the Priest's
Speech is a different tack from saying that there was in prehispanic Tarascan "sacred
history" an already preconstituted Taríacuri (with all of these attributes, including importantly that particular name) whom then the priest simply through his
narrative projects onto Don Francisco. In order to make Don Francisco into the
leader the priest wanted him to be, the priest took it upon himself to make this past
Taríacuri whom he wanted *him* to be.

   This cyclical notion of time thus becomes in the Priest's Speech and the colonial
encounter more generally not a straightjacket of prescribed action but rather more of
a resource, an ideological framework to draw upon as historicity is practiced. This is
akin to Sahlins's (1999:408) useful phrase "the inventiveness of tradition" and focuses
the analytic project on actions in real time that attempt to make sense of the past,
present, and future as one thread or wheel of time in which the most powerful concretizations will be constructed in concordance with larger cosmological precepts,
even as those cosmological precepts are themselves reworked slightly in the process.

NOTES

   1. The full title of the document as originally written is "Relación de las ceremonías y
ritos y población de la provincia de Mechuacan, hecha al Ilustrisimo Señor Don Antonio
de Mendoza, Virrey y Gobernador de esta Nueva España, por su Majestad." The document
is simply referred to in most if not all scholarship with the abbreviated title of *Relación de
Michoacán*, which I will use throughout this book.

2. As discussed most cogently by Angélica Afanador-Pujol (2010) there are discrepancies in the historical sources regarding how this last king died at the orders of Nuño de Guzmán. The second quote that begins the current book is a statement from Don Pedro Cuinierán-gari, an indigenous governor of Michoacán and an interested party who did not want his position questioned. At issue is whether or not Tzintzicha Tangáxoan received a "pagan" or a "Christian" death sentence; in the former he would be immediately burned to death while in the latter he would first be strangled and then burned, with the garroting allowing his soul to escape to heaven as he suffocated and before being burned. Once again, as explained by Afanador-Pujol, the manner of death had serious consequences for the "estate" of the last king. If he had died as a pagan, his property could be legally acquired or confiscated by the Spanish Crown and its representatives. If he had died as a Christian, such confiscation would be illegal.

3. As pointed out by Stone (2004:62–71), an editorial hand changed some of the verbs from present tense into past imperfect tense. This indicates a concern for representing that indigenous practices and beliefs were things of the past that no longer were ongoing. Such a concern for the politics of representation, however, likely indicates that at least some indigenous practices were still ongoing and that this process of rendering them as things of the past was focused on casting the colonial effort of converting and governing the indigenous peoples in the best possible light.

4. Franco Mendoza (2000:277) characterizes the discourse of the Petámuti within the emic framework of modern Purhépecha words: Iórhijpikua is a convocation or official announcement; *aiámpekua* is the information, the main contents of the discourse; *arhíjtspe-kua* is the argumentative exhortation; and *Ka Jurámukua* is the orders that are presented in the manner of conclusions. What I refer to as the "summation" in particular can be understood as a combination of the last two categories.

5. For example, in her discussion of the priest's narrative, Stone states that "The place where the petámuti delivers his oral performance is of crucial importance to the argument advanced in this chapter, which rejects the friar-compiler's framing of part two of the *Relación de Michoacán* as a ceremony frozen in time" (Stone 2004:112). Later, she begins her discussion of this section of the document as follows: "As the petámuti stood, circa 1538–1539, most likely in the ruins of the patio of the royal palace that represented the sacred organization of the fourfold kingdom, he symbolically reenacted for his audience" (Stone 2004:114). Such statements or surmising are not merited by the information contained within the document, which as stated above does not relate where, when, or in what company the narration that is included in the document was told. Rather than simply a framing of a ceremony frozen in time, in the service of colonialist interests as Stone presents them, the friar's introduction in the imperfect past tense of how the chief priest "used to begin" is the most honest presentation of how the narrative actually used to be presented in the past, assuming that his informant was actually retelling what he believed to be fixed text concerning the

origins of the king's ancestors and the kingdom they created. While I have not studied the Escorial manuscript itself, perhaps it is telling that this case of the use of the imperfect is not included in Stone's (2004:62–71) own analysis of the many instances in which the original use of present-tense verbs are changed to the imperfect verb tense, perhaps indicating that the use of the imperfect in the presentation of the priest's narrative was the first (and only) description of the relation of the priest's narrative to the present time.

6. That is, "royal house"; see Cristina Monzón and Andrew Roth-Seneff (Monzón and Roth-Seneff 2016; see also Monzón 1996, Castro Gutiérrez and Monzón García 2008; Castro Gutiérrez 2015) on the possible applicability of the model of a lordly or royal "house" similar to the Nahua *teccalli* or "lord(ly) house." See also Gillespie (2000a, 2000b) and Joyce and Gillespie (2000) on "houses" as kinship groups and associated practices in Mesoamerica and further afield. I do not have the time or space to dedicate to a discussion of how Tarascan kinship appears to have operated, particularly among the noble families, but I feel that the works cited above for Michoacán fit well with applications of the "house model" as in the other citations. Thus the Uacúsecha as a whole, I suspect, could be regarded as one big noble/ royal "house," or, more likely, the Tzintzuntzan, Ihuatzio, and Pátzcuaro "lineages" could be understood as allied and endogamous amongst themselves noble "houses" with the Tzint-zuntzan "house," the so-called Uanacaze, having achieved preeminence among the three by the time the Spaniards arrived in Mesoamerica. At any rate what appears to have definitively been the case is that subordinates who served the leaders of these noble houses, that is, the kings and highest nobility of the kingdom, appear to have been proud to have been affiliated with the house *as servants / subordinates*, the relationship of subservience being inherent to their relationship with, and membership within, the royal house (Monzón and Roth-Seneff 2016; Castro Gutiérrez and Monzón García 2008; Castro Gutiérrez 2015; this is similar to Gillespie's [2000a] discussion of Maya "nested houses" as containing the "family" members but also subordinates and servants within this idiom of membership and identity).

7. Martínez Baracs (2005:156) notes that Don Pedro assumed the governorship in 1530 and held it until his death in 1543, though there are some years in which documentation is poor and other indigenous nobles appear to have held the office, for example, Don Alonso Ecuángari o Tzapícaua, who was governor in 1538. On political alliance achieved through marriage relations and resulting conceptualizations of such affinal relations as fraternal kin relations within the broader context of Tarascan state/elite culture, see Roberto Martínez González (2011; see also Haskell 2008b, 2012).

8. On accommodations and assimilation to the Spanish colonial system (especially judi-cial system, founded as it was on recognitions of lineage and privilege) in Michoacán specifi-cally, see Afanador-Pujol (2015); Delfina López Sarrelangue (1965); Maria de Lourdes Kuthy (1996, 2003); Martínez Baracs (2005); and Hans Roskamp (1997, 2001, 2002, 2003, 2004, 2010b, 2012, 2015; Roskamp and César Villa 2003). Indigenous alliance with the Spaniards and subsequent use of the legal bases of the Spanish colonial and system, including casting

themselves as—and playing the part of—loyal and assimilated subjects, are well established. See, for example, Florine Asselbergs (2006); Louise M. Burkhart (2001); Charles Gibson (1964); Robert S. Haskett (1991, 1996); Robert Hill (1991); James Lockhart (1992); Laura Matthew and Michael Oudijk (Matthew and Oudijk 2007); Dana Velasco et al. (Murillo, Lentz, and Ochoa 2012); Matthew Restall (1997); Yannakakis (2008). In such a complex, fluid, and variable process as colonization, it is necessary to acknowledge that these terms— accommodation, assimilation, resistance, and so on—are problematic and that practices that could be characterized as one could and did slide into another analytic category, or that the same practice could be fit into more than one category depending on perspective, (temporal) scale, and the problematic relationship between intent and effect. For instance, the use of European iconography and language in documents or the adoption of European dress could simultaneously be seen as accommodation and assimilation as well as mere precursors or proximate behaviors to achieve more ultimate goals of contestation and/or resistance. "Hybridity" (as in the case at hand, see Afanador-Pujol [2015] and Espejel Carbajal [2008]; more generally see Ohnuki Tierney [2001, 2005]) as a concept that due to its historicization as opposed to a homogenizing analytical framework can hold together many of these simultaneous contradictory perspectives or implications in colonial contexts has great analytic value in this regard.

  9. The Spaniards were well acquainted with the importance of bodily remains, as numerous Catholic pilgrimage sites across Europe prominently featured remains of saints. However, they might have managed to underestimate the importance of the physical remains of the king in indigenous cultures. As Susan Gillespie (1989:227) writes, "the notion that possession of the king's body is a prerequisite for succession is also revealed in the Aztec stories of Topiltzin Quetzalcoatl, who carefully searched for the bones of his father, Mixcoatl/ Camaxtli/Totepeuh, after the latter had been slain and installed them in a shrine, the Mixocatepetl, prior to killing his father's murderers on top of that shrine and rightfully taking his father's throne." It is interesting to note that the *Relación de Michoacán* (Alcalá 2000:654) contains in the third part of the document a story that is very similar to the myth variants concerning Topiltzin Quetzalcoatl cited by Gillespie. In the myth in the *Relación de Michoacán*, the deity Cupanzieeri plays the ball game against another deity named Achuri hirepi, and the latter wins and sacrifices the former. The son of Cupanzieeri recovers his father's remains but before he can kill Achuri hirepe, he is startled, drops the remains, and miraculously the remains of the father transform into a "deer" with a mane and long tail that the Spanish were understood to be mounted upon.

  10. I draw on the discussions and critiques of numerous scholars working in "historicity" and indigenous historical traditions in Mesoamerica (particularly Boone 2000 and Gillespie 1989, 1998, 2007b, 2008; see also Bricker 1981; Hill 1991; Quiroa 2011) and South America (Fausto and Heckenberger, eds. 2007; Hill 1988; Rappaport 1998; Salomon 1982; Urton 1990; Whitehead 2003). See also Troulliot (1995) for a discussion of historicity in Haiti.

11. As I discuss also in another work (Haskell 2015), the very human-centered nature of the narrative should not necessarily be seen as a purely indigenous point of view due to the fact that the friar-compiler interjected himself into the priest's narrative. The friar-compiler explains right at the beginning of the second part of the *Relación de Michoacán* that in the narrative, it was a common practice for the narrator to state that the god Curicaueri had done such-and-such thing, but the friar's interjection and explanation and the manner in which he continues the story strongly suggest that he required the narrator to include the names of the human characters (Alcalá 2000:341). The exact way in which this altered the narrative is unknowable, however. The manner in which Curicaueri was rendered to be the primary agent in an indigenous version of the narrative could have taken many forms, including simply implying (repetitively so) that the god had willed the actions of the characters into existence. Additionally, it could have been simply understood by an indigenous audience that the god Curicaueri should be recognized as a source of aid for the Uacúsecha, a resource to draw on within their own actions and plans (for a discussion of a somewhat similar phenomenon in Amazonia, see Carlos Fausto and Michael Heckenberger's discussion of historicity "in a shamanic key" [Fausto and Heckenberger 2007]). Still, the fact remains that the narrator was able to produce a fairly large range of named characters (the repetition of Xoropiti and Tarequetzingata as men from a town near and very probably subordinate to Corínguaro and almost immediately afterward as their function as place-names involved in actions involving men from Corínguaro notwithstanding; see chapter 4), and this could suggest that the narrator did not simply fabricate characters and events on an improvised basis when pushed by the friar-compiler to do so. This returns us to the likelihood that in some sense, the priest's narrative was the result of a form of indigenous historiography and involved what I refer to above as institutional and institutionalized knowledge of the past.

12. This bias is, I would contend, still reflected in the practice of referring to the narrative contained in the *Relación de Michoacán* as "the Petámuti's speech" in spite of the fact that the document states that the version recorded in its own pages was the testimony of a priest who knew this history rather than "the," or "a," Petámuti. The document does state that the "official history" was told at a yearly festival in the capital as a preamble to the punishment of wrongdoers and that, moreover, members of another priestly order were dispatched to the towns of the province to recite that history in local, provincial, contexts. The illustration of the oration of the history of the *Uacúsecha* does depict the Petámuti speaking to a group of nobles. This does not necessarily indicate that the Petámuti is speaking in the context of the present of the Colonial era to such a group of congregated nobles, or again if the Petámuti told this story in public at all in the Colonial era. On that note it is important to recognize that, similarly, in the case of the *Cazonci's* burial ceremony, Afanador-Pujol (2015:chap. 6) has argued convincingly that the image is essentially an idealized representation that "recreates" a past that did not necessarily exist, or at least did not exist in such a stereotypic and

straightforward manner. A largely similar point is made by Stone (1994) in her discussion of the royal funeral. Returning to the point at hand, by unconsciously but still erroneously attributing another priest's narrative to "the" Petámuti, however, the assumption remains that the version recorded in the *Relación de Michoacán* is somehow the same as the version told by the Petámuti in years previous, or, at the very least, is the same version that would have been told by the Petámuti had he been available to offer his testimony for the production of the *Relación de Michoacán*.

13. Immediately following his use of the term "sacred history," Roskamp (2012:124; italics in original) includes a parenthetical clause: "others use the term *myth*." Such disagreements and characterizations are part of the reason why I consider it important to explicitly define "myth" and "history" (see chapter 3), even though this debate is largely seen as an old (and unproductive) one in contemporary anthropology. Rather, I take the position that the priest's narrative in the *Relación de Michoacán*, according to my analysis, manages to still confound (in very interesting ways) the specific and supposedly refined etic frameworks for analysis and comparison discussed in chapter 3.

14. Previously this document was known as the *Lienzo de Jucutacato*, but Roskamp (1998) has shown that it originated from Jicalan, or prehispanic Xiuhquilan.

15. Afanador-Pujol (2010, 2015); Claudia Espejel Carbajal (2008); Rodolfo Fernández (2011); Kuthy (2003); Martínez Baracs 2005; Cristina Monzón, Hans Roskamp, and Benedict Warren (Monzón, Roskamp, and Warren 2009); Monzón and Andrew Roth-Seneff (Monzón and Roth-Seneff 1999); Carlos Paredes Martínez (1997); Roskamp (1997, 1998, 2015); Stone (1994, 2004); Warren (1963, 1985).

16. See also the discussion in Carolyn Dean and Dana Leibsohn (Dean and Leibsohn 2003).

17. See also John Comaroff (1982); Jean Comaroff and Comaroff (1991–1997); Fausto and Heckenberger (2007); Gillespie (1989); Hill (1988); Emiko Ohnuki-Tierney (1990a); Renato Rosaldo (1980a, 1980b); Terence Turner (1988a, 1988b); Neil Whitehead (2003).

18. In theorizations of ethnicity/identity, often formulations of what the group is not— that is, a contrast with an other—are powerful demarcations of ethnicity and an important process in the identification as the definition of the negative pole ("what we are not") influences the formulation of the positive pole ("what we are"). See, e.g., Barth (1969); and particularly in how narratives concerning the past and historicity play into the formulation of ethnicity and identity see, e.g., Elizabeth Boone (2000); Gibson (1964):31–34; Gary Gossen (1974); Gillespie (1998); Michael Harkin (1988); Hill (1988); Shepard Krech (2006); Susan McKinnon (1991); Edward Schieffelin and Deborah Gewertz (Schieffelin and Gewertz 1985); Stephen Hugh-Jones (1989); James Peacock (1969); Peter Nabokov (2002); Nestor Quiroa (2011).

19. See, e.g., Florine Asselbergs (2006); Boone (2000, 2007); Boone and Walter Mignolo (Boone and Mignolo 1994); Lori Diel (2008); Eduardo Douglas (2010); Leibsohn (2009);

Roskamp (1998, 2003, 2004); Dennis Tedlock (2010); Robert Williams (2009); Stephanie Wood (2003).

20. This should not be taken to mean that I advocate investigating indigenous historicity solely through documents written in Latin letters, which indigenous scribes adopted fairly quickly (but in the indigenous world also remained less highly valued than more indigenous forms). As Boone (2000) in particular discusses, the ambiguity of the indigenous pictographic systems was an essential aspect of the indigenous practice of historicity. However, the flip side must also be true, that lengthy narratives (of precisely the kind that were written down in Latin letters) or performances that "read" or "interpreted" the ambiguous documents were also part of the indigenous practice of historicity. Only by taking both into account can we come to appreciate the complexity of the entire range of practices. Townsend herself indicates this perspective when she notes that the studies she is reviewing—notably Diel (2008), Eduardo Douglas (2010), and Leibsohn (2009)—do incorporate the many glosses written within/on pictographic documents. By combining "glyphs" and "words," we can indeed know Mesoamerican peoples more deeply. At any rate, the extent to which such issues of working within pictographic documents and documents produced using Latin letters are problematic in the Tarascan area is an open question, as discussed in this chapter.

21. On the importance of language and its specificities in interpreting narrative or any engagement of the past, see, e.g., Allen Christensen (2007); Shelly Errington (1979); Michael Harkin (1988); Dell Hymes (1981); Rena Lederman (1986); and Tedlock (1983, 2010).

22. This "important and indispensable tool" has, however, not been applied widely at all. Turner (1969, 1977, 1985) develops and utilizes it, and Mary Dillon and Thomas Abercrombie's (Dillon and Abercrombie 1988) analysis of an Andean myth similarly examines the syntagmatic properties of the myth. Ronald Engard (1988) employs it in a study of a myth in the grasslands of Cameroon. Pierre-Yves Jacopin (1988) has also published an explicitly syntactic approach to a South American myth. The present work was originally a reappraisal of my own MA thesis (Haskell 2003) that was part of a session at the 2009 meeting of the American Society for Ethnohistory and subsequent work toward an edited volume in collaboration with Susan Gillespie, Jalh Dulanto, Nestor Quiroa, and Carl Wendt. We all used Turner's method to some extent in our explorations of Mesoamerican and Andean narratives, but the collaborators' excellent studies have not yet been published.

23. According to the Priest's Speech and other information in the *Relación de Michoacán*, succession to the kingship passed from father to son almost exclusively, though there are times when it passes to a member of the Uacúsecha that is not a son of the dead king/leader. For example, following Taríacuri's own death, his nephew Hiripan took on oversight of the god Curicaueri and the maintenance of his treasures as opposed to Taríacuri's second son, Hiquíngaxe. I have elsewhere (Haskell 2008b) explained this as his opting for the clearly more "Chichimec" Hiripan over the "Islander" Hiquíngaxe. Elsewhere (Alcalá 2000:631) the *Relación de Michoacán* gives a summation of the deliberations on electing, if that is the

right word, a new king that is rather anonymous and portrayed as a "stereotypical" deliberative session. This representation is then brought into a concrete historical moment following the death of Zuangua, in which Zuangua's son Tzintzicha Tangáxoan suggests that Paquingata, lord of Ihuatzio, should assume the kingship rather than him (Alcalá 2000:659). Whether or not this is an example of displaying the sort of "modesty" that was expected of lords and rulers, it is perhaps nonetheless instructive that it was at least a possibility for this to happen; by the same token it is instructive that Tzintzicha Tangáxoan suggested the lord of Ihuatzio and not of some other place as the potential heir.

24. My analysis reaches many of the same conclusions as that of Afanador-Pujol (2010, 2015); working independently and paying close attention to different media within the document—she on the paintings that illustrated it, primarily, and I on the priest's narrative—we largely agree that Don Francisco Taríacuri is the implicit referent for much of the document's depictions and descriptions. Her analysis of the burial of the last king (Afanador-Pujol 2015:chap. 6) demonstrates that this effort of "ethnographic representation of the past" was constructed to represent king-to-son succession as the normal and preferred way of selecting an heir (thus favoring Don Francisco Taríacuri in the context of its production), even if the text of the document suggests that there might have been a practice of selecting the next king from a pool of eligible Uacúsecha lords (Alcalá 2000:631).

25. On a related point, Afanador-Pujol (2010:fn20) writes that "the possible involvement of Don Francisco and Don Antonio [in the production of the *Relación de Michoacán*] has not yet been explored."

26. Additionally Gillespie (2007a) has examined the contrastive ways in which Mesoamerican artists represented actors (most prominently rulers) who would have occupied three-dimensional space but occupy these artworks in such a way that they have been the subjects of choices concerning which dimension (either depth or verticality) to emphasize. As such, they represent different modes of representing rulers, action, and the temporal process within which the rulers and their actions unfold. Particularly illuminating is her discussion of the Cross Group temples at Palenque and their artwork, which she interprets as indicating that a sacred tree acts as a sort of portal allowing the ruler to interact with his past self. If rulers are equivalent in some ways to trees via their ability to center and thus create the world, and trees at the center enable persons to access other times, then it is perhaps likely that Maya rulers' persons enabled such access as well. In fact, Maya rulers' access to the ancestors and sacred beings in other space-times on behalf of society seems to have been a major part of their ritual function.

2

The Tarascan Kingdom and Its Prehispanic Past in Mesoamerican Context

In order to understand why the cultural practices that provided the institutional-ized ground for the Priest's Speech, as well as why it has traditionally been inter-preted in a predominantly literalist fashion, it is necessary to discuss a wide range of topics having to do with Tarascan society in the prehispanic era and wider issues and debates pertaining to how we understand Mesoamerica more generally. With regard to Tarascan society in particular, because historicity is cultural but also the product of historical processes, a discussion of the development and nature of the kingdom and place of the priesthood within the culture in general and the politi-cal apparatus in particular is essential for an appreciation of points made following the analysis of the Priest's Speech. I argue later that while the speech is advocat-ing for Don Francisco Taríacuri's succession to the governorship is the overarching concern of the priest, part of the reason it is composed the way that it is, as mostly a record of human deeds and events, is due to the fact that the Tarascan political structure was a fairly recent development, and an unprecedented one, in the prehis-panic history of Michoacán.

More widely, other influences in the Priest's Speech must also be addressed and accounted for. Particularly because my argument is more in keeping with a "history as symbol" (Bricker 1981; Gillespie 1989; Gossen 1977; Leach 1990; Richards 1960; Rosaldo 1980a, 1980b; Sahlins 1981, 1985, 2004) interpretive mode as opposed to the assumption of literal history, this chapter presents relevant information con-cerning Tarascan and Mesoamerican understandings of the nature of time and the

DOI: 10.5876/9781607327493.c002

cosmos in which human social action is grounded and with which it shares certain analogous (or homologous, depending on the question of whether an emic or etic perspective is adopted) qualities. In Mesoamerican worldviews, human society, and particularly political legitimacy as the principal of hierarchical superiority over the rest of society, takes part in the same processes and logics of the cosmos in general. This is a key point in the debate over how to interpret Mesoamerican narratives and histories in which there is noted cyclicity and repetition, as a common point of analysts is that histories in Mesoamerica present what should have happened (according to some cosmological precept) rather than what actually did happen (Boone 2000; Bricker 1981; Gillespie 1989).

A common problem to all of these discussions in the prehispanic past of Michoacán is the extent to which Michoacán and Tarascan society were full participants in the Mesoamerican culture area that shaped the nature of these institutions and religious and ideological precepts. It is important to recognize *both* the similarities to the Mesoamerican patterns as well as the differences from them. I discuss below, in this regard, how Michoacán was, according to archaeological research, interacting with Central Mexican peoples during the Epiclassic and Early Postclassic periods. They therefore were influenced by the developing ideologies of rulership that spread throughout Mesoamerica following the collapse of Teotihuacan at the end of the Classic period, if not an earlier spread of such ideologies. The other dominant process in the prehispanic period that must be addressed, along with how it impacted Michoacán, is the migrations from the northern Mesoamerican frontier and beyond into Central Mexico. Obviously the Priest's Story, because it has some similarities and purported connections to these migration tales, has been subjected to modern interpretations that give primacy to those perceived similarities. Such studies have been guided by a literalist bias that largely ignore the insights of culturally particular reasons for producing histories and representations of the past. In so doing, efforts to connect the Priest's Speech to other Mesoamerican ethnohistorical documents and archaeological interpretations—themselves compromised by an overreliance on literalist interpretations of the documentary sources—and thereby construct Michoacán's place in a "real" history of these movements, does damage to these individual representations including the Priest's Speech. The main goal of this chapter, then, is to argue that between the complex spread of an ideology of rulership, similarly complex migrations into Mesoamerica from peripheral areas, and their complex intertwinement in indigenous histories, approaching the Priest's Speech from both an "instrumentalist" perspective focusing on what the priest was trying to accomplish with his representation and a "symbolic" approach appreciating the metaphorical meanings of peoples and places contained in such representations is the most appropriate way to understand the narrative.

THE TARASCAN KINGDOM, AND TARASCAN CULTURE,
AT THE MOMENT OF THE SPANISH CONQUEST

Because Tarascan historicity in the Early Colonial period was shaped in some way by the past and historicity within that past, it is essential to discuss the Tarascan kingdom as it existed in the prehispanic era, as far as we understand it. When Hernán Cortés and his army of conquistadors arrived in what would become the colony of New Spain (and ultimately Mexico) in 1519, the Tarascan kingdom dominated West-Central Mexico. It covered much of the modern state of Michoacán, and small parts of the neighboring states of Jalisco, Querétaro, Guanajuato, Mexico, and possibly Guerrero (see map 1.1). In the central part of this region, Tarascan speakers were the majority, but other ethnicities such as Nahua, Otomí, and Matlatzinca speakers also populated the area (Albiez-Zwieck 2013; Brand 1943; Stanislawski 1947). The extent of the kingdom is known primarily through ethnohistoric documents such as the *Relaciones Geográficas* (1958) and the *Caravajal Visita* (see Warren 1963, 1985), though archaeological evidence has confirmed Tarascan control in some towns, as discussed below. As the dominant political entity of West-Central Mexico, it butted up against the better-known Aztec empire at its eastern boundary, and the two polities had, according to sources on both sides, fought each other in large-scale campaigns on at least two occasions (Hassig 1988:183–184, 206–211; Herrejón Peredo 1978).

The available ethnohistoric and archaeological evidence indicates that the Tarascan state emerged around 1350–1400 CE. Archaeologists, most notably Pollard (e.g., 2008, 2015, 2016; see also Michelet 1995, 1996; Michelet, Pereira, and Migeon 2005; Migeon 1998; Pulido Méndez 2006), tend to view the transformation as occurring on the early side of that timeframe, with antecedent transitions in material culture taking place in the Middle Postclassic (ca. 1100–1350 CE).[1] Ethnohistorians, on the other hand, tend to view the process of state formation occurring at the later end of that time period, more toward 1400–1450 CE based on documentary evidence that contain king lists and purported information concerning the reigns of those kings or, often, outright assumptions concerning likely reigns (e.g., Bravo Ugarte 1962a; Hassig 1988; Herrejón Peredo 1978; Kirchhoff 1956; León 1903; Martínez Baracs 2005).[2] Regardless of which timeframe is posited for the emergence of the state, the available evidence suggests that the Tarascan state expanded through primarily militaristic conquests, though some towns, in particular some in border regions and/or metal-producing regions along the eastern and southern borders (those abutting lands or territories in which Aztec influence or hegemony dominated), were absorbed peacefully, allying themselves with the Tarascan state and promising military service and tribute of metal objects in particular in order to forego violence and maintain some autonomy (Carrasco 1969; Roskamp 1998:174–175; see also Gorenstein 1985; Pollard 1994, 2016b).

There has been much debate concerning what exactly to call this polity due to the ignominious origin of the term "Tarascan." The most likely origin of this term is that it was applied to the Tarascan people because a few indigenous noblewomen were given to Spaniards as wives in the early days of interaction between the two groups. Because the Tarascan term for "in-law" is *tarascue*, the Spaniards were referred to with this word, they heard it often, and they used it to refer to the Tarascan-speaking population (Martínez Baracs 2003, 2005; Warren 1985). The term has taken on negative connotations, however, and offends some indigenous members of this group (see especially Márquez Joaquín 2007 for a discussion of such issues). They prefer to be referred to as Purhépecha, and thus the prehispanic polity has recently been referred to as the Purhépecha state. At the time of the arrival of the Spaniards, however, *purhépecha* meant "commoner" or "laborer," (Martínez Baracs 2003, 2005; Warren 1985) and so to call any hierarchical and centralized political entity by the name applied to commoners would seem to be a contradiction in terms. For such reasons and for consistency with the existing literature, I will simply refer to the political entity as the Tarascan state, with my sincere apologies if I thereby offend any indigenous Purhépecha people.[3]

The kingdom was ruled by a single person, called the Irecha in the Tarascan (Purhépecha) language, from his palace in the capital city of Tzintzuntzan on the shores of Lake Pátzcuaro in central Michoacán. The Irecha ruled with apparently unquestioned authority, as an "autocrat that shared power with no one" (Brand 1971:646; see also Beltrán 1982; Carrasco 1986; García Alcaraz 1976; Gorenstein and Pollard 1983; Pollard 1993b, 2003a). Not only was he the supreme political authority but he also served important religious functions, as he was constructed to be the human representative of the deity Curicaueri and served as one of the sacrificers, a class of the indigenous priesthood (Alcalá 2000). As I (Haskell 2008b, 2012) have argued, part of the reason for the king's unquestioned authority was his ability to discursively and materially co-opt local level lords, in effect encompassing and transforming them into a bureaucratic class that acted with and within his agency, but with little agency of their own. As represented in the (admittedly biased) documents such as the *Relación de Michoacán* pertaining to the king's authority, the king was the center of society, structuring the relations of the wider society that he ruled. This centrality is reflected in various cultural and social practices surrounding the kingship and its place in society: the market was closed following the death of a king, and the populace as a whole ceased activities while mourning the dead king; the king cemented relationships with the lords of the kingdom by marrying sisters or daughters of those lords as well as marrying off women of his court to the lords of the realm; among other rituals of succession, a new king would assume the marital relationships of the dead king, thereby reestablishing the relationships that helped constitute the kingdom; the king was ultimately responsible for selecting the successors to the offices of local-level lords throughout the kingdom and, at least according to the *Relación de Michoacán*, he would bequeath to these lords the insignia of office that symbolized and constituted their authority as his representatives (Alcalá 2000; but see Haskell 2008b; and Rebnegger 2010).[4] The kings in Tzintzuntzan also oversaw a large bureaucracy located within the capital. Some members of this bureaucracy oversaw craft specialists, while there were also officeholders who kept track of various forms of tribute to the royal coffers and storehouses as well as overseers of rotational laborers in royal parcels of land (Alcalá 2000:558–563; Beltrán 1982; Carrasco 1986; García Alcaraz 1976; Pollard 2003b). According to the *Relaciones Geográficas* (1958), in most areas of the kingdom community boundaries, land rights, and other usufruct rights are attributed to the past kings, particularly Tzitzispandáquare (García Alcaraz 1976; Pollard 2003a, 2016b; Roskamp 2010b, 2015), rather than through recourse to the community's purported historical antiquity (as is the case generally in Central Mexico; see, e.g., Boone 2000; Florescano 2002; Gibson 1975; Lockhart 1992; Marcus 1992; Nicholson 1975; see also Oudijk and Romero Frizzi 2003 on titles in Oaxaca).

It should be noted that in interactions with Nahua speakers from the Basin of Mexico and the Spaniards, the Tarascan king or kings came to be called by the title Cazonci or the more Nahua rendering Caltzontzin. There has been much debate about the origins and application of this title, which is largely beyond the purview of the present work, although the proposition of Martínez Baracs (2003:77–78) that Irecha was the title used to refer to all kings of the Tarascan state, and that perhaps the term Cazonci or Caltzontzin was used to refer only to the last one or two kings—Tzintzicha Tangáxoan and perhaps his father, Zuangua—seems most plausible to me. The use of Cazonci or Caltzontzin was possibly as a result of this last king (or last two kings) having come into communication with the Nahua-speaking Aztec emperors, or the fact that the Spaniards only came to know of the Tarascan state and its king through the Aztecs. At any rate, this title and its widespread application becomes important in the Early Colonial period among the highest nobility in Michoacán as descendants of the last king appropriated it and used it in their names (López Sarrelangue 1965).

As is revealed in documentary sources, the king was a member of lineages of the upper nobility that referred to itself collectively as the Uacúsecha, a term that in the Tarascan (Purhépecha) language means "eagles" (e.g., Martínez Baracs 2005:60). Much has been written about the names of these lineages (or sublineages) within the Uacúsecha as related in the *Relación de Michoacán* itself. In a few places in speeches recorded in that document, the named lineages Uanacaze, Eneani, and Zacapu-hireti are mentioned. Not much other evidence of the meaning of these names is given, but I interpret these to be the lineages of the three Uacúsecha capitals of Tzintzuntzan, Ihuatzio, and Pátzcuaro, respectively (see also Stone 2004:123; Afanador-Pujol 2015 also uses Uanacaze to indicate the Tzintzuntzan lineage). According to the priest's narrative contained in the *Relación de Michoacán* analyzed here, the members of these lineages were all descended from a common ancestor (along the male line—the document does not contain information concerning the wives of Uacúsecha members except for those of particularly important marriages of Uacúsecha members, and even then not by name; as I discuss here and earlier [Haskell 2008a], there is a logic to which marriages are recorded and when in the narrative they take place). The section in the second part that relates the names of the Uacúsecha nobles who ruled in each capital also states that the idol of Curicaueri, the primary deity in the Tarascan pantheon and tutelar deity of the Uacúsecha, passed from Pátzcuaro to Ihuatzio immediately following the conquests that effectively created the state, and a generation later it passed to Tzintzuntzan. This indicates that at the time of the Spanish conquest, Tzintzuntzan was the preeminent capital, and had been for at most a few decades. This is supported by a 1543 document discovered and analyzed by Monzón, Roskamp, and Warren (2009; see also Haskell 2013) in which a Nahua-speaking nobleman testified that according to a document in the possession of another member of the Nahua community in Tzintzuntzan, their (Nahua) ancestors aided the king Tzitzispandáquare in conquering Tzintzuntzan and making it the preeminent capital of the kingdom. In spite of these political shifts, however, Pátzcuaro apparently retained some status as a "ritual capital," or the most sacred of the Uacúsecha capitals, as reflected by remarks attributed to the past king within the *Relación de Michoacán* (Alcalá 2000:364).[5]

Archaeological investigations in the Pátzcuaro Basin, the political and demographic core of the kingdom (Pollard 2003b, 2008), suggest that sometime around 1350 CE this basin became integrated politically. This is indicated by material culture such as fine ceramic vessels that mimicked fine wares at Tzintzuntzan as well as by a dramatic shift in mortuary practices in which lords demonstrated ties to the king and upper nobility in Tzintzuntzan through the material culture with which they were buried that originated largely locally from central Michoacán, as opposed to with foreign-derived objects (Pollard and Cahue 1999; see also Pollard 2016a). Similar assemblages of material culture found in other towns throughout the kingdom from about 1400 CE on, including the stylistically consistent fineware ceramics, architectural conventions of temple platforms, and metal objects used for bodily ornamentation, confirm the expanding political dominance of the king in Tzintzuntzan (e.g., Macías Goytia 1989, 1990; Pulido Méndez 2006). I have elsewhere (Haskell 2008b) interpreted the mortuary evidence for changes in the differential treatment of noblemen and noblewomen (Pereira n.d. ; Pollard and Cahue 1999) to indicate hierarchical relations between the king and subordinate lords throughout the kingdom constituted through the kinds of marriage alliances discussed above. Royal or cloistered women from the king's palace who had married into local-level administrative sites likely played an important part in ennobling the lords and their offspring, as they brought with them not only royal blood but also royal dowries of foreign-wealth objects such as archaeologically recovered greenstone beads, shell ornaments, and metal objects.

Due largely to the fact that the first part of the *Relación de Michoacán* was lost, little is known about Tarascan religion in the prehispanic or Early Colonial eras. The primary deity, as noted above, was Curicaueri; he was the tutelar god of the Uacúsecha and therefore the state as a whole. A male deity, he was associated primarily with the sun and fire but also warfare and hunting (Alcalá 2000; Corona Núñez 1957; Monzón 2004; Pollard 1991). The most important female deity was Xarátanga, who embodied fertility and a generalized principle of increase (Monzón 2004:151–153; see also Corona Núñez 1957; Pollard 1991). It has also been suggested that she had lunar associations (Corona Núñez 1957; Pollard 1991). These two deities always went together and were placed or carried out in front of the other deities in battle formation, an indication of their centrality within the political ideology of the Tarascan state. Martínez González (2010, 2011) has also done much to examine the structural oppositions of these two deities and other pairs of deities. Not only were gods engaged in relationships in complementary opposition, but these deities reflected larger complementary social patterns and ecological and economic relations in Michoacán society. The goddess Cuerauáperi was also quite important; she was regarded as the mother/earth goddess (Alcalá 2000; Monzón 2004), and her body—face down and with arms and legs stretched out—was said to be the earth (Francisco Ramírez 1959; see also Monzón 2004; Stone 2004). There were numerous other minor deities who were worshipped in the various towns of the kingdom. They do not seem to have been organized into a pantheon, however, leading Helen Pollard (1991) to suggest that Tarascan religion, in the sense of the state-supported religious activities and beliefs, was likely in the process of consolidation at the time of the Spaniards' arrival.

TARASCAN HISTORICITY: THE ROLE OF THE
PRIESTHOOD IN TARASCAN CULTURE

Any study of Tarascan historicity also must address the manner of historical record keeping among the Tarascans. In other Mesoamerican societies, the elites were literate and wrote down records of their calendrical systems, histories, and other genres of information, so long as "writing" is understood broadly and not restricted to alphabetic or phonetic systems but can include pictographic systems (Boone 2000). Exactly to what degree the Tarascans took part in this Mesoamerican tradition of record keeping is difficult to determine. Within the *Relación de Michoacán*, for example, the friar-compiler states that the indigenous peoples of Michoacán "did not have books" (Alcalá 2000:326). However, this remark perhaps reflects a Spanish definition of books as restricted to bound documents made of paper containing phonetic writing, in the form of letters that signify sounds. Elsewhere in the *Relación de Michoacán*, including in the priest's narrative, characters are said to have stated that they had no need to "count the days" (Alcalá 2000:509), that is, consult calendric/divinatory "books," in their preparations for war. Such remarks seem to indicate that the Uacúsecha eschewed using calendric documents to find auspicious days for certain actions, but it is important to note that this is limited to divining auspicious days for warfare—the Uacúsecha state that they alternatively perform services for their gods in order to petition for success in war. This remark also indicates their knowledge of such books, and their not using books in this way could be understood not as a failing or lacking but simply as a cultural preference. Importantly, there have been studies of the Tarascan monthly (based on the 20-day "months" used as the basis of the yearly or solar calendar throughout Mesoamerica) ritual cycle (Caso 1943), and so the Tarascans did share in broader Mesoamerican constructions of time and the calendar. The *Relación de Michoacán* does contain a description of one of these monthly festivals and the religious observances and practices that comprised it (Alcalá 2000:331–332); this is contained in the only folio of the first section that has survived. The priest's narrative does include references to the timing, in the monthly calendar, of certain events. However, no calendrical documents are known to exist, and perhaps the remarks attributed to characters in the priest's narrative could be taken to indicate, in coordination with this absence, that the Tarascans did not put much effort into producing documents related to keeping or counting the days as in the 260-day "ritual" calendar present in much of the rest of Mesoamerica.[6]

There is evidence that documents of some kind were produced and preserved within Tarascan society. Certainly the Michoacán area did not produce a volume of indigenously authored documents on par with other areas of Mesoamerica such as Central Mexico, the Oaxaca region, or the Maya region. This perhaps indicates that the tradition of writing and producing documents was not as firmly entrenched and elaborated in Michoacán in the prehispanic era. However, there are various Tarascan terms in the sixteenth-century *Diccionario Grande* (1991:218, 327) related to writing, or "painting" in the indigenous idiom (emphasizing the artistic aspects of producing books). The word *carari*, for example, is translated as "painter, scribe."

As discussed by Martínez Baracs (1997:122–123) the *Diccionario Grande* contains several indigenous words related to the art of writing and the products of that art, and so the practice must have been known to them. Stone (2004:77) refers to the proposition that some form of picture writing was well established on the eve of the Spanish arrival in Mexico as "controversial." She also notes the work of Roskamp (1998:31–32, 284), who suggests that any writing tradition in Michoacán was due to Nahua speakers bringing this art into Michoacán at some point in the prehispanic era. This is possible, and perhaps the presence of an indigenous document among the Nahua-speaking nobles of Tzintzuntzan as referred to in the case of the 1543 document mentioned above indicates that, at a minimum, some segment of the nobility was not only familiar with record keeping but actively produced and guarded such documents and that at least some percentage of these specialists was Nahua speaking (Monzón, Roskamp, and Warren 2009). Stone (2004:76) does note that in indigenous society small pieces of paper or cloth with images on them were used to communicate information, particularly in the cases of judicial matters. Such "letters" are depicted in the *Relación de Michoacán* itself and described in various accounts in the ethnohistoric record (Stone 2004:76). In that same vein, Don Francisco Taríacuri supported his claims to land (or tribute from those lands) and valuable objects with *pinturas* (paintings) (López Sarrelangue 1965:171). In the Early Colonial era, Monzón, Roskamp, and Warren (2009:31 nn5 and 8) note that the Purhépecha term *erangaqua* was used to denote a pictographic document or *lienzo* (a large-scale image on a piece of cloth, especially linen, from which the term comes) in the indigenous tradition, while the Spanish term *pintura* was adopted and used to denote documents produced using script composed of Latin letters. On the whole, the evidence suggests that some form of communication and record-keeping existed in Tarascan society, even if it was restricted to a small cadre of professionals and not as developed or widespread as in other areas of Mesoamerica.

On the other hand, there is evidence that public oratory and the recounting of the past (perhaps, but not necessarily, consulting any existing documents beforehand) were quite important and frequent in Tarascan society. Oratory was the responsibility of the priesthood, as evidenced by the priest's narrative in the *Relación de Michoacán* and the information surrounding it. Not only did the chief priest relate his narration in the capital of Tzintzuntzan at the appropriate time during a specific religious festival, but lesser priests were also dispatched to the towns of the realm so that they might also narrate the past to the peoples of those towns (Alcalá 2000:340; see also Haskell 2015 for a discussion of how this discursive phenomena was important in constructing Curicaueri's presence throughout the state). Within the context of the priest's narrative itself, following a certain passage in which Taríacuri prophesies that his nephews will be lords of all of the towns of the region, an interjection (presumably by the friar-compiler) notes that this particular speech by Taríacuri was revered by the Cazonci and he had a priest tell it often, because it was advice that Taríacuri had given "to all of the lords" (Alcalá 2000:468). Furthermore, the framing information that precedes the relation of the second of two sections of the *Relación de Michoacán* which relate stories or events not included in the priest's narrative (discussed at greater length in chapter 1 and chapter 5) indicates that stories of the past were intimately tied with the experience of the landscape (Alcalá 2000:537; this point is also made by Stone 2004[7]). Certain places where events had occurred apparently prompted priests to tell of the events that had transpired there, thereby keeping those tales alive. In the speeches contained in the *Relación de Michoacán* that purport to represent stereotypical speeches by priests made at the installation of a new lord, moreover, the actions of past Uacúsecha individuals in establishing the office to which the lord is being raised are recounted as a means of reestablishing the Uacúsecha's authority and reminding the new officeholder of his duties.

REGIONALISM VERSUS INTERCULTURAL INFLUENCES IN PREHISPANIC MICHOACÁN

The Tarascan kingdom was an essential part of Mesoamerica, and in particular the economic interactions that constituted the "Mesoamerican World System" that shaped political and cultural histories (and vice versa) during the last one or two centuries before Spanish contact.[8] During the late Postclassic period (ca. AD 1350–1520), the Tarascan kingdom constituted the second largest polity in Mesoamerica. Documentary evidence as well as some archaeological evidence suggest that the Tarascan and larger Aztec empires had reached something of a stalemate at the time of Spanish contact, resulting in a fairly rigid border area that to this day roughly aligns with the border between the modern Mexican states of Michoacán and México. In the second half of the fifteenth century, the Aztecs had made a major incursion into Tarascan territory, but this gain by the Aztecs brought a response by the Tarascans in which they regained the lost territory (Hassig 1988; Herrejón Peredo 1978). Documentary sources attest to garrisons or fortified sites on both sides of this uneasy frontier (Hassig 1988; Herrejón Peredo 1978); archaeological research largely backs this up in the vicinity of at least one such garrison site (Silverstein 2000; a garrison site on the Tarascan side at Acámbaro has also been investigated: see Gorenstein 1985).

This standoff between the Tarascans and Aztecs appears to have had some effect on international trade in Postclassic Mesoamerica. For example, obsidian from the Ucareo-Zinapécuaro source zone in the northeast corner of Michoacán, which had been widely exploited and traded throughout Mesoamerica, possibly under the leadership or auspices of the Early Postclassic center of Tula, Hidalgo (Healan 1997; see also Braswell 2003), was in the Late Postclassic much more limited in its distribution and oriented more toward feeding the Tarascan state apparatus (Pollard and Vogel 1994; Pollard 2003b). In addition, the Tarascan kingdom existed at or near the heart of the "West Mexican metallurgical zone" (Hosler 1994, 2009). The production of bronze alloys was integral to the political economy of the Tarascan kingdom itself (e.g., Pollard 1987), and the political apparatus seems to have inserted itself directly in production in at least some contexts (Pollard 1987) but not necessarily all contexts (Hosler 2009; Maldonado 2008, 2012; Maldonado et al. 2009). The investigation of key resources such as these in projects of state formation and the consolidation of power, not to mention the participation of state merchants and/or possibly merchants who were not politically affiliated or co-opted by which these and other resources reached other areas of Mesoamerica, are key problems for archaeologists working in this or any region in Mesoamerica during the Postclassic.

The archaeological record therefore seems to indicate a regionalization of certain commodities in the Late Postclassic that perhaps mirrors wider cultural attitudes and some small level of ignorance of specific dynamics of other cultures in Mesoamerica. Obsidian from regional sources such as Ucareo-Zinapécuaro and Zinaparo did not seem to move beyond Tarascan borders; certainly the Ucareo-Zinapécuaro source area did not flow east as it once had. While Late Postclassic ceramics do take part in certain wider Mesoamerican trends such as the development of miniature bowls and jars, akin to similar developments to the east (Smith, Wharton, and Olson 2003), in terms of decorative style Tarascan ceramics present a readily recognizable contrast to Basin of Mexico ceramic styles. Again, this boundary between distinct ceramic styles is evident at certain points along the militarized frontier between the Tarascan kingdom and Aztec empire. At this point it is an open question of how much the bronze artifacts produced in Tarascan-held territory made its way into international markets, but there is ethnohistoric evidence that indicates that at least some aspect of the metallurgical process felt strong political influence and demand from the Tarascan king and capital (Pollard 1987; Warren 1963). Pollard (2000) has discussed how misperceptions in Basin of Mexico ethnohistoric sources reveal that while the Mexica and other Basin of Mexico peoples had some knowledge of their Tarascan adversaries, this knowledge was imprecise and oftentimes mistaken, suggesting a lack of flow of information.

This arrangement in the Late Postclassic period contrasts with the Early Postclassic period, in particular.[9] In the Early Postclassic, particularly as evidenced by burials at Urichu in the Pátzcuaro Basin, incipient elites sought to demonstrate their status with wealth objects that were either derived from the Basin of Mexico or further afield or were in the style of "Toltec" (in the sense of being Early Postclassic and affiliated with the archaeological site of Tula, Hidalgo). Most spectacular among such Tula-influenced artifacts at Urichu was a set of ceramic flutes (Pollard and Cahue 1999). The archaeological picture that has emerged in Michoacán for the Early Postclassic is largely one of incipient or emerging elites who sought to define their new status by consuming wealth objects that were derived from elsewhere and that could, according to various connotations of "Toltec"—both associated with the site of Tula and with already existing or past centers of power—confer much needed legitimacy to these efforts to distinguish these elites from commoners and potential rivals (Pollard 2008, 2016a). This pattern can be interpreted to be a continuation of contacts between Michoacán and Central Mexico that date at least to the Classic period. Imported Pachuca obsidian was prominent at Erongarícuaro in the Classic period, indicating ties to the Classic period Central Mexican metropolis Teotihuacan (Pollard 2005). Teotihuacan influence has also been identified in the Classic period in the Cuitzeo Basin (Filini 2004). It is necessary to add, moreover, that in Michoacán any such existing or past center of power was necessarily extralocal. These developments of incipient elites and the sites they inhabited and apparently governed reach their height in terms of local sociopolitical and demographic history in the Early Postclassic. There is in Michoacán no presence of local, formerly glorious cities that could be appropriated into local histories to legitimize them. Therefore while the Priest's Speech in the *Relación de Michoacán* does follow some familiar patterns in relation to other Mesoamerican narratives concerning the past and rulership (discussed below), in many ways the deployment of such stories to defend and define the origins of kingship in a local context—embodied by what we know as the Late Postclassic Tarascan kingdom—was a new one. To put this in archaeological terms, from the perspective of the culture area of Mesoamerica as a whole the Tarascan kingdom is a secondary state, having grown out of processes that preceded it and influenced its rise; from a restricted local perspective, the Tarascan kingdom is a primary state with no local precedents to draw on.

It is obvious that this situation directly contrasts with much of the rest of Mesoamerica. As far back as the Late Pre-Classic, certainly, state-level societies arose in Mesoamerica. The Monte Alban State in the valley of Oaxaca is first identifiable at roughly the transition from the Middle Pre-Classic to the Late Pre-Classic. In the Classic period, if not just before its onset, Teotihuacan grew to unprecedented heights in terms of demographic size and cultural influence throughout Mesoamerica. Schele and Mathews (1998) have argued that Teotihuacan is often a definite reference in Classic period Maya inscriptions to a place from which rulership originates; it is possible that already Teotihuacan is only the latest embodiment of such a font of rulership. While the Olmec polities of the Gulf Coat of Veracruz and Tabasco are debated in terms of their status at state-level societies, they (Schele and Mathews 1998:37–40) argue that the earlier Early and Middle Pre-Classic Olmec sites could be earlier iterations of the idea of a "Tollan," or "Place of Cattail Reeds / Place Where People are as Numerous as Cattail Reeds" (this is the translation of Tollan in Nahuatl; in the Maya inscriptions this idea of a place is called Puh [Schele and Mathews 1998:37–40]). What we can say is that apparently from the Pre-Classic period forward in time in Mesoamerica, but definitively with the rise of Teotihuacan and the spread of its influence in the Classic period, there is a cultural pattern that identifies political capitals as an instantiation of a growing list of embodiments of this idea of a place. While this idea was widespread and the Colonial-era narratives concerning the prehispanic past partake in this tradition, from the point of view of Michoacán this tradition appears to have been a purely external force, with no site in the area being on par with a Tollan until the Late Postclassic period and the rise of the Tarascan kingdom.

MODERN WESTERN REPRESENTATIONS OF THE PREHISPANIC PAST AND HYPOTHESIZED LINKS TO OTHER MESOAMERICAN TRADITIONS

Literalist and historicist readings—and as noted in Chapter 1 the majority of studies have a strong undercurrent of historicist assumptions—of the ethnohistoric record have been formulated in response to and as part of a movement to produce a single understanding of the real past that merges ethnohistoric data with archaeological (and other) data. Some ethnohistoric representations as well as other data (particularly linguistic data) indicate that large-scale movements of people occurred in various stages through the Postclassic period in Mesoamerica (see, e.g., Smith 1984; Beekman and Christensen 2003 for synthetic approaches to the sources from archaeological points of view). Of particular importance here is the movement of people from the northern frontier of Mesoamerica southward into areas such as the Basin of Mexico that were and had long been firmly within the culture area; this shifting nature of the northern frontier in Mesoamerica during the Postclassic was recognized as a significant factor in the history of the culture area by Pedro Armillas (1969; see also Hers 2005, 2008; Punzo Díaz 2016; Weigand 2015a). Many archaeologists and ethnohistorians, based on the documents of Early Colonial Mexico (particularly from the Basin of Mexico; see, e.g., Smith 1984), but also using linguistic and biological evidence (e.g., Beekman and Christensen 2003) emphasize the historical veracity of these migrations. While shifting environments and other factors almost undoubtedly led to movements of people from the Epiclassic period (and likely in earlier periods) onward in time, tying any particular archaeological assemblage or human remains to stable and fixed ethnolinguistic groups referred to in the documentary record is quite difficult. In fact, part of Christopher Beekman and Alexander Christensen's anthropological examination of migration as a phenomenon is the recognition that fluidity in identity was an important factor in such movements and the decisions and paths therein (Beekman and Christensen 2003).

In relation to studies of these migrations, ethnohistoric sources from Michoacán and adjacent areas appear to be viewed as sources that might provide an ancillary window onto Nahua traditions of their origins and migrations from the origin place of Aztlán in particular, or alternatively that the Nahua traditions can be used to provide the appropriate background to the account of the priest that appears truncated at its inception in the *Relación de Michoacán* (the first part of the document having been lost, as discussed in chapter 1). In this way some scholars attempt to merge the *Relación de Michoacán* with the more voluminous Nahua corpus of documents in order to somehow prove, explain, or fill in the gaps in what is believed to have been a historical relationship between the two groups (Jiménez Moreno 1948; Roskamp 2010a; for modern analyses of the Nahua migration stories see, e.g., Beekman and Christensen 2003; Smith 1984). The mere fact that a migration story is common to both, combined with the notion that somehow the migration story in the *Relación de Michoacán* seems to be abbreviated or picked up partially into that migration (as it opens in Zacapu), is held up as evidence that there is enough in the stories to indicate some real relationship in the real past between the two peoples. The fact that Purhépecha by most if not all accounts is a linguistic isolate of a few thousand years (see summary in Pollard 1993b:15–16) must be ignored in any such scenario that posits anything approaching a phylogenetic relationship (i.e., one group of people splitting off into "daughter" populations) that is supposedly being represented in these migration stories. I am inclined to follow Pollard's assessment of the potential ties between the archaeological record and supposed migrations into the Lake Pátzcuaro Basin: "While the legendary histories record several episodes of migration of non-Purépecha [*sic*] populations into the region, so far these population movements are not visible in the archaeological record." More recently, Pollard and Dorothy Washburn have argued in a preliminary fashion that judging by consistencies in the structure or layout of design elements in ceramic decorations, there was little ethnolinguistic change in central Michoacán from the Classic period through the Late Postclassic period (Pollard and Washburn n.d.). Begun (2008) has reached a similar conclusion based on long-lived stylistic elements of figurines in the Lake Pátzcuaro Basin from the Classic through the Late Postclassic periods. This would cover the migration(s) that many suppose occurred sometime between the end of the Classic period and the Middle Postclassic period.

In an appropriately cautious analysis of linguistic diversity evident in the *Relaciones Geográficas* (from the 1580s), Espejel Carbajal (2016) notes that when these documents were produced, most non-Purhépecha-speaking communities were located away from the Lake Pátzcuaro Basin and central Michoacán more generally (see also Albiez-Zwieck 2013; Pollard 1994). She also notes the presence of Nahua-speaking communities interspersed throughout central Michoacán at the time of the Spanish incursion into Tarascan territory, as evidenced by comments in the *Relación de Michoacán*, in which communities extant at the time are clearly described as such. However, she cautions that information pertaining to linguistic diversity from the period prior to the formation of the Tarascan kingdom is scarce (Espejel Carbajal 2016:97–98). I concur with this assessment and believe it is important to note furthermore that I find no incontrovertible evidence that the practice of referring to certain places in the Lake Pátzcuaro Basin such as Tzintzuntzan/ Michoacán are named in the *Relación de Michoacán* using their Nahuatl names has anything to do with what these places were called prior to Tarascan state formation. In some discussions (e.g., Roskamp 2010a), there is the apparent assumption that the names used for these locales as well as certain characters (e.g., Naca; see chapter 4) is an indication of how they were referred to in the prehispanic past, with the further assumption of who—speakers of what language—inhabited these places. The fact that Tzintzuntzan is universally referred to as "Mechuacan" in the document (including in the Priest's Speech) is used to infer that it was primarily inhabited by Nahua speakers. While this is possible, it is far from demonstrated that this should be taken as a certainty. It also goes against the observation noted in chapter 1 that the document, due in large part to this use of "Mechuacan" as the name for the capital, is a biased and "Tzintzuntzanist" representation that promotes the view of Tzintzuntzan as the original and proper "Ciudad de Michoacán," which then undercuts Quiroga's movement of the diocese and indigenous government to Pátzcuaro, the current "Ciudad de Michoacán." Alternatively, the priest or any member of the team that produced the document, including the friar could simply be using the name of the place as it became known to the Spaniards through their Nahua allies and interpreters through the intrusion of Spaniards into Tarascan territory and subsequently through the imposition of the colonial order. There is no definitive case to be made based on the evidence in the *Relación de Michoacán* as well as other documentary evidence that Tzintzuntzan or any other locale in the basin was populated *predominantly* by Nahua lords and commoners (see chapter 1, *contra* Castro Gutiérrez 2015:134; Monzón, Roskamp, and Warren 2009; Roskamp 2010a). We know that Tzintzuntzan was home to Nahua speakers, some or many of which were lords, at the time of the Spanish entrance into Michoacán. While there are hints and indications that Nahua speakers were then settled in Tzintzuntzan, the demographic dominance as well as the temporal depth of those inhabitants is frankly speculation that presumes many things, first and foremost of which is that the *Relación de Michoacán* is an accurate representation—the yardstick against which to evaluate other representation, as in Roskamp (2012, 2015)—of a real past and a deep past. A supposition that Tzintzuntzan was heavily populated and dominated by Nahua speakers, only to then be replaced or deposed by immigrant Purhépecha speakers, as occurs in many of these migration scenarios based on interpretations of the Priest's Speech, is at this point far from demonstrated. It is important to not overstate the predominance of the Purhépecha speakers that called north-central Michoacán home to the exclusion of some ethnolinguistic diversity and thereby impose a cultural homogeneity that perhaps never existed (Castro Gutiérrez 2015; Espejel Carbajal 2016; Monzón, Roskamp, and Warren 2009; Roskamp 1998, 2010a), but we should also not jump to unwarranted conclusions that read much into the Priest's Speech and that ignore the reports of the predominance of Purhépecha in this area and archaeological assessments that suggest they had lived there for centuries.

I also point out that the use of kinship terms in the *Relación de Michoacán* and in the Priest's Speech within it has been often misunderstood. For example, upon meeting the fisherman from Xaráquaro who would become Taríacuri's mother, the Uacúsecha lords exclaim that the gods worshipped on the islands of the lake were their "grandfathers" as they traveled the road; they thereby claim to have found their relatives. This is another passage often used in supposing that the Uacúsecha are at least related to the Islanders (the passage also indicates that the Uacúsecha spoke a *serrano* or mountainous dialect of the language of the Islanders—this is commonly assumed to be Purhépecha), but perhaps not related to non-Islander groups (such as the inhabitants of Erongarícuaro and Urichu). If the view is taken that kinship is often expressed to indicate *social* relationships (see especially Castro Gutiérrez 2015:136), then this passage and others in which in-laws and characters engaged in social relationships (especially of marriage alliance) use kinship terms to refer to one another can be understood as more of an indication of forging and maintaining such relationships rather than actual kinship relations.

What I contend are misunderstandings of the ethnohistoric record, and particularly the Priest's Speech within the *Relación de Michoacán*, impact how these processes and the archaeological record of Tarascan territory are investigated and understood at nearly every turn. Readings of the Priest's Speech that are literalist in orientation have influenced archaeological research and interpretations in West Mexico. Zacapu and its environs, the supposed "homeland" of the "Chichimecs" in the priest's speech, was chosen as the site of a major archaeological investigation by Centre de Etudes Mexicaines et Centre-Américaines (CEMCA). As I detail below, the specific place (Zacapu Tacanendan) that was chosen by the priest to begin his narrative has certain symbolic qualities that I suggest were more important than representing the past accurately. While this research found important evidence of settlement pattern shifts, the growth of urbanism, and changes in mortuary behavior, some of the archaeologists involved have been at pains to reconcile their archaeological findings with their interpretations of the Priest's Speech. This has resulted in their insistence on the fact that the "chichimecs" who supposedly moved into the Pátzcuaro Basin from the Zacapu area were actually quite settled and "civilized," that is, the opposite of the typical definition of "Chichimec" (Michelet 1989; Arnauld and Michelet 1991). While the Zacapu project found evidence for dramatic settlement pattern shifts and even the rapid abandonment of some sites, the assumption that the people who abandoned this region went to the Pátzcuaro Basin would be difficult to prove archaeologically and I would contend has been colored by the priest's speech. Population within the Pátzcuaro Basin rose throughout the Postclassic as evidenced by the growth of sites in the southwestern portion of the basin (Pollard 2008). More recent research in the basin has identified previously unknown settlements in the eastern portion of the basin (e.g., Fisher and Leisz 2013), the depopulation of which some time in the Early and/or Middle Postclassic likely had important impacts on the settlement patterns and resource needs for the settlements that survived and thrived into and during the Late Postclassic. At any rate, the question of population movements both within and between the Zacapu and Pátzcuaro Basins is far from settled (Pollard 2016b); the role of such movements and resulting population pressure in the face of declining prime agricultural land in the Pátzcuaro Basin in particular are crucial factors in the formation of a centralized state in the Pátzcuaro Basin (Pollard 1980, 1982, 2008; Pollard and Gorenstein 1980; see also Haskell and Stawski 2016).

In another example of merging archaeological data with historicist readings of the ethnohistoric record, archaeologists have interpreted cultural sequences in the Zacapu Basin, northern Michoacán in the region along the Lerma River, and areas further to the north to indicate population movements going out of northern Michoacán around the end of the Classic period (ca. AD 500–700) and then the return of at least some of these people in the Postclassic (Carot 2005; Carot and Hers 2006; Hers 2005, 2008; Pereira, Michelet, and Migeon 2013). In these interpretations of the archaeological record, changes in ceramic decoration are interpreted to be related to the Purhépecha ethnicity that left northern Michoacán only to return later. Such an emigration to northern sites, presumably to take advantage of agricultural and trading opportunities that were expanding northward at the time, coupled with a return when large-scale habitation of those sites was rendered problematic due to climactic shifts, impacted how and with whom these Purhépecha migrants would have traded. If these migrants are interpreted to be related to the supposed migrants who came to Zacapu only to shortly leave for the Pátzcuaro Basin (and which is an interpretation of the Priest's Speech but not explicitly stated therein as it could be interpreted in a religious mode), then the history of movement and established ties with key trading partners to the north might have been advantageous to this new elite class (a point made explicit by Albiez-Zwieck 2013, who points out the potential importance of these migrants in establishing trade ties but nevertheless remains somewhat skeptical of the interpretations that emphasize ethnic continuity; see also Weigand's [2015a] discussion of mercantilism and sociopolitical structure in the northwest part of Mesoamerica). Any such ethnic continuity would also have had to have been preserved in and through a period of relatively chaotic movements of people, adaptations, and adoptions of different or new political ideologies, and likely some ethnic intermixing, all of which were noted above. I argue that again the archaeological record has been stretched to attempt to reconcile it with certain literalist interpretations of the *Relación de Michoacán* and the priest's narrative. Namely, scholars have tried to posit a shared ethnic identity in relation to a claim of familiarity between the "Chichimec" migrants and the "Islander" autochthons as told by the priest (Alcalá 2000). If such a familiarity existed and can be merged with these archaeological interpretations, this familiarity would be a memory or cultural pattern that would have survived at minimum 500 years of migrations, displacement, and possible ethnic mixing. Once again, these key issues and the ability of archaeological materials to address them have, in my opinion, been co-opted by literalist interpretations of the ethnohistoric record, foremost within that record the Priest's Speech within the *Relación de Michoacán*. It is entirely possible to interpret the archaeological evidence in other ways; the claim of long-lived ethnic homogeneity and the reflection of ethnicity in ceramic material culture is dubious on theoretical grounds, and I would argue the interpretations of the investigators would have been different if the ethnohistoric and archaeological records were kept analytically separate.

In this debate over literalist readings of the Priest's Speech and attempts to link them to the prehispanic past, including archaeological materials, it is important to recognize the fact that the Priest's Speech only says that Curicaueri and Hireticatame arrived at Uirúguarapexo / Zacapu Tacanendan, but does not specify from where, or which direction. More specifically, the speech begins by only stating that Curicaueri began his reign when he arrived at that place. Only after an interjection by the friar summarizing what the narrative will state is it then related that Hireticatame was also there, and that he had carried the god there, and had been gathering firewood for the deity, worshipping it with incense, and performing the war ceremony. I have already discussed the manner in which this place—a round volcanic crater with water inside near Zacapu—is a fitting place to precede the story the priest is about to tell because it foreshadows the relevant elementary categories. It is necessary to emphasize that this place *is the beginning of the story*; the priest consciously chose this place and its meanings to begin his tale. It should not, therefore, be seen as a place and time at which the priest simply picks up a migration story that is already in progress.

This notion of the arrival of Curicaueri specifically and Hireticatame in an ancillary fashion can be compared with other oral and combined oral and literary/material traditions that supplemented the oral performance of storytelling with the various kinds of documents to support the claims of the orator. The performance of a lengthy historical and lineage focused oration is similar to how Mixtec elites legitimated their place in society. As indicated by many scholars, Mixtec elites did not so much "read" their pictorial codices as they used them as mnemonic devices and a form of cosmological authentication (Weiner 1992) or as what Parmentier (1987) called "signs in history." Recently Williams (2009) has argued based on the structure of the *Codex Nuttall* that a more cosmologically oriented origin myth of Mixtec elites is included in this screen-fold-style manuscript, but the structure of the codex made it possible to easily open up and include or keep folded and thus exclude these "pages." These episodes concerning a "war of heaven," as Williams (2009) and before him Byland and Pohl (1994) discuss, serve to provide an orientation to larger cosmological forces and possibly incorporate rival polities within this cosmological/mythological framework. This is a common phenomenon in the Mixtec codices, which typically open with origin scenes that can vary among themselves but that typically represent the emergence of elite lineages from sacred trees. It would thus be entirely keeping with other modes of legitimization to have a more "historical" and according to my analysis and Valerio Valeri's (1990; see also Turner 1988a; and chapter 3) framework, syntagmatic presentation directly follows an episode or episodes of creation, emergence, arrival from a sacred or nonmundane space-time. It is unfortunate that we cannot know in what way the first part of the *Relación de Michoacán* transitioned into the second part that included the Priest's Speech, but I suggest that it provides background information concerning Curicaueri before his arrival on earth, at Uirúguarapexo/Zacapu Tacanendan (Alcalá 2000:341), as a direct prelude to the Priest's Speech and thus serves the same function of a form of cosmological authentication that could be included or omitted based on the circumstances of the oratorical performance.

THE PRIEST'S SPEECH AND POSTCLASSIC
MESOAMERICAN IDEOLOGIES OF RULERSHIP

Studies of the indigenous historical tradition as well as archaeological information help inform us of what comprised those larger influences, particularly in terms of their symbolic content. In the ethnohistoric and archaeological record from throughout

Mesoamerica, the Epiclassic to Postclassic transition is a time of upheaval in trade routes, movements of people, and very likely the spread of a new political ideology with new symbols of power and legitimation (López Austin and López Luján 2000) that could perhaps even be characterized as a Mesoamerican "world religion" (Ringle, Negrón, and Bey 1998) that was readily exported to societies throughout Mesoamerica. This movement, according in particular to Alfredo López Austín and Leonardo López Lujan , left social patterns and political structures that persisted in time and are reflected in the ethnohistoric record both predating the Spanish conquest (López Austin and López Luján 2000; as in the preconquest Mixtec codices: see, e.g., Byland and Pohl 1994; Williams 2009) and postdating it (as in particularly the Central Mexican documents as well as Yucatec and K'iche' Maya documents). A key element of this ideology that influenced ideas of how the past should be represented and made to include constructions of legendary/semidivine origins and rituals of investiture demonstrating ties to ancient capitals and places of power, were movements of people. The most well-known variant (or really, series of variations) of this ideology is the set of related myths and legends of Quetzalcoatl/Topiltzin (e.g., Gillespie 1989; López Austin and López Luján 2000; Nicholson 1957; see also Kowalski and Kristan-Graham 2007). Studies of the *Relación de Michoacán* that read into the document religious, ideological, and metaphorical understandings of indigenous practices and events directly relate to another of the processes that was an important aspect of the Classic-to-Postclassic transition in Mesoamerica—namely, the widespread but complex Quetzalcoatl/Topiltzin phenomenon. Dominique Michelet (1989) and Michelet and Arnauld and Michelet (1991), two archaeologists of the CEMCA Zacapu project, approach the narrative as a mix of historical events, mythological elements, and moralizing fables. Their studies note commonalities with other "historical" narratives and traditions in Mesoamerica as well, perhaps implying that such commonalities might be due more to ideological rather than historical factors (this is also pursued by van Zantwijk 1985:27–28). López Austin and López Luján (2000) formulate a wider explanatory framework to account for many of the similarities in Postclassic and Early Colonial period representations of the past in which Feathered Serpent (or "Quetzalcoatl," to use the Nahuatl name) imagery, metaphors, and characters indicate a widespread political shift in how political legitimacy was conceptualized. This reconceptualization of political ideologies was, in their model, exported and merged with older but likely weakening sociopolitical structures in various areas of Mesoamerica through the Postclassic. In that endeavor they cite approvingly Michelet and Arnauld and Michelet's (1991) position that the "Chichimecs" of the *Relación de Michoacán* should not be understood as "literal" Chichimecs, because they bear many indications of civilized life. López Austin and López Luján (2000) take this observation a step further and indicate that they interpret the narrative of the *Relación de Michoacán* to signify an ideology that had existed in Michoacán that, like elsewhere in Mesoamerica, drew on the ideological formulation that this new political legitimacy derived ultimately from some sacred city (the famed "Tollan"), or cave, or person (the famed "Quetzalcoatl" in some manifestation). While I am in agreement that the formulation in the *Relación de Michoacán* should not be understood literally and therefore that "otherness" and origins from "beyond" are being emphasized as opposed to ties or heritage to a literal social group (as is present in both the original work of Arnauld and Michelet [1991] and López Austin and López Luján [2000]), it is also essential to note that Michoacán and the priest's narrative only fit this grand model if certain glaring departures from the ethnohistoric record of Michoacán compared to the basics of the model are discounted. The most notable example of Michoacán's unique relationship to this phenomenon lies in the fact that nowhere in the priest's narrative is there anything on par with a "Quetzalcoatl"-type figure mentioned.[10] This is evident in the presentation of the narrative and its analysis in chapter 4, and this point is relevant not only with respect to López Austin and López Luján's work but also others who find some commonalities between the priest's narrative and other representations of the prehispanic past that more definitively contain those elements (e.g., as in Arnauld and Michelet's [1991] comparison of the priest's speech with the *Popol Vuh*; see also Olivier and Martínez González 2015).

What can be said for the Epiclassic period into the early years of the Spanish colonial system, then, is that there were numerous commingled and overlapping processes; the two dominant ones appear to have been the spread of a multiethnic or even "world religion" basing political sovereignty on access to certain fonts of historical-cum-cosmic power and a significant movement (or likely multiple movements) of people both into and within Mesoamerica. The two processes could have been intimately related to one another in some contexts but do not necessarily require one another in any particular context. What can be said, however, is that approaches to the ethnohistoric record in Mesoamerica generally and Michoacán in particular have generally privileged underlying literalist as opposed to metaphorical and ideological constructions within that ethnohistoric record. In essence, therefore, such studies have inherently devalued the nature of that complex process of spreading one or more iterations of the Quetzalcoatl "World Religion" or novel political ideology and the ways in which it has constituted the native historical tradition (e.g., Gillespie 1989, 1998, 2007b, 2008), rather than some presupposed events of the past and unproblematically "historical" memories of such that constituted that transition in political ideology.

This brief foray into some issues pertaining to archaeological and ethnohistoric interpretations of the prehispanic past of Michoacán and its relations with the wider Mesoamerican past is intended to highlight how important the *Relación de Michoacán*, and interpretations of that document, are to an area of Mesoamerica that is already poorly understood and understudied. This state of affairs stands in contrast to its importance in Mesoamerica, however. This was a dominant polity in Late Postclassic Mesoamerica; its fortunes and strategies affected the availability of at least two key resources in Mesoamerica. Its productive and distributive organizational structures and the extent to which Tarascan elites inserted themselves into those structures or were perhaps even the driving force behind a few of those structures have important ramifications for economies throughout at least West Mexico and likely most or all of the culture area. However, the place of the Tarascan kingdom within Mesoamerica in these important regards cannot, I contend, be understood until we jettison some old ideas about what exactly the ethnohistoric record, including representations of the prehispanic past and especially the Priest's Speech, should be interpreted to mean. Doing so will require further analysis of the logic and structure evident in individual narratives and documents and the relation between their structural and logical coherence and the aims of impacting the specific sociohistorical contexts in which they were produced. Again, this is the point of historicity as a theoretical construct. We should not analyze narratives as members of broad categories, but rather as specific yet culturally influenced expositions aimed at varying sociohistorical goals.

TARASCAN AND MESOAMERICAN PERCEPTIONS OF TIME AND THE COSMOS

The preceding discussion lends itself to a discussion of Mesoamerican conceptualizations of time and its cyclical nature. Part of the appeal of conceiving of politics in such ideological terms apparently was the ability to fit the rise and fall of various iterations of the Tollan pattern with larger celestial and cosmological cycles, namely, the daily rising and setting of the sun and also its yearly march northward and southward as it rose and set on the horizons and thus being of varying strengths during the year and giving rise to seasonality. As noted above, the available evidence suggests that Tarascan culture and history have a problematic relationship with this Mesoamerican tradition.

Tarascan representations of the past and its relation to the rest of Mesoamerica should be understood in relation to conceptions of time and the cosmos in which time was seen as a complex arrangement of various cycles (e.g., Boone 2007; Bricker 1981; Florescano 1994; Hassig 2001). For my purposes it is enough to merely note that to some extent Mesoamerican peoples, including the Tarascans, constructed human events within the cyclical structure of the cosmos as they understood it. Within the daily and seasonal movements of the sun and other cycles of the movements of celestial bodies, Mesoamerican peoples clearly observed the recurring cycles of the cosmos around them. The indigenous calendrical systems of Mesoamerica also contained their own built-in cycles of the repeating day names (the 20 day signs) and numbers (1 through 13) in the ritual calendar and the yearly north-south movements of the sun through the year in the yearly or solar calendar (18 successive "months" of 20 days each, plus a period of 5 "empty days" that did not belong to a named month). Time and temporal periods were, importantly, qualitative rather than a continual flux or quantitative accumulation. Days, thirteen-day periods that the Spaniards called *trecenas*, years, and even whole cosmic ages or "Suns" were qualitatively different from one another, and to move in time was to shift from one qualitative state of being to another. The day names and perceptions of varying degrees of propitiousness for the day names, along with deities and their qualities that ruled or governed the days, exemplify this.

An important ideological precept in Mesoamerica in general was that humans should fit within these calendrical cycles and the celestial movements around which they were constructed. In this way human deeds were viewed through this integrated sociocosmic lens as extensions or manifestations of larger cosmic events. Maffie (2013) has suggested that this is the case in Aztec philosophy because humans are composed of the same sacred force that comprises the rest of the cosmos; because humans are consubstantial with, for example, the celestial bodies, they are the result of and follow the same general processes and manifest different surficial variants of what is ultimately the same underlying sacred force and its processes of composition and flow. Therefore human actions were interpreted according to, and fit within, the cycles evident in the cosmos. In the Mesoamerican view, furthermore, people or social categories were related to the phenomena of the cosmos as they were embodied by anthropomorphized deities. In this sense, religious and political leaders in particular drew on these deities and the cosmos for their power and efficacy. In the formulation of the *hombre-dios*, or "man-god" (López Austin 1973; see application of this concept to the *Relación de Michoacán* specifically in Martínez González 2010, 2011), Mesoamerican rulers were constructed or understood to possess sacred power that they had obtained or inherited from the gods through various means. Power was also fostered and preserved by maintaining proper relationships with time and the count of the days; people and their actions were expected to be harmonious with the period of time that they were occupying (day, thirteen-day trecenas, years). To do so was to harness good fortune, but to work against these forces was potentially calamitous. These points are essential in understanding how in the indigenous worldview, social categories, and actions, were tied to larger cosmic phenomena and their temporality, and the cyclicity of an integrated sociocosmic world

helps us understand the case of the two Taríacuris and the importance of constructing and relating the past Taríacuri to Don Francisco Taríacuri.

In analyses and discussions of Central Mexican narratives of the past,[11] the presence of four or sometimes five creations is given analytic prominence. The paradigmatic nature of four as the number of directions is also reflected in this number
of creations, and it is very likely that the role of four directional year bearers and
directional world trees is important in representing time in totality as an assembly
of four successive ages or "suns." The cycles are similar in the broad outlines of creation and share certain aspects in pairs (e.g., Graulich 1997:63–95). Furthering the
apparent dominance of paradigmatic repetition, cyclicity, and the functional identity and interchangeability is the fact that in the various Central Mexican sources,
the order of the various creations, or "Suns," are related in different orders. When
some difference among the "suns" is recognized, a concomitant result of analysis is
presented in which four as a ritually important number in Mesoamerica can easily
be produced as two sets of coupled terms, thus once again reducing variation to
purely paradigmatic terms. As for the five, as opposed to four, creations given in
the strictly Mexica sources, this is explained in some respects again in paradigmatic
terms. In Mesoamerican numerology and its relation to cosmological principles,
four is a complete number but five can be regarded as similarly complete but with
the added connotation of "full" (see, e.g., Maffie 2013:212–228). Five directions represent the four directions and associated phenomena plus the center, as in representations of this *quincunx* with the central element depicted in, for example, the
Codex Féjerváry-Meyer, the *Codex Mendoza*, and in more mundane iconic motifs
depicting four elements plus a central fifth element. Five is a complete and proper
number due to this association with the center that defines and organizes the four
surrounding elements, in addition to the composition of the human body with five
digits on four limbs (López Austin 1988). The number 5 also constitutes a full number or a kind of numerological precipice, however. Counting beyond 5 results in a
transition into chaos and improper, profane, or polluting numbers (until multiples
of 4 and 5 can be reached). Ross Hassig (2001) adopts this numerological stance
of paradigmatic significance in arguing that Mexica priests and scholars added in
a fifth sun in their representations of the cosmos and its ages to produce a more
profound sense of finality should the current sun end. In other words, the difference between Mexica and other sources can be framed in terms of the implications
of what sun the composers of these representations understood themselves to be
in. In the traditions that identify four suns (including the present one, from the
point of view of the producer of the representation), then while this sun might end,
there might be another sun; the Mexica sources that identify the present sun as the
fifth admits no such possibility. Hassig interprets this representation as providing

further motivation within the ideological framework that underpinned Mexica warfare and expansionism—warfare is necessary to perpetuate the cosmos through human sacrifice, and if this is not achieved then there will not be any future suns that might arise in the case of the destruction of the present one.

Such conceptualizations of time as discrete and qualitatively different from one unit of time to the next apply within the set of day names, for example, but the repetition of the cycle provides for a means to connect time across these cycles through the paradigmatic repetition of the day name. This is part of the function of the repetition and qualitative character of the calendar—it enables prophesying by knowing that years with the day sign "Rabbit" are stereotypically years of famine and "Flint" years are typically associated with founding or abandoning cities (López Austin 1973:101). The repetition of the calendar and of named periods within the calendar therefore establishes and conserves through time connectedness of the cycles. There is therefore a complication in any calendrical system: time switches from one discrete and qualitatively different state to another and ultimately repeats itself, but how can this transferral between days and then larger units of time—such that days then repeat themselves—be ensured? In such systems, the boundaries between the discrete units are times that are fraught with both danger (as in the five "empty" days or the end of a fifty-two-year cycle at which fires must be extinguished and a new fire for all of society be drilled, in Mexica-dominated Basin of Mexico) and power. Anthropological studies of cyclical notions of time composed of discrete units have emphasized that the boundaries between units of time are simultaneously dangerous because they are neither time period but powerful because they touch and unite both time periods involved in the transferral of time. Boundary figures themselves become part of the logical armature that ensures the proper transferral of time, and so their role of transferral, union, and disjuncture is itself cyclical and repetitive. In other words, boundary figures are essential paradigmatic operators that due to their function are constructed to be similar and have similar effects in time.

In Mesoamerican thought there existed, then, a system in which both the internal qualities of the units of time were encompassed by names or signs, and the boundaries between units—and the means by which they were mediated as they were brought together, exchanged time, and were separated—were marked paradigmatically with similar names. Furthermore, time was not simply the flow of time but rather was a complex conceptualization of "space-time" and thus time was always "in place." This facilitated the transposition of temporal conceptualizations of firmly inhabiting the internal category as well as marking the boundary to spatial conceptualizations. To be unambiguously in place was powerful; to mark the boundary between places and a fortiori nothingness and liminality opened up new possibilities for creation as creative ordering.

To bring the discussion full circle, and to relate it to an understanding of the Priest's Speech, the qualitative nature of time and periods of time in Mesoamerican thought provides a foundation of time that is more concerned with divination than providing a framework for historical record keeping (Dibble 1971). We see this use of the calendar, in fact, in the Priest's Speech itself when one characters asks if they should "count the days" (see chapter 4), that is, use the calendar to keep track of the days and determine a fortuitous day for an undertaking. Divination is linked to the repetitive nature of the calendar system and the fact that day signs and therefore years that took their names from day signs came to have had positive or negative associations (e.g., López Austin 1973). Taken to its logical conclusion, this means that the future is knowable thanks to this system and the ability to project the repetition of these systems into that future—one must only look to the past and present in order to know what the future holds. This is what Gibson (1975:319; see also Carrasco [1980:302–303] and Todorov [1984:74]) calls "prophetic history." When this is taken yet a step further, the unity and cyclicity of the temporal succession mean that in keeping with the discussion of historicity in the next chapter, past, present, and future are viewed to some extent simultaneously, thanks to the paradigmatic associations created by the repeating day signs, and worked and reworked in concert when new revelations arise. Writing on the inclusion of ideograms in Aztec pictorial documents, specifically the *Codex Mendoza* and *Codex Fejérváry-Mayer*, Maffie (2013:524–525; emphasis in original) notes that they function to "both *describe* existence and *prescribe* a way for humans to exist. They describe the way things *are* as well as prescribe how things *ought* to be." The nature of what ought applies not merely to present, future-oriented action, but also applies in some contexts to the past and what ought to have happened. This is why in Aztec and Mesoamerican conceptions of history and how it should be engaged, it was conceived as a continual process in which there were no fixed texts and existing knowledge, materialized in books, was subject to revision (Gillespie 1989:xxvii). The cosmos, time and its discrete nature(s), events both cosmic and human, all become symbols to be worked and reworked in pursuit of a greater understanding of the overarching nature of not just humans and their societies but ultimately the whole of reality.

CONCLUSION

It is difficult to disentangle the Priest's Speech in the *Relación de Michoacán* from the complexities and uncertainties of the prehispanic past both in Michoacán and Mesoamerica more generally, but it is necessary to do so. While Mesoamerican ethnohistoric and archaeological data sources seem to indicate the same kinds of processes, it must be remembered that multiple scenarios and explanations might exist for such widespread shared patterns, ranging from real events and processes such as migrations from the north to the development and spread of a complex ideological structure that draws part of its power from its cyclicity and multiple iterations. In this regard archaeological data and interpretations should be kept analytically separate, and with the advent of finer-grained analyses, such as those of Pollard and Washburn (n.d.) and Elsa Jadot (2016), we are entering a period in which the issues related to movements of populations can more securely be addressed. Similarly, the independent study and analysis of ethnohistoric and archaeological materials are essential. Understanding ethnohistoric documents entails understanding the cultural and ideological factors that structured the representations, thereby influencing how the past is represented and whose interests those representations served (Leach 1990).

Building on that latter point, we cannot begin to understand the Priest's Narrative without understanding the sociostructural and sociohistorical context in which he produced his narrative. He was part of a class of learned men, charged with carrying out the ritual prerequisites for the kingship, as a stand-in for the gods, that kept the kingdom and the cosmos functioning properly. As such, they were also responsible for the preservation of historical as well as ritual/religious knowledge—and I contend that at the very least there were some occasions in which the two should be integrated into a common vision of the temporal flow, if indeed this was not a constant concern that informed multiple levels of everyday existence. In the context of the imposition of Spanish colonialism and the Spaniards' efforts at the extirpation of idolatry as well as a weakening and even disappearing sense of a sovereign power at the heart of indigenous society, the priesthood in general was perhaps the most in danger of losing their position in the developing encounter. It is also essential to recognize that while the prehispanic era is murky and it is impossible to know for sure to what extent the priest that formulated this narrative had been influenced by wider, pan-Mesoamerican themes and tropes, there are indications of Michoacán's participation in material culture and informational flows that likely would have brought wider Mesoamerican beliefs and ideological structures to Michoacán at various times in the past. Thus while there are noticeable commonalities between the Priest's Speech and other Mesoamerican representations, the extent to which those flows influenced institutionalized knowledge among the Tarascan priesthood remains largely unresolved—and I suggest a need to problematize not only those commonalities but also the local factors and idiosyncrasies that perhaps are responsible for the differences. In this regard it has been important to point out that state formation in Michoacán has only occurred, as best we understand, once. The priest's sense of the past and the institutional/structural factors that must have existed in a recursive relationship with knowledge and modes of representing that past, both constituting and being constitutive of the priesthood and its practice of historicity, must have been affected by this fairly shallow history of states in Michoacán, in contrast to other areas of Mesoamerica, on which grounds I argue that we should expect a certain level of divergence from the broader Mesoamerican pattern.

NOTES

1. The archaeological assessments concerning the timing of the development of the Tarascan state in the Zacapu Basin are difficult to evaluate and compare to the Pátzcuaro Basin because a Middle Postclassic phase was only recently separated out from the Late Postclassic material culture. This means that until recently the "Late Postclassic" in the publications related to their projects covers from 1200–1522 CE). Pollard, personal communication.

2. See Haskell (2013) for a possible/tentative reconciliation of the two timeframes based on the document and discussion published in Monzón, Roskamp, and Warren (2009). Also, it should be stated that the discrepancy between ethnohistoric sources and archaeological materials is not entirely problematic or unexpected, due to the different nature of the evidence and what can be gleaned from the evidence. Archaeology deals in longer-term trends, developments, and evolutions of things such as ceramic technologies and decorations among other artifact categories. History, on the other hand, deals of course with remembered or written-down events, i.e., compact and seemingly transformational short-term actions. On the relationship between the two different kinds of temporalities, see, e.g., Raymond Fogelson (1989), J. Hexter (1971), A. Bernard Knapp (1992); and Sahlins (2004). The same phenomenon, an apparent but not necessarily contradictory discrepancy between archaeological interpretations of settlement and material cultural transformations at larger timescales compared to "eventful" histories in ethnohistoric accounts, can be found in many investigations of sociopolitical transformations, including the development of the Inka state-cum-empire (see especially Bauer and Smit 2015; see also Bauer 2004; Bauer and Covey 2002). The problem arises when archaeologists and ethnohistorians assume that they should reflect the same past and reflect that past in the same manner, oftentimes implicitly by attempting to fit them together.

3. I should also state that even though the Tarascan kingdom was populated by multiple ethnic groups, as just discussed, and that one such ethnic group was the Tarascan or Purhépecha people, in this book for the sake of simplicity I use Tarascans and "peoples of Michoacán" interchangeably. In this usage, "Tarascans" takes on more of a connotation of "subjects of the Tarascan king." Similarly, my usage of "the Tarascan area" should be understood in political rather than ethnic terms. This usage, then, allows for a discussion of "Tarascan" historicity as it was practiced by indigenous peoples, and particularly elites, within the Tarascan state even though there is good evidence that at least some of the elites were not ethnically

Tarascan but were Nahua as well as Matlatzinca speakers (Monzón, Roskamp, and Warren 2009; Roskamp 2010a, 2012). Moreover, some of these Nahua-speaking elites appear to have made up a portion of the nobility tasked with keeping historical records to the extent that indigenous documents existed (see discussion in chapter 3; Monzón, Roskamp, and Warren 2009; Roskamp 2010a).

4. See Haskell (2008b, 2012) for archaeological evidence from the important secondary center of Erongarícuaro that indicates that elites there were manufacturing or sponsoring the manufacturing of elite insignia made from obsidian. The relationship appears to have been a complex arrangement, however, given other material evidence for these elites being provisioned and monitored by the central or higher levels of the state bureaucracy. The various implications of these material arrangements are discussed in Haskell (2008b).

5. It is at least plausible to see such remarks as posturing in the Colonial period within the document but in relation to the movement of the diocese by Quiroga occurring at the time—indicating that the newly established seat of the diocese was or had always been an important religious place could be seen as reflecting a stance in favor of the move. The recognition of the document's role in these issues (Bravo Ugarte 1962b; Martínez Baracs 2005; Roskamp 1998; Stone 2004) at least raises this possibility.

6. It is also important to note that in other areas of Mesoamerica, a strong calendric tradition does not necessarily correlate with the detailed and specific "fixing" of events in "historical" time. Rather, human events and calendric associations were often manipulated according to sociocosmic precepts of when in the calendar certain kinds of actions *should* have happened (e.g., Boone 2000; Bricker 1981; Carlson 1980; Gillespie 1989, López Austin 1973). In the same vein, claiming that an event happened on or in a certain period of time (a certain day or year for example) was a way of framing that action and how it should be understood, for example as a "new beginning" politically that was characterized as such with a date associated with beginnings in the calendric system (see, e.g., Boone 2000, 2007; Davies 1987:25; Furst 1978; López Austin 1973; Marcus 1992; Umberger 1982).

7. The intimate relationship between places/landscapes and narratives concerning the past is widespread and has received much excellent anthropological and social scientific attention. See, e.g., Keith Basso (1996); Stephen Feld and Basso (1996); Eric Hirsch (2006, 2007); Richard Parmentier (1987); and Schama (1995).

8. On the Mesoamerican "World System" during the Late Postclassic period (AD 1350–1520) see especially Smith and Berdan (2003).

9. It is worth noting that the interceding period, the Middle Postclassic, as the period in which this transition between international influences and networks influencing the regional polities in the Early Postclassic and a more regionally focused and insular regional arrangement in the Late Postclassic is very poorly understood at the moment.

10. I presented a paper that was an early stage of the formulation of the ideas presented here on precisely this issue (Haskell n.d.). In that paper I argued that essentially Taríacuri

shares more in common, syntagmatically speaking, with the Inka Pachacuti, whose name means "the world reversed." Tarascan kings, as I demonstrate in chapter 4, gain legitimacy from an entirely localized people with no explicit ties to the Tollan/Quetzalcoatl phenomenon. They are "northern Chichimecs" who intermix with settled agriculturalist (but also in this context apparently aquaculturalist) lake dwellers, and so in only the most generalized terms some of the same dichotomies exist. The associations of Quetzalcoatl-influenced rulership and with Venus / the Morning Star that are well known have no parallel in the *Relación de Michoacán*; as I demonstrate the Corínguaro category of the narrative, which has Venus associations, is nonetheless associated with a combined precipitator/temporizer role (in terms of the effects on the narrative, this category functions in the first half of the narrative as temporizers and in the second half as precipitators; these terms are explained in chapter 3 and their effects are documented and explained in terms of the syntagmatic arrangement in 4). Furthermore, a key aspect of López Austin and López Luján's (2000) model is that the Feathered Serpent political ideology is useful because it bridges ethnic boundaries and incorporates what were previously disparate or antagonistic ethnic populations under a singular banner under which the roles of governance can be sorted out. In point of fact, while the *Relación de Michoacán* does share superficial similarities like a "Triple Alliance" akin to how the political arrangement in the Basin of Mexico was represented (but see Gillespie 1998), this Triple Alliance of the *Relación de Michoacán* is explicitly composed of members of the same ethnic group—namely, the Uacúsecha. Therefore while certain symbolic numbers and arrangements might be commonalities between the different regional traditions, it seems a stretch of logic and the nature of the evidence to assert that the application of the pattern in Michoacán, if it existed, functioned to incorporate different ethnicities and thereby bridge or overcome such differences within a political ideology.

11. Narratives from the Basin of Mexico and neighboring areas to the east (i.e., the Puebla and Tlaxcala areas) that include the presence of previous eras or suns are as follows: *Anales de Cuauhtitlan, Codex Vaticanus A, Historia de los Mexicanos por sus Pinturas, Histoyre du Mechique, Leyenda de los Soles, Memoriales e historia de los Indios de la Nueva España*, Muñoz Camargo's *Historia de Tlaxcala*, and some of the works of Fernando de Alva Ixtlilxochitl. See, e.g., Graulich 1997:63–95).

3

The Methodological and Theoretical Background
to the Analysis of the Priest's Speech

Historicity and Narrative Structure

By engaging "historicity" as a theoretical tool, new light can be shed on the manner in which the *Relación de Michoacán* and its contents—namely, the Priest's Speech that comprises almost all of the second part of the document—were not stereotypic or timeless reproductions but novel and agentic acts that responded to the sociohistorical context of their production. The narrative made specific rhetorical points and constructed an overarching vision of the relationship between the past and present in order to advocate for a path forward into the future. Moreover, the priest's narrative can contribute to cross-cultural studies of particular historicities by illuminating how one of the complex cultures of Mesoamerica engaged its past in an effort to shape the present and future very shortly after the Spaniards' initial steps of imposing a colonial system. This chapter lays the foundation for the analysis of the priest's narrative, and therefore sets the terms on which these two contributions can be made. First, I discuss historicity and how and why it can be useful in illuminating cultural productions and understandings of the past. Historicity emphasizes that such engagement is ongoing and always in process; therefore it is always potentially in flux. This is not to say that it is practiced in a cultural and historical vacuum in which cultural actors are free to fabricate not only representations of the past but the tropes and structures through which they convey meaning. On the contrary, historicity is "resolutely cultural" (Lambek 2002:4) and is therefore structured by a multitude of shared practices, institutions, and webs of signification.

DOI: 10.5876/9781607327493.c003

The relation between historicity and structure is a complex and reflexive one. Historicity is practiced within certain structures and is molded by them. Its products—representations (concretizations; see below) of the relation between the past, present, and future—are therefore shaped by and produce meaning in relation to those structures. By becoming intersubjective phenomenon, they recursively contribute to those very structures and reproduce and/or potentially transform them. Particularly in the case of sophisticated forms of symbolic action such as narrative, such representations shape those structures at various levels, not only in terms of their explicit or surficial messages but also the forms that they take and the deeper-level meanings that they make manifest, and the way they actively construct and oftentimes reify organizing principles of society. Historicity, then, could be said to exist only through its practice and the products of its practice. In order to analyze the practice of historicity as the ongoing and open-ended production of representations in coordination with the historical actions of others, in a manner that can analyze the various levels of meaning-making and thus the reproduction and transformation of structure, what is needed is a definition of structure that is processual rather than static and a method of narrative analysis that makes possible the investigation of deeper levels of meaning.

In both of these regards, anthropologist Terence Turner's integration of the applicability of Swiss psychologist Jean Piaget's developmental and processual definition of structure to anthropology (Turner 1973, 1977) and the poiesis involved in constructing and structuring narrative with multiple levels of meaning (Turner 1969, 1977, 1985) provide the theoretical and methodological grounding for the present work. Turner's formulation and application of these two threads were mutually informative, as I discuss in this chapter. The processual nature of Piaget's structuralism, which is discussed following the definition and discussion of historicity, is a suitable theoretical foundation for an approach to historicity that is structured but also structuring; that is open to contingency, change, and transformation; and that confronts and engages novel events by incorporating them within and through knowledge of the past. This structuralism, combined with the work of the Prague School of Linguists (see Turner 1973, 1977) allows for the analysis of narrative as extensively developed by Turner (1969, 1977, 1985, 2017).[1] This method of narrative analysis, its theoretical underpinnings, and its implications are presented following the brief introduction of Piaget's structuralism. It is also important to note, for those predisposed to dismissing anything that calls itself "structuralist," that Turner's works on narrative vociferously demonstrate the failings of structuralist analysis of myth as formulated by the anthropologist Claude Levi-Strauss in painstaking detail. They do so while rebuilding a structuralism based on the temporally constituted construction and organization of relations among characters and actions in time (especially narrative time/sequence). Such an approach is neither timeless nor incapable of incorporating change, both frequent and entirely valid criticisms of Levi-Strauss's approach to narrative. In short, Turner's work enumerates everything wrong with Levi-Strauss's approach, discusses how and why it went wrong, and corrects those errors both in theory (Turner 1969, 1973, 1977) and as demonstrated methodologically in the course of analyses of narrative that incorporate the sequential or syntagmatic axis of any narrative form (Turner 1969, 1985). It is Turner's approach, by accounting for the structure in both paradigmatic and syntagmatic terms, that renders complete analysis of the logic of a single narrative possible and comparison with other narratives helpful but not essential. This approach therefore makes the analysis of historicity at a single moment in time as reflected by one particular narrative possible.

With this method and its terms and concepts in hand, the present chapter concludes with a discussion of genres of narrative and their role in constituting various modes of historical consciousness. Genres and modes of historical consciousness are part of the cultural matrix that structures and is structured by the practice of historicity and the production of representations of the past, present, and future. It is important to understand how different genres such as "history" and "myth" help constitute different modes of consciousness, particularly in light of the functions of narrative and the poietic manner in which it organizes and relates the actions and events that comprise it. The discussion of these genres and modes of social consciousness is presented here as a prelude to their problematic application to the priest's narrative in chapter 5, following the presentation of the complete analysis in chapter 4. By understanding how narrative structures the events that it relates, we find it becomes evident that every narrative has at least the potential to exert a control over both the internal relations and therefore meanings of the events it contains as well as the "real world" upon which it draws and of which it casts itself as a powerful simulacrum. Narratives, whether they might seem "historical" or "mythical," can convey meanings through their deeper-level relations by constructing an invariance of structure that subsumes and incorporates potentially random surface events, thereby constructing and reifying a vision of a cultural structure that can do the same.

HISTORICITY AND SOCIAL ACTION, HISTORICITY AS PROCESS

"Historicity" is commonly understood by anthropologists as the culturally variable mode in which the past is engaged and used in the present (Fausto and Heckenberger 2007; Hirsch and Stewart 2005; Lambek 2002; Ohnuki-Tierney 1990b; Whitehead 2003). Historicity should moreover be conceptualized as a practice that is integral to living historically and temporally (Hirsch and Stewart

2005:262; see also Carr 1986). Eric Hirsch and Charles Stewart go so far as to describe historicity as an encompassing concept on par with sociality and temporality (Hirsch and Stewart 2005:262, 271). This is because historicity is not merely the engagement of the past for its own sake, but integrates the events and structures of the past and present in order to help chart a way forward in the present and into a future that is being formulated through this very practice (Hirsch and Stewart 2005:271; see also Carr 1986). In this way, "historical consciousness or historicity encompasses the complex relations of past, present, and future suffusing and emerging from production and practice, rather than simply the objectified knowledge *of* the past" (Lambek 2002:17). The continual engagements through which historicity is practiced give form and meaning to the projects of social life, as they constitute and potentially transform the social structure. Historicity is intertwined with and explicitly concerned with action and is itself an important form of symbolic action (Peel 1984; Turner 1969). Therefore it is "both reproduced and left emergent" (Lambek 2002:18). This emergent quality and its relation to action and historical context means that "historicity is itself historical" (Whitehead 2003:xii)—it can and does change as it is practiced.

The flipside to saying that historicity is historical is to say that it is "resolutely cultural" (Lambek 2002:4). Even though it is open to change, it remains structured and influenced by cultural schemas. For example, it is practiced in a particular language or other media with their own conventions.[2] It occurs within and makes reference to social institutions (particularly as they foster or inhibit social memory and how it is represented).[3] It also references materialities and their physical relations and temporal endurance.[4] It incorporates metaphysical understandings of the nature of the world and time.[5] Finally, it engages theories of social agency within those conceptions of the cosmos and its temporalities.[6] The practice of historicity is also inherently multiple, due to its culturally embedded nature and its practice among different factions or segments of the social structure (e.g., Appadurai 1981; Lambek 2002; Leach 1965). The practice of historicity produces not simply multiple representations of the past (Ohnuki-Tierney 1990b:20) but multiple kinds, or genres, of representations (see, e.g., Boone [2000] on various genres of representations in late prehistoric and colonial Central Mexico and the Mixteca and Hanks [1987] on the nature of genre in oratorical productions; see also Nabokov 2002; Peel 1984; Turner 1988a; Valeri 1990). Each genre or mode of representation, moreover, carries its own affordances and limitations for how the past is constructed and presented, influencing the content and form of what is being constructed (Boone 2000; Turner 1988b; see also Hanks 1987). Historicity as practiced by multiple individuals occupying various social positions and undertaking various projects (e.g., Carr 1986; Ortner 1990) also contributes to the multiplicity of historicity. Finally, the process of evaluating the multiplicity of productions in relation to one another is also to some extent influenced by cultural structures, as theorized in Arjun Appadurai's (1981) discussion of the shared framework in which such judgments and valuations are made.

There is another reason that historicity is always multiple in its practice, which is due to its intimate relation to social action (Carr 1986). In any society, there will of course be multiple social projects, each with their own temporalities. Different kinds of projects require various historicities to carry them forward and provide temporal and cultural context for those actions (Carr 1986; Hugh-Jones 1989; Rüsen 2005; Sahlins 2004; Tonkin 1992; Turner 1988a). Social projects are also built upon conceptions of the nature of agency, in the sense of the metaphysics behind the efficacy of social action (Fausto and Heckenberger 2007), as well as the culturally accepted or doxic mode of carrying out some task (Bourdieu 1977). Particularly in the case of projects that involve another subjectivity, historicity is often an essential aspect of bringing into view the nature of the subjectivities involved, which has been borne out in numerous studies of indigenous interaction within the expanding colonialist and capitalist world system (Gillespie 1989; Gow 2001; Hugh-Jones 1989; Sahlins 1981, 1985; Salomon 1999; Turner 1988a, 1988b; see also Mali 2003; Viveiros de Castro 2012:94–96, 114–116).

Exactly what to call the products of such ongoing practice is a potentially thorny issue, however. Following William Hanks (2000:12) I have settled on the term "concretization," which owes its roots to phenomenological philosophy and specifically the work of Roman Ingarden (1973). I will henceforth avoid the term "representation," which appears in the literature (e.g., Ohnuki-Tierney 1990a, 1990b; Lambek 2002; Tonkin 1992), in order to escape the potential perception that any one product of historicity simply "re-presents" what had been a previously existing product. Such a connotation would move the present project of analysis and interpretation away from precisely the formulation of historicity as ongoing and flexible in which I am attempting to ground it. In this phenomenologically grounded understanding and use of "concretizations" of historicity, what is being concretized is an intersubjective *experience* of the construction of, and engagement with, the past and its relation with the present and future. This experience is inherently intersubjective because concretization only occurs as any particular act of construction and engagement meets and is comprehended by an audience, which will have its own culturally and historically influenced frameworks for that comprehension. This is why it was important in chapter 1 to discuss how the audience and potential intended audience of the priest's narrative are to some extent unknown in a specific sense (with the exception of Viceroy Mendoza). I suggest following Cynthia Stone (2004) and Martínez Baracs (2005) that those involved in the document's production understood that the new materiality of the book, translating and transforming what had apparently been mostly oral performances, meant that it could (and likely should) be made to encounter other audiences beyond merely the viceroy. Concretizations exist within a temporal flow (Hanks 2000; see also Tonkin 1992:7); they are produced, meet an audience, and are remembered even as they might be reworked in the process. "Concretization" is not without its own connotations that I wish to avoid, however. What is *not* being "concretized" and pinned down, is "the past" as a static and finalized representation, nor is "historicity" solidified as some isolable, definable, and reified singular entity within a cultural matrix.

Such a conceptualization of historicity as a process comprised of the ongoing production of concretizations is a useful background for the case study of Tarascan historicity as concretized in the priest's narrative for a few reasons. First, it is grounded in a phenomenological approach that emphasizes how people experience, in an intersubjective manner, the production of their social worlds. The arrangement between Tarascan and Spanish societies was precisely what needed to be reworked and transformed through experience and meaningful action. Second, it emphasizes that historicity as it is practiced is not something that is fixed and singular but as something that is flexible and multiple. Therefore historicity as a concept incorporates multiple viewpoints from various members of society. Understanding any particular concretization entails understanding the social and cultural contexts of those involved. Moreover, this conceptualization expects that complex projects such as the *Relación de Michoacán* might or are likely to include multiple viewpoints and therefore multiple concretizations of the past, present, and future. Historicity and concretization make possible the investigation of the interrelations of these various viewpoints and concretizations to better appreciate the Tarascan culture, including its fissure lines that were rapidly opening up in the colonial context (see chapter 1). Third, and finally, this conceptualization has the advantage of mirroring to a great extent how Mesoamerican peoples themselves practiced historicity. Particularly in the pre-Columbian era, but also as historicity continued to be practiced to some extent into the Colonial era, documents did not stand alone as concretizations of historicity. While elites consulted documents in private or among themselves (and they possessed libraries of manuscripts in their residences, which also functioned politically as seats of government; e.g., Boone 2000; Diel 2008; Douglas 2010; see also Hill 1991), in their most powerful social contexts documents were read or sung aloud to an audience by skilled performers/orators (Boone 2000; Christensen 2007:34; Florescano 1994:122–123; Hanks 2000:12; Tedlock 1996; Williams 2009). That is to say, the documents themselves (or, as seems to have been the case with the priest's narrative contained in the *Relación de Michoacán*, previous concretizations that were later remembered) were but key players among a cast in the production of concretizations, the practice of historicity. Each performance had its own internal dynamic in addition to relations with factors outside of itself (i.e., its sociohistorical context), and the internal and external dynamics mutually influenced one another in intertwining visions of past, present, and future. The performativity of historicity is evident in the purportedly institutionalized context of the priest's narrative as it was said to have been related in the past. The addresses to various factions and segments of indigenous society in the narrative contained in the *Relación de Michoacán* seem to indicate that it was a performance intended for an audience, and illustrations in the document serve to reinforce and reify the narrative being intended for an audience comprised of the realm's nobility. This is the case even if that audience was not present at its telling, which we cannot be sure of either way at this point in time. This aspect of Mesoamerican historicity is lost in particular when we are confronted by documents written in Latin script that appear inert and self-evident. The process of writing essentially fixed and made static what was otherwise a flexible and performative process, particularly in the eyes of modern scholars (Boone 2000:6–7; Florescano 1994:122–123). Once again, this is precisely *not* what I intend by my use of the term "concretization." To work within a framework that implicitly accepts the finality of such a fixing process would result in the erroneous equation of these documents with comprehensive, overdetermined, reified, and falsely "authoritative" representations that would purport to equal *the* historicity of some particular culture. Rather, not only should they not be regarded as authoritative exemplars of any particular historicity, but to believe that any particular concretization might "best exemplify" a culture's historicity is to render historicity a concept that is static and singular rather than ongoing and multiple. Such a view is, to some extent, a pitfall to which some of the interpretations of the priest's narrative examined in the introductory chapter have fallen prey (see chapter 1). It is important, however, to keep in mind that this narrative was only one particular concretization of the past, with its attendant biases (see chapters 1 and 2); it just so happens that it was the one that was written down and concretized in what is a more static media and with the authority of recognition by the Spanish colonial administrators or some faction therein. The recognition that concretizations were multiple and open to contestation and reinterpretation, however, should not ignore power relations within that culture. Particularly in the hierarchical societies of Mesoamerica, the practice of historicity among the nobility and the concretizations that resulted were more powerful or efficacious precisely because these were the people who had access to oral traditions and written or pictographic documents and who, moreover, were educated and trained in oratory.

There is, in relation to this point, a recognizable tension between the fluid and ongoing production of historicity on the one hand and the perception of "authority" within any concretization on the other hand. In a practice in which the past and its relation to the present is continually subjected to transformation, it was

nonetheless important that each concretization, each new construction and transformation, be an account that would be interpreted as possessing the authority of
the past and presenting a persuasive argument based in some part on evidence of
and from the past (e.g., in the manner of Weiner's [1992] "cosmological authentication"; see also Parmentier 1987). This relation of the "authority" of any narrative as flowing from the past and bringing it into the present was also necessarily
bound up with the political ideology of the society in which it is told (Boone 2000;
Christensen 2007; Feeley-Harnik 1978; Lambek 2002; López Austin and López
Luján 2000; Valeri 1990). It also was constituted in Mesoamerica through conceptualizations of, and training in, skilled oratory as well as noble or secret words,
dialects, and even riddles (Christensen 2007; Edmonson 1986; López Austin and
López Luján 2000; Maffie 2013:103–110). Building on this notion of education and
training, an important aspect of the "authority" of any narrative was, as I discuss
below, the "content of the form" (White 1987; see also Herrnstein Smith 1980 and
White 1980) as narrative, or the extent to which the medium of the message is an
integral part of its meaning (Dillon and Abercrombie 1988:77) insofar as the composition and organization of the narrative—its structure—makes it compelling and
rhetorically powerful. The capacity to produce such powerful narratives was likely
a skill cultivated within the indigenous priestly orders and therefore part of the
structural power relations in Tarascan culture.[7] Authority concerning the past as a
legitimizing factor for the indigenous hierarchy became an even more heightened
concern within the developing colonial situation, and the importance of narratives
of the past and of other forms of evidence concerning the past was magnified by the
transition to the more static media of alphabetic writing in which such forms would
take on new longevities thanks to their material form. In the project that became
the Relación de Michoacán in particular, there was likely a conscious attempt on the
part of the priest to make his speech a convincing one that carried the weight of the
past because of the purposes toward which he intended and moreover to which he
imagined it would be put in the future, especially in relation to the possibility that
it would be deployed in the Spanish legal system (see chapter 1).

A CRITIQUE OF STRUCTURALISM AS APPLIED TO MYTH

While the practice of historicity is fluid and flexible, it is nonetheless also structured. The precise way in which "structure" should be conceptualized has been a
fundamental problem, or source of debate, in the social sciences (see, especially,
Sewell 2005). For pragmatic as well as theoretical reasons, I focus the following
critique on "structuralism" and its notion of "structure" particularly as formulated
by Claude Lévi-Strauss (e.g., Lévi-Strauss 1955, 1963, 1966, 1967a, 1967b). On the

pragmatic side, some will see my use of "structure" and "structuralism" throughout this chapter and the book and assume I am working from within a Lévi-Straussian tradition. This is not the case. However, "structuralism" in the Lévi-Straussian tradition became an important movement, particularly in relation to the analysis of narratives (mostly myths), thanks in large part to Lévi-Strauss's (1969, 1973, 1978, 1988) own prodigious works on Amerindian myths. Clearing the ground of terminological holdovers and misconceptions from Lévi-Straussian structuralism, which live on in the minds of followers and detractors alike (see, e.g., discussions in Gow 2001; and Descola 2016) is necessary in order to present exactly what the method of analysis discussed in this chapter and used in the book takes as its basic definitions and understandings and ultimately what it can accomplish in terms of illuminating symbolic cultural forms such as narratives.

As formulated by Lévi-Strauss (1963; see also Hawkes 1977; Leach 1976), "structuralism" focused on the structures of culture, understood to be the organization of relations of relations within the totality of cultural practices. This is to say that specific signs employed in cultural practices and particularly symbolic forms such as myth and ritual were not in and of themselves important, but only relations between signs, and more than this, relations among relations of signs. For example, in Lévi-Strauss's (1955) study of the Oedipus myth through which most nonanthropologists (and many anthropologists) are familiar with his theory and methods, it is not merely individual signs but categories of related signs, and relations between categories, that are key to understanding that myth, or any other narrative for that matter. Through the relation of one category to another, for example the juxtaposition of the contrast between the autochthonous origin of humankind and its denial with the contrast between the perception that humans are born from one (just the mother) and the understanding that humans are the biological product of a mother and father, the larger juxtaposition of the two contrasts or oppositions of sign categories constitutes the myth as a way of working through contradictions inherent in social relations. Structural anthropology in Lévi-Strauss's work became the delineation of such related paradigmatic signs and categories of signs (e.g., autochthonous origins or human reproduction) as the stable framework of signification within a culture, and ultimately the theoretical proposition that all cultural forms are constituted by the organization of such signs into binary oppositions. More than investigating any particular cultural practice, moreover, "structuralism" as practiced by Lévi-Strauss came to investigate cultural practices writ large and in general as generated by the structure of the mind as it orders the world into stable bundles of relations, commonly taking the form of binary contrasts.

Keeping with his discussion of myth, as it obviously is of the greatest concern to the investigation of narrative, one of Lévi-Strauss' key insights into a property of myth is that it presents a paradox of forward progression of irreversible actions as a sequence but constructs or presents them in a way that makes the meaning of the story and the actions it contains timeless. "On the one hand, a myth always refers to events alleged to have taken place in time: before the world was created, or during its first stages—anyway, long ago. But what gives the myth an operational value is that the specific pattern described is everlasting; it explains the present and the past as well as the future" (Lévi-Strauss 1963:209). This "operational value" is constructed by the relationship, as Lévi-Strauss (mis)understood it (see discussion below), between "diachrony" and "synchrony." Lévi-Strauss's key insight, which quickly becomes lost in his analytical program, is that myth (or any narrative; see below) serves to somehow or another fuse the diachronic relations within or as synchronic relations. To understand this insight, we must first define and focus on what "synchronic" means and how Lévi-Strauss applied it, as it became a key aspect of Lévi-Straussian structuralism as he developed his analyses and theory of myth. As defined by the linguist Ferdinand de Saussure (1959), whose work Lévi-Strauss adopted and adapted to a great extent, language exists as a system at any given point in time. Synchronic analyses of the rules of a language could be achieved through the statistical compilation of individual speech acts (*parole*), which only exist historically in a temporal flow, into a structured and orderly *langue*. *Langue* is therefore the locus of the multiple rules of relations among signs within which meaning is intelligible. Only within this analytically abstracted langue can the shared rules as they exist at any point be identified and studied.

Lévi-Strauss's basic insight was that even though myth was presented as a sequence, its real meaning—as detectable only at the abstracted level of langue and only revealed in large numbers of myth "variants," which were themselves largely decontextualized—was in its timelessness, the fact that the relations and meanings of its story reflected timeless aspects of social reproduction. He misunderstood this timelessness as the synchronic aspect of the myth, and he associated the sequence of its actions with its diachronic aspect (Lévi-Strauss 1963). His applications of these terms were actually misunderstandings (Turner 1969, 1977; see also, e.g., Engard 1988; Jacopin 1988; Ohnuki-Tierney 1990b). In terms of his goals of analysis, he sought to examine what he mistook to be the synchronic aspect, the timelessness, of myth. This he claimed to achieve by *discarding* the sequence of the myth, what he misunderstood as its diachronic aspect. What he is then left with, purportedly manifesting the "synchronic" or "timelessness" of the myth, is a context-free jumble of signs. These signs were actually a hodgepodge of various so-called mythemes, which served as his basic units of analysis and which could include characters and their innate characteristics, actions, and relations between actors (see critique in Turner 1969, 1977) and which requires a substantial amount of interpretation to organize into various categories based on what the interpreter *presumes* to be their paradigmatic content. These categories of paradigmatically related signs, and the relations between the categories, are then said to reveal the meaning of the myth. Through such organization of the categories and their relationships, the contrast or contradiction between one set of relations is transformed into, or mediated by, another contradictory relation such that the mutually contradictory relations help explain or at least express something that is eternal about social life and its contradictions that might otherwise be inexpressible (Lévi-Strauss 1963:239; Turner 1977:108–109).

Within such a "context-free" (Turner 1977:116) method of analysis, which pays no attention to the location of such actions or characters within the sequence and narrational juxtaposition with other such paradigmatic categories, the analysis is determined by the whims and suspicions of the analyst (Turner 1977:118). The overall effect is to seem as if the analyst is making things up as the analysis proceeds (see, e.g., Turner 1977:104–105). Furthermore, the basic process for analyzing a myth in Lévi-Strauss's discussion of the Oedipus myth comes to be left by the wayside (Turner 1977:110) in his voluminous other studies of Amerindian myths (the *Mythologiques*; Lévi-Strauss 1969, 1973, 1978, 1988). His key insight concerning the nature of the relationship between synchronic relations overcoming the diachrony of myth (again, as he misapplied these terms), however, remains a key part of how he interprets myth and its operative value, which is to continually subordinate time and historical process to synchronically defined paradigmatic relations (Turner 1977:110). This paradigmatic focus is then applied *between* myths, analyzing "transformations" in groups of related myths or myth "variants." In this endeavor, the changes or substitutions of terms from one myth to another reveal paradigmatic associations between the substituted variant terms. Due, once again, to his misapplication of the terms "synchronic" and "diachronic," and his dismissal of the latter, relations among paradigmatically organized signs found among variants were all he had left to work with. In Lévi-Straussian structuralism, structural relations between units of expression, which is precisely where meaning was thought to reside, did not change even as the units of expression changed. Therefore in his view, "structure" (i.e., "synchrony") trumped "history" (i.e., "diachrony") because the historical events that were used and manipulated within a myth were subordinated to the structure that was already evident in other myths as each novel sign was slotted into the paradigmatic categories that the analyst had devised. Thus, in the words of Turner (1977:119), Lévi-Strauss's focus on the synchronic relations between paradigmatically related signs among different variants of a myth became "an inverted and fetishized projection" of the failing of his method, which was its inability to study the production of meaning within any particular myth.

As recent discussions (Fausto and Heckenberger 2007; Gow 2001; Whitehead 2003) have noted, Lévi-Strauss's work was not completely ahistorical—transformations of myths took place in time. Fausto and Heckenberger (2007:10), describing the works in an important volume on historicity in South America that self-consciously saw itself as a reaction against Lévi-Strauss (Hill 1988), note that the studies which comprise it "are good examples of what Lévi-Strauss had in mind when he proposed this [hot/cold; see below] distinction. By exploring how Indian-white relations are incorporated into and expressed by ritual performances and narratives, the contributors show how certain cultural devices absorb new events and relations. The fact that this necessarily implies change does not contradict Lévi-Strauss's argument, since the latter is predicated not upon stability and fixity but upon the notion of structural transformation–the sort of transformation that structures his *Mythologiques*" (Fausto and Heckenberger 2007:10).

The problem, however, with Lévi-Strauss's work and his notion of structure is that it fundamentally cannot investigate agency and social action, either "outside" the narrative in the form of the narrator who selects and puts in motion the transformations of the myth that Lévi-Strauss relies upon, or "inside" the narrative as a story that is about people (or animals, deities, etc.) *doing things in time*. All of this is to say that in Lévi-Strauss's analytic program nothing really changes, because each variant could only be equivalent to a preexisting sign and both could only occupy a place in a preexisting arrangement of relations of signs. Hence, structure according to Lévi-Strauss *always* trumps history—it engulfs and minimizes or neutralizes novelty and the potential for transformation. This is an oversimplified formulation of structure and narrative in relation to history and agency and misses many important aspects of their interrelation (Jacopin 1988; Turner 1969, 1977; see below). "Structure," as historical anthropology has shown in quite enlightening ways, is bound up in action (Ortner 1990; Rosaldo 1980a, 1980b; Sahlins 1981, 1985, 2004; Tonkin, McDonald, and Chapman 1989). The same is true in narrative, and what gives narrative its rhetorical power *as social action* is precisely its temporal (syntagmatic) aspect, which allows it to relate what changes, what stays the same, and the complex relations between continuity and change (see below). The investigation of narrative, then, need not reduce the problem being investigated to the manner in which narrative(s) effect the triumph of structure over history, but how in action structure and agency move through time in a coordinated way, working to change some things and conserve others. Finally, as I discuss below, the method of analysis developed by Turner (see also Jacopin 1988) has a depth or hierarchy within its conceptualization of change and conservation that more accurately reflects, and makes possible the analysis of, the varying depths of cultural structures or schemas and their transformations.

In order for such problems to be investigated in narrative, however, the syntagmatic axis must be incorporated within the analysis. Lévi-Strauss's misunderstanding of diachrony and the temporal nature of any utterance was a serious mistake; the rules for organizing the sequence exist prior to and outside of the utterance as syntactical rules already known to the speaker. To merely begin a sentence involves knowing such rules and what category of word (noun, verb, etc.) with which to begin. This does not necessarily mean that a speaker has a clear idea or formulation of what she or he will say (nor does it eliminate the possibility of adding onto utterances, and this applies a fortiori to narrative), but the speaker does know the syntactic rules for producing a meaningful and coherent speech act as she or he goes along. In short, syntactical rules exist synchronically, at any given point along with the relations among paradigmatic categories that allow for grouping but also distinction between related words. The syntactic structure, in fact, is a set of combinatorial rules for how such words will be selected from various paradigmatic categories at given points in the sequence of the utterance.

This discussion of the shortcomings of structuralism and the structuralist study of myth have helped to clear important theoretical ground while also noting that they do not allow for the investigation of any single narrative in relation to its cultural and historical context, let alone the important matter of the purpose, agency, and vision possessed by the narrator and manifested in any single narrative.

HISTORICITY AND STRUCTURE AS CONSTRUCTION

What is needed is a different concept of structure that allows for change and agency and sees them as meaningful. Such a concept of structure and additionally the complex relation between structure and agency, has largely been the focus of the social sciences since the "historical turn" beginning in roughly the late 1970s. Numerous texts have been foundational to that enterprise (e.g., Bourdieu 1977; Giddens 1984; Sahlins 1981, 1985), but for reasons of consistency of theoretical background and inspiration, I focus on the structuralism of Swiss psychologist Jean Piaget. At the outset of this discussion I should note that Piaget's structuralism bears little relation to that of Lévi-Strauss, and Piaget himself critiqued Lévi-Strauss's brand of structuralism (see Turner 1973:370–373). Rather, Piaget's studies reveal structure as a process of construction, of *building* relations and relations of relations. Particularly as discussed and employed by anthropologists Turner (1973) and other cognitive anthropologists such as Christina Toren (1999) and Bradd Shore (1996), Piaget's work is extremely relevant as a comprehensive conception of structure-as-construction, and it informs Turner's own work on narrative structure as a similar matter of construction. Finally, inherent in this Piagettian model of structure as construction is a sense of hierarchy, in the sense that some rules of organization are more powerful and generalized than others. This is an essential point, with regard to the present study, as narratives convey meaning at different levels of their organization all the way up to the entire narrative and its relation to the sociohistorical context in which it is told.

As defined by Piaget, structure is not something that is static, a "being," but is something that is in an active and continual state of construction or "becoming" (Piaget 1971:139). It is defined as a "self-regulating transformational system" (Piaget 1971:113); in the terminology adopted by Toren (1999:121, also 7–9) it is "autopoietic—self-creating or self-organising." Because structure in this sense is active construction and becoming, these complementary processes of regulation and transformation that characterize structure are "never in principle finished but open always to further elaboration" (Toren 1999:10). For Piaget, mental structures are constructed through interaction with the world. Each action, or operation, involves the formulation of a desired end and then the selection of the necessary objects and the ends to which such objects can be put (Turner 1977:126–127). Children learn by observing their actions and constructing generalized models or schemas of the way in which their interactions affect the world. This is what Toren (1999:9) describes as assimilation, in which an object and tasks to which it can be put are incorporated within a mental model or schema, with which the subject tends to reproduce repetitively. Through a range of such actions and the attendant process of assimilation, models and schemas are constructed out of cases (Shore 1996:367–368). Within the process of accommodation, "schemas themselves are transformed (or even created) by their encounter with novel experiences" (Shore 1996:368). In certain instances a particular schema might be insufficient to explain observed phenomena brought about by novel actions, objects, and outcomes, and so "adaptive pressure leads the subject to attempt to subsume the new accommodations together with its old structure under principles of a higher order, abstract and general enough to serve as common denominators for both" (Turner 1973:355). This construction of more generalized rules that encompass a wider variety of objects, operations, results, and so on, is the "equilibration" of the previously formulated structure of rules and schemas with the novel and the contradictory information. The constructive aspect of formulating more generalized and generalizable rules, according to Piaget, is constructed through reflective abstraction concerning the various contexts, objects, and results, of social action. Within these generalized and higher-order rules, however, there is the organization and compartmentalization of the lower-order rules that formerly were sufficient for the cognitive representation of and action within the world. "Equilibration, or the adaptive coordination of the actions of the subject with reference to its objective milieu, is only possible on the basis of the organization of its accommodations to that environment into a coherent pattern or structure" (Turner 1973:355). To summarize these basic points, Piaget's model of structure as construction is temporal, it is based on actions within the world that simultaneously involve the combined selection of categories of objects and actions (and thus is, I contend, consistent with the phenomenological roots of the approach to historicity discussed above), and it is hierarchical in the sense that some structures are more encompassing in terms of the scope of phenomena to which they pertain and actions which they regulate. It is necessary to note that in all of these aspects of construction, Piaget's conception of construction as transformation is genuinely transformative in nature—the structure changes insofar as it assimilates, accommodates, and equilibrates novel information with preexisting schemas of information. It changes by becoming more generalized and by adding levels and organizing lower-order schemas within those levels, among other transformations. In this way it differs from Lévi-Straussian structuralism, in which so-called transformations are in fact merely substitutions of one sign in place of another, with the result that the various categories in play and their relations to one another do not change.

I have more to say with respect to levels and narrative analysis below in terms of the construction of larger and larger units of narrative, but it is also necessary to discuss Piaget's dismissal of "figurative" or symbolic thought and practices that employ figurative thought such as myth, ritual, and art (Piaget 1971:14; Turner 1973:352–353). Toren (1999:113) seeks to correct this characterization of an acultural scientist, "one who cannot help but seek a rational grasp of the world," by emphasizing the inherently intersubjective and resolutely cultural messages that are incorporated by children and all subjects. "When we incorporate inter-subjectivity into his model, it becomes plain that the meanings we make of the peopled world are themselves constituted in an encounter with the meanings already made, and still being made, by others" (Toren 1999:10). Such meanings include, obviously, those constructed by modes of practice that rely heavily on forms of "figurative thought." In his discussion of Piaget's work, Turner (1973) similarly endeavors to provide a corrective to Piaget's focus on purely logical and operative structures and hence the exclusion of figurative thought. First, Turner (1973:352–353) notes that figurative forms actually do encode precisely the kinds of operations and transformations that interested Piaget. "In both senses, 'figurative' symbolic forms are capable of encoding and expressing dynamic principles and relations. In other words, figurative symbolism can assert a determinate paradigm of relationships as a dominant principle ordering a series of variations or contrasts, in a way that expresses, at the same time, a particular 'sensibility' or subjective relationship to the phenomena it represents" (Turner 1973:353).

The latter half of this quote leads to a second important point that Turner raises in relation to Piaget's work, in which part of the progressive development of the intellect is what Piaget termed "decentering," or the "mobility of the ego" (Turner 1973:352). This means that through the construction of mental schemas, the subject is able to assume the perspective of some other object or subject. Turner (1973:352–354) suggests that in concert with this "decentering" is a cultural process of "recentering" in which a "sensibility" or "subjective relationship" (to use the terms from the above quote) between the individual and the collective social structure are forged (such processes are also the kind of culturally determined messages and meanings within which children learn as examined in ethnographic detail by Toren [1999]; see also Turner 1985). This process of recentering, of constructing the relationship between the individual's identity/sense of self and the collectivity both in the arena of intersubjective actions and within the internal subjectivity of the individual as he or she has been the product of such interactions, is effected through precisely the kinds of figurative thought such as religion, myth, ritual, and art that Piaget dismissed (Toren 1999; Turner 1973:352–354). In relation to this point, the discussion of figurative thought as contributing to the construction of the subjective orientation to the processes through which the collectivity is constructed and structured usefully foreshadows the specific and special relationship constructed through the narrative form between subjective, individual experience (felt or sensed as disorderly "diachrony") and the larger and stable processes or operations through which the collective order is constructed. This process of recentering and producing the relation between the individual and the collective order also will produce culturally specific sensibilities affecting how agency, from mundane daily efficaciousness to cosmologically more encompassing power that transgresses ordinary conceptual boundaries, is understood (as implied in Fausto and Heckenberger 2007).

Here it is useful to pause and point out the relation of these aspects of Piaget's structuralism to the unique historical moment in which the Tarascans, and particularly the Tarascan elite and the priest narrating history, found themselves. This context developed its own "structure of the conjuncture," as Sahlins (1985:xiv) termed the unique development of structural dynamics in a relatively short period of cultural contact and change. While the interrelations between indigenes and Spaniards are the usual "structure" that is focused upon by historians and scholars of colonialism, it needs to be explicitly stated that within or as part of such ongoing interactions, the indigenous Tarascans were developing their own schemas of this interrelationship as both a precursor of action and a transformed result of those actions (see comments on Tarascan conceptions of the Spanish in particular and the wider accommodations of meaning and meaning-making in chapter 5). They were attempting to understand the Spaniards, and the relation of the Spaniards to their own world, through operations carried out by actors in the real world, responses to such actions, and the formulation of organizing principles that explained the dialectic of interactions between the two sides. As an alien culture that abided by logics and principles (and with technologies) different from their own, such formulations would have required the higher-order integration of their own understandings of the world with their observations of the novel information gleaned from the actions of the Spaniards and generalizations of their "nature" for lack of a better word (Viveiros de Castro [2012:94–95, 114–116] illustrates just such an encounter in a context of contact in the Antilles). Turner (1988b) has termed this "ethno-ethno-history" (different from Fogelson's [1974] prior use/invention of the term), to indicate the study of how other cultures have formulated models of colonialist society as they have interacted with it. In situations of culture contact, these models of the alien society were essential to action by indigenous society as they sought to interact with the colonizing society (e.g., Gillespie 2008; Hugh-Jones 1989; Jacopin 1988; Lockhart 1993; Sahlins 1981, 1985; Schroeder 1998, 2010; Turner 1988a, b; Wood 2003). At a more general level, moreover, as part of any interactions there must have been some goal in mind, meaning that a higher-order model of how the two societies should interact and exist in relation to one another needed to be constructed. In the case of the Spanish colonization of the societies of Mesoamerica, it was obvious fairly early on that concessions and adaptations would need to be made by indigenous society. Therefore more encompassing models of the relations between indigenous society and colonizing society in which there was some level of cultural exchange were necessary, even as such adaptations would need to be synthesized within indigenous society while drawing some boundary between indigenous society and the colonizing one. As Peel (1984:111) notes, making history in terms of future-oriented action was bound up with making history as the process of constructing a sense of collective self that has not only been the result of historical processes but also had, and could, cohere through time thanks to the conservation of the principles and operations through which indigenous society could and would (hopefully) reproduce itself even in the face of antithetical forces. In so doing, "the past" as concretized can detail specific events that produced a certain social order and/or moments in which the social order was threatened but managed to reassert itself. Alternatively such concretizations could advocate and make manifest social reproduction through a persistent iteration of past instances in which that order is stereotypically and unproblematically reproduced (as in Valeri 1990; see the discussion of genres and modes of historical consciousness below). Indeed, there is no reason why these multiple modes could not be simultaneously employed or interwoven, and both would demonstrate the perseverance of a cohesive social order, only differing according to the various individual and/or collective (and even supernatural) agencies that might be responsible for such structuring through time. At the most general level and the level of concretization as social action, then, both indigenous and colonialist sides had to either reiterate or reformulate whose metaphysical understandings of the cosmos and social action within it should apply to and in some sense regulate the structure of that conjuncture.

HISTORICITY, NARRATIVE, AND POIESIS

David Carr (1986), in an approach grounded in phenomenological philosophy (particularly the writings of Edmund Husserl and Martin Heidegger), discusses how historicity and narrative are integral to social action; because agents are constantly acting and engaging in social projects, historicity by the same token should be conceptualized as a practice that is ongoing. In Carr's (1986:50–99) discussion, historicity, and the formulation of narratives of social action or projects involve continually "taking stock" of the project up to the present, examining what has been accomplished, what remains to be done, how certain actions have succeeded or failed, and so forth. The kinds of narratives and the manner in which they are constructed, in coordination with the past, will influence the course of action moving forward. Carr's phenomenologically grounded discussion of the projects of social life and "taking stock" is a useful background, and a point to which I return later, that highlights the generalized importance of narrative to the actions and lives of individuals. The work of Turner (1969, 1977, 1985, 2017) adds the complex relation of the individual to the rest of the collectivity (decentering and recentering, above) as constructed within narrative to this generalized phenomenological grounding. In other words, Turner addresses the role of narrative in the constitution of the relation between the individual and society and the kinds of projects that should be undertaken and why, as well as who should be involved and why that are constitutive of both that relation between society and the individual and the intertwined histories that they follow and produce.

The point of narrative is that it tells a story that is relevant to action, and that in telling a story, narrative "models" (Turner 1969:34) the real world. That is, it incorporates aspects of the real world into its own narrative world, and proceeds to relate how things, people, and the actions that involve them are interrelated through time in a dialectic of actions. In the terminology of Piaget, we might say that the narrative performs "operations" upon the things and people in the form of actions, and then through the sequence of the narrative these operations subsequently become the instigations for new rounds of operations (following Turner 1977). In this respect, the apparent "diachrony," the flow of time in which things change and do so irrevocably, mimics the subjective experience and temporal orientation of any member of society. Therefore the plot of the narrative is familiar to the individual as something akin to "the actual, relatively disorderly subjective experience of social processes and historical time" (Turner 1969:33).

This relationship of the sequence of the narrative (its diachrony and "disorderly" nature) to the real world is, however, something of an illusion. Narratives are not, in fact, disorderly and random, but are highly structured forms. They are structured not only according to their paradigmatic content, or the categories of actors, things, and places, but also in the sequence of the action. The sequence of operations performed among those paradigmatic elements has a structure of its own. This aspect is the syntactic, or syntagmatic, structure of narrative—the rules and organizing principles underlying the sequential and combinatorial (Turner 1977:121) ordering of the actions and transformations produced through the course of the narrative. This syntagmatic structure is part of the synchronic structure of language and symbolic forms, or the structure of relations among signs that exists at any given moment in time. This was the original formulation of the synchronic aspects of language as originally formulated by the linguist de Saussure (1959), as noted above.

The complex relation between the perceived disorderly diachrony familiar to listeners as a model of their everyday lives and the synchronic syntagmatic structure of the sequential arrangement of the actions of the narrative is part of the special power of narrative. "From the subjective point of view of the listener, this temporal arrangement at once reflects his personal experience of social events, replete as it is bound to be with tension, conflict, and deviation (all within a framework of irreversible time), and provides a model for reconciling it with the ideally synchronic normative structure of the collective order. This integration of individual experience, essentially diachronic and deviant in character, with the relatively "synchronic" principles of the normative order is the central concern of traditional narrative forms" (Turner 1969:63).

The structure and orderliness of the narrative as played out in time therefore demonstrates the imposition of order upon the seeming chaos of everyday experience and historical time (and its events) as understood by the listener. This order, the actively structuring capacity of narrative, is manifested by what Turner calls the "invariance of structure." Even as actions and operations within the narrative serve to change relations within that narrative, those changes are in fact carried out according to consistent "schemata of knowing, willing, judging, etc." (Turner 1969:65; I point out that these activities are intimately bound up with agency). In addition, narratives exist in a tension between their internal dynamic of the motivations and agency of the characters in relation to one another and the external dynamic in which the narrator is the one who actually constructs the actions and motivations of the characters: "In other words, myth belongs to two different orders of things, which, though they are distinct, are inseparable. From the internal point of view, myth is a self-contained structure: it is equipped with a set of specific rules or a syntax that governs mythical speech. From the external point of view, myth has a specific social function that depends on the social structure and on the nature of the society in which it takes place" (Jacopin 1988:133).

It should be added that the relation of a narrative to its social function, and specifically the narrative's ability to achieve the fulfillment of the function, is constituted by the narrator's agency and skill in crafting that narrative. An audience might only be cognizant of the internal motivations, as the narrator hides her or his role and can manipulate and structure such actions in anticipation of actions to come, thereby actively constructing a sense of order that is felt by but remains latent among that audience, just as the narrator skillfully paints herself or himself as merely the vehicle of the story.

Returning to the larger concern with the value and function of narrative, through narrative and its capacity to incorporate the real world and its events, the seemingly random events and processes of history are given shape *in time* (the time of the narrative, that is). Through that act of incorporation, this internal world is a prime representational vehicle for time as the "mode in which society continually resynthesizes itself" (Turner 1969:35). This relation is why narratives often take on a dialectical form in which disorder as a negation of the general order is itself negated through the unfolding plot and structure of the narrative (following Turner 1969:42, 61). Not only is order restored, but the subjective experience of the listener incorporates the lesson or meaning of the narrative, which is that the structure of the collectivity can overcome and reorganize itself in the face of random events that threaten it.

Moreover, because narratives are concerned with embodying and constructing "the real world" in microcosm, such narratives take on an iterative or performative quality (Searle 1969) as the internal world of the narrative is projected out into the external world (Jacopin 1988:133; Ricouer 1985; White 1980; see also discussion in Carr 1998). The self-evident structure of the narrative itself is intended to effect the transference to the real world of its logical and patterned construction of events, which serves in the real world to make sense out of what might otherwise appear random events. Such a projection often is a backdrop to the proposal of a course of action that logically follows the constructed meanings of the narrative sequence as it has been crafted. By incorporating the outside world and events of the past within itself and ordering that world and its history, narratives do not merely advocate for a position or course of events; they provide and make convincing the very framework of understanding and thereby potentially transforming the meaning of aspects of the real world. This is the full power behind Peel's observation concerning the dual meaning of "making history" that are bound up with one another. Members of the audience are free to reject this framework and its transformed understanding of the world, but part of the rhetorical power of narratives thus constructed is to be persuasive by the very nature of their organization and their logical ordering of their events. The meaning of the narrative *as social action* is not merely in its content but in its form and the ability of that form to construct and assert order in general and certain kinds of order in particular, the latter being what the content of the narrative is all about (following Dillon and Abercrombie 1988:77).

A METHOD FOR THE SYNTAGMATIC AND PARADIGMATIC ANALYSIS OF STRUCTURE

The preceding discussion of Piaget's structuralism and general properties of narrative, brief though it is, helps set the background for Turner's method of narrative analysis and theory of narrative as poiesis. Turner developed the method and theory of narrative analysis and construction in a series of three publications (Turner 1969, 1977, 1985; see also Turner 2017). The 1977 paper provides the most extensive critique of Lévi-Straussian structuralism and the most detailed reformulation of structuralist theory and method out of the three. It also contains a short snippet of his analysis of the Oedipus story.[8] Turner's entire analysis of the Oedipus story, with a shorter critique of Lévi-Strauss, can be found in his 1969 paper. His 1985 paper is a complete analysis of a Kayapó (an Amazonian culture) myth of the origin of cooking fire.

Turner's method corrects the errors of Lévi-Strauss by reinstituting the sequential or syntagmatic axis of narrative structure, which allows him to develop a rigorous method for analyzing individual narratives. In Turner's method the basic unit of analysis is the "episode" (Turner 1977:133; Turner's analyses in his 1969 and 1985 papers demonstrate how narrative analysis based on episodes is achieved). An episode is defined as a unit of narrative in which some relationship changes.[9] The action and change occurs within what Turner (1977:133–135, also 116, 156) calls "dimensions" that help to organize the action and characters involved into related categories; therefore, these dimensions help to construct the paradigmatic structure even as the action of the narrative and its transformations are what reveals or makes these dimensions manifest. The framework of dimensions and the changes that occur within those dimensions, for example, could be composed of relations between kin; or nonkin (as in marriage relations); or different generations or age sets; or differently gendered characters; or people of different locations, social classes, and so on. This framework is what helps make the change, or "event" relevant or meaningful, and helps provide paradigmatic links to other episodes and places in the syntagmatic sequence. The events of the

narrative, moreover, relate the different categories at play within the framework
to one another. Within each dimension of this framework, there might be different "surface components" or "signs" (Turner 1977:139) in which the relations are
changed, say from a normal or positive relation to a negative relation, while the
dimension is preserved. For example, the episodes of Oedipus killing his father
and later marrying his mother occur within and tie together multiple dimensions
of the framework—knowledge (more on this below), kin relations, marriage relations, and succession—while containing and transforming negative and positive
relations. While the different dimensions of the framework might not all be present in any given episode, they can be switched one for another, likely in patterned
(structured) ways (more on this below). So one episode might tell of an event that
involves relations between kinsmen that also involves multiple generations (e.g.,
father and son) while another episode could involve kinsmen within the same
generation (e.g., siblings), and this could further be transformed in succeeding
episodes to involve relations among nonkin within the same age-group (e.g., marriage). Together, the episodes build a framework in which the multiple dimensions are made part of the story and help to give it its meaning and relate it to the
society in which it is told.

    The actors of the narrative, moreover, are partly built out of this framework and
the events of the story that occur within it. Rather than the context-free approach
exemplified by Lévi-Strauss (and used by others), Turner's method relies on context for the definition of actors and their paradigmatic content by their actions and
the juxtapositions with one another created by those actions within the narrative
(Turner 1985:53). These dimensions help constitute characters and their paradigmatic content as, for example, masculine, the son of another character, a member
of a social class, an outsider, and so forth. Moreover, the events that involve such
characters and their potential transformations can take on paradigmatic qualities
of their own, as they establish a category of action to be repeated and/or transformed later on in the narrative. Yet another possibility established in the action
of the narrative is the unification of multiple paradigmatic aspects within specific
characters, and the manner in which characteristics of the characters change (see
below), is an important way in which the narrative relates the multiple aspects of
the framework to each other, defining but reworking them and the characters and
actions of the narrative. For example, a character might unite within his person
masculinity and membership within a social class or origin from a particular place,
only to have the content of his character subject to transformation—he can be
"feminized" or "domesticated" (to draw an example from Sahlins's [1985:chapter 3]
discussion of divine kingship in Polynesia). This leads us to the recognition that
the "paradigms"—the categories, characters, and aspects of the framework—are

not immutable as Lévi-Strauss would have it. Indeed, the transformation of the categories is often the point of telling a story. Furthermore, the way that aspects of the framework are combined or reworked through the action of the story can potentially build upon itself, as the combination of aspects creates wholly new categories that encompass multiple preexisting aspects of the framework. By allowing for change, Turner's method allows for an examination of how that change is explained through the contextually related coordination of various transformations within the narrative, that is, one transformation is explained through its relation to others (e.g., Turner 1969:59–61; 1977:159).

Certain categories or aspects of the framework can also function as what Turner calls "temporizers" and "precipitators" (Turner 1977:156–158). Temporizers prevent something that would otherwise happen, while precipitators serve to bring about some action or event that would not have happened without their intervention. Knowledge, or lack thereof, plays the role of a key temporizer/precipitator in the Oedipus story, best exemplified when Oedipus kills his own father because he does not know who he is (here the lack of knowledge is a precipitator) and later solves the riddle of the Sphinx (here knowledge gained as a man but not really any particular kind of man—i.e., a man lacking a kin/family name—is a temporizer) (Turner 1969). Temporizers and precipitators illustrate the fact that paradigmatic categories come to possess syntagmatic properties as they affect the sequence or plot of the narrative. In relation to the instigation or prevention of action embodied by these paradigmatic categories, furthermore, Turner (1977:151–158; see also 1985:68–69, 102) describes how the actions of episodes are frequently related to one another via a handful of processes that he calls operations. One episode might constitute a reversal of the action of the previous episode, for instance, as an inverse action is carried out or there is a switch of who is agent and who is object among the cast of characters (Turner 1985:68–69). Alternatively, due to the transformation of a character, as when a boy becomes a man, the character's relation to another character or dimension can "pivot"—what was previously dangerous space to a boy is now where he is comfortable and expected to be as a man, for example (Turner 1985:83). Characters might also be "polarized" into two characters who possess antithetical properties, or two characters (with certain properties) might be "condensed" into one (Turner 1977:154–155; see also 1969:62). By recognizing that the manner in which episodes can be linked one to another via certain consistent operations such as reversal, the manner in which these operations link certain contiguous episodes to one another in consistent and patterned ways constructs larger-order units of narrative. A series of episodes that are united through such syntagmatic operations or a common subject matter in their content that serves to string several episodes together might be related to and contrasted with another series that are united by a different process and/or some different subject matter that is consistent within that set of episodes. The ability to build larger units of narrative, with their own qualities (paradigmatic significance) is another key aspect of Turner's structuralist method. In this regard, Turner draws on Piaget's analyses of how novel information and events instigate the construction of higher-order levels or models that incorporate the smaller and seemingly disparate episodes and their dimensions, organizing and structuring them. This construction of higher-order structures of relations out of the lower-order episodes and units is, of course, a process that proceeds in step with the construction of the lower-order units themselves. These lower-order units are produced with an eye toward how they factor into the production of the higher-order units. This is the manner, in fact, in which various events, dimensions, characters, and ultimately meanings are organized into a total and coherent structure even though no single episode could possibly involve all of these aspects.

The preceding points are all related to an important theoretical insight, that the paradigmatic and syntagmatic axes of narrative "relativize" one another (Turner 1977:145; Turner himself draws on Jakobson's [1960] study of poetry). A simpler way of saying this is that they are made to behave or function like the other. Through the plot and structure of the narrative, paradigmatic categories (characters, social groups, animals) take on temporally manifested properties, and the content of those categories drives (or stalls) the action of the narrative. Contiguous episodes become paradigmatic units defined by common dimensions (e.g., relations between kin or nonkin) or syntagmatic operations (e.g., reversal, polarization/condensation), or both. Furthermore, the way that these units of narrative sequence are themselves manipulated, transformed, and added together once again displays paradigmatic properties. The two axes, by mutually informing one another as they work together to constrain and organize the seemingly random "surface signs" of individual episodes, exert a power over the narrative and its organization of events, actions, and characters (Turner 1977:143–145). It is the invariance of structure, now conceived of as the syntagmatically and paradigmatically coordinated construction of surface variation, that gives narrative its "timeless" quality.[10] "A narrative, on this view, is a symbolic mechanism for doing two basic things; firstly, for asserting that a common order underlies a superficially varying universe of actions and relations, and secondly, for elevating this common order from the level of a set of residual constraints underlying discrete sets of relations to the level of the general principle or force responsible for creating the common pattern it manifests" (Turner 1977:147).

To carry this point further, telling a good (well-structured) story is a way of demonstrating one's own ability to make sense of the world, and to elevate that interpretation into a persuasive argument by what seems to be its own internal force (also

Turner 1977:159). A well-crafted story is constructed such that it seems to organize and tell itself, and is thus constructed to appear self-evident in its meaning and structure—as if there could be no other way. This is narrative's power: to appear natural and given as opposed to a potentially biased account of persons, events, social structures, and processes. This property of narrative obviously relates to the issue of the authority of the narrative, discussed above in terms of its ability to construct a vision of the past that is persuasive to others because it presents an ordered and seemingly self-evident story. Once produced, a narrative and its autopoietic character shape wider understandings of the social world in which it is told and helps to orient social action.

GENRES OF NARRATIVE: NARRATIVE STRUCTURE
AND THE MYTH VERSUS HISTORY DEBATE

With an understanding of the function of the narrative form in general (not only of myth) as well as the relation of variation within invariance, it is now possible and appropriate to discuss how anthropologists have defined and characterized "myth" and "history" in detailed terms. This brief exercise in etic categorization will serve as the backdrop for my discussion of the priest's narrative and its structure, meaning, and effect in chapter 5. Following the discussion of definitions of "myth" and "history" as genres, however, I will also note here that in practice the specific status of any particular narrative in relation to those categories can be difficult to discern, and there has been a growing trend in anthropological analysis to investigate how particular narratives blur those lines and/or incorporate multiple "mythic" and "historical" viewpoints within single narratives or other forms of discourse. This discussion also returns us to the cultural and intersubjective concretizations of historicity and the forms they take, particularly as they are "structured" aspects of culture. Within the structure as it is perceived and engaged at any point in time are conceptualizations of how information is to be communicated in terms of the form, arrangement, and purpose of a communicative act. These genres of communication have, when it comes to investigating historicity, often been reduced to the analytical distinction between myth and history, and some evaluation concerning which predominates in a given culture.

As understood by anthropologists, the etic genres of myth and history are the results of, and serve to reproduce, different understandings of the nature of time and social action and its efficacy through or within time. Furthermore, anthropologists have discussed the differences between societies in which one or the other genre is interpreted to dominate the practice of historicity, characterizing some societies as exhibiting a "mythic mode of consciousness" and others a "historical mode of consciousness." This division recapitulates Lévi-Strauss's dichotomy between "cold" and "hot" societies discussed in the introductory chapter and above in this chapter. Mesoamerica has not escaped this dichotomy, and as discussed in chapter 1, historians, archaeologists, and others have long since assumed that the narratives and documents constructed and written by Mesoamerican peoples are most properly considered histories and that, due to their possession of a calendrical system, Mesoamerican peoples were "historically minded" (Davies 1973, 1980, 1987; Nicholson 1957; Radin 1920; Smith 1984; for contrastive positions of history and time—even dates—as symbols, see, e.g., Furst 1978; Gillespie 1989; León Portilla 1988; López Austin 1973; Marcus 1992). There have been many theoretical and substantive refutations of such simple dichotomization between different approaches to the past (e.g., Hugh-Jones 1989; Rosaldo 1980a, 1980b; Turner 1988a), and Mesoamerican scholars have increasingly voiced the observation that the dichotomy between myth and history applies in a problematic way, if at all, to Mesoamerican engagements of the past (Boone 2000; Diel 2008; Gillespie 1989; Marcus 1992). Therefore both outside and within Mesoamerican studies, and both theoretically and substantively, anthropologists have sought to move past this faulty analytical framework, to paraphrase Whitehead (2003:xi; see chapter 1). Even with the recognition of such progress, I believe it remains instructive in the case of the priest's narrative contained in the *Relación de Michoacán* to discuss and confront such positions regarding history and myth head on. Such an endeavor makes possible a detailed discussion in chapter 5, following the analysis of the narrative in chapter 4, of the ways in which that narrative conforms to characterizations of both myth and history and thus confounds simple categorization. The unique way in which it conforms to such characterizations in different ways, however, also helps us understand what exactly the narrative is doing and how it was constructed to perform the rhetorical feats that it does.

The most commonsense place to start is with a layperson's (or, at least a Western layperson's) understanding of myth and history. Simply put, "history" is what really happened. The label also applies to any story that tells what really happened. On the other hand, "myth" contains what could not have happened, that is, what is physically impossible or unlikely. The characterization of history has remained relatively unproblematic at a basic level. It has been recognized that relating everything that happened is impossible, and such a goal misses the point of telling a story in the first place, which is to distill events down to the most important factors, events, processes, and so on (see, e.g., Hexter 1971; White 1980). In this vein Edmund Leach's (1965) definition that "history" need not include everything, but should maximize its "real" content and minimize events that did not happen is useful. Within this framework, the role of history, and historical narratives, has remained faithful to this goal of representing some real past (as gleaned from sources) and not inventing or fabricating any aspect of the past. Historical modes of consciousness, of which Western academic history is a variant, are said to produce a historical mindedness in which understanding the past for its own sake is important. In light of the above discussion of the narrative function, structure, and narrativity, however, narratives can be factual on one level but presented in such a manner that their underlying meaning is a distortion of the actual processes that produced the past. Therefore biases, the implicit inclusion of certain points of view, and the manner of "emplotment" (White 1973) complicate the definition of history as a narrative that is true at all levels. For example, any history of American history could be factual on its face but through the devices just enumerated, decisions concerning inclusion or omission of certain events or persons, and the overall principle of "invariance" that lies beneath and motivates such decisions, that history could convey a more mythic meaning such as the idea of American Exceptionalism and continuous progress (e.g., Loewen 2009).

In the face of such a developing comparative problem, anthropologists who must deal with non-Western narratives and other forms of historical representation have necessarily sought to define history in contrast to myth in more analytic terms rather than simply based on facticity. In Turner's (1988b:252) anthropological classification of modes of consciousness, "history . . . is concerned precisely with the level of particular relations among particular events." Similarly, Valeri (1990:157) states that in more "historical" forms of representation, the "syntagmatic relations are established between events qua events, as defined in their position in the temporal chain," and that "[t]he chain of events that forms becomes the major argument for justifying any future event: An event is legitimate because it is appropriate at that point in time." In the "historical" endeavor, thus characterized, getting sequentiality and cause-and-effect relationships (those between "events qua events") correct is essential. Such relationships are fundamental to understanding that the flow of events as one action was a response to another and therefore that the significance of those events emerges from the preservation of those relationships. The past can be and is applied to understanding the present, as in either an analogic mode that preserves such relations or direct effects on paradigmatic categories extant in the present, and not according to a mode in which paradigmatic categories are reworked such that relations of recycling or repetition are produced. Historians (including cross-cultural practitioners) might differ as to what kind of "events" they grant primacy, but getting events, their consequences, and their relation to the present right is the main goal of history.

Turner's classification takes this seemingly straightforward category and distinguishes between two different "levels" of historical consciousness. The "minor level" is concerned with historical events and their remembrance in terms of their own internal relations, but such events are seen as "merely replicating the same essential pattern of human or social nature, that is, varying within the limits of the social structure" (Turner 1988b:253). This somewhat complicated definition is rendered more understandable through comparison with his definition of what he calls the "major level of historical consciousness," in which there exists "the conception of historical events and processes as bringing about changes in the sociocultural structure itself" (Turner 1988b:253). Through this contrast, the minor level might be characterized as the recording of true events that occur and recur due to the tensions inherent in the social system but do not meaningfully change or transform that social structure. Turner's own example in this regard is the fissioning of Amazonian villages. If a change in the social structure, for example in relations between villages or the emergence of some hierarchical authority within the village to prevent fissioning, was due to events—the actions of some agent—that are remembered and orated, this would be characteristic of the "major level" of historical consciousness. It likely goes without saying but is nonetheless important to explicitly point out that the societies of Mesoamerica in general are known to have undergone such structural transformations in the numerous examples of the rise and disintegration of state-level societies. Moreover, their narratives and documents contained the kinds of stories concerning precisely those transformations that are the subjects of what Turner would place in the "major level" category; the priest's narrative contained in the *Relación de Michoacán* is explicitly concerned with how the Tarascan kingdom came to be where previously there was no centralized state.

The case of myth, particularly in the layman's usage, is contrasted with history at almost every turn. Whereas history is true, myth is often unreal and fanciful, telling of things that could not possibly have happened from a scientific or rational point of view.[11] It is also a mode of explaining the nature of the cosmos and of reality in a nonscientific way that depends heavily on constructing metaphorical and other symbolic or trope-based relations between perceived phenomena. Particularly as Western positivist history came of age, myth and similar nonscientific understandings became denigrated as the products of irrational thought, the corrupted memories and traditions of a real past, or both (e.g., Burke 1990). Most anthropological approaches to myth have in common the idea that myth, through the supernatural events and explanations that it relates and the differences between them and the social world as it is experienced in the present, explains the nature of the cosmos and the social order within it as determined by supernatural events and not due to its own internal dynamic. In contrast to the emphasis on syntagmatic relations between events in historical representation, "mythic" representations relate to the present mainly through paradigmatic relations which "are established between events as members of classes of action, that is, as instantiations of the rules" (Valeri 1990:157). Within such a formulation, membership of a past action within the same class as a present action serves to legitimate and provide cosmological validation of the present action. The relationship between past and present is, moreover, one of at least potentially "mutual conditioning" (Peel 1984:113–114; Valeri 1990:161); the past could inform action in the present as it happens (as in the "mytho-praxis" of Sahlins 1985:54, 55, 120, 144) or the past could be reworked in order for it to legitimate or otherwise render comprehensible some apparently novel event within the present (e.g., Bricker 1981, Gillespie 1989, 1998, 2008). The effect of myth and its deployment in social action, then, is to render the social structure timeless because it has its origins in a kind of metaphysical space-time that is fundamentally different from the everyday world of experience that occurred long ago and which cannot be undone by human agency (following Hugh-Jones 1989; Turner 1988a, 1988b; Valeri 1990).

It is essential to point out that myth and history, as etic categories of the various genres that exist in any society and their typified modes of structuring social action and its meaning, frequently exist side-by-side and are complementary with one another within any cultural context. Such complementarity can provide differing but mutually supportive rationales for understandings of the cosmos and the efficacy of actions by various agents within the cosmos (Fausto and Heckenberger 2007; Gillespie 1989; Hugh-Jones 1989; Marcus 1992; Sahlins 1985; Turner 1988a, 1988b; Valeri 1990). At times, as Turner (1988a; see also Hugh-Jones 1989) demonstrates, different genres and the modes of consciousness they both construct and are influenced by are brought together in order to inform the separate but related matters of interpretation and action. It is furthermore necessary to point out that, as recognized by Hanks (1987) in his combination of Mikhail Bakhtin's (1981) theories of narrative and Pierre Bourdieu's (1977) practice theory, while genres of narratives exist at any given moment, genres are something that are the products of practice that can appropriate but potentially transform the "rules" concerning any such genres. Through the concretization of narratives that comprise them, genres are always at least potentially being worked and reworked, possibly transformed and reinvented in the process. Genres might be interwoven in order to invent new hybrid genres that seek to integrate and combine the genres and their modes of understanding the social world and the actions through which it takes shape. Particularly in the case of various modes of consciousness, each of which purport to explain different aspects of the world in its metaphysical aspect (myth) and in its everyday human aspect (history), integrating these two visions can be a powerful means to rhetorically convey the cause-and-effect relations of the actions that produced a social structure at any given point but also the metaphysical underpinnings of *why* any particular actions were successful. On this point it is useful to recognize the work of Fausto and Heckenberger (2007), who remind us that agency is always culturally constructed, and in many cultures often entails accessing or manifesting supernatural powers (see, e.g., Freidel, Schele, and Parker 2001; López Austin 1973; Marcus 1992). In other words, the supernatural world and efficacy in the mundane world often mutually implicate one another.

As Bakhtin (1981) states, moreover, narrative is a highly complex form of communication that often includes various means of discourse and reportage, woven into an integrated whole. This is certainly the case for the Priest's Speech as recorded in the *Relación de Michoacán*, which mostly tells a story in the third person, often takes on the role of characters in the form of reported (and/or purported) speeches, and even included commentaries pertaining to the present. Through such a wide range of means of conveying information, we should expect that these smaller units of narrative were deployed to score individual rhetorical points and were probably related to the number of contentious disagreements between the large number of factions competing with one another in the colonial present (as in the work of especially Martínez Baracs 2005; Roskamp 1998, 2010a, 2012; Stone 2004). As a complex whole, however, narrative has the ability to not only relate disparate elements and score isolated points, but to integrate all of the means through which such points are conveyed into a coordinated rhetorical feat that has an overarching meaning. It has, in other words, the ability to integrate various conceptualizations of "history" and "myth" and all of the understandings of human and metaphysical worlds that are encompassed by these terms into a coherent vision of action in the past and for action in the present. In this sense, the specific genre or the mode of consciousness that is brought to bear on a particular issue exists in a complex relationship with the rhetorical point being made in the construction of a vision of the resolution of that issue. It could perhaps be said that the nature and complexity of the rhetorical point and the social context in which it seeks to be made drive the nature and complexity of the symbolic form (see especially Turner 1988a).

On a final note, if the Priest's Speech was about reconstituting indigenous society, if only but at the very least indirectly by suggesting the person to whom that task should fall, it *should* have invoked various understandings of social and metaphysical properties and processes. Confronted by the Spaniards, their god, and Christian theology, the kinds of construction and resynthesizing that were needed existed at all levels of explanation and justification, from the mundane matters of cause-and-effect in the course of human interaction to the divine will of the apparently competing gods, interpreted to be behind the actions of both sides. Unfortunately, the first section of the *Relación de Michoacán*, which contained accounts of the indigenous gods and the festivals in their honor, has been lost. I suggest that the priest's narrative, which was contiguous in terms of the sequence of the document as a whole, carried on certain paradigmatic themes and perhaps even a common syntagmatic structure. In addition, in the extant two sections of the document and apart from the Priest's Speech, we do get a glimpse, through various vignettes and asides, of how the indigenous Tarascans sought to make sense of the Spaniards and their alien theology. It is essential to remember that in the indigenous formulation, as in the formulation of the Spaniards themselves, the power of the Spaniards was in some way related to their worship of their god. Particularly when various passages of the *Relación de Michoacán* are read as intertexts (Hanks 2000) along with the Priest's Speech and the meanings of that narrative as presented here, such passages help us understand the specific argument that the priest is making in terms of the human interrelations between his own society and Spanish society and the relations between the indigenous gods and the Christian god, with each set of relations merely a proxy and outgrowth of the other. I discuss the meanings of some of these vignettes in relation to the meanings of the priest's narrative in chapter 5.

CONCLUSION

Turner's method of narrative analysis is a rigorous method that fundamentally reformulates the structural study of myth and how "structure" is itself conceived. By integrating the syntagmatic axis of the production of meaning, the method fundamentally reconstructs a vision of how we should understand narrative and its deployment in (and as) social action. Within this method, "structure" becomes less a static arrangement of elements that constricts agents, and more a concept that, understood as something that cultural agents *do through narrative*, defines and makes meaningful and perhaps possible yet further social action. To structure experience within narrative is to produce a persuasive, because organized and coherent (i.e., structured), point of view within which social action can be described and reworked at multiple scales and within multiple genres. In this way, Turner's method of narrative analysis, and his concept of structure, is not opposed to agency or action as in the perceived dichotomy between structure and agency (or history). Rather, structure in the verb form ("to structure") *is* coterminous with agency. Particularly in symbolic forms such as narrative that serve to establish, to varying degrees, the terms in which the world and actions within it are perceived, their production often is a precondition for action at the same time that it can be a call to action. This was the case with the priest's narrative.[12] In the next chapter I present my analysis of that narrative and begin to demonstrate and discuss the manner in which it is a call for a specific state of affairs (Don Francisco Taríacuri's succession to the governorship) but also how it constructs the general importance and propriety of that advocated state of affairs.

NOTES

1. The manuscript of this book was finalized before the publication of Terence Turner's (2017) book *The Fire of the Jaguar*. Based on publicity for the book, it appears to carry on and more thoroughly contextualize Turner's analysis of the Kayapó myth of the acquisition of fire from jaguars and theorize its role in and as a primary means of Kayapó socialization. Owing to Turner's passing in 2015, this will no doubt be his final pronouncement and cap to his oeuvre on both narrative structure and how it functions in social context.

2. See, e.g., Boone (2000); Errington (1979); Lederman (1986); Nabokov (2002); Joanne Rappaport (1998); Renato Rosaldo (1980a, 1980b); Tedlock (1983); and Gary Urton (2003).

3. See, e.g., Gillian Feeley-Harnik (1978); Gillespie (1989); Michael Lambek (2002); John McCall 2000; Suzanne Oakdale (2001); Sahlins (1985, 2004); Urton (1990); and Zuidema (1964, 1990).

4. See, e.g., Gillespie (2015), David Haskell (2015), Barbara Mills and William Walker (Mills and Walker 2008); Parmentier (1987); Roger Sansi-Roca (2005); and Jonathan Walz (2015).

5. See, e.g., Maurice Bloch (1977); Boone (2007); Enrique Florescano (1994); Clifford Geertz (1973); Alfred Gell (1992); Ross Hassig (2001); Miguel León-Portilla (1988); and Nancy Munn (1992).

6. See, e.g., Fausto and Heckenberger (2007); Gillespie (1989, 2008); Turner (1988b); and Roy Wagner (2001); but see also Krech (2006).

7. Compare how I have contrasted the Priest's Speech as convincing due to its coherence and structure and structuring characteristics with an emic understanding from nearby Aztec culture of "well ordered" speech as discussed recently by Maffie (2013). Aztec sensibilities of well-ordered speech are grounded in an all-encompassing process metaphysic in which what is the most powerful or what we might call "sacred" objectifications of the Nahuatl term *teotl* (which is really coterminous with the cosmos itself and its generation and transformation) is "that which is well-rooted, well ordered, and well-balanced," and to be these things means an existence that is "disclosing teotl's diachronic balancing, ordering, and unifying of complementary polarities" (Maffie 2013:103). Maffie (2013:109–110) goes on to discuss Teotlatolli, which he glosses as "sacred or teotlized words or language" and which "included the speeches made by the *tlatoani* ('ruler') and high priest . . . The Aztecs viewed such spoken words as beneficial, nourishing, renewing, life-sustaining, and conveying life-energy." It follows that the power behind such life-sustaining power of such speech is its well-ordered property and its being well-rooted in *teotl*, which are according to Maffie the same thing.

8. Following this snippet, Turner himself notes the amount of space needed to carry out an analysis at his level of detail and rigor. "We may pause here long enough to note that this entire section [the preceding 6 pages of text and diagrams] has been taken up with the structural analysis of a single episode, consisting of a single sentence, of the saga of the house of

Labdacus" (Turner 1977:138). Obviously analyzing the priest's narrative, which is written on seventy-eight folios of the *Relación de Michoacán*, at this level of detail would be impossible or nearly so. Therefore I follow his method at a somewhat larger scale of episodes in which not every action is analyzed, but significant changes in interpersonal relations and arrangements are the basic units of analysis, while the coordinated nature of these smaller changes make up the "larger" aspects of the structure of the narrative. I believe the results still demonstrate the promise of applying Turner's method somewhere above the level of detail at which he applies his own method.

9. Turner (1985:64) elsewhere offers a more inscrutable, if more technically precise and expanded, definition of an episode: "A single cluster of contextually juxtaposed interactions among interdependent symbolic elements . . . [displaying] the conservation of the unity of a group of relationships—as a logical 'totality.' This unity is manifested at the most fundamental level of narrative structure as an inverse correlation of the transformation of the relations in question, which has the effect of conserving a constant proportion of polarization and integration among the elements constituting an episode. The minimal set of inversely coordinated transformations of the relations among contextually juxtaposed symbolic elements that conserves an invariant balance of separation and integration—or in formal terms, contrast and identity—constitutes an episode." In other words, I believe what Turner is saying is that something is preserved, i.e., the cast of characters, the dimensions (marriage, descent and succession among kin, etc.), even while one of the relations among them is transformed.

10. It should be obvious that this "timelessness" is contrary to Lévi-Strauss's analyses in which the purely paradigmatic juxtapositioning or arrangement of categories that is the purview of the *analyst* makes myths "timeless."

11. It should be noted that the distinction of what constitutes impossibility, fanciful events, and the nature of the intervention of non- or superhuman agents, is culturally relative and subjective. It turns on culturally particular definitions of the nature of reality and the possibility of the intervention of such agents, and the nature of evidence for perceiving and judging the nature of such interventions.

12. Furthermore, Maffie's analysis of Aztec metaphysics could perhaps be stretched slightly to provide an emic endorsement of the approach and hierarchical definition of structure and structuring discussed in this chapter. "Agonistic inamic unity (Maffie's term for the tension-filled struggle between two things interacting and thus becoming one) is an *unchanging* pattern of change according to which everything changes . . . Borrowing terms from Western philosophy, we might say that agonistic inamic unity is a stable, *second-order* pattern of *first-order* orderings and disorderings according to which first-order orderings and disorderings are unstable, short-lived, and impermanent . . . In sum, agonistic inamic unity is an enduring rhythmic reiterative pattern in the becoming, changing and processing of teotl and hence in the becoming, changing and processing of reality, cosmos, and all things" (Maffie 2013:139).

4

Analysis of the Priest's Narrative in the *Relación de Michoacán*

The analysis of the priest's narrative as recorded in the *Relación de Michoacán*, drawing on Turner's (1969, 1977, 1985, 2017) method of analysis in which both the paradigmatic *and* syntagmatic axes are analyzed, is presented below.

Before beginning the analysis of the narrative, a brief summary of the paradigmatic framework and the general transformation of those paradigms of the narrative will help make the analysis more understandable. The heart of the meaning of the narrative is the relation between two categories of characters, the Uacúsecha "Chichimecs" and the "Islanders" (see figure 4.1 for a representation of the Uacúsecha family tree showing participation in these elementary categories).[1] I have written elsewhere and in slightly greater detail on these paradigmatic categories and the evidence for their role and construction in the narrative in my earlier works on the subject (Haskell 2003, 2008a). This evidence should become evident through the course of the narrative. In my delineation of these elementary categories, I focus on the metaphorical meanings of the characters and the names that are used to refer to them. Thus, while Uacúsecha members are referred to as "Chichimecs," a name that Nahua speakers used to refer to the uncivilized peoples at the northern border of Mesoamerica (see chapter 2), whether or not the Uacúsecha were actually such a kind of people is not particularly relevant. Rather, the name is used to characterize these people as occupying a particular place in the sociocosmic world (see chapter 1; see also Gillespie 1989). What is relevant are the metaphorical or paradigmatic relations that this name implied. As I have suggested elsewhere,

DOI: 10.5876/9781607327493.c004

the characters of the narrative should be understood as exemplars of what Sahlins (1985:89) calls "elementary categories,"[2] "abstract but fundamental categories represented in persons." In contrast to the "Chichimec" category, the "Islander" category is constructed and composed of the location, subsistence practices, and patron deities of the peoples of the various islands within Lake Pátzcuaro, primarily Xaráquaro and Pacandan. It is important to note that the categorization of a certain character at a certain point in the narrative (because they do change, which is the point of the narrative; see chapter 3) is not necessarily a matter of lineage or lineal heritage but of "comportment" (as recognized by Martínez González 2010:45), though to some extent comportment is grounded in, or the result of, heritage. While the two should be kept analytically separate, they do implicate one another. Between the two categories thus constructed through the places and personages, the universe is essentially dichotomized into these two meaningful and thus powerful categories. Furthermore, through the course of the narrative, not only are these elementary categories constructed through reference to practices, places, and heritage, but "the alleged actions between these persons display the right relations between the categories, a process of their combination and organization" (Sahlins 1985:89). Having noted that I take the metaphorical meanings rather than literal identity to be more salient to understanding the narrative's meaning, I will henceforth refrain from using quotation marks for these labels.

Within the construction of "elementary categories" in the priest's narrative, the Uacúsecha Chichimecs are, at least in the initial episodes of the narrative, associated with foreign (in particular northern) origins, hunting, warfare, a nomadic or unsettled way of life (akin to the Latin concept of *celeritas*; see Dumézil 1949) and worship of a male solar deity Curicaueri that also has associations with hunting and warfare and is physically manifested in a piece of obsidian. Uacúsecha is a name that members of the king's ancestors used to refer to themselves at various points in the narrative, and the word means "eagles" in the Purhépecha language.[3] Due to the fact that high-flying (and raptorial) birds are often associated with the sun in Mesoamerican and world religions, this name is consistent with their qualities as solar and celestial. It also fits well with how dynasties in other parts of Mesoamerica symbolically appropriated such qualities—the Mexica, for example, represented themselves as related to eagles and other sky-dwelling and predatorial or "war-like" birds such as hummingbirds. On the other hand, the Islanders are the more ancient inhabitants of the lake basin; are fully sedentary, relying on farming and fishing; and variously worship feminine deities that are in some way related to the water, the land, and fertility in a general sense (see, e.g., Corona Núñez 1957; Monzón 2004; Pollard 1991). Through the course of the narrative, and due to its actions, the Uacúsecha Chichimec category is also transformed into possessors of legitimate

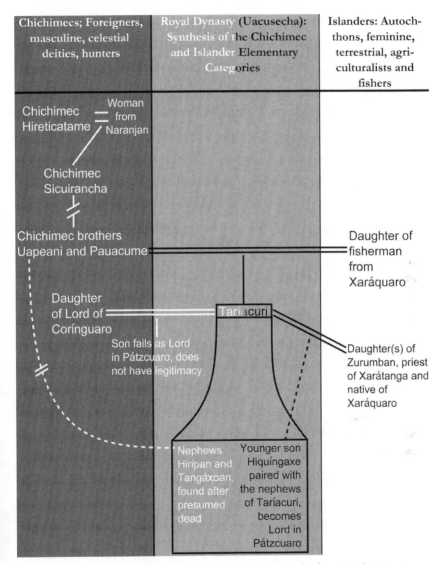

Chichimecs; Foreigners, masculine, celestial deities, hunters	Royal Dynasty (Uacusecha): Synthesis of the Chichimec and Islander Elementary Categories	Islanders: Autochthons, feminine, terrestrial, agriculturalists and fishers

Chichimec Hireticatame = Woman from Naranjan

Chichimec Sicuirancha

Chichimec brothers Uapeani and Pauacume

Daughter of fisherman from Xaráquaro

Daughter of Lord of Corínguaro = Taríacuri

Son fails as Lord in Pátzcuaro, does not have legitimacy

Daughter(s) of Zurumban, priest of Xarátanga and native of Xaráquaro

Nephews Hiripan and Tangáxoan, found after presumed dead

Younger son Hiquíngaxe paired with the nephews of Taríacuri, becomes Lord in Pátzcuaro

FIGURE 4.1. Representation of the genealogy of the Uacúsecha, locating characters within appropriate "elementary categories." Two hatch marks through a line of descent indicate the passing of at least one generation between the characters shown. Dashed lines indicate a relationship in which parentage is not explicitly stated or is problematic for some reason. The duality embodied by Taríacuri is reproduced as the "triumvirate" of Hiripan, Tangáxoan, and Hiquíngaxe. Reprinted with permission from Cambridge University Press from Haskell 2008a.

political and ritual/moral authority—they become kings. Concomitantly, the Islander category comes to be defined as the subservient category—in cases in which they are not the subordinate allies of the Uacúsecha, they become the conquered as opposed to the conquerors.

This transformation—the construction of the kingship by the Uacúsecha—is explained within and through an indigenous "cultural logic" (Haskell 2008a; Fischer 1999) of the relations between these elementary categories. Through the course of the narrative, the Uacúsecha, already embodying the "Chichimec" category, comes to encompass (Dumont 1980; see also Haskell 2008a, 2008b; Turner 1984) within itself the opposed but complementary Islander category. By encompassing the Islander paradigmatic content, the Uacúsecha constructs itself as a novel, synthetic, and hierarchically superior term that can differentiate itself from the other two categories, which of course can only embody and practice the paradigmatic content of one of the two elementary categories (Haskell 2008a; see also Sahlins 1985:99). The specific manner in which this is achieved by the Uacúsecha and manifested in the actions of the narrative will be related through the course of its presentation and analysis in this chapter, but it should be no surprise given the discussions of the personages at play in the Early Colonial era and the past, and the relations between such personages across time, that Taríacuri played an instrumental role in this encompassment. Figure 4.1 is a diagram of these categories and the membership of various characters within them; it should also serve as a useful reference for the reader concerning genealogical relationships of the members of the Uacúsecha lineage.

In a more detailed sense of the relations between episodes, the analysis presented below reveals how the narrative is an ordered series of transformations involving characters and their actions. The presentation of the narrative is arranged according to one of the results of the analysis and the primary point of this entire work, which is the "pivoting" (see chapter 3) of the narrative's structure and the paradigmatic nature of its main protagonist, Taríacuri, at its midway point. In addition, the framework of the narrative in terms of its "dimensions" (see chapter 3), is also organized in the syntagmatic axis such that these dimensions are involved in the various episodes in a structured way. Therefore I have divided presentation of the narrative and my analysis into two halves. The first half contains the narrative up to but not including Taríacuri's pivoting. The second half of the chapter presents and analyzes the narrative including and then following this pivoting event and reveals how the second half of the narrative progresses in a structurally regulated way in and of itself, but also how the syntagmatic relations of paradigmatic events create the effect of the pivoting of the entire narrative itself. Following this introduction, the summaries of the episodes are italicized and the analysis of the episodes is left in standard script.

THE FIRST HALF OF THE NARRATIVE

The narrative begins with the arrival of Hireticatame, with his god Curicaueri, at a mountain named Uirúguarapexo near Zacapu Tacanendan. (See figure 4.2 for a map showing the locations of places mentioned in the narrative.) *Hireticatame marries a daughter of the lord of the nearby town of Naranjan, at that lord's suggestion. It is said that the lord of Naranjan believes that the Naranjans could appropriate some of the god Curicaueri's power through the marriage. Hireticatame warns his new in-laws not to take the deer that he shoots, and especially to not ruin their skins, because they are offerings to his god Curicaueri. Hireticatame's wife bears a son, named Sicuirancha. One day Hireticatame shoots, but only wounds, a deer at a place called Querequaro. The next day he encounters his in-laws butchering the deer and ruining the skin. Hireticatame chides his in-laws, and they shove him to the ground. Enraged, Hireticatame shoots one of them. He returns to his house to retrieve his wife and son so that they may all flee. At Querequaro, however, the wife asks if they can go back and retrieve her god, Uatzoriquare. They do, and flee again, settling at a place called Zichaxuquero. There they build temples and a house.*

In the next episode, the Naranjans seek revenge not long after Sicuirancha becomes a man. Hireticatame prepares for battle by making arrows. When the Naranjans come for him he kills many of them, but he eventually runs out of arrows and is beaten to death. The Naranjans carry off the god Curicaueri. Sicuirancha comes home and goes off after the god, who has caused the Naranjans to be sick. Sicuirancha retrieves the god and moves to Uayameo, a place on the northern shore of Lake Pátzcuaro.

The second episode is a reversal of the first in its essential elements, its dimensions. The death of the in-law from Naranjan in the first episode is reversed with Hireticatame's own death in the second episode. The locales of the deaths are also reversed: Hireticatame shoots his in-law in the open field where his in-laws butcher the deer and its skin,[4] while Hireticatame is killed inside his own house. Sicuirancha's birth in the first episode is reversed by his status as having reached the age of maturity—he is now a man. In fact, it is that maturation that in a narrative sense enables the story to kill off Hireticatame, as Sicuirancha is now available to carry the Chichimec mantle and perhaps more significantly the idol of Curicuaeri.[5] The transition from wild/uncultured space in these events is repeated in the movements of Hireticatame and Sicuirancha, who move from the mountain near Zacapu to Zichaxuquero and ultimately to Uayameo in the Pátzcuaro Basin, which is for all intents and purposes the center of the world, and a symbolic microcosm of the world, within the narrative (Pollard 1993b:135; Stone 2004).

The two episodes together form a larger paradigm concerning relations between in-laws and ultimately the proper match for the Uacúsecha Chichimecs. The

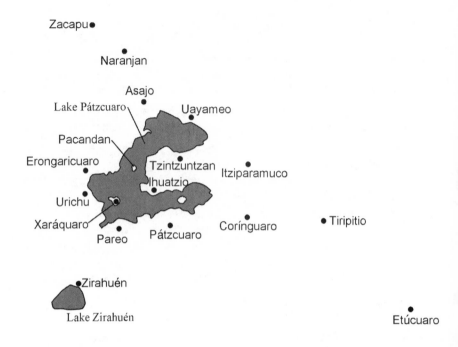

FIGURE 4.2. The locations of places mentioned in the chief priest's story. The most relevant factor is the directionality of the places; it is these relations of north/south and east/west that are most salient for understanding especially the inverted qualities of certain characteristics of the second half of the narrative in relation to the first. The location of Tariaran has not been confirmed, but numerous scholars have interpreted contextual clues and believe it is somewhere south of Lake Zirahuén (e.g., Espejel Carbajal 2000, 2008; Kirchhoff 1956).

relation with the Naranjans falls apart on its own accord due to the behavior of the Naranjans. The god of the Naranjans reveals a clue to the incompatibility in paradigmatic terms. According to Tudela (Alcalá 1956:20), the name Uatzoriquare means "heat," thereby revealing a similarity to the solar deity of the Chichimecs. Hireticatame's Uacúsecha Chichimecs and the Naranjans are similarly undifferentiated with regard to their origins and location in space—they are both north and outside of the Pátzcuaro Basin. The marriage with paradigmatically similar or undifferentiated characters will be contrasted with other marriages in order to reveal a suitable match for the Uacúsecha Chichimecs.[6]

Finally, the initial place where Curicaueri (and by extension Hireticatame) arrives acts as a microcosm of the essential paradigmatic categories and as a foreshadowing of their importance. Seler ([1905] 1993:18) commented long ago on the meaning of this first place of arrival, but the paradigmatic qualities of the place have received scant attention since his work.[7] He translates *tacanendan* as "where it is full of water inside" and the mountain name he adjusts to Uiringuarampexo, which means "on the back of the completely (frequently or repeatedly) round one." He suggests these names point to a mountain he refers to as the "Volcán del Agua," which is two leagues from the town of Zacapu and which the eighteenth-century Franciscan chronicler Beaumont claimed was a wonder of nature for its roundness. Today this extinct volcano north of the town of Zacapu, with a steep-walled basin at its top that is partially filled with water, is known as "El Tecolote" (Espejel Carbajal 2008:278–279), and archaeological sites in its surrounding area were registered by the CEMCA project in 1983–1987 (see Michelet 1992). With the two elements of mountain and water, this origin place possesses the two characteristics that help to establish (and foreshadow) the dimensional framework that comprises the Chichimec and Islander identities at the outset of the narrative.

Generations pass at Uayameo, and two brothers, Uapeani and Pauacume, are the leaders of the Chichimecs. The priests of the goddess Xarátanga in Tzintzuntzan are said to carry firewood to the temples to a place near Uayameo, while the Chichimec leaders take firewood to Xarátanga's temples in a barrio of Tzintzuntzan. At one fiesta, the priests of Xarátanga drink too much and dress themselves in the adornments (made of maize seeds and beans) of the goddess. This angers the goddess, who causes the pulque (an alcoholic beverage made of fermented maguey juice) *they are drinking to make them ill. They look for some fish to eat to help their sickness, but Xarátanga hides the fish. All they can find is a large snake, which they eat. They then start turning into snakes themselves, enter the lake, and swim toward Uayameo. They shout at the Chichimecs, who are frightened and flee from that place. Four different factions of Chichimecs scatter in different directions, the most notable of which* [aside from the Uacúsecha themselves] *is the faction who takes their god Urendequavecara and settles in Corínguaro. The priests of Xarátanga then climb Mt. Tariacaherio* [a mountain just west of Tzintzuntzan and near the center of the lake basin as a whole; Pollard 1993b] *and burrow into the ground. This leaves the Uacúsecha brothers Uapeani and Pauacume roaming the mountains surrounding Lake Pátzcuaro. The goddess Xarátanga is taken to Tariaran* (a place that is apparently south of the Pátzcuaro Basin; see, e.g., Espejel Carbajal 2000; Kirchhoff 1956).[8]

With the introduction of the two brothers, Uapeani and Pauacume, the Uacúsecha Chichimecs are led for the first time by two characters simultaneously. Previously the Uacúsecha had been led by only one male leader at a time. The two brothers are undifferentiated with respect to their Chichimec character and lineage, and they also carry out their actions together. Their relation as brothers introduces the dimension of seniority as an important one. However, the seniority between the two is somewhat ambiguous. The difference between them as older (senior) and younger (junior) brother is negated by their names, as Pauacume means "first born" whereas Uapeani is derived from "son" (according to Tudela's note in Alcalá 1956:23). However, Pauacume is said to be the younger brother, while Uapeani is the elder, contradicting the inferred seniority of Pauacume according to their names. I suggest that the play on names further demonstrates that the two are as undifferentiated as possible and specifically that this lack of differentiation is transferred to their paradigmatic content—they are both firmly Chichimec characters, as the narrative proceeds to indicate through their actions.

This episode begins with an exchange relation between the Chichimecs and the priests of Xarátanga in which the same good (firewood) is exchanged.[9] The relation is largely pointless, because the end result of the exchange is the same as the initial conditions—both groups possess firewood as they did before. Moreover, the narrative explains that the priests of Xarátanga would follow one path from Tzintzuntzan to Uayameo while the Chichimecs followed another to go in the opposite direction, and so the two groups never even meet each other on the road to expand on their relationship. The unproductive and overly distant relationship—without any contact the maintenance of their separate identities is guaranteed—between the Chichimecs and the priests of Xarátanga is ended, and inverted, by the actions of the priests of Xarátanga. Their actions of appropriating the goddess's adornments cause humans and the goddess to become too close to one another, erasing the distinction between the two. This leads to the transformation of the priests into snakes, which is universally interpreted as a bad omen by the characters of the narrative. Ultimately Xarátanga is taken out of the basin—a reversal of the initial conditions of the narrative—while the Uacúsecha Chichimecs remain inside the basin, though they are restricted to the higher elevations ringing the lake. As a result of the priest's actions and the omen, the reciprocal, unproductive, and distant relation is brought to an end—it is transformed into a relation that is nearly nonexistent due to the movement of the priests of Xarátanga and therefore the goddess herself outside of the Lake Pátzcuaro Basin. Furthermore, this episode is an inversion of the episode involving Hireticatame and the deer whose skin was butchered by the Naranjans. The priests of Xarátanga are not in-laws but have a relationship based on exchange,

FIGURE 4.3. Line drawing of illustration ??? from the *Relación de Michoacán* depicting the encounter of the Uacúsecha with the fisherman from Xaráquaro. The fisherman's daughter in time marries into the Uacúsecha and gives birth to Taríacuri. Note the elevated position of the Uacúsecha, as if they are on a hillside or have come down from the mountains, as in the narrative, as well as the solar icon on the back of one of the Uacúsecha member's jackets.

and they instigate the separation of the Chichimecs and themselves by becoming too close to the goddess themselves. In contrast, the Naranjans are in-laws, but they instigate the dissolution of their relationship by butchering the deer and ruining the skin, which prevents Hireticatame from fulfilling his obligation to the god Curicaueri, in effect rendering Hireticatame too distant from Curicaueri. Finally, the episode involving Hireticatame ends with his son Sicuirancha settling in a proper town on the shores of Lake Pátzcuaro, while the interactions with the priests of Xarátanga results in their position on the mountains.

In the next episode the Uacúsecha come down from the mountain and spot a fisherman from the island of Xaráquaro (figure 4.3). The Uacúsecha and the fisherman exchange fish and hunted food, both of which are cooked on a fire started by the Uacúsecha, who, the narrative explains, always walk with fire for they are Chichimecs. After asking the fisher about the different islands of the lake and their inhabitants, the Uacúsecha brothers ask if the fisherman has a daughter. At first he says no, but the brothers press the issue and, in a moment of foreshadowing, explain the reason why they ask.

"We say it because Curicaueri will conquer this land, and you will stand partly on the land and partly in the water, and we will stand partly in the water and partly on land as well, and we will live together as one, you and us" (Alcalá 2000:355). *The fisher relents and explains that he has a daughter but she is very young. The Uacúsecha brothers say that is not an issue and tell the fisher to meet them the next day with his daughter so that she can join them. They go back up the mountain, and the next day they meet the fisherman and take his daughter, and settle in a place called Tarimichundiro, a barrio of Pátzcuaro toward the lake and therefore lower than Pátzcuaro proper. When the girl comes of age, Pauacume marries her and she becomes pregnant and gives birth to Taríacuri. In time, the lords of Xaráquaro learn of Pauacume's marriage to a woman of their village and the birth of Taríacuri. They invite the Uacúsecha to come live with them on the island of Xaráquaro and marry more of their daughters. The Xaráquaros make the Uacúsecha brothers sacrificers, shave their heads in a certain manner, and give them "tweezers"* (an adornment characteristically worn by priests) *to wear around their necks.*

This episode sees the Uacúsecha invert their movement from up to down of the previous episode by moving down to Tarimichundiro first and then the low island of Xaráquaro. This movement only occurs, however, with the permanent acquisition of a female Islander character as a wife—the fact that they go back up the mountain after their first interaction with the fisherman is significant. Because they do not have an Islander woman, their proper place is still the mountains and hillsides. The relation between the Uacúsecha Chichimecs and the Islander fisherman is also a reversal of their relationship with the priests of Xarátanga. Rather than exchanging the same thing, they now exchange complementary items with the fisherman.[10] The complementary and productive relationship leads to a new relation between in-laws that produces Taríacuri, a dual Islander/Chichimec character who, the narrative foreshadows, will be lord.[11] The establishment of Taríacuri as a dually constituted character inverts the establishment of the Corínguaro category in the previous episode.[12] As becomes clear shortly, the Corínguaros are essentially neither Chichimec (because they adopt an agricultural lifestyle and quit their Chichimec ways) nor autochthonous and lake-dwelling Islanders (because like the Uacúsecha, they are a result of the split of the Chichimecs following the omen of the snake).

The end result is a marriage that contrasts with the marriage of the initial episode between Hireticatame and the Naranjan woman. The present marriage of Pauacume and the Islander girl involves complementary opposites in nearly every regard. The Chichimecs are foreigners, whereas the Islanders of Xaráquaro are autochthons in the Pátzcuaro Basin who are even called "Hurendetiecha." This translates to "those who are in first place" according to Seler (1993:21) or "those who have knowledge" according to the *Diccionario Grande* (1991). Pedro Márquez Joaquín (2000:711) translates "Hurendetiecha" as "those who are skillful." This is based on the meaning of *hurendi*, which means "one who is wise or prudent." These translations would make the Islanders of Xaráquaro roughly equivalent to the "Toltecs" of Mexica and wider Nahua myth/history (see Gillespie 1989; Graulich 1997; López Austin and López Luján 2000; but see further discussion and the points on which the comparison breaks down in chapter 6).[13] The Chichimecs worship a male, solar-oriented deity while the Islanders worship a female deity. The Chichimecs are hunters who catch game, while the Islanders are fishers and farmers. The complementary opposition of the present episode stands in clear contrast to the redundancy of the categories involved in Hireticatame's marriage.

Furthermore, this episode is the first in which the autochthonous Islanders are cast as an ennobling source of legitimacy.[14] With their interactions with the Xaráquaros, having been raised to the rank of priests (sacrificers), the Uacúsecha attain the trappings of nobility and rank, symbolized primarily by the lip plugs but also the tweezers,[15] for the first time. Thus their original status as lacking any social status is reversed in this episode, at least to a certain extent or if only in a partial way. I say partial because while the position of priest is elevated above the commoners it is nonetheless subordinate to the status of lord, a fact that becomes readily apparent in the next episode and through its repetition in the priest's narrative and in the rest of the *Relación de Michoacán* as a characteristic of Tarascan political structure.

In the next episode the Corínguaros learn of these events and convince the Xaráquaros to cast the Uacúsecha out of Xaráquaro. The Xaráquaros oblige, and not only cast them out but also remove the lip plugs and the tweezers of the Uacúsecha brothers. The Uacúsecha brothers do not return to Tarimichundiro but search for the location of the temple foundations in Pátzcuaro proper that had been foretold to them. They find four unique stones there in Pátzcuaro and begin to clear the trees of the area.

This episode reverses the movement of the Uacúsecha from up to down in the previous episode as the Uacúsecha go up to Pátzcuaro proper. They return without their Islander wives, who remain in Xaráquaro, thus also reversing the previous conjunction of Chichimec and Islander categories, thereby again helping to construct the paradigmatic content of the category. The two events (upward movement and separation) reiterate the fact that the Uacúsecha cannot live at lower elevations when separated from Islander characters. Concomitant with this movement and separation from the Islanders is the fact that they are stripped of their insignia of rank, as members of the priesthood, reversing the previous bestowal of those insignia. Therefore at this point in the narrative, the Chichimec identity is not fit for the priesthood, but more immediately, neither is it yet associated with the possession of legitimate authority. The Uacúsecha brothers do not control their own ability to possess the trappings of nobility and authority, but are reliant upon others to bestow such objects upon them and are subject to the whims of those others. The role that the Corínguaros play throughout the narrative also finds its first instantiation in this episode. The Uacúsecha are separated from their wives and in-laws only due to the intervention of the Corínguaros. The Corínguaros act as what Turner (1977:156–158) calls "precipitators," or a paradigm that instigates something that would not otherwise happen. The fact that the Uacúsecha are separated from the Islanders only due to the intervention of the Corínguaros is significant in itself because it contrasts with Hireticatame's marriage with the woman from Naranjan, which essentially self-destructed. This contrast indicates that the conjunction of Chichimec and Islander is correct and complementary (just as was foreshadowed by the words of the Uacúsecha, who explained that together they would rule as one with the Islanders). The fact that the Corínguaros do intervene, however, allows for the relationship between the Uacúsecha Chichimecs and the Islanders to be reconstituted later in the narrative with different specific relations within the same dimensions of the possession (or dispossession) of legitimate authority and seniority versus subordination.

In the next episode the Corínguaros fear that the Uacúsecha will not forget the wrongs they have done them, and so they propose a war between the two peoples. The two groups war with one another, and in the fighting Uapeani and Pauacume are injured. The fighting ends (indecisively), *and Uapeani and Pauacume recover in the Eagle House in Tarimichundiro.*[16] *Some Islanders come to visit them, but the Corínguaros send a woman to spy on the Uacúsecha to see how bad their injuries are. Inside the Eagle House the woman spy's cover is blown and the Islanders leave angrily, saying that the Chichimecs are two-faced and some have come to ambush them* (implying, I believe, that the Islanders believed the Uacúsecha and Corínguaros have planned the ambush together).

Once again the Corínguaros instigate the action of the narrative, as the battle they propose sets the stage for a reunion between the Uacúsecha Chichimecs and their Islander in-laws. That reunion takes place in the Uacúsecha Chichimec settlement of Tarimichundiro in contrast to the previous union on the island of Xaráquaro, thereby inverting the place of their conjunction from the Islander's home to the Uacúsecha Chichimecs' home. The movement of the Uacúsecha back to Tarimichundiro reverses their movement up to Pátzcuaro in the previous episode. It furthermore makes possible, or even necessitates according to the logic of the interactions being constructed, that the Islanders come visit them. The Corínguaro spy instigates another separation of the Uacúsecha Chichimecs and the Islanders, thereby again revealing that an out-side force is needed to separate the two groups and that their union does not dissolve on its own accord. By the end of the episode, the Uacúsecha find themselves with-out their Islander in-laws but also down and out of the mountains. Given previous actions and circumstances, this appears to be a dangerous development.

The Corínguaros once again intervene in the next episode, as they convince the Xaráquaros to tell the Uacúsecha Chichimecs that their wives on Xaráquaro cry for them and that they should come for their wives. The Corínguaros desire to ambush the Uacúsecha on their way to the island. The plot fails the first time, but the second time Uapeani is shot and killed immediately while Pauacume runs away and tries to climb a mountain but is shot and killed on the mountain slope. The elders/advisors of the Uacúsecha Chichimec brothers encounter the Islanders poking the bodies with oars and offer a ransom for the bodies. The Islanders object that they did not kill the brothers, but the advisors do not believe it. Eventually the Islanders relent and take the ransom, while the bodies of the brothers are taken to Pátzcuaro and buried under the temples there.

The dangerous status of the Uacúsecha Chichimecs is tragically resolved, as only in death are they returned to the higher elevations of Pátzcuaro befitting their char-acter and lack of an accompanying and complementary Islander element. Moreover, rather than taking place at either Xaráquaro or Tarimichundiro, the brothers are killed between the two places. The sequence of episodes involving the Uacúsecha Chichimecs and Xaráquaros has until now oscillated between one group traveling to the territory of the other as a proxy for addressing the underlying tension within their union over who should be the dominant group and who should be the sub-ordinate group. This tension was introduced explicitly when the Uacúsecha were made (subordinate) sacrificers on Xaráquaro. That subordinate status, moreover, followed the prophecy involved with the acquisition in marriage of the fisherman's daughter in which it is made clear that though they will stand together (in rule), it will be Curicaueri who conquers, that is, that he (and by extension the Uacúsecha) will rule supreme. The murder of the brothers by the Corínguaros ends, but never really resolves, this tension over how these complementary categories should be joined together.

With the deaths of Pauacume and Uapeani, the focus of the narrative turns to relations between differentiated characters within the Uacúsecha in the next epi-sode. In the next generation, Taríacuri is differentiated from his cousins Zetaco and Aramen, the sons of Uapeani. The undifferentiated brothers Pauacume and Uapeani, both Chichimec, have not transformed the political landscape but have through Pauacume's marriage to the Islander woman and the resulting birth of Taríacuri, set the stage for such a transformation.

The three lords (Zetaco, Aramen, and Taríacuri) live in Tarimichundiro, and because it is foretold that Taríacuri will be king,[17] three elders/advisors educate him constantly about how to be a good lord and servant to the gods (Curicaueri in particular). In contrast, Zetaco and Aramen go about getting drunk and running around with women. On occasion, they take Taríacuri with them—he rides on their shoulders on such escapades. The three advisors banish Zetaco and Aramen to a place called Uacanambaro to keep them from being bad influences on Taríacuri. With his cousins gone, Taríacuri roams the mountains gathering wood and making fires on the hilltops. The fires frighten the people of Xaráquaro, who do not go ashore because of them.

Due to his parentage, Taríacuri is both a Chichimec and Islander character.[18] Through the actions of this episode, Taríacuri emerges as an "Islander" in contrast to his cousins, who exhibit wild and unconstrained behavior. Even when his cousins take Taríacuri out running around with them, he does not move on his own power and is motionless in relation to them (i.e., from their perspective) because he rides on their shoulders. Within the Uacúsecha, Taríacuri's and his partial Islander content is junior to his older cousins' seniority, as they are the sons of Uapeani, older brother of Pauacume. Once his cousins are banished and removed from the equation, however, Taríacuri becomes a Chichimec, but now in relation to the immobile Islanders of Xaráquaro. He moves up from Tarimichundiro to the hilltops. The transformation of Taríacuri within the episode demonstrates that Taríacuri is an "Islander" character in relation to his Chichimec cousins, but in relation to actual Islanders he acts as a Chichimec. On a final note, the nature of Taríacuri's Chichimecness in which he roams the mountains is born of piety, as the gathering of firewood and setting of bonfires on the hilltops are exemplary and an offering to the gods (particularly his solar/fire god Curicaueri), in contrast to his cousins' impropriety and lasciviousness.

The Xaráquaros ask Zurumban for (military) help against Taríacuri in the next episode. Zurumban, a native of Xaráquaro and favored priest/lord of the goddess Xarátanga in Tariaran, agrees to help. He sends a messenger named Naca to both Xaráquaro and Corínguaro to organize an alliance.[19] Taríacuri finds out about the plot and enlists his cousins to capture Naca. After pretending to be hunting, Zetaco and Aramen shoot Naca in the back, and Naca remarks that only Chichimecs deceive in such a manner. Taríacuri orders Naca to be sacrificed, and then arranges for Zurumban (along with the lords of Xaráquaro and Corínguaro) to be tricked into eating part of Naca's body. Upon finding out that he has eaten a bit of his priest, Zurumban is enraged and casts Zetaco and Aramen out from Uacanambaro, removing their lip plugs as he does so. Taríacuri flees from Tarimichundiro. Zetaco and Aramen ask Taríacuri how they should find food, and Taríacuri suggests that they take some food from Curicaueri's granaries. An explanatory tangent in the text states that anyone who takes food from the deity's granaries should become a slave.[20] Taríacuri eventually settles at Pátzcuaro, while Zetaco resides on a mountain and Aramen settles at the foot of a mountain slope.

Zetaco and Aramen initially play the role of Chichimecs, which is explicitly commented upon, but now in relation to Naca. This reverses the previous juxtaposition of their Chichimec qualities with Taríacuri's Islander nature—a relation within the Uacúsecha—to a juxtaposition that is external to it between the Uacúsecha and Islanders. Once Naca is taken to Taríacuri, Taríacuri orders Naca to be sacrificed and takes on the active role of hatching the plan to trick Zurumban into eating part of Naca. In this manner Taríacuri pushes his cousins to the sidelines himself, as opposed to his elder advisors as in the previous episode. Because Zurumban's revenge ultimately falls upon Zetaco and Aramen more than it does Taríacuri, however, their status is reduced in comparison to Taríacuri's. The action of the episode equates Taríacuri with his cousins as a Chichimec because he deceives Zurumban into eating Naca just as his cousins deceive Naca in the first place. However, it also equates Taríacuri with Zurumban because both are responsible for a diminution of the status of Zetaco and Aramen—Zurumban strips them of their insignia and Taríacuri instructs them to take food from Curicaueri's granary, which should, but apparently does not (at least not in any concrete actions or repercussions that are discussed in the narrative) result in their becoming slaves. Earlier in the episode it is also evident that Taríacuri exercises some authority over his cousins, telling them what to do. Through the actions of the episode, Zurumban (and by extension Taríacuri to a certain degree) reprises the role played by the Islanders of Xaráquaro as the group that can confer but also revoke status and legitimacy on the Uacúsecha. This is appropriate, since he is said to be a native of Xaráquaro and he is the priest of Xarátanga, a female deity related to fertility similar to the goddesses of the Islands. The paradigm of Islanders as an ennobling source of status is being constructed beyond the Xaráquaros to include Zurumban and to Taríacuri's Islander side of his character. This episode adds the ability to have and/or confer legitimate status and authority to the distinction previously drawn between Taríacuri and his cousins in terms of movement and immobility.

The next episode begins with Taríacuri (now residing in Pátzcuaro) instituting a market in Pareo. Aramen meets the wife of the lord of Xaráquaro there repeatedly to carry on an affair. The wife's husband finds out about the affair and orders his underlings to kill Aramen. Aramen is shot in his house, and then climbs up a mountain and dies. Taríacuri learns of the murder and flees from Pátzcuaro. He intends to go to a place named Condembaro by traveling through Corínguaro territory. He offers feathers to the lord of Corínguaro for safe passage, but the lord of Corínguaro insists that Taríacuri settle in his territory. Taríacuri ends up settling on the mountain Hoataropexo, in between Pátzcuaro and Corínguaro. [An important note: upon the death of Aramen his brother Zetaco never again appears in the narrative.]

Aramen attempts to re-create the relation with the Xaráquaros that Pauacume had initiated when he married the fisherman's daughter by having an affair with the Xaráquaro lord's wife. The present relation is outside of marriage, however, and must be done secretly at the market. The result is that once again, the Xaráquaros (as representatives of the Islander category) are the agents in the transformation of the status of a Uacúsecha man by killing him. Aramen's Chichimec status at the foot of a slope at the end of the previous episode is conserved in the event of his death, as he is shot in his house but does not die until he climbs a mountain, thereby indicating in his final moments his proper place, much like the death of Pauacume in particular. However, Aramen is part of the senior branch of the Uacúsecha lineage as Uapeani's son, whereas Pauacume was the founder of the junior branch—thus the relative seniority/juniority of the individuals involved is reversed. With Aramen (and Zetaco) gone, Taríacuri is the lone Uacúsecha, and he immediately settles on a mountain to indicate his status in the absence of his cousins and in relation to the other groups of the Pátzcuaro Basin. In this episode, we see that the Uacúsecha, as it has been constituted in this latest iteration of characteristics and statuses, with a junior Islander character ostensibly possessing authority over his senior Chichimec cousins, has failed. It has failed, moreover, in no small part due to the wild and improper nature of the Chichimec behavior exhibited by Zetaco and particularly Aramen. This point becomes readily apparent in time, when we meet their sons.

In the next episode the lord of Corínguaro suggests that Taríacuri marry his daughter. Taríacuri accepts, and shortly after coming to live with Taríacuri this daughter gives birth to a son, Curátame. She frequently goes back to Corínguaro, however, and gets drunk with the priests there. On one occasion she does not return, and so Taríacuri goes to Corínguaro, carrying a deer that he has killed. The lord of the town asks Taríacuri why his wife is not traveling with him, and Taríacuri explains that his wife has not returned home. He claims to come only to offer the deer to Urendequavecara, the god of Corínguaro. He also refuses pulque, saying that if he were to drink he would attack the Corínguaros because they gave him a bad raiser of children. The Corínguaros look for Taríacuri's wife, find her, and bring her to her father, Chanhori, who asks why she leaves her husband. She lies to her father, saying that everyday Taríacuri insults her brothers, calling them men who are not valiant and are "women," and saying he will kill them. Chanhori says that these must be Taríacuri's words because women do not speak in such a way. He nonetheless sends his daughter back to live with Taríacuri. On the way, she sleeps with the elders who accompany her at places named Xoropiti and Tarequetzingata. Upon arriving at Taríacuri's house she says that she had gone out for fish, and she gives Taríacuri a fish. Taríacuri gives a piece to his god Curicaueri but throws the rest away, saying "we do not eat brothel fish." He then goes out on the mountains and gathers wood for the temples.

Within this episode, the wife's infidelity drives Taríacuri out of his house to an even higher elevation as he goes out to gather wood at the end of the episode. In other words his Chichimec status intensifies following his wife's infidelities. The exchange of deer for fish that is negated establishes a paradigmatic link with the marriage of Pauacume to the Xaráquaro fisherman's daughter, when upon their meeting the Uacúsecha Chichimecs shared hunted game (rabbits) and the fisherman shared his fish. Because the present exchange is negated, however, the link serves to highlight the *contrast* between the present marriage and the previous marriage of the Uacúsecha and Xaráquaros.

The stated desire on the part of both the Naranjans at the outset of the narrative and the Corínguaros in the present episode is to try to stake a claim on the god Curicaueri through alliances constituted by the marriages between the Uacúsecha and both the Naranjan and Corínguaro women. Like the earlier marriage of Hireticatame, the present marriage is, in terms of the paradigms established in the narrative, composed of the wrong categories. The Corínguaros and Uacúsecha Chichimecs are both represented by celestial male deities and are foreigners to the Pátzcuaro Basin by reason of their origin if not their present location (Corínguaro is east of the basin, Pátzcuaro within the basin). The patron deity of the Corínguaros, Urendequavecara, is associated with Venus / the Morning Star (Corona Núñez 1957; Monzón 2004), and he was with the Chichimecs when they settled at Uayameo (Espejel Carbajal 2008:146). He is generally interpreted to be a "brother" of Curicaueri and one of the Tiripemencha or five male deities who represent the four cardinal directions (plus the center) (Pollard 1991). Both marriages are initiated by the in-laws (first the Naranjans and now the Corínguaros) with the explicit goal of taking the powerful god Curicaueri from the Uacúsecha.[21] Just like Hireticatame's marriage, moreover, Taríacuri's marriage is in trouble due to its own internal incompatibilities; no outside involvement from others is needed in order to create discord in contrast to the marriages involving the Uacúsecha and the Xaráquaros.

In addition, many of the dimensions of the marriage to the Naranjan woman are repeated but reversed. Taríacuri manages to kill but also maintain possession of a deer and offer it to the Corínguaro god, reversing Hireticatame's earlier inability to offer deerskin coverings to the Uacúsecha god Curicaueri. He refuses pulque, forestalling any hostilities, thus reversing Hireticatame's murder of a brother-in-law. The murder of many Naranjan in-laws by Hireticatame is reversed, moreover, in the fact that the words of Taríacuri's wife that he plans on murdering them are a lie. Thus not only are no in-laws killed, but there is a demonstrated lack of intent to engage in violence and even restraint from any action (drinking alcohol) that might instigate it in the present episode.

In the next episode two men from Itziparamuco named Xoropiti and Tarequetzingata come to Taríacuri's house on Hoataropexo and claim that they want to bleed their ears as sacrifice to the gods. Taríacuri's wife dresses herself prettily and greets the visitors, and proceeds to pour them some pulque. Taríacuri does not drink and instead leaves his house to go out and gather wood on the mountains, but he tells his visitors that they are welcome to stay and drink. The next morning he returns to his house and finds that his wife has slept with the men, who have set out for their home village. Taríacuri goes out to the mountains again and gathers wood, not even stopping to eat.

Taríacuri's wife sleeps with her own categorical kinsmen again—Itziparamuco is, we learn later in the narrative, subject to Corínguaro. Moreover, the names of the men are simply the repeated names of the places where the Corínguaro elders slept with Taríacuri's wife in the preceding episode. This episode therefore repeats the incestuous action but reverses the location of the action in the previous episode from his wife's natal town to her new home. She cannot, in other words, remain faithful to Taríacuri regardless of her location or situation. Taríacuri's intensifying Chichimecness, additionally, threatens to destroy him. The narrative even states that he is gaunt and white from his behavior. The current iteration of Taríacuri's Chichimec behavior, in other words, does not appear to be something that can be maintained.

Once again, this episode hearkens back to but reverses key element of Hireticatame's marriage to the Naranjan woman. Here, the Corínguaro wife is the reason for the incompatibility of the match. Earlier the conflict was directly with the in-laws; Hireticatame and his wife fled and settled at Zichaxuquero together. Earlier it is the skin of the deer that is ruined whereas here it is the wife's skin, that is, her sash and paint-covered skin that is "ruined" (in disarray). There are three interrelated and patterned transformations at play here. In the dealings with the Naranjans the deer is missing but found by the in-laws, who ruin its skin, while the wife remains faithful to the husband (even escaping with Hireticatame and her son, inverting the Corínguaro princess's flaw as a bad mother). In the relations with the Corínguaros, the deer is present and accounted for (and offered as a sacrifice as already noted) while the wife is missing but found by the in-laws, who also are the ones responsible for "ruining" her "skin"—and she was missing due to her infidelity which involved those same in-laws. In addition, these two episodes in which interaction is exclusively between the Uacúsecha and the Corínguaros forms its own paradigmatic set, which plays the same role that we have already seen the Corínguaros play. However, whereas before that role is paradigmatic and *in praesentia* as the direct precipitators between the Uacúsecha and Islanders serving as the cause of both the conjunctions and disjunctions, in this set they play the role in terms of the syntagmatic aspect of the narrative and drive its action. This set takes place after the latest round of Uacúsecha-Islander interactions has concluded and apparently does not have any reason to continue, and it provides the rationale for the next round of Uacúsecha-Islander interactions. In other words, previously the narrative has placed the Corínguaro characters in between the Uacúsecha and Islander characters as precipitators, whereas this set of Corínguaro-focused episodes come between and instigate episodes involving the Uacúsecha and Islanders. The paradigmatic quality of the Corínguaros is extended to the level of a syntagmatic phenomena, and in the process this syntagmatic unit and its effects in the narrative sequence takes on the paradigmatic qualities of the Corínguaro category.

THE NARRATIVE, TARÍACURI, AND THE WORLD TURN

Taríacuri's destructive Chichimecness requires a remedy if the story is to proceed.

In the next episode Taríacuri's aunt tricks him into eating something and tells him to seek out another wife and to visit Zurumban, and that he and Zurumban are to be lords. Taríacuri goes, and Zurumban challenges Taríacuri to shoot a humming-bird. Taríacuri successfully shoots the bird. He then instructs Zurumban to retrieve the arrow and the bird, which miraculously is not dead but flutters in Zurumban's hands. Zurumban exclaims at Taríacuri's feat that he "is certainly a Chichimec for this bird is not that large, and was it not something to shoot it for it is so small?" (Alcalá 2000:417). Zurumban then invites Taríacuri to have some pulque, and Taríacuri accepts. Zurumban also instructs his daughters to come, and tells them to spend the night with Taríacuri. Taríacuri does not sleep with the women, but stays up all night holding vigil and plotting with his elder advisors. In the morning he blackens himself with smoke from a brazier. The two women remark to Zurumban that they did not sleep with Taríacuri and that he is crazy and does not have sex. Zurumban responds that Taríacuri is indeed a lord. Taríacuri then requests that he and Zurumban go to where the idols are kept, and there he lectures Zurumban, telling him that he should not get drunk so often but rather should make war and enrich Xarátanga's coffers. Taríacuri says that Zurumban can claim it is not he but instead Taríacuri that is conducting these raids. Taríacuri closes by saying: "Truly, Zurumban, I am making you a lord if you do this, for you are not a lord but of low class and a beggar, and now I am making you a lord and do you this favor" (Alcalá 2000:422).

Zurumban bursts into tears and says, "Oh! Lord Son-in-law! These words you brought with you are those of a king. I will do it, all that you have said to me" (Alcalá 2000:422). *They go and eat, and then Zurumban has the two daughters gather up their finest clothing and jewelry. The ladies go live at Hoataropexo, and Taríacuri gathers wood once again for the temples.*

The present episode is a reversal of the previous episodes because we see Taríacuri's self-destruction due to his first marriage end with a more successful marriage to an Islander's daughters. That reversal is most poignantly represented by Taríacuri's lack of color because he has been roaming the mountains constantly and not eating. He was white and gaunt. Upon shooting the hummingbird, however, we learn that Taríacuri has painted himself black with soot in honor of his god Curicaueri; he also allows Zurumban to apply some yellow paint to his body. Afanador-Pujol (2015:170) suggests, based on her analyses of the illustrations of the *Relación de Michoacán*, that yellow and especially yellow body-paint was associated with the Islanders. Therefore the combined painting of black and yellow on Taríacuri's body perhaps indicates both a Chichimec and Curicaueri-associated identity as well as an Islander identity associated with the worship of Xarátanga. In addition, an aunt of Taríacuri tricks him into eating some food by telling him some Islanders have come to see him; when he is prepared for the Islanders (who are not coming) and having regained enough of his strength from the food, she changes the subject to Taríacuri's plight and advises him to go and see Zurumban.

Most significantly for the course of the entire narrative, in this episode Taríacuri pivots (see chapter 3), as he essentially switches places with Zurumban. Pivoting in this sense entails that not only one or two elements of the dimensions are reversed but also that from the perspective of the pivoting character, all of the values for each dimension are reversed. The course of the entire episode is set up by Taríacuri's success in shooting the hummingbird, which explicitly (because it is remarked upon by Zurumban) demonstrates his Chichimecness.[22] Immediately upon shooting the bird, however, Taríacuri takes on what had previously been the Islander role in relation to Zurumban. Zurumban becomes the mobile one, fetching the bird, while Taríacuri stands in place. Taríacuri also becomes the lordly and ennobling one, saying that he is making Zurumban a lord. This power has, until now, been associated with the Islander category.

In the marriage to Zurumban's daughters, who bring their feminine and autochthonous wealth as a dowry, Taríacuri and the Uacúsecha Chichimecs acquire not only a permanent contingent of female Islanders but also the wealth and legitimacy that they possess. Therefore there is an ironic tension when Taríacuri states that he is making Zurumban a lord because, at the same time, Taríacuri is acquiring the Islander wealth that helps legitimate his newfound authority. The tension between the two is also evident in the manner in which Taríacuri achieves the acquisition of the feminine wealth; not through outright warfare, conquest, and killing (yet) but rather by answering a challenge to shoot a hummingbird, which does not die. Taríacuri answers the challenge, demonstrating his Chichimec skill and hunting prowess, and even wins spoils, but through an activity that is a game or at least is not real warfare. This tension is really over two ideologies of authority. The one already in place emphasizes legitimacy based on ancient occupation of the land, symbolized or indexed by the accumulated wealth resulting from working the land since time immemorial.[23] The new ideology emphasizes piety toward the gods, and Curicaueri as a "king-maker" in particular, manifested as a war-hungry disposition (war casualties placate the gods) that he advises Zurumban to adopt. As a result of this episode, however, the Uacúsecha have staked a claim on and have thereby encompassed *both* kinds of legitimacy. This encompassment is symbolized by the combination of the black and yellow body decoration, the marriage and appropriation of feminine wealth, Taríacuri's sequentially manifested ability to be both Chichimec and Islander, and now the resulting ambiguity thanks to the new dual significance of the underlying rationale for Taríacuri's lordly and ennobling behavior.

Much like the similarity between the marriages to the Naranjan and Corínguaro women, this episode contains paradigmatic associations with the marriage to the daughter of the fisherman from Xaráquaro. The complementary categories— Chichimec and Islander—are the same. Like that marriage and unlike the other two, this marriage does not end due to the actions of the parties themselves; in fact, this marriage remains intact. Both the present marriage and the Xaráquaro marriage involve delayed consummation: the fisherman's daughter must be brought to the Uacúsecha and then come of age, whereas the present (and apparently sexually available) daughters of Zurumban are forced to wait until a proper marriage can take place.

There remains an important difference between the two Islander-Chichimec unions, however, and this difference explains why the Corínguaro category was called upon to end the first union. By shooting the hummingbird and winning Zurumban's daughters, Taríacuri essentially transforms himself. Indeed, as explained above, as soon as he shoots the hummingbird he and Zurumban pivot. His Chichimec quality is what allows him to transform himself. Contrast this with the earlier marriage between the fisherman's daughter and Pauacume. It might be objected that as a prelude to that union, the Chichimec brothers Uapeani and Pauacume provided the fisherman with a story to tell his kinsmen to secure the marriage, but in the end this ruse appears unnecessary as the Islanders do not mind the alliance and in fact want to build upon it. In so doing, the Islanders invite the Chichimecs back to the island of Xaráquaro and marry their daughters to them, in the process making them priests/sacrificers and giving them their first trapping of nobility. In other words, in that preceding iteration the Islanders play the role of transformative agents, changing the status of the Chichimecs. This is a necessary first step in Islander-Chichimec relations, primarily because it produced Taríacuri, but if it were to be conserved it would maintain the Chichimecs in a subordinate role as the subjects of the transformation accomplished by others in contrast to the dominant status of transforming agent we see here in Taríacuri's pivoting.

This episode, in which Taríacuri pivots and displays the ability to be both a Chichimec and an Islander in relation to both Chichimec and Islander non-Uacúsecha characters, is the key episode of the entire narrative in both its paradigmatic and syntagmatic aspects. In its paradigmatic aspects, the Uacúsecha Chichimecs are transformed into a category composed of both fully Chichimec and fully Islander qualities and statuses, thereby creating a new and overarching category that separates the Uacúsecha from the rest of society and defines their legitimacy. The rest of the narrative protects this difference. For example, the rest of the narrative does not record any other marriages between Uacúsecha characters and non-Uacúsecha characters. In its syntagmatic aspect, moreover, this episode in which Taríacuri pivots is the central point about which the rest of the narrative pivots. Following this event, the narrative proceeds to "work," which is to say build associations between events through both their syntagmatic ordering and their paradigmatic content, in two directions. The first direction is the simple forward moving plot of the narrative, with the same general pattern of reversing the values of certain dimensions from episode to episode, as in the analysis thus far. The second direction is an inversion of the episodes of the narrative to this point. These inverted actions are paradigmatically associated with the actions of the first half—they involve the same kinds of characters and the same themes. They are also related syntagmatically, as these paradigmatically related but inverted events occur in reverse order in relation to their ordering in the first half of the narrative, working back through those same paradigmatic themes in a manner similar to chiasmus (see chapter 6). The manner in which the paradigmatic content of the episodes line up in their syntagmatic ordering is diagrammed in figure 4.4. Furthermore, the manner in which the paradigmatic content is transformed or inverted within this structure of the pivoting of the narrative is diagrammed in figure 4.5. The specific nature of these paradigmatic inversions are noted in the analysis of the episodes below.

This episode in all of its detail contains an abundance of symbolism, more than can be dealt with comprehensively here. However, it is important to consider the

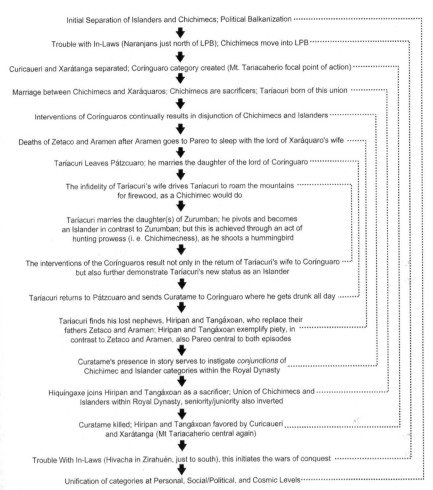

Initial Separation of Islanders and Chichimecs; Political Balkanization

Trouble with In-Laws (Naranjans just north of LPB); Chichimecs move into LPB

Curicaueri and Xarátanga separated; Corínguaro category created (Mt. Tariacaherio focal point of action)

Marriage between Chichimecs and Xaráquaros; Chichimecs are sacrificers; Taríacuri born of this union

Interventions of Corínguaros continually results in disjunction of Chichimecs and Islanders

Deaths of Zetaco and Aramen after Aramen goes to Pareo to sleep with the lord of Xaráquaro's wife

Taríacuri Leaves Pátzcuaro; he marries the daughter of the lord of Corínguaro

The infidelity of Taríacuri's wife drives Taríacuri to roam the mountains for firewood, as a Chichimec would do

Taríacuri marries the daughter(s) of Zurumban; he pivots and becomes an Islander in contrast to Zurumban; but this is achieved through an act of hunting prowess (i. e. Chichimecness), as he shoots a hummingbird

The interventions of the Corínguaros result not only in the return of Taríacuri's wife to Corínguaro but also further demonstrate Taríacuri's new status as an Islander

Taríacuri returns to Pátzcuaro and sends Curatame to Corínguaro where he gets drunk all day

Taríacuri finds his lost nephews, Hiripan and Tangáxoan, who replace their fathers Zetaco and Aramen; Hiripan and Tangáxoan exemplify piety, in contrast to Zetaco and Aramen, also Pareo central to both episodes

Curatame's presence in story serves to instigate *conjunctions* of Chichimec and Islander categories within the Royal Dynasty

Hiquíngaxe joins Hiripan and Tangáxoan as a sacrificer; Union of Chichimecs and Islanders within Royal Dynasty, seniority/juniority also inverted

Curatame killed; Hiripan and Tangáxoan favored by Curicaueri and Xarátanga (Mt Tariacaherio central again)

Trouble With In-Laws (Hivacha in Zirahuén, just to south), this initiates the wars of conquest

Unification of categories at Personal, Social/Political, and Cosmic Levels

FIGURE 4.4. Schematic representation of summaries of episodes of the Priest's Speech. The episodes are arranged sequentially moving from top to bottom, but the lines at right connect the paradigmatically similar episodes of the two halves of the narrative to one another. Taríacuri's pivoting in his interaction with Zurumban serves as the focal point around which these linkages are produced; the effect is much like the poetic device known as chiasmus.

role of the hummingbird and its rejuvenation because I propose that the fact that the hummingbird is brought back to life is linked to Taríacuri's rebirth and rejuvenation. When it comes to the hummingbird, the normal expectation is that because it has been shot with an arrow it should be dead. The narrative comments

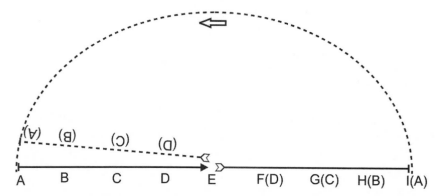

FIGURE 4.5. Abstracted representation of the "folding back" effect produced by the paradigmatic linkages between the episodes of the second half of the narrative and those of the first half. In this image, the inverted and mirrored nature of the forward-moving episodes [labeled F(D), G(C), H(B), and I(A)] is indicated visually by their upside-down placement over the corresponding episodes of the first half of the narrative.

upon the rather miraculous fact that the hummingbird does not die but flutters in Zurumban's hands as he carries it. Hummingbirds have bright, iridescent feathers, and for this reason they are commonly associated with the sun (e.g., Hunt 1977).[24] I suggest that this is an allusion to a belief among Mesoamerican peoples, most notably the Aztecs, that this is stereotypical behavior for hummingbirds. "It rejuvenates itself. . . . In the winter, it hibernates. It inserts its bill in a tree. [hanging] there, it shrieks, it shrivels, molts. And when [the tree] rejuvenates, when the sun warms, when the tree sprouts, when it leafs out, at this time [the hummingbird] also grows feathers once again. And when it thunders for rain, at that time it awakens, moves, comes to life" (Sahagún 1950–1982:11:24).

A link is established between Taríacuri and the hummingbird by virtue of him shooting the hummingbird, a link that likely constitutes the importance of rebirth and transformation at issue in this episode. Moreover, in this episode the hummingbird is enclosed by Zurumban as it flutters inside his hands and the morning after shooting the hummingbird Taríacuri is enclosed in a rich, doubled blanket after he has colored himself with soot and smoke.

Taríacuri is also linked to the hummingbird via his name as birds that both mark the transition to the summer, the strengthening sun, and the coming of the rains. Seler ([1905] 1993:23) suggests that Taríacuri's name is a rendering of *tareácuri*, the Tarascan name for a mockingbird or, as in Sahagún, specifically the curved-billed thrasher. In Sahagún's writing, the curved-billed thrasher is characterized (aside from its physical characteristics) thusly: "And in winter it does not sing, it does not cry out, it does not produce songs. When the rains comes, when they threaten, when it becomes warm, then it begins to sing. Toward whence the wind comes, there it settles facing it, continuing to call, to sing" (Sahagún 1950–1982:11: 52).

Note here that not only is there a common association with the hummingbird insofar as it is rejuvenated when warmer weather and the rains set in, but also there is a link to the wind and Taríacuri's name as the bird is said to face the wind and sing in the direction of it. The curved-bill thrasher makes one other appearance in Sahagún's work, in the description of the Aztec ceremony of Atl Caualo or Quiahuitl eua (Sahagún 1950–1982:2:45). It is said to sing its song when the rains have come, and the overall significance of the festival is to bring the rains and worship the Aztec Rain God Tlaloc. Broda (1976, 1982) suggests that the Aztec rain ceremony was celebrated around the Spring Equinox, which would be just before the rainy season begins. In Michoacán (much as in the Basin of Mexico), the rainy season sets in in May, as the sun is about a month to a month-and-a-half away from its northernmost (and strongest) point at the summer solstice; in other words its rejuvenation will be complete at this point (on the movements of the sun in Mesoamerican thought, see, e.g., Coggins 1980; Hunt 1977; Leon Portilla 1988; see also with respect to the priest's narrative itself Martínez González [2010:48] relates certain elements of the story to the sun's daily and yearly movements). Seler ([1905] 1993:23) also notes that Taríacuri's name relates to the Tarascan word for wind (*tariata*), and given the slight difference between his name and the name of the bird I believe it to be likely that his personal name is more closely related to the wind but is also a metaphor or pun on the name of the bird. Because the concepts—the strengthening sun, wind, storms and the transition to the rainy season, birds and their behavior—are all related the specific meaning of the name Taríacuri is largely moot, and the polysemy is the significant point.

Unfortunately the priest's narrative does not state what time of year this episode takes place, but the associations are clear. Taríacuri is associated with the hummingbird and through his name to another bird whose behavior is strongly seasonal, with rejuvenation of life in general, with the onset of the rains, and likely most importantly with the reborn and strengthening sun. It might seem paradoxical that Taríacuri is being associated with a stronger sun in precisely the moment when he pivots to being an Islander in contrast to his Chichimec side that is associated with Curicaueri and therefore the sun. First, it is necessary to point out that in rites of passage, a liminal stage or social death is necessary in order for a new identity to be realized. Taríacuri's path in the recent set of episodes, culminating in his pivoting here, can be read as just such a rite of passage, a transformation. Previously he had grown gaunt and weak as a Chichimec, and here he is reborn as an Islander. Second, the shared timeframe of the coming of the rains and the strengthening sun indicates that this period of the solar year is one of at least dual significance and that one such significance is the rains and what they bring, that is, fertility of the land. This aspect of the symbolism of the timeframe is easily accommodated with Taríacuri's new Islander nature, as the Islanders and their deities represent fertility and the fecundity of the land that is realized thanks to rain. Finally, it is true that in the immediate aftermath of this pivoting, Taríacuri takes on an Islander as opposed to a Chichimec identity. This is only true at one level—the surface level—of the meaning and implications of what is happening in this point of the narrative. At a higher level, Taríacuri is effecting the encompassment of the Islander category within the Chichimec category—Islander qualities are being appropriated by the Chichimecs and merged as a subordinate element with the original Chichimec qualities (see Haskell 2008a, 2012). It is this encompassment that legitimizes the Uacúsecha; they are the ones who actively incorporate the complementary element within themselves (in this sense it is not simply Chichimecness as such that is superior to the Islander category, but it is the Chichimecs' ability to encompass and come to represent both elementary categories). Taríacuri can only effectively manifest one identity at a time—he is here transitioning from Chichimec to Islander—but in totality he is expressing his ability to be both and to transform himself from one to the other in order to do so. As the sole member of the Uacúsecha at this point in the narrative, moreover, he is representative of the Uacúsecha as a whole. To summarize, Taríacuri and the Uacúsecha are indeed getting stronger by encompassing the Islander qualities and being able to act as an Islander, and this is fitting given the association of the two birds with the strengthening sun and the solar associations of the Chichimecs and their deity Curicaueri.

The centrality of Taríacuri and his pivoting is also revealed in the genealogical tree contained within the *Relación de Michoacán* (Alcalá 2000:545). This depiction of the Uacúsecha characters is obviously related to the priest's narrative,[25] as it shows the manner in which the Uacúsecha lords died according to the narrative (this is carried forward in time past the conclusion of the narrative to show the manner in which Tzintzicha Tangáxoan was killed as well). As Stone (2004:83) recognized, Taríacuri is placed at the midpoint of the oak that comprises the literal tree upon which the family tree is represented and which depicts Hireticatame as its roots and Tzintzicha Tangáxoan at the top in the center. Taríacuri is also the closest Uacúsecha member to the trunk of that tree; the total effect is to locate him at the center of the tree that represents the Uacúsecha as a whole. It is also interesting that Taríacuri is not superimposed directly on the trunk of the tree but is placed just to the right of the trunk. Therefore he sits directly under Don Francisco Taríacuri, who is to the right of his father at the top of the genealogical tree (see figure 1.3). This same paradigmatic centrality of Taríacuri is also perhaps confirmed by the similarity his name shares with the mountain that is located to the west of Tzintzuntzan. The mountain Tariacaherio (presently known as Cerro Tariaqueri or Tariak'eri and which is located just west of Tzintzuntzan), as it is referred to in the *Relación de Michoacán*, occupies a central position within the Pátzcuaro Basin as a whole. In the priest's narrative the character Taríacuri does not perform any actions on this mountain, and as he is established in Pátzcuaro within the narrative it is difficult to see how the similar names could be the result of naming the mountain after the character (at least as he is known from the Priest's Speech). I suggest that the names of both the character and the mountain are derived from a shared centrality within their respective contexts, one narrative and the other geographical or spatial.

Taríacuri's first wife returns to her native town of Corínguaro immediately after Taríacuri's marriage to the daughters of Zurumban. The lord of Corínguaro is affronted and goes to Hoataropexo and takes over Curicaueri's temple there, casting the idol to a corner and having the temple painted in red and white for his god Urendequavecara. Taríacuri and the Uacúsecha Chichimecs leave and go to one place and then another, where Taríacuri builds a temple out of earth. The Corínguaros attack him there, but the god Curicaueri inflicts illnesses on the Corínguaros, allowing the Uacúsecha Chichimecs to sacrifice them in great numbers. They place the Corínguaros' heads on pikes, and the number of heads on pikes is said to have cast a great shadow. Taríacuri remarks that his (ex)-wife has acted like a valiant man because she has caused the gods to be fed with sacrificial victims. The Corínguaros vow to not forget this offense and attempt to spy on Taríacuri to see how they might attack him. Zurumban's son participates in the spying, and because he is Zurumban's son and Taríacuri and Zurumban had just become allies through marriage relations, the son enters Taríacuri's house freely. Taríacuri's aunt learns what is going on and enters Taríacuri's house while he is with the son. She says that she has heard that Zurumban's son is helping the Corínguaros by entering Taríacuri's house. Taríacuri is angry and tells her that the man he is with is Zurumban's son and tells her to get out. Zurumban's son is no longer at ease and so he leaves, but Taríacuri gives him a load of fish to take to Zurumban and follows soon after to ask Zurumban where he might settle. Zurumban pretends to be compassionate, even putting saliva on his face to imitate tears, but instructs Taríacuri to settle somewhere else. This begins a short peregrination in which the Uacúsecha Chichimecs settle in place after place, staying in each only a matter of days. Finally they settle in a place where they can gather firewood for the temples.

This episode inverts the paradigmatic content of the episodes prior to Taríacuri's pivoting. Most fundamentally the marriage to the Corínguaro woman is dissolved, reversing its initiation prior to Taríacuri's pivoting. In addition, Taríacuri's first wife's extramarital relations with her kinsmen is an act of categorical incest, as two persons from the same category have come together in a procreative act. The sacrifices and radical disjuncture of the Corínguaro soldiers' bodies, as their heads are detached from their bodies and placed on spikes, inverts this while still preserving the dimension of the Corínguaro category. In other words, prior to Taríacuri's pivoting, two Corínguaro characters became one (through sexual relations) while after that pivoting, each one Corínguaro soldier becomes two (through decapitation and sacrifice). The gender relations are inverted as well. Previously Taríacuri's wife had lied and said that Taríacuri had called her kinsmen women, which her kinsmen believed, saying her words were not those of a woman. In the present episode Taríacuri metaphorically relates his wife to a valiant man, both inverting who is being labeled the opposite gender (a Corínguaro woman in place of Corínguaro men) while also ironically although discursively realizing the ex-wife's ability to be a man, the impossibility of which caused her kinsmen to believe her lie.

Furthermore, the intervention of the Corínguaros, in their role as precipitators, causes Taríacuri to encounter his new brother- and father-in-law. In this way the actions concerning the Corínguaros not only invert the paradigmatic content from just prior to Taríacuri's pivoting, but in this way serve to move the narrative forward at the same time. In his dealings with Zurumban and his son, this episode reverses the previous episodes in which Taríacuri pivots. First, Taríacuri is unwilling to take his aunt's advice concerning Zurumban's son, whereas he had followed her advice in eating something and going to see Zurumban in the previous episode. Furthermore, the dynamic between Taríacuri and Zurumban has obviously been inverted. In the present episode Zurumban feigns crying in sympathy, whereas previously he had indeed cried upon hearing Taríacuri's advice/chastisement. More important, Zurumban is in control and playing the role of authoritative one as he determines Taríacuri's fate, an obvious reversal of the previous episode. Taríacuri's movements do invert his position by the end of the episode, however, as he has moved off of the mountain Hoataropexo and has settled in a town. These factors confirm his new Islander identity as result of his pivoting and reverse his increasing Chichimecness that had led to and culminated in that very pivoting. In addition, the manner in which Taríacuri's aunt is included in the narrative is reversed. Previously she had tricked Taríacuri into eating food, saying that Islanders had come to see him when they had not. Here she tells the truth, as Taríacuri and Zurumban's son (an Islander) have already sat to eat, but is punished for her words. In the previous episode she causes a conjunction of the Chichimec and Islander categories, whereas here she causes a disjunction because Zurumban's son says that he cannot stay after having heard the aunt's accusations (even though they are true).

The lords of Corínguaro then demand the jewels and riches that they hear Taríacuri has gained by going on raids. Taríacuri refuses and instead gives them arrows of various colors; he gives the names of the various colors of arrows and says that they are the precious jewels and other riches that they have asked for. The Corínguaro messengers at first protest that this is not what they came for but relent and take the arrows back to Corínguaro, but the Corínguaro lords [Chanhori's sons are beginning to take over for their father] *do not know what to do with them, and they break the arrows. Chanhori chides his sons for having done so, saying that perhaps the arrows were somehow sacred. Shortly thereafter the people of Pacandan, the Corínguaros, and the people of Tariaran fight over Pátzcuaro. Taríacuri refuses to help them, but soon another embassy from Xaráquaro asks the same thing of him, because the Xaráquaros had just suffered a defeat at the hands of the people of Pacandan. Taríacuri tells the Xaráquaros to sell themselves into slavery and then he will help them and return to Pátzcuaro. They do this, and so at night Taríacuri climbs a mountain in Pátzcuaro and blows a small whistle imitating the cry of an eagle. This causes the warring parties to flee from Pátzcuaro, and Taríacuri resettles there.*

The riches requested by the Corínguaros stand in for the riches acquired through Taríacuri's marriage to Zurumban's daughters, through the sequential relation between the plot of the story and the fact that the narrative does not mention any such raids. Therefore this episode reveals both Taríacuri's ability to preserve the riches and the autochthonous legitimacy they symbolize as well as the Corínguaros' failure to appropriate the Chichimec hunting/warrior identity of the Uacúsecha, represented metonymically by the arrows. Because the Corínguaros fail in this regard, the Uacúsecha preserve their own hunting/warrior associations along with their newly acquired Islander wealth. By doing so their status as a dually composed and encompassing category is preserved. Taríacuri's status as an Islander is also preserved, as he is in control of the others' status and fate when he tells the rival groups to sell themselves into slavery. The duality of Taríacuri as a character remains present but can only be signified singly at any one point in time by the action and juxtapositions being constructed in the narrative; here his nature as a Chichimec is signified as he climbs a mountain and imitates the eagle in addition to his now developing Islander character. This duality is present, but in coordination with his pivoting he increasingly is signified as an Islander as his Chichimec identity is transferred to other characters, as will soon be made evident. The events that have transpired with the Corínguaros mirror and reverse the events involving the Corínguaros before Taríacuri pivots, namely his ill-fated marriage to the Corínguaro princess. Note that just prior to that marriage Taríacuri was forced to leave Pátzcuaro, reversed by his return to Pátzcuaro in this episode.

After his return to Pátzcuaro, Taríacuri immediately begins to inquire about his nephews, the sons of Zetaco and Aramen. The narrative explains that these nephews have purposefully not been mentioned following the deaths of Zetaco and Aramen so as to make them seem dead. The narrative goes on to chronicle the story of the nephews and how they ultimately are reunited with Taríacuri. The nephews travel with their mother from town to town in an arc from the west to northwest of the Pátzcuaro Basin.[26] They temporarily live in Asaveto [Asajo], where they live off of scraps of food they find in the marketplace. A lord from Corínguaro who was ruling from Hetoquaro in eastern Michoacán inquires about them [the reason is not explicitly given], but this causes them to flee and travel down the western side of Lake Pátzcuaro. First they go to Erongarícuaro, then to Urichu, and finally to Pareo, thus tracing a counterclockwise path along towns on the western edge of the lake to the southwest and then south of the lake.[27] At the first two towns they promise to do services for the lords, but are ultimately expelled by those lords because they are constantly gathering wood for the temples rather than performing those services. At Pareo, however, the lord of that town recognizes the nephews as true Chichimec lords and refuses to accept their proposed household service, telling them instead to take firewood to the temples in Pátzcuaro. They are recognized in Pátzcuaro by Taríacuri's advisors, but they escape and only the third time they go to Pátzcuaro are they reunited with their uncle. Taríacuri then arranges for them to settle in a place called Yauacuytiro, and the two nephews gather wood for the temples.

The episodes with the Corínguaros and the battle over, and Taríacuri's return to, Pátzcuaro set the stage for a new round of interactions between Chichimec and Islander characters. Whereas in the previous episode that interaction is between the groups, in this episode that intergroup scale of interaction is reversed to be within the Uacúsecha. The emergence of Hiripan and Tangáxoan in the narrative is a reversal of the death and disappearance of their fathers, Zetaco and Aramen. It soon becomes obvious that Hiripan and Tangáxoan fulfill the same Chichimec roles that their fathers occupied in relation to Taríacuri. While Zetaco and Aramen's impropriety, lasciviousness, and running around marked their Chichimecness, their sons' roaming Chichimecness is marked instead by their piety (gathering wood in the mountains). The role of Pareo and the numerous trips there further links these episodes paradigmatically. Aramen met the wife of the lord of Xaráquaro repeatedly by traveling to the market at Pareo to carry out his affair, while this generation of Chichimec characters travel from Pareo to Pátzcuaro three times, despite being recognized on the very first trip, preserving the symmetry of the multiple trips from the episode in the first half. Even the nephews' peregrination to the north/northwest of the Pátzcuaro Basin is an inversion of their fathers' settlement in Uacanambaro— Seler (1993:24) speculates that Uacanambaro is within Zurumban's territory, and therefore would be located between Lake Pátzcuaro and Tariaran to the south. Taríacuri's junior position in relation to his cousins Zetaco and Aramen in the earlier constitution of the Uacúsecha is also inverted. With his present combination with his nephews, Taríacuri, as the Islander element within the Uacúsecha, is now senior (due to his status in an older generation) to the Chichimec element (his nephews).

Taríacuri decides to make Curátame [the son of the Corínguaro Princess] lord in Pátzcuaro, and Taríacuri then takes up residence in a barrio of Pátzcuaro named Cutu. Curátame has a disagreement with Taríacuri, and derides Taríacuri as an Islander, saying he cannot therefore be lord. Taríacuri retorts that Curátame is an upstart and lacks the necessary legitimacy to be lord, and states that Hiripan and Tangáxoan are the true lords. Taríacuri returns to Cutu having not given Curátame the feathers that he had intended to give his son, and apparently decides to install a lesser noble lord in Pátzcuaro instead of Curátame. Not coincidentally, the narrative informs us that Hiripan and Tangáxoan have been out on the mountains gathering wood the entire time.

Here Taríacuri's transformation into an Islander is complete.[28] He is no longer up, but has moved down to Cutu. His Islander status as explicitly commented upon by Curátame negates the possibility of returning as lord in Pátzcuaro, and he instead makes a lesser noble lord there, apparently in place of Curátame.[29] The fact that neither Curátame nor Taríacuri is ultimately said to take over as lord is significant; Taríacuri initially steps aside as lord so that his son can begin his own rule, but following the disagreement he removes Curátame from that rule and still returns to Cutu rather than rule himself. Rather, this act of returning to Cutu rather than resuming his own rule, even after Curátame's insult, confirms that his transition into an Islander is complete, as now he is not lord and resides in a ward at a lower elevation than Pátzcuaro proper. His final movement is contrasted with the status of Hiripan and Tangáxoan,[30] who are up in the mountains; as their Chichimec status and piety is reinforced, Taríacuri not coincidentally remarks that they are the true lords. Taríacuri's remark that his nephews will be lords therefore reverses the fate that befalls their fathers, Zetaco and Aramen, when Taríacuri instructed them to eat food from Curicaueri's granary.

In the episodes that follow, the rancor and rivalry that mark the relationship between Curátame and his cousins Hiripan and Tangáxoan repeatedly serve to bring the nephews into interactions with Taríacuri, their Islander counterpart. In one such interaction, the nephews avoid a feast thrown by Curátame, instead preferring to spy on their enemies in the mountains. Taríacuri has likewise spurned his son's feast, and has gone to eat with his people at the foot of a mountain. Hiripan and Tangáxoan happen upon their uncle's feast, and Taríacuri suggests they go to Curátame's feast. They refuse, saying that there are "bad women" there and that the nobles mix with the commoners. Taríacuri then goes on to tell his nephews of the tragedies that are occurring in other towns. Foremost among these tragedies is the tale of Chapa, a lord from Corínguaro to whom Taríacuri had given a piece of the god Curicaueri. Chapa and Curicaueri have had great success in battle, and Chapa established himself in a place far to the east, near Lake Cuitzeo, named Hetoquaro. In time, however, Chapa marries a woman from Corínguaro and began taking all of his sacrificial victims to Corínguaro rather than back to Curicaueri in Pátzcuaro. Eventually everything the lord had built in Hetoquaro fell to ruin as priests left off their insignia and danced with commoners, the cloistered women similarly danced with the people, young girls bore children, the elder women started making arrows and building temples, and the place was overrun with weeds, before a drought came to the place. Similarly, a lord in Zacapu sought a dream from the god Querenda Angápeti, and so he slept first on a mountain and then progressively higher up the steps of the temple. The god recognized this as an impropriety and said that the lord should marry a commoner woman and that they should only see each other every twenty days. The lord died and his wife ruled as lord, carrying a shield and club. Taríacuri explains that such behavior in these places and others meant that now or very soon there would be a political landscape that would be ripe for conquest and reorganization. He explains that the nephews will be lords over all the towns.

In this episode Taríacuri tells of disasters that have befallen certain towns, explaining why they will not have lords and saying that Hiripan and Tangáxoan will be kings and rule over these towns. The two lengthy stories are similar in basic elements but represent inversions of each other. Both Chapa and the Zacapu lord begin as lesser nobles, as they are said to be of questionable parentage. Chapa does not take sacrifices to offer to Curicaueri in Pátzcuaro and thus fails to fulfill his relationship to that god, as Taríacuri's remark implies. The Zacapu lord, on the other hand, gets too close spatially to the god Querenda Angápeti, sleeping higher and higher on the steps on the temple. As a result, Querenda Angápeti orders the man to marry a woman but live apart from that woman, only seeing her every twenty days. Therefore a married man and a woman are permitted to only have limited sexual contact. In contrast, the priests in Hetoquaro leave off their insignia and dance with the commoners, and the cloistered women similarly dance with the people. Male/female relationships that are improperly close to each other in one story become male/female relationships that are too distant. Both stories end with women performing men's roles (building temples, making knives, acting as a lord, etc.) and gender imbalance (the absence of men) that guarantees that there will be no lord in those towns.

Both of these stories document relationships between humans and gods, nobles and commoners, and men and women. The relationships in these areas, which are either too distant or too close between gods and humans, men and women, and nobles and commoners, ultimately result in the abandonment of or illegitimate rule in these towns. They thus stand in contrast to the behavior of Hiripan and Tangáxoan in the previous and present episode, whose proper actions and now explicit desire to avoid the same disasters that have occurred in other places prompt Taríacuri to approvingly advise them and tell them that they will be kings over all these towns. It is also necessary to note that Curátame's feast is the event that puts this sequence into motion, bringing Taríacuri and his nephews together so that the nephews can demonstrate their piety in direct interaction with their uncle. Therefore Curátame takes on the role of precipitator, which is fitting owing to his Corínguaro identity that he inherited from his mother.

In the following episode, Hiripan and Tangáxoan set up an ambush and capture an Islander named Zapiuatame. They take him to Taríacuri, but it is clear that Tangáxoan wants to sacrifice him. After conversing with Taríacuri, Zapiuatame leaves with an oar on his shoulder to return home. Taríacuri tells his nephews that Zapiuatame wants to place himself under the protection of the god Curicaueri. While Zapiuatame is returning, he is chased by a second group of Islanders as he and his people cross the lake. Hiripan and Tangáxoan have stationed themselves as spies on a mountain and shoot at the second group, forcing them to give up the chase. Zapiuatame and his people therefore join Hiripan and Tangáxoan, and they establish themselves at or near Ihuatzio.[31] They are prosperous and enjoy success in both farming and going on military/hunting forays.

The great success of Hiripan and Tangáxoan with their new Islander allies indicates the suitable nature of their combination, composed of both Chichimec and Islander categories. It is important that their success involves both farming and going on military/hunting forays, demonstrating their capacity to be successful in both economic activities owing to this combination of Islander and Chichimec categories. This episode contrasts with previous episodes in which Curátame, as the Corínguaro character within the Uacúsecha, attempts to have Hiripan and Tangáxoan join him and which the nephews refuse to do. As the Islander companion of Hiripan and Tangáxoan, Zapiuatame also replaces Taríacuri as the Islander character that is most closely affiliated with Hiripan and Tangáxoan. Zapiuatame and his people are not Uacúsecha members, obviously, and therefore an intra-Uacúsecha combination of Islander and Chichimec characters (Hiripan and Tangáxoan with Taríacuri) is transformed into one between Uacúsecha Chichimec characters and non-Uacúsecha Islanders.

Furthermore, the negated sacrifice of Zapiuatame is linked paradigmatically to the episode in the first half of the narrative in which Taríacuri sacrifices Zurumban's priest, Naca, and tricks Zurumban into eating part of Naca. Both episodes involve relations between the Uacúsecha and the Islanders, but the role of Taríacuri is reversed as here Taríacuri is the mitigating factor that prevents the sacrifice of Zapiuatame, whereas earlier he was the driving force behind the sacrifice of Naca as revenge against Zurumban. Even the fact that Hiripan and Tangáxoan have to shoot at the second group of Islanders that is chasing Zapiuatame and his people preserves the shooting involved in the episode involving their fathers in which Aramen shoots Naca in the back. The paradigmatic association between the present episode and that earlier one is thus constructed and requires this element of intrigue and shots fired because Zapiuatame's actions in the current episode are entirely peaceful and would not otherwise require Hiripan and Tangáxoan to shoot at anyone.[32]

Angered over the success of his cousins, Curátame sends messengers to Taríacuri demanding to know the meaning of their actions, rhetorically asking where they will be lords [i.e., because Curátame is lord in Pátzcuaro, they have no place to be lord]. *Taríacuri tells the messengers to go ask his nephews directly. Upon hearing Curátame's questions, Tangáxoan flies into a fit of rage. He says that he and Hiripan will indeed be lords, and will be lords in Pátzcuaro. The nephews then go tell Taríacuri what has transpired. Taríacuri suggests that they take his son Hiquíngaxe back to live with them and be sacrificer. Hiquíngaxe agrees to join his cousins, gathers up his arrows, and travels ahead while Hiripan and Tangáxoan inform Taríacuri. On their way the three do penance in a cave. Hiripan and Tangáxoan eat only raw plants while they give their cousin toasted maize kernels to eat. When Hiquíngaxe asks them why they do not eat the maize, Hiripan begins weeping and says that this is how they eat and that Hiquíngaxe can go back if he wishes. Hiquíngaxe says to stop weeping because they are making him start to cry.*

Once again Curátame, as the Corínguaro character in the Uacúsecha, plays the role of precipitator. His insult causes the nephews to visit Taríacuri. This latest episode involves a transformation of the scale of the relation between Chichimec and Islander characters to one *within* the Uacúsecha lineage. Taríacuri's son Hiquíngaxe, who has until now not been mentioned within the narrative, becomes the Islander counterpart to the Chichimec characters of Hiripan and Tangáxoan. Hiquíngaxe's parentage is never stated, though it is possible or even likely that he is the product of Taríacuri's marriage with Zurumban's daughter. Hiquíngaxe is, at any rate, demonstrably different from his cousins as indicated by the different foods they eat— Hiripan and Tangáxoan eat raw and semiwild foods as opposed to Hiquíngaxe's meal of toasted (i.e., cooked[33]) corn, corn being the domesticated/cultured food par excellence throughout Mesoamerica. He appears to be essentially a reproduction of Taríacuri's Islander nature.[34] The union of Hiquíngaxe with Hiripan and Tangáxoan is therefore a transformation of the relation between Hiripan and Tangáxoan and Zapiuatame's Islanders. As was indicated, there is nothing fundamentally wrong with that previous iteration of the relation between the Uacúsecha Chichimecs and Zapiuatame's Islanders—the narrative clearly states that they were successful. This is why Curátame's intervention is needed to instigate this new event in which Hiquíngaxe is added to the composition of the Uacúsecha, just as the relations between Uapeani and Pauacume with the Xaráquaros in the first half of the narrative were successful and some outside force was required to come between them in order to demonstrate the propriety of their relation but also provide for its transformation in order to achieve a more proper union. The new conjunction, however, involves only members of the Uacúsecha lineage, and so the intergroup composition has been transformed into one within the Uacúsecha. The Uacúsecha lineage also now contains Islander and Chichimec characters within the same generation for the first time since the deaths of Zetaco and Aramen. Hiquíngaxe, as the son of Taríacuri, is junior to his Chichimec cousins, thus reversing the previous relation between Taríacuri and his nephews, in which Taríacuri advised his nephews as their elder. It thereby restores the seniority of the Chichimec side of the Uacúsecha and the junior status of the Islander character. However, earlier Taríacuri plays the role of leader as he told his cousins what to do, while here Hiquíngaxe as sacrificer as opposed to lord/leader is clearly subordinate to his cousins. Hiripan and Tangáxoan are the determining factor in Hiquíngaxe's consumption that distinguishes him from them, for example. The role of Hiquíngaxe as sacrificer further links this episode to the relation between the Uacúsecha and the Islanders of Xaráquaro in the first half of the narrative. Now it is the Islander character, rather than the Chichimecs Uapeani and Pauacume who fills the role of sacrificer, and the present episode demonstrates the appropriate subservience of the Islander/sacrificer character to the Chichimec lords.

The fact that the three Uacúsecha lords do penance in a cave at this point in time is highly significant and symbolic in terms of widespread symbolism in Mesoamerica of caves as access points between this world and the underworld (and even upper world), and particularly as a kind of origin point or "birthplace" from which humanity emerges. Pertaining to the priest's narrative itself, Afanador-Pujol (2015:58; she cites Boone 2000:187 concerning Texcocan sources) points out the link between this episode and the theme of caves as places of origin and specifically "among Texcocan manuscripts of central Mexico, the founding of a polity." Similarly, Gillespie's (1989:43–44, 162, 115, 178) paradigmatic analysis of Nahua histories and a logic of Mexica rulership indicates that Chicomoztoc (the "Seven Caves" that is an initial homeland of the Nahua groups) and caves more generally constitute boundary markers of both the initiation and termination of eras as well as their ends. Caves as birthplaces mark not only the birthplace of humans in general but they are then also linked to the "births" of specific *kinds* of humans, namely, kings (see also Roskamp's [1998] analysis of the *Linezo de Jicalan* in Michoacán and for more general Mesoamerican coverage López Austin and López Luján [2000]). Afanador-Pujol states that the three lords in the narrative are in the cave having "met to discuss their plans to consolidate the region under their rule" (Afanador-Pujol 2015:58); in point of fact, no such discussion takes place in the cave. A dispute over the lordship and perhaps regional supremacy is present in only a latent sense (since the dispute is overtly over Pátzcuaro), but that is the *pretext* and instigating action of Curátame, which has served to unite Hiripan and Tangáxoan with Hiquíngaxe. As the title of the "chapter" of the narrative in the *Relación de Michoacán* indicates, the main reason for occupying the cave seems to be the act of doing penance.[35] This is likely related to the broadly employed trope of representing the ancestors of lords as impoverished but pious (it is their piety that effects their transformation) that can be found in many of the Central Mexican sources as well as the *Popol Vuh*.

The syntagmatic relations serve to demonstrate that the unity of these three is the origin point, marked by the cave, of the Uacúsecha as properly constituted—and, as we shall see shortly, ready to embark on the conquests of the region that bring the unified kingdom into being. Interestingly, the narrative notes that Hiquíngaxe packs up his arrows and sets off for the settlement of his cousins, thereby indicating his Chichimec character. This is an important feature, because it serves to differentiate him from the Islander companion of Hiripan and Tangáxoan who essentially serves as his predecessor, namely, Zapiuatame (who carries an oar in his encounter with Taríacuri's nephews). As just discussed, the most important distinction between Hiquíngaxe and Zapiuatame is the fact that Hiquíngaxe is a member of the Chichimec-cum-totality Uacúsecha, as indicated by those arrows. Once the three young lords are in the cave, however, the distinction between Hiripan and Tangáxoan on the one hand and Hiquíngaxe on the other is made clear. Hiquíngaxe *in this moment* takes on the identity of cultured or civilized Islander (and ultimately sacrificer), while his cousins play the role of uncivilized Chichimecs. In this way the locus of the cave and its role in constituting the nature of the interaction between the three lords mark the fact that the Uacúsecha, as now formulated, is ready to emerge into their destiny of encompassing Chichimecs and ruling a unified kingdom that they will establish.[36] The proper *kinds of humans* and their proper arrangement or alliance that will create the kingdom and the kingship at its heart have been created within the cave, and thus the cave serves to mark this as the arrangement

FIGURE 4.6. Line drawing of a part of illustration 17 from the Relación de Michoacán in which Taríacuri gives Hiripan, Tangáxoan, and Hiquíngaxe a piece of obsidian wrapped in a cloth bundle that represents or embodies the god Curicaueri. Reproduced with permission from School for Advanced Research Press from Haskell 2015.

that will be the founders of the kingdom, essentially foreshadowing this triumvirate's success. The symbolism would have almost assuredly been clear to indigenous subjects given the widespread association of caves with power and origins to indigenous cosmologies and ideological beliefs.[37]

In the next episode, Taríacuri gives the three young lords a share of the god Curicaueri as represented by an obsidian blade (figure 4.6) (the idol of Curicaueri appears to have been an obsidian core from which blades were periodically knapped; see Haskell 2015, also Darras 1998; Martínez González 2011). *The three lords build a large religious complex, including a temple, a house for the priests, an eagle house, a house for warriors, and an ark for the idol itself. They inform Taríacuri, who is enraged because such a complex requires sacrifices, which the young lords cannot yet attain. Taríacuri shoots an arrow at them but misses as they scuttle out his door. In order to redeem the young lords, Taríacuri sends a messenger to the lord of Pacandan and asks that lord to arrange for 100 of his men to be captured and then sacrificed for the new temple complex. After some mixed messages and confusion, during which a messenger delivers a message to Hiripan and Tangáxoan rather than Taríacuri and subsequently leaves the nephews with an oar on his shoulder, the end result is that sixty men from Pacandan are captured by the young lords. Forty are sacrificed in Pátzcuaro, and twenty are taken to Ihuatzio for the dedication of the new temple complex. The narrative adds that the young lords then also capture 100 men for the new temples on a foray in Itziparamuco.*

In this episode the Uacúsecha display their ability to placate the gods and avert disaster, as Taríacuri arranges for sacrificial victims to remedy the offense to the Uacúsecha god Curicaueri. The inclusion within the story of the foray into Itziparamuco is relevant in two regards. First, it establishes the focus on attaining sacrificial victims from Pacandan—in the structure of the narrative the first sacrifices at the new temple complex had to be Islanders.[38] This relation between the Uacúsecha Chichimecs and Islanders reverses the previous relation in which Zapiuatame and his Islander contingent joins Hiripan and Tangáxoan. Aside from the broad categorical similarities involved (Chichimec-Islander), the two episodes are further linked by the fact that in the misunderstandings and back-and-forth negotiations, a messenger from Pacandan leaves after talking to Hiripan and Tangáxoan with an oar on his shoulder, just as Zapiuatame had. The narrative has already reversed that Islander-Chichimec combination by introducing Hiquíngaxe and pairing him with the nephews, but that relation existed at a different scale than the current one as the present relation involves characters within the Uacúsecha. With regards to interactions at the intergroup level between Chichimecs and Islanders, now the narrative is not constructing a new combination but rather a new possible fate for Islanders in their interactions with Chichimecs. Whereas previously the Islanders led by Zapiuatame became allies of the Uacúsecha lords, here they are transformed into sacrificial victims. Together the two episodes demonstrate the possible grounds upon which the relationships between Uacúsecha Chichimec and Islanders can exist: either they can ally themselves with the Uacúsecha (as subordinates) or they can become sacrificial victims for the Uacúsecha god Curicaueri. The attainment of sacrificial victims from Itziparamuco in this episode also becomes significant in a subsequent episode.

The next episode begins with the murder of Curátame as ordered by Taríacuri. Just as Curátame was about to drink his ninth cup of wine, Tangáxoan struck him with a club

and then beat him to death. Hiripan, Tangáxoan, and Hiquíngaxe then make bon-
fires [a sign of military aggression] *atop nearby mountains and at Ihuatzio. Taríacuri*
summons the three lords, because he is afraid they have traveled too close to the bound-
aries of their enemies. In the course of the conversation, Taríacuri asks Hiripan and
Tangáxoan if they did not encounter the gods, because the mountaintops are high places
that the gods frequently come down to touch. After first denying it, Tangáxoan states
that he was visited by the goddess Xarátanga in a dream. Xarátanga asked him to
return her to Tzintzuntzan/Ihuatzio and to make her some new adornments, and tells
him that if he did this she would favor him and insure riches and women in his house.
Hiripan then confesses that Curicaueri visited him in a dream as well and promised to
make him successful.

Curátame's drunkenness leads Taríacuri to want to have him killed, and this drunkenness is his undoing in his final moments. Curátame's improper behavior is contrasted with the immediately subsequent actions of the three young lords; as a result
of their making bonfires, they are visited in dreams by the gods and promised riches
and success. In this way their actions are the reversal of their actions in the previous
episode, in which they build too large of a religious complex and require the efforts
of their uncle, Taríacuri. Here they take matters into their own hands by building
bonfires, and as a sign of war and thus the potential for the capture of sacrificial victims (present but arranged for by Taríacuri previously and absent but directly implicated by Hiripan and Tangáxoan here) that would feed the gods. Due to this action
they are rewarded with contact with the gods rather than threatened by a relationship to Curicaueri that is dangerously distant. Moreover, by appearing to Hiripan
and Tangáxoan in dreams and promising to favor them, worship of the two gods is
united within the Uacúsecha for the first time.[39] This reverses the arrangement that
has held for the entire narrative up to this point—the fact that the two gods favored
separate peoples/towns; Curicaueri was the god of the Uacúsecha while Xarátanga
was the principal goddess of the Islanders, or at least her chief priest (Zurumban)
was an Islander. In addition, by returning her to Tzintzuntzan/Ihuatzio, Tangáxoan
reverses her displacement from that place after her priests turned into snakes early
in the narrative. Following that omen, not only is Xarátanga moved to Tariaran, but
the Corínguaro category is created when the different groups of Chichimecs scatter
to many places. Therefore the death of Curátame, as the Corínguaro element within
the Uacúsecha, here reverses the birth of the Corínguaro people but at the intra-
Uacúsecha scale, conserving a pattern in this second half of the narrative.

The people of Itziparamuco ask their allies/lords in Corínguaro to assist them
against the Uacúsecha after they see the bonfires that the Uacúsecha have made. The

Corínguaros deny help, saying there is nothing to be afraid of. [The fact that only a short time earlier, the Uacúsecha had taken 100 people from Itziparamuco to be sacrificed at the new temple complex in Ihuatzio would seem to contradict the Corínguaros' interpretation of events.] *The people of Itziparamuco, seemingly confined to their fate, decide to get drunk and then abandon their town. Amidst the drunkenness a woman who is later identified to be the goddess Auicanime appears to the daughter-in-law of the lord of Itziparamuco and says she is hungry, and will trade an unusually large mole for some ears of corn. The daughter-in-law agrees and takes the mole and singes it to remove the skin and fur and then cooks it. She feeds it to her husband, who begins to inquire about their baby son, checks the crib, and discovers that his wife has cooked the baby. In his rage he kills her. The townspeople find out, and the lord tells what has happened. The lord then states that surely the gods are starving and that they have all lost their heads.* [The friar explains in his prologue (Alcalá 2000:329) that this expression means that they already envision their fate as sacrificial victims in which their heads will be cut off and placed on pikes, and the expression transposes this expected future into the present tense, as the event that is interpreted to inevitably seal their fate has already happened.]

The events of the current episode present an inverted appearance of the gods from the previous episode. As opposed to the goddess Xarátanga and Curicaueri favoring the members of the Uacúsecha, the goddess Auicanime causes a tragedy in Itziparamuco. The explanation given, that the gods must be starving, is likely a reference to the need to feed the gods with sacrificial victims; the people of Itziparamuco certainly see their own sacrifices to the gods as an eventuality. Moreover, given the aggressive stance taken by the Uacúsecha and the stated fears of the people of Itziparamuco, it is apparent that the Uacúsecha will be the sacrificers for the gods, in effect correcting the situation—the starving status of the gods—that has led to this tragedy.

In addition, this episode is linked paradigmatically to the episode in the first half of the narrative in which the priests of Xarátanga eat snake and become snakes themselves. In both episodes the animals in question are ground-dwelling animals. The narrative even explains that the snake and mole were both singed before cooking to allow for the removal of the skin. The inversion comes in two regards. The first is the role of the goddesses; Xarátanga hides the fish that her priests desire to catch and eat, thus forcing them to eat the snake, while Auicanime gives the daughter-in-law the mole/baby so that she might give it to her husband to eat. Second, in the episode of the first half of the narrative, the transformation from human to animal occurs after the humans eat the animal whereas in the present episode the transformation occurs prior to the eating, as somehow the baby is substituted for the mole.[40]

In the next episode Taríacuri asks the three young lords to take a fish to his brother-in-law, Lord Hivacha in Zirahuén. They do, and first Hivacha asks them if they should not talk of war and count the days [i.e., use the calendar to divine auspicious days for actions, as was widely practiced in the rest of Mesoamerica, including among the Mexica/Aztecs; Roskamp 2010a]. *Tangáxoan is insulted at the suggestion, saying that they are Chichimecs who only need to hold vigil to their god Curicaueri to prepare for war. Nevertheless they all sit, and Hivacha brings out food for his people but the Uacúsecha lords are not given any, nor are they given any blankets or shirts.*[41] *After this insulting breach of lordly etiquette, the Uacúsecha lords are enraged and leave. Hivacha's majordomo chases after them and apologizes for the actions of his master. He also gives them feathers so that they might remember him and spare his life and the lives of his family. Once they have returned to Ihuatzio, Hiripan climbs a tree, but a rotten limb breaks and he falls. Tangáxoan and Hiquíngaxe fear he is dead but together they revive him.*

This episode involves improper relations between in-laws (Hivacha is a son of Zurumban) and among lords. The *Relación de Michoacán* (Alcalá 2000:599–603) explains elsewhere that generosity was expected of lords; they were to give food and cloth goods to anyone who came calling on them. Furthermore, the gift proffered by the Uacúsecha lords is not reciprocated, as Hivacha gives food and cloth goods only to his own people. Hivacha's majordomo, in contrast to Hivacha, apologizes for his master's actions and gives the lords some feathers, asking that they spare his life. The gift of the fish is reciprocated within the episode, but only belatedly, only by a third party, and without the approval of Hivacha, who has no knowledge of the actions of his majordomo. In other words, Hivacha still remains culpable for his improper behavior.

In addition, the "death" of Hiripan and his subsequent revival by Tangáxoan and Hiquíngaxe is significant.[42] No longer are new characters added to the cast as it is presently constituted—nor, significantly, are any essential Uacúsecha members removed or killed off by the plot. The cast threatens to be changed with the apparent death of Hiripan, but Tangáxoan and Hiquíngaxe negate the apparent transformation, indicating that the trio is composed of the right elements in the right proportions as demonstrated in this act to conserve the Uacúsecha as it presently exists. It is also important that Tangáxoan and Hiquíngaxe, as Chichimec and Islander characters within the Uacúsecha, respectively, revive Hiripan together. Due to their combined dual nature (now in both social and cosmic terms, as Curicaueri and Xarátanga favor members of the Uacúsecha) and efforts, the Uacúsecha lineage and more specifically the trio of young lords (i.e., without the help of Taríacuri) has the ability to reproduce itself as a duality. This is an important point in light of the fact that in the second half of the narrative, none of the Uacúsecha members have entered into any marriages. The Uacúsecha's dual Chichimec/Islander identity was produced first by Taríacuri's own dual nature and finalized by Taríacuri's pivoting and acquisition of Zurumban's daughters as wives and the feminine wealth that they brought with them. The second half of the narrative has been an exercise in reproducing that duality in the succeeding generation and in the right proportions, with two Chichimec characters who are senior and one Islander character who is junior leaving no ambiguity over which category is the dominant one.[43] The collapse of the major action to the intra-Uacúsecha scale is also, as noted above, constituted in the interactions with Curátame, his role as the main precipitator in relation to his Uacúsecha kinsmen, and finally his death as the inversion of the birth of the Corínguaro category in the first half of the narrative.

The next episode is the denouement of the entire narrative, and centers around the Uacúsecha lords' desire to recompense the insult they received from Hivacha. Taríacuri asks if they desire to go to war against Hivacha, and the three lords answer that they do, and name some lords that will help them. Taríacuri tells them to wait a day while he arranges for more allies. After he has done so, he tells the three lords to meet him on a hill, where he explains to them that Tangáxoan will be lord in Tzintzuntzan, Hiripan will be lord in Ihuatzio, and Hiquíngaxe will be lord in Pátzcuaro. According to Taríacuri, together they will rule over the entire region. He then explains the plan of attack. The young lords agree, and they attack and conquer Zirahuén. Hivacha is among the first to die in the fighting, and many captives are taken to Pátzcuaro and sacrificed. Hivacha's majordomo and his family are spared, however, because he reminds the Uacúsecha lords of his gift of the feathers. The Uacúsecha lords and their allies go on to conquer many other towns. After the first round of conquests, which include Zacapu and Tariaran, Taríacuri dies and the three young lords bury him in Pátzcuaro. After a few days the young trio of lords then embark upon more conquests. Following these conquests, the Uacúsecha must pacify the people so that they will not run off with their wealth but will instead give their wealth to the Uacúsecha and work the land so that they might be prosperous. To that end, the Uacúsecha lords institute offices of local lords.

Here the failed exchange relation between Hivacha and the Uacúsecha lords is transformed (and syntagmatically reversed) into two separate, but paired, proper exchange relations through the military conquest of Zirahuén. Together, they sum up and unite the previous but syntagmatically disparate fates of members of the Islander category in the episodes involving Zapiuatame and his people allying themselves with the Uacúsecha and then the sacrifices from Pacandan following the construction of the temple complex at Ihuatzio. First, the Uacúsecha establish a proper exchange relation with the gods by sacrificing the captives from Zirahuén.

By providing sacrifices for the gods, they feed the gods, who are starving as was indicated in the episode involving the tragedy in Itziparamuco. Second, the exchange relation between conquered and conqueror is established with the realization of the exchange between Hivacha's majordomo and the Uacúsecha lords that was initiated in the previous episode. In short, the lives of the conquered are spared in exchange for their wealth (or their labor, as that which produces wealth). The two exchanges are thus simultaneously existing alternate paths for the rectification of impropriety, and at the same time involve the establishment of proper hierarchical relations of guarantors of the sociocosmic and moral order, allies and proper subjects, and improper subjects/wrongdoers.

The paired episodes involving Hivacha's insults and the conquest of Zirahuén and much of the region are, furthermore, reversals of the episodes that began the narrative involving Hireticatame's quarrel with his in-laws the Naranjans. In both sets of episodes, improper actions by in-laws are the events that instigate further action. In the initial episodes Hireticatame shoots and kills a brother-in-law only to be killed later, whereas now Hivacha (Taríacuri's brother-in-law) is killed and Hiripan's "death" as a death within the Uacúsecha preserves a measure of symmetry between the sets of episodes. In terms of the inversions involved between the two sets, by butchering the deer's skin, the Naranjans prevent Hireticatame (by way of his wife's labor) from making a blanket for the god Curicaueri, that is, fulfilling an exchange obligation with the god. In the present set of episodes, Hivacha's actions instigate the Uacúsecha wars of conquest and the offering of sacrifices to the gods in the fulfillment of an exchange obligation. In addition, the locale of the in-laws involved in the action are reversed: Naranjan sits north of Lake Pátzcuaro between Zacapu (the original home of the Chichimecs and Curicaueri) and the lake whereas Zirahuén sits south of Lake Pátzcuaro between the lake and Tariaran (home of Xarátanga and her priest Zurumban throughout much of the narrative). Finally, the initial separation between the Uacúsecha Chichimecs and the Islanders as well as the political balkanization of the region are reversed through the Uacúsecha wars of conquest. The Uacúsecha-led alliance that conquers the region also includes Islanders, and following the conquests it is stated that Islanders took charge of the side of the left hand (i.e., the south) and the Chichimecs took charge of the side of the right hand (i.e., the north).[44]

Therefore with the advent of a unified kingdom composed of Chichimecs and Islanders but dominated politically by the Uacúsecha (who have encompassed both the Chichimec and Islander categories, including on the cosmic plane of deities), the syntagmatic and paradigmatic structure of the second half of the narrative has completely reversed the syntagmatic and paradigmatic structure of the first half of the narrative. The ability of Taríacuri to pivot and become an Islander is at the same time the point at which the entire narrative pivots, or better, folds back upon itself. The visual metaphor of the narrative folding back upon itself is particularly apt, as the paradigmatically linked elements "line up" with one another while at the same time they are inverted mirror-images of each other (as images on a folded piece of paper will face one another and as depicted in figure 4.5).

CONCLUSION

As revealed in the analysis presented in this chapter, Taríacuri's own personal pivoting is the singular event around which the entire narrative pivots. The events and details of the second half conserve the same paradigmatic dimensions but invert the relations within those dimensions. This is established, moreover, not merely through the paradigmatic content, but also their syntagmatic arrangement. Events at the end of the narrative reproduce but invert the episodes at the beginning of the narrative, while episodes of the second half that are closer to the middle (Taríacuri's pivoting) are related to episodes of the first half that are similarly closer to that midpoint. Taríacuri thus is structurally merged with the plot of the story, which is obviously the establishment of the Tarascan state.

In addition to this overarching structure of pivoting and the paradigmatic inversion/reversal of the actions of the first half of the narrative by the action of the second half, there are the smaller level interepisodic reversals through which the plot not only takes shape but which motivates its progression. In this manner, and as presented above, each episode reverses in some way the content of its predecessor, as when Hireticatame first kills his in-laws near Naranjan in wild space only to subsequently be killed by them in the cultured space of his house. At slightly larger levels, groups of episodes bundled together form larger paradigms that are also reversals or transformations of one another. For example, the relationship between the Uacúsecha brothers Uapeani and Pauacume and the Xaráquaros that in its first instance is one based on intermarriage and alliance is transformed, with an intervening sequence of episodes involving the Corínguaros that serves as precipitator, into a sequence of episodes in which the relationship between the Uacúsecha and Islander category now personified by Zurumban is one in which Taríacuri's hunting prowess sets in motion his appropriation of Islander wealth and a relation between the two groups in which the Uacúsecha are superordinate and the Islanders are subordinate. It is that appropriation and Taríacuri's pivoting that produce the Uacúsecha as an encompassing and superior novel, dual term—the act and the symbolic hierarchy are essentially the same thing. In this way the entire narrative is a well-structured and hierarchically organized series of reversals and inversions that is consistent in its poietic construction and the devices it employs to generate the action, the surface content of the plot. In this way, Taríacuri's pivoting is the most hierarchically encompassing manifestation of the lower-order reversals of the narrative structure—pivoting is simply reversal writ large, a totalizing vision of reversal that fundamentally reworks the relation of the categories at play and what the content of the characters signifies (following Turner 1985; see also Dillon and Abercrombie 1988). Through this conservation, or the "invariance" of structure (Turner 1977; see chap. 3), the narrative brings into existence not only a logically ordered and thus meaningful account of the past, but it exemplifies the very conservation that the priest is advocating for Tarascan society as a whole, as represented as a microcosm within the narrative. At the center of that society is of course the kingship through which the society was united and formed and around which it should continue to revolve in the present according to the priest. The "Chichimecness" that defines the kingship and made possible its encompassment of the Islander category is also conserved throughout the narrative and in fact is the driving force behind its unfolding. This is also a point in advocacy of Don Francisco Taríacuri to assume the position of indigenous leadership and conserve Uacúsecha dominance. I address this and the larger issues regarding the narrative as an example of the indigenous practice of historicity in chapter 5.

NOTES

1. Long ago, Eduard Seler ([1905] 1993:19) recognized that in the narrative, the "Chichimecs" are "intentionally contrasted with the agrarian tribes of the surrounding villages and the fishing population of the lake." Seler believed, however, that the narrative was basically a fixed one that had been kept alive in Tzintzuntzan and interprets it in literalist rather than "poetic" or ideological terms.

2. Martínez González (2010:45) agrees for the need to consider these categories as "elementary categories" in the manner Sahlins advocates. However, Martínez González (2010:45) constructs his own list of associations for the two categories that he identifies, those categories being "locals" and "foreigners" (a transformation of my "Islanders" and "Chichimecs"). In this way, he identifies as "Chichimec" qualities: bringing firewood for their gods, practicing autosacrifice, offering cloth and food to visitors, not forgetting their injuries or insults they have suffered, passing the time making arrows; furthermore, they are chaste, do not drink (alcoholic beverages), are good hunters, and are young and poor. The "Islanders" can be understood to represent, roughly, the opposite of these characteristics (Martínez González 2010:47). My point is not to quibble with certain of these characteristics (my differences of opinion are evident in my analysis) but to reiterate that the point of the narrative is precisely the *transformation* of the categories or the appropriation of various aspects of one category by another. Sahlins (1985:102–103) puts it best: "the total scheme, in its true

mode of movement, is more than any given static set of contrasts. . . . A structural analysis would not be worthy of the name were it content with some extended table of parallel binary oppositions, or even with the proportions of the classic A:B::C:D from derived from such a table. . . . The logic of the whole lies in the generative development of the categories, by which alone may be motivated all static and partial expressions of it."

3. It should also be noted that I use Uacúsecha to refer to all members of the royal dynasty that have descended from the founder, Hireticatame, as is told in the priest's narrative. In other documents from Michoacán, members of the royal dynasty are depicted with eagles. For example, the Carapan corpus including the *Codex Plancarte* [1959; see also Roskamp 1997, 1998, 2003]) displays members of the royal family with an eagle and the words "Uacus / Trongo Real" ("Eagle Royal Trunk or Tree"), and there the founding progenitor is named not Hireticatame but rather Uacusticatame. This usage is consistent with, for example, Helen Pollard's (2003a) use of the term Uacúsecha as synonymous with members of the royal lineage and consequently members of the upper nobility (the strata from which kings in Tzintzuntzan would be selected as well as the heads of the other two "capitals" of Ihuatzio and Pátzcuaro) at the time of the Spaniards arrival in Michoacán. Alternatively, Afanador-Pujol (2010, 2015) prefers to use the designation "Uanacaze" when referring to the members of the highest elite, essentially the members of Tzintzicha Tangáxoan's lineage. These usages are not contradictory; Uacúsecha as used in the priest's narrative and elsewhere seems to refer to, as stated above, all members of the royal lineage that are descended from Hireticatame (including the royal families / houses of Ihuatzio and Pátzcuaro) while the most parsimonious interpretation of Uanacaze is that it refers specifically to the ruling family at Tzintzuntzan, that is, the family of Tzintzicha Tangáxoan. Eneani and Zacapu hireti seem to be the family names of the ruling families of Ihuatzio and Pátzcuaro respectively. Finally, it is interesting to note that Uanacaze, as the family name for the royal family of Tzintzuntzan and therefore the family most closely associated with the kingship, means *serrano* ("mountain-dweller") according to Martínez Baracs (2003:66; 2005:60–61). I believe that this fits with the general proposition of this book, that Tarascan ideological concepts of kingship can be broadly understood within a framework that Sahlins (1985) termed the "Stranger King," the particularities of which can then be examined using the priest's narrative and other sources (see also Haskell 2003, 2008a, 2012).

4. On deer and deer sacrifice in the *Relación de Michoacán* and in prehispanic Michoacán more generally, see also Brigitte Faugère (1998, 2008). Faugère links deer sacrifice to a beginning, and if her association between the deer and a regenerating sun about to rise at dawn is correct, it is interesting and symbolically significant that this first episode involves a quarrel over a deer and its sacrifice for the sake of the god Curicaueri. Martínez González (2010:49) has also commented on the likely significance of a deer being killed at the outset of a narrative that can, according to his work, be associated with solar movements and a metaphor of the day in certain ways. At nearly the opposite end of Mesoamerica spatially as

well as in the chronology of Mesoamerican civilization, the relatively recent and spectacular finds of the Pre-Classic murals at the Maya site of San Bartolo, in which the sacrifice of a deer seems to happen in a sacred time-space before our own and as a way for the world to begin, is particularly noteworthy imagery of the importance of deer in ritual and offerings (Saturno et al. 2005; Saturno 2009). Working somewhat within the "perspectivist"/"animist" debate between Viveiros de Castro (e.g., Viveiros de Castro 2012) and Descola (e.g., Descola 2005), Dimitri Karadimas (2012) notes that in many Amazonian and wider Amerindian ontologies deer are the material symbol of prey par excellence. To be prey is to be (someone's) deer, and to be a deer is to be (someone's) prey. Again, it is very likely significant that a narrative ostensibly about rulership constructed through conquest opens with a sequence of episodes concerning the fate of a deer, that is, prey, and, if the analogy can be stretched as it commonly is in the ontologies discussed in the works above, war captives / sacrificial victims.

5. It is possible to interpret the name Sicuirancha as paradigmatically associated with his role in the narrative. Seler ([1905] 1993:19) translates various versions of the root *sicui-* plus certain suffixes thusly: *sicui-ri* = "hide," *sicui-ni* = "take the hide off," *sicui-ra-ni* = "to have the hide taken off." The *Diccionario Grande* (1991) is not far off from these meanings, giving *sicuirani* = "quitarse la postilla, o caerse ella" (to take off a scab or have it fall off) and *sicuiri* = "cuero, correa" (leather, hide, a strap or band made of such material). The *Diccionario Grande* information confirms a sense of a covering or skin as the root and derivations thereof indicating a removal of that covering. I suggest that this is unlikely to be a coincidence in a pair of episodes in which the in-laws butcher the hide of a deer (against the expressed warnings of Hireticatame) and thus render it unusable. This violation is then improper in both a moral/legal sense as well as a functional/usable sense. In fact, a closer examination of the structure of the narrative and the strict order of presentation that would more closely follow Turner's (1969, 1977; see 3) detailed analyses would likely reveal that in the first episode Sicuirancha's birth, as a successful bringing of a character whose name means "taking the hide off" into the world, is both matched with Hireticatame's warning of the religious purpose of the hides of deer and sets up the contrast with the next episode in which the hide if unsuccessfully taken off and Sicuirancha's status as a child is reversed. As stated in 3, to analyze the entire narrative at the level of detail that might reveal such structural juxtapositions, on par with Turner's efforts, would be an enormous undertaking. I reiterate that what is presented in the body of this book is an analysis that is fine grained enough to perceive the underlying guiding principle of its construction, namely, the fact that the narrative revolves around Taríacuri and his pivoting.

6. Martínez González (2011:89–90) objects that the union is not as incompatible as I suppose, because after all it produces Sicuirancha, who is able to carry on the responsibilities of his father's lineage (namely, care for Curicaueri). In this regard Martínez González is, in my opinion, interpreting the sequence in the narrative too closely within the paradigm of López Austin's "Hombre-Dios," in focusing on the "fitness" of Sicuirancha to take the place

of his father as a result of his heritage and its presumed "purity." I deal with this issue in the main text as well as later in footnote 12. The robbery of Uatzoriquare as a victory over the Naranjans is also given as evidence for the positive effects of the union. It is interesting to note that, as Espejel Carbajal (2008:2:264) points out, Hireticatame remarks that Uatzoriquare is a "liberal" god and that he "gives food to the people" (Alcalá 2000:346). In such a role, I suggest the god essentially reproduces the role of lords in general and in particular Uacúsecha lords, who are supposed to act on behalf of Curicaueri, to give food and cloth to the people and to those that come calling on them (Alcalá 2000:327, 602). It is possible to interpret therefore an implicit competition between Curicaueri and Uatzoriquare over who will, in effect, care and provide for the people—which deity will reign. By "stealing" Uatzoriquare and by placing the idol in the ark of Curicaueri, Uatzoriquare is in effect encompassed within or as part of Curicaueri's ark and identity (See Haskell 2015 on the importance of the ark as a physical body for the idol). This interpretation would seem to fit well with part of the stated goal of the Naranjans in the first place, as the Naranjans recognize Curicaueri as a powerful god and Naranjans propose the marriage so that *they* could appropriate *him*—the sequence of action therefore serves to invert the goals of the Naranjans' scheming. Additionally, in this analysis the union does drive the action forward (namely, toward Lake Pátzcuaro), and the union does possess similarities and differences with other unions, as we will see. If the union were of a *perfect* match, Sicuirancha would play a more direct role in forming a unified kingdom (as we will see he does not do so), and furthermore the deaths on both sides, and the outright refusal of the Naranjans to adhere to Hireticatame's one request that causes those deaths, demonstrate the incompatibility of the union.

7. In an endnote, Martínez González (2010:65) comments on this place, and includes a statement from the chronicler Alonso de la Rea (1996:68–82) concerning its perfect roundness and the supposed location of a temple on its slopes. Martínez González suggests that the allusion in this naming of place is related to "fertility" but does not recognize its importance as a microcosm that itself foreshadows the importance of the relation between mountainous places and peoples and water-based associations of lower elevations and the fertility that water brings.

8. María Isabel Terán Elizondo (2000:288) characterizes the event of the separation of the Chichimec factions as "between history and myth" and states that the whole episode is "narratively structured within the schema of "transgression" and "punishment." While this is true, the specific elements of the episode reveal its relation to what has preceded it. It should further be noted that this episode in its essential elements is not unique to Mesoamerica, or in world literatures (e.g., de Heusch 1982) concerning the founding of sacred kingship systems. Gillespie (1989:216–219) discusses the paradigmatic links between Aztec documents that describe drunkenness as the root of the downfall of the various narrative concretizations of Ce Acatl Topiltzin Quetzalcoatl and the dispersal of groups of people, the latter being specifically relevant to the present episode. Drinking too much pulque

results in both instances in a disjunction; in some of the stories (as every instantiation of the highly problematic story of Ce Acatl Topiltzin Quetzalcoatl is at least slightly different as the story developed over time, as Gillespie shows) the first king and founder of the kingship is separated from that office due to some impermissible act caused by drinking too much. In another story the Huaxtec leader of a bygone era became drunk, and as a result he and his people had to leave and travel to the Gulf Coast. Following soon after their departure, the people of all nations split up (the story is from Sahagún 1950–1982:10:193–194). These disjunctive stories of transgression and separation can be furthermore linked to not merely moralizing concerning the negative consequences of inebriation, but to the place of alcoholic—fermented—beverages in symbolic classification systems. Derived from natural foods (maguey juice in the case of pulque), they are rendered cultural through the labor and appropriation of humans, only to be allowed to ferment ("rot") in order to achieve their intoxicating effects, which are furthermore taken advantage of and rendered cultural once again through the establishment of cultural rules and norms concerning proper consumption of such beverages. The drink itself, in other words, violates stable classificatory boundaries by being both natural and cultural, rotten and yet still desirable (interpreting alcoholic beverages in this manner draws on, among others, Lévi-Strauss 1969:294).

9. Fernández (2011:151–166) teases out the multiple metonymic meanings of bringing firewood to the temples, among which are it is an act of dedication to the gods and thus piety; it is an act of paying tribute, and firewood often stands for all manner of tribute; it is the enactment of political subjugation to another authority such as a lord. Additionally, Felipe Castro Gutiérrez and Cristina Monzón García (2008:35–36) discuss how the idiom of gathering community supplies, and in particular firewood, is an expression of the integration of community, superior-subordinate relationships, and the power that defines the latter and thereby helps constitute the former.

10. Martínez González (2010:51; see also Michelet 1989:111) describe this exchange as somewhat "ritualized" but also note the hierarchization of the food exchanged as constituted by the Islander's remark that the cooked game the Chichimecs give them is "real food." Martínez González contends that in the social hierarchy of the kingdom and its manifestation in everyday consumption, game is consumed by the nobility while, especially as confirmed by the *Relación de Ajuchitlan* (in *Relaciones Geográficas del Siglo XVI* [1958]), fish is the food of the commoners.

11. Stone (2004:99) recognizes the importance of the relations established with the Islanders in this episode. In her analysis of the illustration of this meeting and its placement of elements, she comes to the conclusion that "the manner in which the fisherman is positioned, with the base of his canoe touching the mainland and the tip of his paddle the island shore, converts him into a metaphorical bridge for the Uacúsecha lords who, through him—or, more precisely, his absent daughter—gain access to the domain of the original inhabitants, the locus of female power and the cult of the moon goddess Xarátanga." Fernández

(2011:53) writes that with these interactions, the Chichimec lords reanimate the intergroup relations that had been interrupted by the omen of the priests and priestesses of Xarátanga turning into snakes. This is true, but fails to appreciate what is different this time around, in terms of the different goods being exchanged.

12. In my opinion, numerous authors (Krippner-Martinez 2001; Martínez González 2010, 2011; Stone 2004:135) misunderstand this relationship between the Uacúsecha Chichimecs and the Islanders, mostly due to an overemphasis on maintaining a "purity" of "lineage" that ultimately derives from Alfredo López Austin's (1973) formulation of the Hombre-Dios or "man-god" ideology of Mesoamerican rulership. In that formulation, lineage serves to bind descendants to the god, just as their ancestors had been. I contend that the priest's narrative is not about lineage "purity" at all but uses the metaphor of kinship and elementary categories to construct individual Uacúsecha characters and the Uacúsecha as a whole as a dually composed entity. Insisting that Taríacuri's "Islander" heritage on his mother's side is a "disadvantage" (Stone 2004:135; although on the same page she sees his dual nature as being related to his "success as a visionary and a prophet") also is embedded within a restrictive vision of the relation between any two entities such that they must be mutually exclusive and antagonistic. As I discuss here and in my earlier work, the whole point of the narrative follows a different logic of the relation between two entities, that of encompassment as defined by Dumont (1980; see Haskell 2008a, 2008b, also 2012).

13. While many Mesoamerican scholars and particularly ethnohistorians focus on the Toltecs of the past, "toltec" was used, perhaps primarily, to indicate great or highly skilled craftspersons in the present (Sahagún 1950–1982:10:165). When speaking of the "ancient" Toltecs, the *Florentine Codex* (Sahagún 1950–1982:10:165) states that "[t]here [was] no real word for their name. Their name is taken from—it comes from—their manner of life, their works," that is, their knowledge and skill in all manner of crafts.

14. Afanador-Pujol (2015:131) states that the relationship between the Uacúsecha and the Islanders is "never one of equals." This ambiguous statement seems to indicate that it is the Uacúsecha who gain the upper hand, exemplified by Taríacuri's "rejection" of the amoral qualities of his relatives, including the Islanders (Afanador-Pujol 2015:132). In point of fact, the relationship is not one of equality as Afanador-Pujol states, but in this first half of the narrative the Uacúsecha are at the mercy of the Islanders (the Islanders later dispossess the Uacúsecha of the markers of status that they had bestowed on them and they arrange for the deaths of Pauacume and Uapeani, for example). The measures of revenge that the Uacúsecha manage to exact upon the Islanders and other characters are clearly outside the norms of "civilized" behavior, as those groups see it (especially in the example of the sacrifice and fate of Naca that is to come), with the possible exception of the isolation of the Xaráquaros by Taríacuri's bonfires if warfare was an accepted pattern of prestate culture, as it appears to have been.

15. Tweezers, which are an ornament worn around the neck and which are depicted in the illustrations of members of the priesthood in the *Relación de Michoacán*, are only known

to have been made of metal. Metalworking and smelting was considered in Michoacán and Mesoamerica more generally to be associated with (sacred) knowledge (e.g., Hosler 1994), and so again this fits with the characterization of the Islanders as wise and skillful artisans.

16. The "Eagle House" as represented in the *Relación de Michoacán* is a structure that is used for holding vigil and has militaristic associations; it is likely homologous to the better known Mexica/Aztec House of the Eagle Warriors (Berdan and Anawalt 1992:143, 222; Sahagún 1950–1982: 8:43), which has been excavated archaeologically and analyzed to confirm ritual activities through chemical analysis (Barba et al. 1996). Another "Eagle House" was excavated at the Early Postclassic site of Tula, Hidalgo (Healan 2011).

17. In fact, Taríacuri never becomes "king" in the sense of the ruler of a unified polity. He dies during the initial conquests that establish a unified polity that were led by his nephews Hiripan and Tangáxoan and his son Hiquíngaxe. Perhaps this is a prophecy that is directed toward or related to Don Francisco Taríacuri's proposed succession to his father's throne.

18. Stone (2004:96) similarly recognizes the importance of the dual quality of Taríacuri: "To narrate the life of Taríacuri is also to tell the story of the symbolic union of the male and female lines of descent, the former related to the cult of the sun and fire god Curicaueri, associated with the nomadic Uacúsecha or Eagle Chichimecs; the latter, to the cult of the moon and water goddess Xarátanga, associated with the Hurendetiecha, the original inhabitants or sedentary fisherfolk of Lake Pátzcuaro." Similarly, Martínez González (2010) agrees with the importance of a symbolic union between opposed categories, but in his study he generalizes the contrast between "Islanders" and "Chichimecs" to a contrast between "locals" and "foreigners." I do not necessarily agree with this slight transformation in the interpretation of the priest's narrative specifically, as it overlooks the symbolic importance of water and fertility. In his study, however, it is important to recognize that the distinction between locals and outsiders is a widespread organizing principle in Michoacán through a long timespan, and therefore is likely played out in a number of permutations and contexts.

19. If Hans Roskamp's (2010a:81) suggestion that the priests of Xarátanga were Nahua speakers and thus Naca's name is a shortened version of the Nahua word *nacatl*, meaning "meat," turns out to be true, then clearly this would be an instance of naming this character after his fate; I doubt it would have been such a coincidence that a person named as such would turn out to be consumed as meat.

20. This aside or explanatory tangent was possibly included in the narrative at the behest of the friar-compiler who acted as questioner/compiler in the production of the document. It is unlikely that any indigenous members of the audience would have been unaware that the penalty for taking food from the gods' granaries would have been enslavement, particularly due to the fact that the narrative was itself told at the yearly festival at which criminals were punished. Regardless, the role of Taríacuri as the lordly one is essential, and the meaning of his suggestion would have been known by the audience either with or without the inclusion of such a tangent in any prehispanic version of the narrative.

21. Castro Gutiérrez (2015:136) uses particularly the current episode involving the marriage to the Corínguaro princess and the desire to take Curicaueri from the Uacúsecha as justification for believing that "inheritance was determined through the female line." While Chanhori, the lord of Corínguaro does indeed say, "It will please the gods for you to bear a child by him, and thus we shall take away Curicaueri, who is a very great god" (Alcalá 2000:402–404; translation is by Castro Gutiérrez), I interpret this as not evidence of a set-in-stone rule of matrilineal inheritance but rather as a process of making a claim on the god, a claim that could be utilized to overwhelm the claim of male inheritance within the Uacúsecha. If a house model (see discussion in note 6 in Chapter 1) can be applied to the Tarascan elites in particular, then we need to understand kinship at a fundamental level and marriage relations and the task of kin-group reproduction within that larger umbrella of kinship as more of a transactional phenomenon and not a prescriptive phenomenon. In other words, kinship, including inheritance, is worked out by making claims and then supporting those claims over and above the claims of the other kin groups—houses—involved. This viewpoint is reinforced by the fact that in every other instance of inheritance, the lordship and the deity Curicaueri that guarantees it passes from father to son. At times the deity himself must step in to preserve this relationship (in precisely a transactional/performative move), but it is preserved. See also Pollard (1993b:59).

22. Afanador-Pujol (2015:119–120) notes that stories of Uacúsecha (/Chichimec) hunting prowess would have found a certain amount of respect and admiration among the Spanish and European royals and upper nobility. While this might be true, the symbolism of the hunting prowess, the selection of the specific prey, and the symbolism of that prey in particular as it relates to symbolic death and regeneration, appears entirely indigenous.

23. The similarity to the Mexica and wider Basin of Mexico stories in which a marriage between the Mexica and an ancient place and its ruling dynasty (in that case the Culhua of Culhuacan) that is also related to fertility and agrarian productivity is worth noting (see Gillespie 1989).

24. Hummingbirds are in Mesoamerican symbolism also associated with warfare, as hummingbirds are aggressive and fearless in their dealings with other birds. The Mexica patron deity, Huitzilopochtli, has the root for hummingbird in his name and is often depicted in a hummingbird guise or costume. Tzintzuntzan is named after this diminutive bird but because of this further symbolic association with warfare, the city name could be understood not merely as "Place of the Hummingbird" but also "Place of War."

25. Afanador-Pujol (2010) argues that the family tree was composed visually to make essentially the same argument that I am making for the oratory of the priest's narrative—that Don Francisco, or one of Tzintzicha Tangáxoan's two sons at least, is the legitimate heir to what remains of their father's kingdom.

26. The two nephews apparently share a mother but perhaps have different fathers (Zetaco and Aramen), causing Fernández (2011:62), for example, to rhetorically ask, "one [mother]

for the two?" In point of fact the *Relación de Michoacán* is remarkably casual about stating the parentage of certain characters, in particular the mothers of certain characters. In the case of Zetaco and Aramen and their relation to Hiripan and Tangáxoan, the name of the wife/mother or her town of origin is never stated, and the specific paternity of the nephews is never given—they are simply the offspring of Zetaco and Aramen. I believe this should be taken as an indication that they should be viewed simply as paradigmatic replacements of their fathers as Chichimec characters within the Uacúsecha.

27. This counterclockwise path re-creates the pattern of the initial counterclockwise migration of Uapeani and Pauacume following the omen of the snake. The counterclockwise direction is typical in many Mesoamerican narratives and representations, as it mimics the counterclockwise path of the sun as it rises in the east, sets in the west, and travels through the underworld to be reborn in the east the next day. Stories of the Mexicas' arrival in the Basin of Mexico follow this general pattern, first arriving in the western area of the basin and then engaging in relations with Culhuacan of the south.

28. In relation to the importance of comportment concerning Taríacuri's characterization as belonging to one category or the other, Martínez González (2010:45, 2011:89) notes that "the case of Taríacuri is particularly notable: while in his chaste and warrior-like youth, Taríacuri is called Chichimec, while as he grows old and begins to be surrounded by women [the narrative] begins to record his Islander origin." This statement recognizes the important temporal distinction/transformation in Taríacuri's "career" but fails to account for the logic behind the transformation as well as the initiation in that transformation as something that occurs almost immediately after his "pivoting" as just analyzed and not in some ambiguous process of growing old.

29. Stone (2004:120) observes that Curátame "is repeatedly encoded in the story told by the Petámuti as the paradigm of those with a penchant for debauchery." This is of course due to his Corínguaro side, the debauchery of whom has already been made evident in the narrative. It should also be noted that later on the narrative heavily implies through reported speech of Curátame that he is indeed lord in Pátzcuaro. It is unclear whether Curátame becomes lord of Pátzcuaro again at a later date and this is not related to the audience, or if the inclusion of the lesser noble is not in reality what happened. It is possible in the later episodes in which Curátame is clearly acting as lord in Pátzcuaro that the priest narrating the story simply forgot the detail about this lesser noble being made lord in Pátzcuaro. I choose to interpret that detail of the lesser noble becoming lord in this episode as solely necessary to construct Taríacuri's Islander nature at this point in the narrative sequence and its structure and make clear that it was not related to an issue of generational succession. Once the juxtaposition of this nameless lesser lord with both Curátame and Taríacuri had served this purpose, it was no longer necessary as a part of the overall story.

30. Stone (2004:126) agrees with the characterization of Hiripan and Tangáxoan to come: "Unlike Taríacuri, who embodies both masculine and feminine attributes . . . , Hiripan and

Tangáxoan are consistently encoded in the narrative as pure Chichimecs, archetypal hunters who owe their allegiance exclusively to the male solar god Curícaueri." This is for the most part true but ignores the fact that Tangáxoan is visited by the goddess Xarátanga in a dream and restores her temples and worship in Tzintzuntzan, as we soon see.

31. Technically, Hiripan and Tangáxoan establish themselves with their new Islander cohorts at a place called Queretapuzicuyo or Quereta paranzicuyo. Espejel Carbajal's (2008) notes for reading the *Relación de Michoacán* indicate that this place is in or near Tzintzuntzan. She also notes that Quereta paranzicuyo, Quereta ychanzicuyo, and Querétaro are likely the same place. In a footnote in the 1956 version, Tudela (Alcalá 1956:119) states that this name means "place of the ball court," and the only ball court in the Pátzcuaro Basin was located at Ihuatzio.

32. Regarding the alliance between Zapiuatame and his Islander followers and the Uacúsecha characters Hiripan and Tangáxoan, Afanador-Pujol (2015:88, also 92, 132–135) states that the importance of this episode (and possibly the reason for its inclusion in the story) is to link Don Pedro with the Uanacaze but in a subordinate fashion. The narrative therefore gives a historical justification for Don Pedro's affiliation with the kings in general and Tzintzicha Tangáxoan in particular and paints him and his kin group in a favorable light. It also unavoidably does so by making clear that Don Pedro and the Islanders in general might have been allied but were explicitly not equals—they were at the mercy of the Uacúsecha and placed themselves under the protection of the Uacúsecha (and Taríacuri). The episode, in the reading here and in Afanador-Pujol's (2015) work, establishes an allied but subordinate relationship between the two groups, in which the other possibility for the Islanders was sacrifice, as we will see in the rest of the narrative. Afanador-Pujol's work makes these linked fates in the illustrations of the *Relación de Michoacán* evident, as in the image of the burial of the king in which the role of Islanders as servants and sacrificial victims are merged or simultaneously represented in the artwork (Afanador-Pujol 2015:chap. 6). With regard to methodological concerns discussed in the previous chapter in particular, Afanador-Pujol (2015:133–134) seems to claim, by linking the two episodes together, that this alliance between the Uacúsecha and Zapiuatame's Islanders sets the stage, so to speak, for the Uacúsecha conquests of the many towns of the kingdom due to the gods favoring Uacúsecha members and appearing to Hiripan and Tangáxoan. Such an argument essentially ignores the intervening episodes that are discussed shortly, the most important of which is the pairing of Hiquíngaxe as sacrificer with Hiripan and Tangáxoan. It is this addition to the marauding "Chichimecs" Hiripan and Tangáxoan that produces the Uacúsecha as a complete, because complementary, sociocosmic totality on its own and without nonlineage members. Such a misinterpretation is the result of exactly the kind of "context free" approaches to the material that begs for an appreciation of the syntagmatic development and ordered transformations of the narrative.

33. In his multiple volumes on Amerindian myths, Levi-Strauss recognized the essential role of cooking as a cultural transformation, indeed *the* cultural transformation, that enables

for proper socialization and ultimately other cultural institutions to take place (the first volume of his *Mythologiques* is, after all, entitled *The Raw and the Cooked*; Lévi-Strauss 1969). Similarly, one of Turner's publications that has formed the methodological basis for the present study is his analysis of the Kayapó narrative of the origins of cooking fire, in which food cooked by a jaguar is essential for the main character to regain his strength following a period of isolation, defeat his jaguar surrogate mother, become a man, and steal cooking fire to show to his village so that they, too, might steal cooking fire and transform themselves into properly cultured beings (Turner 1985).

34. Martínez González (2010:45, 2011:88) discusses comportment as partially constituting the categorical affiliation of the characters, and claims that Hiquíngaxe is a "Chichimec" in spite of the fact that he is not solely dedicated to hunting and leads a fairly sedentary lifestyle. This is true to some extent due to his place as a member of the Uacúsecha, but as my analysis and his contextual difference in contrast to his cousins demonstrate, the point is that he is contrasted with his cousins and is an Islander character within the Uacúsecha.

35. The chapter is entitled: "Como Curátame envió por Hirepan y Tangáxoan que hacían penitencia en una cueva y de la respuesta que dieron."

36. On a related note, it is perhaps significant that in the genealogical tree in the *Relación de Michoacán*, this triumvirate of lords is the first in the sequence of lords to be shown with bows and arrows, indicating kingship (Afanador-Pujol 2015:147; and I would add kingship as manifested through and symbolized by warfare and the possession of the means of warfare/conquest). This triumvirate certainly is the group that, according to the narrative, establishes a unified kingdom, making them the first kings of such a kingdom. It is also the case, however, that the other Uacúsecha lords shown in the tree are depicted not with bows and arrows but with the instruments/weapons of their death, which, in Afanador-Pujol's (2015:144) own discussion, likens them to Christian saints who were commonly depicted with the weapons by which they became martyrs for their faith. The two desires, to show the earlier members of the lineage as martyrs and then subsequent members as powerful lords, are not at cross-purposes or mutually exclusive because the triumvirate was after all the group to unify the area, and they did not die by violent means. Taríacuri himself, additionally, was the architect of the kingdom as the main advisor of his son and nephews but was never king himself according to the narrative. Therefore his depiction without a bow and arrow nor accompanied by the instrument of his death reinforces the account in the narrative and the fact that the triumvirate were indeed the first to be kings of a unified kingdom, but also indicates Taríacuri's ambiguous and anomalous character.

37. Afanador-Pujol (2015:124) also notes that the poverty of this scene in the cave was perhaps intended to mimic European notions of hermetic religious figures and their own poverty and penance. While this is plausible and I do not doubt that it could have been received as such, this seems an unnecessary position given the widespread importance of caves in Mesoamerican cosmologies, though perhaps the priest-narrator emphasized this happy

coincidence between the two religious traditions. I believe, however, that the episode's great est import focused on the fact that the Uacúsecha was now, as evidenced by the episodes to come, properly constituted. It should also be noted that this episode fits nicely with the work of Nigel Davies (1987), who suggested that the Mexica histories paint a "rags to riches" story that emphasizes the struggle and piety of the Mexica protagonists. Such meaning is partially constitutive of the meaning of passages such as those in the Mexica histories and here in the *Relación de Michoacán*, but it does not approach the fuller understanding of the symbolism of beginnings and new eras, and especially not *why* a new beginning happens when it does and why it is undertaken by specific kinds of characters, as discussed here.

38. Again, Afanador-Pujol's (2015:chap. 6) discussion of the role of Islander sacrificial vic tims in the burial rite of the Cazonci is relevant here as an "ethnographic" parallel to the past as constructed in this episode, as in footnote 32.

39. Fernández (2011:72) perceives the importance of the dreams and messages of Tangáxoan and remarks that "in this symbolic moment of their history, the Uacúsecha have in their favor and with 'legitimacy,' the two most prominent gods of the Michoacano Olympus."

40. Both moles and snakes, as animals that burrow into the earth and thus come into con tact with the underworld, are associated with that underworld and with death. Brand (1951) reports that small figurines of gophers and similar burrowing mammals were placed at the entrance of caves on the mountain Zirate, the tallest mountain of the area.

41. Paul Kirchhoff (1956) misunderstands the affront committed by Hivacha when he interprets the schism between Hivacha and Hiripan and Tangáxoan to be based on his suggestion that they "count the days," thereby exhibiting fundamental cultural differences between the two groups that cannot be resolved. While this suggestion does anger the two Uacúsecha lords, they go on to sit with Hivacha. The real instigation for their abrupt depar ture is indicated by the fact that it comes only after they are not given anything to eat or any of the blankets.

42. Afanador-Pujol (2015:58, 135) notes, concerning this particular event of this episode that in other Mesoamerican codices a broken/breaking tree is used to symbolized a bro ken alliance (her example, cited in an endnote [200n92], is the Central Mexican *Tira de la Peregrinación*, a pictorial history of the migration of the Mexica). I take no issue with this symbolism and reading, as certainly the event could drive home Hivacha's impropriety as a pretext for war; my point is that its syntagmatic juxtapositioning with what comes directly before and after, and how it compares to events in the first half of the narrative is significant as well.

43. This reading of the working out of the right proportions of the categories in play within the Uacúsecha differs from that of James Krippner-Martinez (2001:59), who sees the transi tion from Taríacuri to Hiripan and Tangáxoan as one in which "lineage" is emphasized as something to be preserved, and Taríacuri carefully insures that his nephews will carry on his lineages duty to the god Curicaueri. Krippner-Martinez thus reads of the surface contents of

the narrative—Taríacuri's instructions to his nephews to be pious and serve Curicaueri—but does not see the deeper structural arrangements that dictate that the nephews also must be paired with some member of the Islander category.

44. Not coincidentally, the southern portion of the kingdom is lower in elevation, hotter, and produces different commodities than the northern area, key among them cotton, copper, and tropical birds. The northern half is firmly part of the Mexican neo-Volcanic axis and central Altiplano, possessing a more temperate climate (Pollard 1982, 1993b).

5

Tarascan Historicity in and through the Priest's Speech in the *Relación de Michoacán*

INTRODUCTION: THE PRIEST, THE TWO TARÍACURIS, AND THE FUTURE

Having presented the analysis of the priest's narrative in detail, the structure and meaning of the narrative and the full meaning of Taríacuri can be examined. The manner in which the priest constructs Taríacuri is indicative of indigenous ideologies of the nature of the kingship, and furthermore relates that kingship to Don Francisco Taríacuri as its heir through that symbolic and agentic construction and the shared name that links them. A key aspect of the narrative revealed by the analysis is its structured transformations, organized according to both syntagmatic and paradigmatic principles. Each episode constitutes a reversal of some aspect of the previous episode, and these reversals and the development of the paradigmatic framework of the narrative build larger-order units of narrative in syntagmatic terms. Those larger-order units then work to reverse and invert the paradigmatic arrangements (e.g., Chichimec supremacy/seniority over Islander subordination, or an intergroup conflict is transformed into an intragroup conflict) in the unfolding action. At the largest unit of narrative structure, the narrative pivots at its central episode, Taríacuri's pivoting from Chichimec to Islander and the appropriation of Islander wealth and legitimacy within the Chichimec category. Taríacuri's pivoting is also the pivot of the narrative, as the second half of the narrative is a paradigmatic reversal that is ordered in syntagmatic fashion—much like in the use of chiasmus (see chapter 6)—of the first half of the narrative, before Taríacuri's pivoting. It is this orderliness that has not garnered scholarly attention but which, I argue, was the foundation of the narrative's

DOI: 10.5876/9781607327493.c005

rhetorical power. By organizing the past and relating it to the present in this way, future events that are an extension of this past and the present are rendered not only appropriate but self-evident. Because of the poiesis at work in the priest's effort and the narrative he produced, the succession of Don Francisco Taríacuri to whatever could be reconstituted of the kingship (and the kingdom that it symbolized and embodied) that was not only created by, but *personified by*, Taríacuri took on the characteristics of not mere random historical process but rather revealed truth.

In addition, this constructed nature of the narrative and the other information contained within the *Relación de Michoacán* reveals some important insights into how historicity was practiced in the Tarascan state by the nobility and the priesthood. This active practice was informed by certain ideological constructs of how the past and its relationship to the present should be understood within Tarascan culture. Most often such constructs are cast as either "mythic" or "historical." Within the debates over how the narrative should be interpreted, however, the analysis of the preceding chapter suggests that this dichotomy is insufficient for any detailed understanding of how the past was actually engaged and constructed. Rather than attempting to fit the priest's narrative into this dichotomous framework, I suggest that instead we should investigate each particular concretization as an instantiation within a specific sociohistorical context with a unique meaning that weaves together potentially differing perspectives on the past, different temporalities, and different notions of agency within those temporalities, in order to produce that meaning. This places the focus not simply on the past as an isolable entity, but on how the past is actively engaged to construct and convey theories of agency and change, which are thereby used to inform and guide the course of action in the present.

TARÍACURI AS A NOVEL AND CENTRAL AGENCY

Recall from chapters 1 and 4 that Taríacuri is the production of the interaction of the Chichimec and Islander "elementary categories." Those elementary categories essentially represent the totality of the cosmos through their complementary opposition; they represent the celestial and the terrestrial, masculinity and femininity, hunting versus agriculture and aquaculture, and *celeritas* and *gravitas*. Taríacuri is both dually composed of these complementary categories, due to his parentage, and also works to further integrate and embody the combination of their power. That combination and embodiment is, as I have discussed here and elsewhere (Haskell 2008a, 2008b, 2012), a relation of encompassment in which Taríacuri's nature and the nature of Chichimecness attain a novel power because they have the power to represent not merely the original symbolic content of the Chichimec category but now also the symbolic content of the Islander category.

In addition, the relationship of Taríacuri's composition in "lineage" terms is related to his subsequent ability to produce himself and the Chichimec category as an encompassing power. The former not only appears as a foreshadowing of Taríacuri's greatness (as in the wording of the Priest' Speech itself; Alcalá 2000:355, 357) but also in the form of the latter. It is that lineage-based, dual Chichimec-Islander that constitutes Taríacuri's autopoietic nature as a self-producing production. From a certain perspective, perhaps it could be said with the benefit of hindsight, the Chichimec-cum-Uacúsecha characters that precede Taríacuri and especially his father, Pauacume, are guided to the initial production of Taríacuri. The quarrel with the Naranjans, for example, must take place in order to send the Chichimecs on their way toward the Pátzcuaro Basin. The same can be said for the omen of Xarátanga's priests and priestesses causing the Chichimecs to leave Uayameo. Of course, this is exactly what is happening—from the narrator's (the priest's) point of view, which ultimately through the act of narration and concretization in the mind's ear of the audience, becomes the audience's point of view by the end of the narrative. Taríacuri, as a special kind of character and agent, is able to play both Chichimec and Islander roles; in relation to his cousins Zetaco and Aramen, he can play the staid and stately figure that avoids the pitfalls of wild and lascivious behavior, while in relation to Zurumban he can play the prototypical Chichimec. Note, furthermore, that it is the former "Islander" qualities along with the other details of Taríacuri's early career that enable and place Taríacuri in the position to interact with Zurumban as the Chichimec, as he eventually shoots the hummingbird and wins (as opposed to being granted) the daughters and wealth symbolic of the Islander category. This dual nature is necessary for the Chichimec quality of Taríacuri to shine through as *the* paradigmatic category associated with change, transformation, and thus autopoietic construction.

The centrality of Taríacuri's shooting of the hummingbird and wider interaction with Zurumban is constructed by the syntagmatic arrangement of the halves of the narrative that precede and follow this episode. Taríacuri is a central figure in both paradigmatic and syntagmatic terms. In the second half of the narrative, Taríacuri essentially reproduces his own duality, simply as various sociocosmic levels. His own singular duality is reproduced by the trio of young lords, his nephews Hiripan and Tangáxoan, and his second son, Hiquíngaxe. Along the way Taríacuri himself must direct this composition even as he deals with the fallout from his first son, Curátame (who is partly Corínguaro), and educate the three young lords so that they will be successful as the central, encompassing term of the Uacúsecha that constitutes the kingdom and the kingship. In other words the inward-focused production of Taríacuri as a fully dually composed character is turned inside out and expanded upon and transformed into the dually composed Uacúsecha, the kingdom that they conquered, and the self-producing (as autopoiesis and through conquest) kingship and encompassing relations of subordinate lords as secondary copies of the king and therefore transformed Chichimecs (Haskell 2008b). As I discussed in chapter 1, the effect of the merger of Taríacuri's personal pivoting with the syntagmatic-paradigmatic pivoting is to merge Taríacuri with a generalized principle of agency and transformation. He is, in essence, the supreme agent. This quality is brought to light in stark contrast with the category that, as opposed to Taríacuri's dual nature, constitutes essentially a null category—the Corínguaros. Taríacuri is both Chichimec and Islander, whereas the Corínguaros are neither Chichimec nor Islander; he is all agency, and their efforts are doomed to fail. Not only does this contrast help us understand the priest's goal and the logical production of categories and their qualities, but it ties these qualities and the logical and repeated sequences of action-to-outcome as an explanatory exercise in the nature and facticity (from the point of view that the priest is advocating) of political legitimacy.

CORÍNGUAROS AS ANTIAGENTS

Taríacuri's (and the Uacúsecha's) foil throughout the narrative, the Corínguaros, further demonstrate how agency is manifested in the narrative and provide a counterpoint to Taríacuri's manifestation as all agency and as the kingship. In contrast to Taríacuri's pervasive and transformative agency, characters from Corínguaro are cast as bumbling, and even blasphemous, characters whose own self-interested actions only end up setting the stage for the successful actions of the Uacúsecha. They are antiagents and therefore antikings. The status of the Corínguaros as antikings is revealed both in the content of the category and the repetitive paradigmatic units of sequentially organized events within the narrative. The two modes in which their status as antiagents is revealed are, of course, logically interrelated. It is the content of the category that causes their ineptitude in action (even as, narrationally speaking, the ineptitude in action reveals the content of the category). The Corínguaros are, as even Kirchhoff (1956) recognized, "ex-Chichimecas." Having settled and taken up agriculture, they are no longer true Chichimecs. They are also not the autochthonous fisher/agriculturalists that the Xaráquaros and followers of Xarátanga are. They are, in effect, a category with no meaningful content according to the dimensional or paradigmatic structure of the narrative, neither Islander nor Chichimec.

Their origin is, moreover, directly followed by the relations between the Uacúsecha and the Islanders of Xaráquaro that engenders Taríacuri and constitutes the Uacúsecha as a synthesis of the Chichimec and Islander categories. Out of the initial opposition of Islander and Chichimec, then, the narrative creates first an entity that is neither (the Corínguaros) followed by a category that is both, balancing the one with the other.[1] Later in the narrative and following Taríacuri's pivoting (not coincidentally), the emptiness of the Corínguaro category is again confirmed when they demand that Taríacuri hand over riches. Taríacuri gives them arrows with varicolored tips instead, which the Corínguaros break. As noted in chapter 4, they fail to appropriate either the riches, which are linked via syntagmatic contiguity with the riches Taríacuri had gained along with the daughters of Zurumban (Islander priest of Xarátanga) through his second marriage, or the hunting prowess of the Chichimecs as indexically signified by the arrows.

Throughout the narrative Corínguaro characters serve as precipitators (Turner 1977:156–158). That is to say, they make things happen that otherwise would not. In every instance, at either the smaller intraepisodic level or the larger interepisodic level, what their actions cause is the conjunction, increasingly in the right proportions, of the Chichimec and Islander elements, first between the larger categories and then in the Uacúsecha itself by the "Corínguaro" character within the Uacúsecha (Curátame). In this way the Corínguaros unwittingly serve to facilitate the Uacúsecha's rise to power rather than their own; their actions do not benefit themselves and thus they do not act with agency. This characterization is neatly summarized in one tellingly disastrous sequence in which Taríacuri gives a Corínguaro lord a piece of the god Curicaueri and that lord establishes himself in the town of Etúcuaro (Hetoquaro), to the east of the Pátzcuaro Basin (Alcalá 2000:460–463). The lord enjoys much success but in time stops bringing sacrificial victims back to Pátzcuaro to be sacrificed to the god. After a while the polity that he builds suffers catastrophes and is abandoned. Therefore we see that even when given the perfect chance to be favored by the god Curicaueri, and thereby to act agentically and perhaps even be kings, the Corínguaros manage to fail in spectacular fashion. Their lack of agency, and their relation opposite Taríacuri, only serves to highlight the drastically uneven construction of agency and the ability of certain agencies to drive the historical and temporal process in the narrative.

THE PRIEST'S SPEECH AND THE FUTURE OF THE TARASCAN KINGDOM: THE PRESENT TARÍACURI AND THE PAST TARÍACURI

In her discussion of the priest's narrative, Stone (2004:112–114) emphatically posits that the priest's narrative is not merely about the past but is in fact a call to action, directed at the lords and populace of the kingdom. As part of this call to action, it offers a hint of a vision of who and what will be successful in such a confusing and chaotic colonial situation. Stone focuses on the morality, piety, and work ethic that pervades the priest's narrative (particularly as they are displayed by Chichimec characters; the same is also noted by Afanador-Pujol 2015), but she also recognizes that the priest understood the importance of a cultural broker. By this Stone means someone who could appropriate the essential aspects of both indigenous and Spanish society, act as a mystic seer and shrewd tactician, and ultimately reconstitute the Tarascan kingdom in one form or another within the situation that the Tarascan elite in particular found themselves. The priest was arguing, in short, that the indigenous lords and people needed another Taríacuri, someone who could lead them and someone they in turn should follow. Stone (2004:148–149) suggests that Bishop Vasco de Quiroga was being singled out in the priest's narrative through allusions, grounded in the resignification of place through actions of the narrative, to some of Quiroga's actions, most notably the founding of the *pueblo-hospital* Santa Fe de la Laguna (see chapter 1). The suggestion of Quiroga is not without merit, but upon closer examination of the evidence presented by Stone that the priest is advocating for Quiroga as the future leader of the people of Michoacán is lacking, and the debate over the identity of this new Taríacuri is instructive of the contrast between Stone's method and the method I have employed in my analysis of the priest's narrative.

Quiroga has, since his death if not earlier during his life and work in Michoacán, taken on almost mythological status himself. He came to be referred to by the indigenous peoples of Michoacán as Tata Vasco, or "Father Vasco," a name that reflects their understanding of his relationship with them (and not simply his position within the Catholic Church), as he was and is "extolled as the creator of the new social order" (Pollard 1993b:3; he is remembered, among other things, for assigning craft specialties to the various towns of the Pátzcuaro Basin as part of his pueblo-hospital program). However, examining the specific evidence within the *Relación de Michoacán* and the arguments put forth by Stone reveals that the indigenous priest who crafted his narrative as it is recorded in the *Relación de Michoacán* was not likely to have been referring to Quiroga. First, Stone states that Quiroga was seen by indigenous peoples as a civilizing force. This is *perhaps* likely, even at the time of the production of the *Relación de Michoacán*, as he and Spanish colonial policies that he likely represented and personified brought peoples down from the mountains and remote areas and settled them in towns. Quiroga also established the pueblo-hospital at Santa Fe and the earlier pueblo-hospital in Mexico City (see Martínez Baracs 2005; Stone 2004:149–151; Warren 1963 on the pueblo-hospitals; see also Bernardino Verástique (2000) for a discussion of Quiroga's career). However, the evidence Stone cites on Quiroga as a civilizing personality is testimony by an elder in Pátzcuaro, who might have favored Quiroga's move to Pátzcuaro and who therefore sought to cast Quiroga in the best and most positive and effective light (Stone 2004:149). Furthermore, there is the issue of the mythology surrounding his discovery of a spring at the site upon which his great cathedral in Pátzcuaro would be built

(León [1903] 1984:209–210). This miracle occurred at, and the cathedral would be built at, the site of the indigenous temples of Pátzcuaro, which had been foretold to them in their peregrination as related in the priest's narrative (see chapter 4). The "metaphorical" "mapping of place" that Stone (2004) identifies within the narrative thereby constructs a link between the foretold foundation of the ancient temples of Pátzcuaro and the miraculous, divine, and possibly preordained placement by Quiroga of his cathedral on that same spot.

Stone (2004:151) states that she is "not suggesting there was a consensus among all the indigenous peoples of the region at the time of the compilation of [the *Relación de Michoacán*] regarding Quiroga's role in the fulfillment of prophecy." She does, however, see a direct relation between Taríacuri, that is, the Taríacuri crafted within the priest's narrative, and Quiroga (Stone 2004:152). Part of her advocacy for viewing Quiroga as the indigenously perceived "new Taríacuri" is the framing of Santa Fe within the *Relación de Michoacán*. Within the priest's narrative, Quiroga's hospital at Santa Fe is prominent in the episodes said to have occurred at Uayameo early in the narrative. Santa Fe is explicitly mentioned on four straight folios when discussing places or directions of movement. It is impossible to know whether these references, in which the indigenous place is named, and then an aside is inserted noting the relationship to Santa Fe, were spoken by the native priest or were interjected by the friar-compiler. It is worth noting that it was Don Pedro Cuinierángari who had sold the land for the hospital to Quiroga (apparently out of his wife's dowry; see chapter 1), but that the Tzintzuntzan nobility objected to the construction and Quiroga had to bring *tecos* (i.e., Nahua speakers) in to build it (Warren 1963). It is also impossible to know if these references to Santa Fe were included by the priest simply as part of the hybrid colonial-indigenous transformations underway in order to facilitate communication. In this respect, the references could have been included in order to more concretely ground the action for the benefit of the audience, particularly the one known individual who was to receive the document, Viceroy Mendoza. Afanador-Pujol (2014, 2015) has argued convincingly that the indigenous artists who painted the landscape scenes of the document employed a novel landscape perspective technique that they imagined would make place more legible to Mendoza. The narrative references linking the current landscape to the past landscape could have served analogous purposes, and both could have been sly but important strategies to make their case in the Infante lawsuit (see chapter 1) more successful simply by offering more readily comprehended testimony and representations. Nonetheless, it is possible that by mentioning Santa Fe and by the very fact that Uayameo plays a role as an important place as the first settlement of the Uacúsecha within the Pátzcuaro Basin, a paradigmatic link is constructed between the Uacúsecha and Quiroga, as the hospital was Quiroga's first construction project upon his arrival in the Pátzcuaro Basin and the place was the location of the first Uacúsecha settlement within the basin.

Furthermore, in the part of the narrative that tells of when the foretold foundations of the temples at Pátzcuaro were discovered, Quiroga is present, though not by name: "'This is the place our gods tell us is called Zacapu Hamúcutin Pátzcuaro. Let us see what it is like.' So they went along following the water . . . [Thus] did they arrive at the spring [the one in] the patio of the lord bishop that flows farther up, to where the large bell is, in a little hill that is formed there" (Stone 2004:137; translation and insertions in brackets are by her, of Alcalá 2000:363–364).[2] In addition, the *Relación de Michoacán* (Alcalá 2000:655) relates a tale in which a poor old woman claimed that the gods had told her that they would rise up from Ihuatzio (which was the capital at the time that this woman is said to have had her vision) and go to Tzintzuntzan (which became the capital during the reign of Tzitzispandáquare; Alcalá 2000:542; see also Monzón, Roskamp, and Warren 2009; Haskell 2013), and then they would rise up again and "'go to our first dwelling place called Uayameo' where Santa Fe is now constructed" (translation is that of Stone 2004:147; the voice is that of the gods). This tale, however, is contained within the third part of the *Relación de Michoacán*, the "ethnographic" section, and specifically within a chapter dedicated to prophecies pertaining to the coming of the Spaniards and the events of the conquest (and thus *not* within the priest's narrative). As such, it is possible that this tale was related by Don Pedro Cuinierángari, the main informant for this third section. Don Pedro was opportunistic in his relations with the Spaniards. It is therefore curious that Stone presents such information from this section, which is outside of any narrative or testimony of the priest, within the chapter that is ostensibly an analysis of the Priest's Speech of the *Relación de Michoacán*. In her search for metaphorical linkages, she ignores the possibility or even likelihood that the narrating priest and other indigenous informants, including Don Pedro, would have differing opinions of the future of relations between indigenous society and the encroaching Spanish colonial order. Therefore I believe it is entirely likely that certain passages in the *Relación de Michoacán* could indeed advocate for Quiroga as a new leader, but that the Priest' Speech does not. To conflate the priest's narrative with other sections of the document is to ignore the very important and related view of the document as a palimpsest that brings together many competing visions of the future and the very multiplicity of viewpoints from which historicity was envisioned and practiced, both of which Stone advocates elsewhere in her work (Stone 2004:21, 151).

There is another way in which Quiroga is possibly referenced by the Priest's Speech, as illuminated by the analysis of that narrative presented here. The story of the Uacúsecha is essentially a story of foreigners appropriating autochthonous wealth and certain customs and ultimately establishing their own rule over the inhabitants of the land. The paradigmatic linkages between the Uacúsecha Conquest and the Spanish Conquest that was underway at the time of the production of the *Relación de Michoacán*, of invading outsiders conquering indigenous peoples and appropriating their wealth while forging integrated but hierarchical relations, are not difficult to see. Part of Quiroga's success was founded on his foresight to include the indigenous peoples in certain aspects of decision making (Krippner-Martinez 2001:71–106, 151–179). This is evident in the use of Don Pedro and certain unknown indigenous individuals in selection of Uayameo as the location of the pueblo-hospital of Santa Fe (see above; Stone 2004:149–151). Therefore Quiroga appears to be just as keen at managing to appropriate some aspects of indigenous culture and history as Taríacuri and the Uacúsecha had been, according to the priest. I address, and argue against, such an interpretation of the structure of the priest's narrative below.

The hypothesis that Quiroga was the focal point in the *Relación de Michoacán* and particularly the priest's narrative is elsewhere contradicted by Stone's own remarks concerning other aspects of the priest's narrative. She states in other passages that the priest is "giving voice to the patron god of the Uacúsecha, [and that] his words read as an indictment of their allies and subject peoples" (Stone 2004:129). The gods are said to lament their fate through the priest in the opening and closing remarks, the "address" and "summation" as I have referred to them (Alcalá 2000:340, 525–530; see also Stone 2004:122), that bracket his narrative of the past in the second part of the *Relación de Michoacán*. In the "address" by the priest to his audience before the narrative begins, Curicaueri plays an essential role, as the priest states that they have all assembled to hear the god's grievances against them and because he bemoans his fate (Alcalá 2000:340; see also Stone 2004:123). Regarding the "summation," it is emphasized that the priest speaks in one instance in the first person as the god Curicaueri (Stone 2004:116; the passage in the *Relación de Michoacán* is from Alcalá 2000:529). Finally, Stone states that the priest's grievances (and thus Curicaueri's grievances) are that the people of Michoacán have not fulfilled their promises and duty to support the king and remain faithful to the old ways: "In this context the act of remaining faithful to tradition is tantamount to personal allegiance to the cazonci [the king; see chapter 2], which is incompatible with loyalty to any rival lord, including, presumably, the Spanish crown and its representatives, such as Christian missionaries and colonial administrators" (Stone 2004:129).

With this passage, it becomes obvious that the priest cannot be advocating for Quiroga to be the one to lead the indigenous peoples, as he fits into that category perfectly as a representative of a rival lord and, it should be emphasized, a rival god. Furthermore, Quiroga cannot be the new Taríacuri in any strict sense because he is not a dually composed figure. He might have "left his mark upon the landscape" just as Taríacuri had (Stone 2004:113), and he might have even been viewed as an "organizer and visionary" as Stone (2004:113) characterizes him, but he was not a Taríacuri in the manner that Taríacuri is constructed in the narrative. He was a Spaniard and unapologetic representative of the Spanish king and the Christian god, even if he did allow some indigenous peoples to influence the manner in which the processes whereby both the Spanish king and his deity would be imposed.

SPANIARDS AS A DEVELOPMENT OF THE CORÍNGUARO CATEGORY

The syntagmatic and paradigmatic structure of the narrative itself yields further insights into how the priest himself, and perhaps other indigenous peoples, viewed the various factions of Spaniards and their relation to indigenous society. The indigenous nobility were, according to the text of the *Relación de Michoacán*, having a hard time deciding what exactly to make of the Spaniards. I propose that the indigenous elites, most notably the indigenous priests, saw the Spaniards as a transformation of the "antiagents" that the Corínguaros defined. In the priest's narrative, the category of antiagent continuously moves eastward. Their initial creation moved them from the Pátzcuaro Basin east to Corínguaro. Chapa, son of the original Corínguaro lord, established himself in Etúcuaro, south of the Cuitzeo Basin and fairly close to the eastern limits of Michoacán, as has been mentioned in chapter 4. It is even possible that the Tarascans viewed their great rivals, the Mexica/Aztecs, as a kind of transformation of antiagents. Although they considered their rivals powerful, the Tarascans derided them for only offering songs (rather than firewood) to their gods (Alcalá 2000:325).[3] Therefore from the Tarascan point of view, the Mexica lacked certain cultural and moral characteristics that retarded their efforts in war.

The Spaniards, having come from even farther east than the Mexica, were the final transformation of antiagents, though in their attempts to understand the Spaniards, the Tarascans cast them as a kind of anti-antiagent.[4] The Spaniards were clearly not impotent, as the Corínguaros were. In explaining the Spaniards' power, however, the Tarascans denied their humanity, normatively defined according to indigenous concepts, in a couple of ways. As related in the third section of the *Relación de Michoacán*, when the Spaniards kept demanding the king's gold and other treasure, Tzintzicha Tangáxoan pondered to his lesser lords why they wanted so much gold, and then answered his own question by saying that "those gods must eat it, that is why they want so much" (Alcalá 2000:674).[5] This might appear an amusing commentary on the greediness of the Spaniards and the search for a rational explanation of why they required so much cast in human terms. It directly juxtaposes, however, the Spaniards and their "divinity" with the indigenous words and conceptualizations of the precious metals at issue and their place within the cosmos. The *Relación de Michoacán* (Alcalá 2000:522) explains that gold was, perhaps metaphorically, understood to be the "excrement of the sun" and silver similarly was "excrement of the moon." Particularly if the sun and moon were understood as transformations of divinities as the more extensive Central Mexican sources suggest (e.g., the Leyenda de los Soles in the *Codex Chimalpopoca* [Bierhorst 1992]; see also Hunt [1977] and López Austin [1993] on the importance of metaphor and transformations in Mesoamerican cosmology), Tzintzicha Tangáxoan's suggestion that the Spaniards ate, rather than excreted, the precious metals was an ironic inversion of their understanding of the cosmos and the role of divinity within the world.

In a later passage, the *Relación de Michoacán* states that following the arrival of the Spaniards in Michoacán and the passage of enough time to at least be familiar with some aspects of the Spaniards' daily routine, the Tarascan elite saw the Spaniards in some way as gods and great men, at least partly because they did not get drunk and eat the same kinds of food as them (Alcalá 2000:678). They were at great pains to figure out the friars, however, who wanted neither silver nor gold, dressed so poorly, and did not take wives or have relations with women. The indigenous priests supposed that the friars were walking dead and that at night they took off their habits, became skeletons, and went to the underworld where their women lived. Moreover, they thought that the friars had never been children, that they did not have mothers, and that they had been born with their habits on (Alcalá 2000:679). These anecdotal speculations together suggest that in the eyes of the indigenous Tarascans, the Spaniards were the opposite of antiagents, that is, they were indeed powerful beings, but they were powerful because in some way they were opposed to humanity as they understood it.

In order to counter such powerful but asocial and by some formulation nonhuman beings, a new leader was needed, one who could appropriate those powers of the Spaniards, while being able to divine the way forward according to some mix of Spanish, traditional, and adapted or novel beliefs. Particularly from the viewpoint of the priest who narrated this story, what was needed was a new visionary who did more than simply living in both worlds but could weave the two worlds into a single world in which the indigenes (and the indigenous gods) would still play a favorable, if not dominant, role. I have already indicated that as a result of my analysis, Don Francisco Taríacuri is implicated as the one to reconstitute the kingdom, or at least to weave a way forward that incorporated the old (prehispanic) order and the increasingly imposed Spanish colonial order in a way that would be the most advantageous possible for indigenous society and the Uacúsecha within it. Don Francisco Taríacuri is the choice of the priest to succeed his father and restore the position of supreme indigenous authority to the Uacúsecha lineage not merely because of his lineage—his Chichimecness—but because of the meaning of his lineage and heritage as it was constructed as a powerful, autopoietic, and encompassing nature. The restoration of Don Francisco Taríacuri would of course follow prehispanic succession patterns as they are presented in multiple places in the *Relación de Michoacán* and therefore reestablish a measure of indigenous continuity in the face of Spanish incursions and usurpation of their ultimate authority.[6] There is more to the matter than mere intralineage succession (as Krippner-Martinez [2001] and Martínez González [2010] would have it), however. As constructed in the narrative, while Taríacuri is a dually composed character, it is his Chichimecness that remains superior to his Islander nature. His Chichimecness is what allows his paradigmatic content of his character to incorporate and subordinate, in other words encompass (Haskell 2008a, b), the Islander nature. Recall that it is his shooting of the hummingbird, a demonstration of hunting prowess par excellence, through which he acquires the wealth and Islander women that signify the autochthonous wealth of the land. By the same token, Don Francisco Taríacuri, through his lineage and innate "Chichimecness," should have had this capacity to incorporate and subordinate the paradigmatic content of the new social category in play in the Early Colonial era, the Spaniards. According to indigenous conceptualizations, his lineage and identity perhaps established him as having comparable divine force to that of the Spaniards, particularly if he was understood to have appropriated some of the Spaniards' perceived powers thanks to his time spent as a youth in the court of the viceroy and his Spanish education.

Don Francisco's Chichimecness was precisely what was needed in contrast to, or following, the governorship of the "Islander" Don Pedro Cuinierángari. Don Pedro is explicitly stated to be descended from the Islanders (including Zapiuatame) allied with the Uacúsecha at the initiation of their war against Hivacha (Alcalá 2000:512). In addition, Stone (2004:157) points out that he is depicted in the frontispiece of the *Relación de Michoacán* with a fish on his hat, which she explains could be related to the fact that he was from Michoacán (the name is Nahuatl for "place of the owners of fish" [Martínez Baracs 1997:161–162]) or his fishermen heritage as an Islander. She also notes (Stone 2004:157) that it is perhaps no coincidence that Don Pedro took as his Christian name that of the apostle Peter, who was a fisherman himself. The fact that Don Pedro Cuinierángari was an "Islander" is what made him unfit for the governorship in the eyes of the priest, and likely other members of the indigenous nobility; as a categorical Islander, Don Pedro did not possess the autopoietic quality, that transformative capacity for self-production and therefore the production of society that was an ideological feature of the indigenous kingship, that the Uacúsecha Chichimecs possessed. This lack in Don Pedro's character and its importance as a feature of Uacúsecha Chichimec identity extends a fortiori to the ability to transform and actively resynthesize society when such a transformation was called for. While Don Pedro's career as an opportunist and schemer has been commented upon as from certain perspectives—he always sought to cast himself in the best possible light and forge a path of upward social mobility for himself—the fact remains that from a certain (Uacúsecha and traditional) point of view Don Pedro's career was made possible first by Tzintzicha Tangáxoan's actions in recementing the apparently foundational alliance with the Islanders through marriage and subsequently Cortés's selection of Don Pedro as an indigenous leader, which was itself only possible because Tzintzicha Tangáxoan's sons, including Don Francisco Taríacuri, had not yet reached maturity.

By the same token, Quiroga must not have possessed this nature either, and the possibility that he and the Spaniards' paradigmatic content would incorporate and subordinate the indigenous world, which was already apparent to the priest and other indigenous persons, was precisely what needed to be reversed. Therefore the point suggested above that Quiroga did share some paradigmatic quality with Taríacuri and the Uacúsecha in general, that is, their foreign origins, can now be addressed and the case for Quiroga as the new Taríacuri can be fully refuted. While Quiroga was thus a foreigner and had some limited inclination toward allowing the indigenous Tarascans some room to integrate traditional places and meanings with aspects of the new Catholic faith and administrative apparatus of Spanish colonialism, he was not a foreigner who possessed any sort of "Chichimecness" defined as an autopoietic quality. He fell far short of Don Francisco Taríacuri's ability to appropriate the culture of the colonial other: there are no indications that he learned Purhépecha, for example. Only the real Chichimecs possessed this autopoietic and encompassing quality, and the construction of the legendary Taríacuri as the embodiment or singular instantiation of that quality and of its more generalized attribution to the Uacúsecha as a whole indicates that it was this quality that was defined as the sine qua non that should characterize true indigenous leadership. Indeed, with the presence of the Spaniards and their imposition of colonial authority, it was this autopoietic quality that would lead to or was evidence of the wider ability to forge the new society that would somehow blend the two worlds together and take the place of the old kingdom. In the Early Colonial period it was now the autochthonous figure, rendered so in relation to the incoming colonizers, who would appropriate the powers of the foreigners and possess the vision necessary for their combination, as opposed to the foreigner taking on this role in the prehispanic period as constructed within the priest's narrative. Thus the arrival of the Spaniards and their imposition of a new colonial order can be read as triggering a new era that was itself a transformation of the reversal operation that is ubiquitous in the priest's narrative and in particular Taríacuri's pivoting as a reversal on a grand scale; here the understanding of an advocated course is a transformation in which the quality, that is, Chichimecness, that is fundamentally transformative is conserved while the statuses of the groups in relation to one another (autochthons versus newcomers) is reversed.

In this way, the essential role of Chichimecness as that paradigmatic character-istic that encompasses its contrary, which is not only present in the narrative but is its constitutive and organizing principle, is preserved. Only the surface variations, the roles of one social category as "foreigner" and the other as "prior inhabitant," have been reversed. In coordination with the fact that Quiroga was not, in any significant way, a dually composed figure who had assimilated and appropriated "the other" on par with Don Francisco Taríacuri, as well as the evidence discussed above that the priest explicitly takes on the view and voice of the indigenous gods (particularly Curicaueri), the view that Quiroga was being constructed as the new Taríacuri and thus new leader of the indigenous peoples of Michoacán at least in the rhetoric of the priest and his narrative, must be rejected.

The point of this discussion is not only to settle whom the priest was referring to as the future leader of the indigenous peoples of Michoacán. Rather, the point highlights a larger theoretical one concerning how historicity was practiced by the Tarascan priest (and to some extent other indigenous Tarascans) and to both advocate and pursue a significant methodological shift in how we interpret the actions of agents as they relate the past to the present. I have critiqued Stone's work because it is the clearest and most valuable exposition to date of how the priest's narrative related to the context in which that priest found himself.[7] Through her specific method, with its emphasis on only the metaphorical/paradigmatic resig-nification of places and people and which is essentially context free, I believe she has shortchanged the priest and the manner in which he produced a novel con-cretization of the past and its inherent relation to the present and future. Stone's work draws on literary criticism as well as the work of López Austin (1993) to explore the "remythification" (Stone 2004:4) of the events and places of the past through their relation to the events of the present. The result is to analyze each paradigmatic relationship, established through spatial relationships, in isolation from the other relations that comprised and made the narrative as a whole mean-ingful. With the approach used in the present work, we see that not only have places or events been "remythified" and symbolically adjusted to include links to the present but, rather, that *the entire narrative* is remythified or as I would pre-fer re-constructed, re-produced, and re-concretized by the priest. This process of novel concretization took place not only as it was formulated by the priest but also as it met with an audience that could follow the syntagmatic juxtapositioning of paradigmatic elements within the narrative itself and therefore to understand the underlying structure of the narrative. The entire narrative and its sequence is an act of poiesis, and the result of that poiesis is an entirely new paradigm manifested by the total structure of the narrative, the paradigm of "Taríacuri." The construction of the past Taríacuri is obviously related to the reality of a new Taríacuri in the present and the priest's perception that he should lead indigenous society forward in the colonial encounter; the constructed centrality of Taríacuri is linked writ large to the present and to Don Francisco Taríacuri's advocated role as leader of indigenous society in addition to the myriad smaller ways the narrative links itself to the present through "remapping" place and the individual moralizing fables of which it is comprised. With the present analysis and discussion, it becomes evident that particularly the indigenous priesthood held on to the notion that indigenous society could still be reconstituted by indigenes; that they envisioned the power struggles between themselves and the Spaniards as one potentially still in flux and in which they could ultimately gain the upper hand; that they could appropriate aspects of the foreign culture for their own benefit and not, as colonialist history would have them, to actively participate in their own assimilation and subordination; and finally that *their* indigenous understanding of the cosmos and its temporalities (including human history) was still the place to look for answers in addressing all of the above. Whether such perceptions extended beyond the priesthood is questionable, as discussed in chapter 1. The nobility, including Don Francisco Taríacuri himself, seem to have sought the best possible status for themselves without violent or overt confrontation by this point. Perhaps the most that can be said is that Don Francisco Taríacuri and other nobles were happy to have the Priest's Speech in their favor but they simultaneously "mapped out" the best possible avenues for themselves in multiple potential futures.

The foregoing discussion indicates that the issue is one of finding and using a method that allows for the analysis of a single narrative in its internal relations constructed as an interconnected whole, but also in relation to the singular context in which it is produced. The method employed here enables the isolation of a single narrative and thus voice from the palimpsest that was the larger document and therefore makes possible the analytical comparison with other voices. This analytical process recognizes commonly developing symbols and frameworks of understanding within the "structure of the conjuncture" (Sahlins 1985:xiv) but maintains at least the possibility of their separate usage and deployment by individual actors. This in turn makes possible a greater appreciation of the variations in the practice of historicity that might be due to differences in knowledge, agency, class status, gender, and historical contingency.

Finally, the approach of Stone and others also renders analytically impossible an appreciation of the degree to which the priest's narrative (or any single narrative)

exhibits not simply a poetic understanding based on the "truth" evident in interpreting metaphorical relations and transformations (Stone 2004:115), but the more
active and powerful poiesis—construction and organization *as revelation*—evident
in the narrative through the syntagmatic and paradigmatic analysis. As discussed
in chapter 3, this aspect of poiesis, of constructing order out of seemingly random
surface variations, makes the narrative as a whole take on a rhetorical power as it is
interpreted to be revealed truth. It is a constructed order that needs nothing beyond
itself precisely because it is a self-constructing and totalizing order that processually
constructs and incorporates the entire cosmos, including the inescapable fact of the
Spanish presence and their efforts to impose their own order. This process of construction as revelation is important; through the poiesis of the narrative *as a process*
(i.e., in time), the narrative and narrator behind it continually introduce variation
in the form of new events, but in a manner in which they only serve to further
demonstrate the contiguity of the underlying principles of order that maintains
itself through and in the face of this new variation. This is the poiesis of authority
that I discussed in chapter 3, in which part of the rhetorical force, and thereby its
meaning, lies in the nature of the message *as a narrative*. To the extent that narrative subsumes within itself the "real world," comes to stand for it, and even exert a
certain power over it (see chapter 3), this poiesis is more than simply an ordering or
construction of the narrative itself but potentially remakes the world. By re-creating
the world in narrative, that narrative produces and reveals the truth of the narrative
world to the real world, the world of direct experience and action. Thus the real
world comes to possess a new, constructed reality, and part of that reality in this
case is the very potential of being reproduced even as it incorporates novelty, so
that its order and the operations that have produced that order can be actively witnessed, comprehended, and consequently reproduced. Of course, all of this is from
the point of view of the priest, but in formulating his narrative it was these intranar-
rative capabilities to frame and affect the world outside his narrative, with which it
shared several contiguities, that would take root and compel through social action
the bending of the real future to the outcome he was casting as inevitable. In order
for an outcome to be possible, it helps to first cast that outcome as proper, logical,
and perhaps even inevitable or preordained.

PREHISPANIC AND COLONIAL TARASCAN HISTORICITY IN PRACTICE

I want to be clear at the outset that I eschew categorizing the narrative as either
myth or history, largely because I find the dichotomy, either as defined by Western
historiography or anthropologists (see chapter 3), constraining and obstructive
at times. I hope that my suggestions as to why the *Relación de Michoacán* is so

concerned with plausible human events, rather than what seem to contemporary Western eyes to be supernatural or outlandish occurrences, does reveal something about the relation between the desire of the Tarascan elites to legitimate the state apparatus and the likely constraints on their ability to do so. Even within such constraints, however, these supposedly human events nonetheless carry the import of sociocosmic categories and are constructed in a way that the relations of the human categories manifest an indigenous logic of how such sociocosmic categories should relate to one another. I also refrain from developing a neologism for what I consider the Priest's Speech to be; I am only offering here the manner in which both "myth" and "history" are mutually misleading.

The definitions and discussions of myth and history in chapter 3 are problematic when applied to the priest's narrative in the *Relación de Michoacán*. That narrative does reveal that a "historical mode of consciousness" existed in some form among the indigenous peoples of Michoacán, though, as I discuss, it cannot properly be called a "history," as understood within a Western academic viewpoint. The recent analysis (Monzón, Roskamp, and Warren 2009) of a 1543 document in the Tarascan language concerning the move of the capital of the kingdom from Ihuatzio to Tzintzuntzan by Tangáxoan's son (and Don Francisco Taríacuri's great-grandfather) Tzitzispandáquare demonstrates that the Tarascan nobility's memory and knowledge of the past were not limited to what was recorded in the priest's narrative contained in the *Relación de Michoacán*, nor is that narrative the sum total of all indigenous knowledge of the past. The subject of the 1543 document, the move of the supreme capital from Ihuatzio to Tzintzuntzan, is almost completely ignored in the *Relación de Michoacán*. In the latter, the history of the Tarascan kingdom after the conquest of the region by Hiripan, Tangáxoan, and Hiquíngaxe; pacification of the people; and installation of local lords is dealt with incredibly briefly and in almost purely genealogical fashion (Alcalá 2000:541–543). These events are also *not* contained within the priest's narrative, but are in a separate chapter following the priest's summation. It is therefore impossible to say who related the information about the capital's move for inclusion in the *Relación de Michoacán*, though it could have still been the same priest. While it is outside of the scope of this book (but see Haskell 2013), the information contained in the 1543 document, provided by a member of the high nobility as he read or interpreted an indigenous and perhaps prehispanic document that has since been lost or destroyed, is full of conflict and intrigue and certainly "noteworthy" if the goal of the priest's narrative in the *Relación de Michoacán* was to tell a complete history of the Tarascan kingdom.

Furthermore, the two stories included in the second part of the *Relación de Michoacán* but not as part of the priest's narrative (see chapter 1) are informative in this regard. Both stories, whose authorship is similarly unknown, though again both could have been related by the same priest, point to the ability and desire of the members of the priesthood to keep and tell stories about the past outside of the bounds of the narrative of the creation of the kingdom. These apparently common tellings could have been part of a more generalized practice that existed in an atomistic fashion that did not require any overarching narrative structure in the various narrational events. In the case of the story of Taríacuri's son Tamapucheca, the telling only seems to have been triggered by the mention of Tamapucheca in the Priest's Speech. In the case of the story of Taríacuri's daughter who kills a Corínguaro noble, the point in telling this story seems to have been grounded in keeping alive the significance of a place. I would speculate that the memory of places and the inhabitation of stories in the landscape would have been a prominent instigator of the concretization of narratives concerning the past. Regardless, the fact that they were remembered but not included within the larger narrative leaves modern interpreters to choose from two options regarding the nature of narrative production in the Tarascan kingdom. Either the Tarascan priests and upper nobility were historians in the Western sense, and these tales were omitted because the priest who relayed this speech for the *Relación de Michoacán* felt they were not essential to the plot and had no real historical consequences, or the priest chose to ignore the question of how the consequences of these events factored into the Uacúsecha's rise to dominance and rather chose to structure the narrative as he did, with all attendant effects on the meaning thereby created as discussed above. I believe the second option is more likely—particularly if a daughter of Taríacuri had killed a nobleman from Corínguaro, this would almost assuredly have instigated a new round of hostilities between the two polities that must have had some impact on the Uacúsecha's rise to power.

This should serve as a cautionary tale to fellow archaeologists and anthropologists who use the priest's narrative either as a model for the processes of state formation (Pollard 1982, 2008; Michelet, Pereira, and Migeon 2005; Michelet 1996; see chapter 2), or as a source of historical data from which to identify patterns in the participation of characters/groups in political-economic activities and processes that would have played a role in the formation of the Tarascan state (Kirchhoff 1956; López Austin 1981). To put it bluntly, there is no way of knowing the kinds or number of events that are skewed, omitted, or fabricated in the process of producing this good story.

The two episodes contained in the *Relación de Michoacán* but not within the priest's narrative as well as the publication and discussion of the 1543 document can be used in combination with my analysis of the priest's narrative in order to comment on the practice of historicity in Tarascan society more widely. My analysis reveals that for the priest to have constructed the narrative in the way that he did, with all the meanings and implications that have been discussed, he needed a rather expansive repository of events from which he could pick out certain events and string them together. Therefore I suggest that the priesthood and perhaps other nobles had institutional motivation and abilities for remembering the past and keeping it alive through retelling and concretizing certain events and perhaps even recording those events in documents. The introduction of the anecdote concerning Taríacuri's daughter (Alcalá 2000:537–540) as well as the last king's stated affinity for the story of Taríacuri's lecture to Hiripan and Tangáxoan, which he purportedly had the priests tell often (Alcalá 2000:468), suggest the practice of telling and retelling such stories whenever there was an occasion for their oration was common among the nobility. The evidence from the *Relación de Michoacán* does indicate, therefore, that the Tarascan priests and upper nobility, at least, did have a strongly developed "historical mode of consciousness" (Turner 1988b; see chapter 3) that served to keep alive remembrances and representations of the past.

The view that the Tarascans possessed a "historical mode of consciousness" is further buttressed by the characteristics of the priest's narrative itself. Its human-centric plot and recognition of human agency in social transformations accord well with the attempts to define a historical mode of consciousness discussed in chapter 3. The narrative of the Uacúsecha is primarily a story about humans and their actions, and ultimately how the actions of humans led to a very dramatic social transformation. Not only does it generally eschew a reliance on the actions of the gods (two direct acts of vengeance by Curicaueri against the Naranjans and Corínguaros notwithstanding; see Haskell 2015 for an explanation of this eruption of the divinity's will into the world) to explain social transformations, but it also explicitly asserts that human actions have important consequences. Furthermore, the characters at the beginning of the story are as relatable and capable of the same sorts of achievements and subject to the same kinds of constraints as are the characters at the end of the story. Therefore the narrative contains a view of time and events as uniform, and uniformly subject to the actions of individuals who possess the ability to change the course of history. This is one reason for rejecting what I contend is the largely arbitrary decision by modern historians and archaeologists to cast certain characters as "legendary" or "mythical" while later characters are deemed "historical" and are even given dates for their lives and reigns.

The editorial oversight of the friar-compiler must be recognized in this regard. The friar-compiler explains very close to the beginning of the second part of the *Relación de Michoacán* that in the narrative, it was a common practice for the narrator to state that the god Curicaueri had done such-and-such thing, but the friar pushed the narrator to include the names of the human characters (see chapter 1, also Haskell 2015). The exact way in which the friar's demand altered the narrative is unknowable, however. The manner in which Curicaueri was rendered to be the primary agent in an indigenous version of the narrative could have taken many forms, including simply implying (but repetitively so) that the god had willed the actions of the characters into existence. The fact that the narrator was able, after all, to produce a fairly large range of named characters could suggest that the narrator did not simply fabricate characters and events in a completely improvised or ad hoc fashion to suit the demands of the friar-compiler.[8]

I believe there is another possible explanation for why the priest's narrative relates essentially the deeds of humans, rather than gods, though it is important to emphasize that the two explanations are not mutually exclusive.[9] First, in keeping with the above arguments, we cannot simply assume that the narrative relates the deeds of humans because it accurately records the past as they were indeed carried out by humans. I admit this is a possibility, however, and in this vein I cannot refute Kirchhoff's (1956) position that the narrative records events that really did happen in the past. It is perhaps even likely that some or most of the events described in the narrative actually did happen. This is emphatically not the same thing, however, as believing that the narrative is an accurate representation of how the Tarascan state actually formed or came into existence. To be fair to Kirchhoff, he never does explicitly claim that the narrative is, on the whole, a "good" history insofar as it gets the sequence of events and, more important, relations of cause and effect right. But he certainly does imply that because the narrative "must have been" memorized and stereotypically reproduced down through generations of priests, the Tarascans must have been historically minded, added "eyewitness" and personal recollections to their histories in "real time," and therefore kept an accurate record of events and were adept at relating the continuous stream of events one to another to the exclusion of a concern with how they relate to the present or at least the subordination of the latter (importance in the present) to the former (relations within the past as such).

The preceding analysis demonstrates however that Tarascan historicity was not practiced for the sake of preserving the past as it actually happened, nor were the indigenous practitioners of historicity concerned with sifting through their various concretizations of the past, whatever form those documents took, in order to reconstruct the past as it actually happened. Any event within oral history or written history was viewed and engaged in practice in an atomistic fashion. It could be selected and put to use in a novel concretization of the past that, in its underlying structure and overarching message, could be tailored to a specific argument or rhetorical point that existed in relation to the context in which it was produced. While the Priest's Speech suggests that a certain kind of historical mode of consciousness existed among the elites and especially the priests of the Tarascan state, I have argued that the production of a concretization of the past in terms of its own internal relations and for its own sake was not the governing principle behind the selection and combination of its elements. Rather, by choosing the episodes and ordering them as the narrator did, the structure of the narrative merges Taríacuri with syntagmatic processes of transformation. The central meaning of the narrative is that kings possess an extraordinary capacity for transformation due to their "Chichimecness" and having inherited that Chichimecness from their predecessor(s). As not only an embodiment but as the originator of the kinship and kingdom, Taríacuri is the epitome of that Chichimecness as revealed in his ability to transform his dual nature as potentiality into a lasting hierarchical duality at several scales—himself, the Uacúsecha (personified by Hiripan, Tangáxoan, and Hiquíngaxe), and ultimately the kingdom itself. This autopoietic nature or self-transformative nature is what constitutes his and the Uacúsecha's ability to transform society around them. Just like Taríacuri, the trio of young lords—Hiripan, Tangáxoan, and Hiquíngaxe—that follow him are and become superagents unrivaled by any other structural position within society; their achievement is not simply the concentration and monopolization of power but also the transformation of local offices of leadership into posts dependent upon them for their legitimation. It is interesting to note that while in the priest's narrative this decision to create the offices of local leadership is the result of a discussion among all three lords (even if Hiripan is stereotypically represented as calling together the other two and leading any discussion that is required), elsewhere in the ritual that elevated a successor to just such a local office in the third part of the document, only Hiripan and Tangáxoan are mentioned as having established the office to which the lord is being raised (Alcalá 2000:604). Furthermore, they are explicitly referred to as the *leñadores*, a clear reference to their devotion to Curicaueri and their Chichimec nature. The implication and tension between the two concretizations are clear; while a duality of Islander and Chichimec qualities is necessary to create a unified kingdom as a sociocosmic totality according to the priest's narrative, and perhaps the wealth that helps cement and consecrate that process of ennoblement in some way can be traced back to the Islander category, it is nonetheless the Chichimec category that has by now (thanks to Taríacuri no less) encompassed and appropriated that wealth, essentially making it a Chichimec quality as well as their original male/solar/foreign usurper qualities. The concretization elsewhere in the *Relación de Michoacán* is thus understandable as an emphasis of this point and the recognition that it is Chichimecness that is behind that encompassment, Chichimecness is therefore associated with transformations of selves and others, raising subordinate lords to their offices is inherently a transformative act, and thus the only appropriate Uacúsecha members to recognize in this passage are the Chichimec characters in the equation.[10] Their paradigmatically monopolized but syntagmatically manifested transformational capacity drives the action of the narrative at the same time that the narrative is what reveals it. This institutionally constructed capacity for the transformation of others is then implicitly handed down to all successor kings by a notably uncomplicated line of succession following the priest's narrative. The link between Taríacuri and Don Francisco as the present inheritor of that nature and as the rightful heir to a position of indigenous authority through the paradigmatic linkage of their name and that syntagmatic list of kingly succession is inescapable.

The rest of the *Relación de Michoacán* portrays this transformative capacity in the "ethnographic present" of the moment of contact with the Spaniards (see Haskell 2008b). Kings are involved in all transformations: they transform criminals into sacrificial victims, captives into food for the gods, autonomous populations into subjects, select members of the conquered into lords through consecration as such (and nonkin lords into beholden affines through marriage relations), and generally chaos into order. Therefore the broader meaning of the narrative is to put forward an exegesis on the nature of agency and power in indigenous society. Explicitly stated, the structure of the narrative serves to explain the kingship (both its development and its characteristics) from the vantage point and in relation to the necessities of the present society and therefore to concretize the necessity of the Uacúsecha *to that society*. The structure of the present takes precedence over the internal relations of the past and the past for its own sake. The transformational capacity of the Uacúsecha is rendered timeless—it has always been there, even if its presence and effects can only be explained and manifested through a sequence of events (just as, again, Taríacuri has always existed as his greatness is foretold the moment the marriage that produces him has been arranged and then consummated). This is what Turner and Levi-Strauss before him identified as the basic function of myth—to create the perception of timelessness, to celebrate the triumph of invariance over surface variations. Note that if this agency is constructed and perceived to be timeless, then it should also be perceived to continue into the present even in spite of the events of history. I suggest that the priest's narrative relates rather ordinary deeds of humans because it wanted to locate the transformative agency of the kings within the directly observable social structure, the practices that produce that social structure, and as the proper outcome of at least some actual historical events. Those events of the past and practices of the present might have manifested and evidenced the divine will of Curicaueri and thereby constituted the Uacúsecha's differential agency vis-à-vis the rest of society, but once in place the effects of that agency needed no explanations outside of the bounds of daily experience. Grounded in this way in everyday experience, so too would the priest's advocated course of action be grounded in normal experience. Success—supporting Don Francisco Taríacuri and helping ensure he became indigenous leader—is defined as achievable in thoroughly human terms and therefore as firmly in the realm of both the possible and the present. What is needed for indigenous society is this person, Don Francisco Taríacuri, who is here, now, and who has the same capacities that are needed to transform the social landscape as the kings that preceded him, particularly Taríacuri who embodied and forged the category of "king" in the first place. All we (the indigenous peoples, according to the priest) must do is support him and make sure he becomes governor.

CONCLUSION

The Priest's Speech could be characterized in any number of ways, as a "historical myth," a "mythical history," a "myth" produced within a "historical mode of consciousness," a "sacred charter," or some equivalent phrase or characterization. Understanding the aims of the narrative in any specificity and the manner in which its construction and concretization related to those aims, however, requires seeing past the categories of myth and history and examining the rhetorical points made by the narrative, the manner in which those points are established and rendered through paradigmatic construction and conservation, how such conservation is constructed and achieved through the time of the narrative, and the various factors that influenced the specific selection and arrangement of the episodes of the narrative. Therefore I also suggest that what is more important than getting overly entangled in semantic debates over history and myth is the analysis of how each specific concretization manifests its own characteristics and structure and how the poietic construction of each narrative is related to the context in which it is told. By doing so we learn much more than if we posit "Tarascan historicity" to be a unitary phenomenon that was more "historical" rather than "mythic" (or vice versa). Focusing on each particular construction, each concretization, moreover, allows for the analytic possibility that both historical and mythic modes are present and interwoven, in whatever relation that the agent who produced the concretization deemed appropriate. In addition, this mode of analysis yields insights that go beyond the discussion of the priest's narrative and other concretizations as a form of propaganda or "sacred history" (as in the work of Roskamp [2010a, 2010b, 2015]). Propaganda or the imputation of bias is seeing in the documents a conscious effort to cast the characters in the best light possible through omitting unflattering events or simply fabricating "events" that flatter royal ancestors and in Mesoamerica to tie royal dynasties to cosmologically informed precepts concerning what constitutes legitimate authority. As I have demonstrated, however, an approach grounded in this model of propaganda and bias based on fissures in the social structure fails to account for the complex and intricate composition of the narratives that do indeed serve to legitimate claims to rulership. Similarly, calling the Priest's Speech "sacred history" is accurate and yet to fully appreciate the priest's skill and intent we must go further than analyses that have employed this term. "Sacred history" as currently used implies that the history is sacred on two distinct but related bases: because it comes from the past and because it talks about the past.[11] In such an analytical mode sacred history functions because it is (or must be taken as) sacred, because it constructs linkages between the present and past sources of sacral authority, but so long as these two conditions are met then the analysis is complete and the concretization is rendered as sacred history and its sociological function understood. While biases based on social structure and factionalism therein are taken into consideration, such an approach has had difficulty in analyzing exactly why different concretizations should represent various links to sacred deities, personages, and/or places through different temporally constituted timeframes. The analysis presented here also discusses time, temporality, and social action in a way that a propaganda or "sacred history" model does not theorize. Propaganda or sacred history are not necessarily incorrect ways of approaching Mesoamerican narratives and other concretizations; they are insufficient if we are to appreciate the full scope of what indigenous artists were doing. Propaganda and sacred history take as their points of departure the unquestioned authority of the agents doing the concretizing (viz. the priests/literati) to concretize the past and linkages to a sacred time-space, thus legitimating the present and whatever faction the concretizing agent hopes to be legitimating within that social structure. Anthropological theory since at least the "historical turn" in the 1970s has heavily critiqued and questioned such "totalizing" and hegemonically unchallenged cultural production. My analysis takes into account the views and judgments of the audience when possible, or at least as in the case examined here the need for an agent endowed with a cultural repertoire of both historical/cosmological knowledge and artistic skill in composition to put his best foot forward in crafting a concretization that legitimated a certain viewpoint not simply because of its content but also due to the composition of that content as something that was coherently organized and thus, as I argued above, "sacred" from another (indigenous) frame of reference beyond that relation to the past—its "well ordered" properties (Maffie 2013; see endnote 7, Chapter 3). In addition, in contexts of cultural contact, colonization, and variable accommodation and resistance, "sacred" immediately becomes a contentious and highly problematic point of departure. The definition of indigenous historicity as relying on so-called sacred history, while true for the reasons outlined above, becomes insufficient once the fact that indigenous peoples understood that the various factions of Spaniards now constituted important and even essential new audiences for such concretizations. Despite their differences, the Spaniards regarded indigenous history as anything but sacred. Indigenous peoples must have been aware of this fact, and indeed the *Relación de Michoacán* presents us with the interjection of the friar when he explains that he has pressed the priest to avoid narrating this history as a history of Curicaueri. Surely the friar's rationale behind this instruction would not have escaped the priest, and this is but one example of the larger effort to literally demonize and render illegitimate the indigenous gods and beliefs. In such contexts, then, indigenous priests and literati had to draw upon not simply their insistence of sacredness, nor not simply the translation of the symbolic content of sacredness at play in these concretizations into the Spanish mindset, but rather on a poietic sense of narrative invariance and inevitability as a construct of the sequence and coherence of the story being told.

NOTES

1. I likely would not have recognized this fact if Susan Gillespie had not shared her work on the *Popol Vuh* with me; in sections devoted to methodology and the logical development of categories this act of balancing, including of categories that are both/neither, is discussed as an important feature of classificatory systems as revealed in Mesoamerican narratives and cosmologies.

2. Stone (2004:140) interprets these references to Don Pedro and to Quiroga due not to the friar's intrusion into the text, supposing that a Franciscan friar would not have to remind his Spanish audience of such present events. I find this point dubious. Moreover, she suggests that the inclusions are by the priest and intended for an indigenous audience "because of their symbolic significance" (Stone 2004:140). Again, this is offered as evidence linking Quiroga to Pátzcuaro and his supposed inheritance of the mantle of leader of the indigenous peoples. I suggest it is just as likely that *if* these elements were included by the priest, they were included to remind the indigenous audience just how much the state of affairs had deteriorated from the prehispanic dominance of the Uacúsecha by explicitly linking the prophesied temple foundations to an occupancy by a non-Uacúsecha lord and to what perhaps was the sacrilegious presence of Quiroga in subordinating the old temples and the past they represented by superimposing himself and his works in that place (particularly to a member of the priesthood, whose influence was waning fast).

3. This observation appears incorrect given what we know of the Mexica, but it is the opinion of record, having been written down in the *Relación de Michoacán*. For more on this and similar misunderstandings/mischaracterizations across the Tarascan/Aztec frontier, see Pollard (2000).

4. The inspiration for this discussion comes from Turner's (1988b) discussion, based on the work of Da Matta (1970), of "anti-myth." An antimyth is a symbolic inversion of an indigenous myth that by the process of inversion seeks to explain the "other," in this case European colonists and their descendants, as an inversion of the indigenous identity and

processes of native enculturation and cultural reproduction. I am currently working on analyzing the story contained in the *Relación de Michoacán* of the horses of the Spaniards as related to deer and one variant of the ball-game genre of myths. In that work I hope to show that the teller of the tale advocates for understanding the Spaniards' success not as the result of their own inherent agency but rather as originating in the failure of indigenous society to properly remember their ways and ancestors.

5. The association of Spaniards with gods has been a controversial topic in Mesoamerican studies. It is known, however, that indigenous peoples referred to Pedro de Alvarado as "Tonatiuh," a Nahua solar deity (as in the *Codex Telleriano-Remensis*, see Quiñones Keber 1995:folio 46r; see also Gillespie 1989:229). On the whole, interactions between the Spaniards and indigenous peoples (most prominently the Mexica and other Nahua peoples of Central Mexico) indicate that indigenous peoples regarded the Spaniards at least at first as something on par with their own deified or semidivine rulers—whom, for instance, commoners were not supposed to be able to look directly in the eyes/face of due to their greater possession of *teotl*, or sacred force, and especially their *tonalli*, the sacred force associated specifically with heat and brightness (Gillespie 1989:219; López Austin 1973).

6. It should be remembered, however, that the representation in the written as well as visual aspects of the *Relación de Michoacán* of uncomplicated succession from father to son is an argument for present and future reality and not necessarily an accurate representation of the totality of past reality. See, especially, Afanador-Pujol (2015:chap. 6) and Stone (1994) on the visual representation of the burial of the Cazonci within the *Relación de Michoacán* as an effort to portray a unique event (the burial of a particular Cazonci, i.e., Zuangua) as merely a token of a stereotypical (i.e., unproblematically reproduced) pattern. Elsewhere in the *Relación de Michoacán*, regarding Zuangua's successor, in fact, the written content of the third ("ethnographic") part of the document states that in addition to or in competition with the father-son succession in which a son co-rules with his father for a time, upon the death of a king elders gather and elect the new king from a pool of close male relatives and members of the lineages of Tzintzuntzan, Ihuatzio, and Pátzcuaro (i.e., Uacúsecha lineages).

7. Afanador-Pujol's (2015) analysis of the illustrations within the *Relación de Michoacán* and accompanying the narrative must also be acknowledged for its rigor and understanding of the role of context at the smallest of (visual) scales. Her fine work nevertheless pertains to a different medium than the narrative and different agents than the narrative and its creator that Stone and now I have focused on. Alternatively, while Roskamp has compared the priest's narrative to other concretizations of the past, his focus has lain more in the analysis of those other documents and therefore other pasts with the priest's narrative as a sort of benchmark (see discussion in chap. 2). The work of Michelet (1989) and Marie Charlotte Arnauld and Michelet (1991) has similarly engaged the priest's narrative in relation to its context, but their analyses resulted mainly in characterizing certain passages as allegorical and moralizing for the present. In short, their analyses do not present a coherent vision of the

narrative as a call to action or a call that links the past as concretized to a future that should be realized and worked toward.

8. The case of Xoropiti and Tarequetzingata serving as the names of places and subsequently characters in the episodes concerning the infidelities of Taríacuri's first wife are a notable exception to this production of unique names and places. The case of Sicuirancha's name and its possible relationship to the unsuccessfully flayed deer early in the narrative and the case of Zurumban's priest Naca possibly being named "meat" in Nahuatl could be other instances of the formulation of a personal name as a marker of some paradigmatic category (see notes 5 (on Sicuirancha's name), 19 (on meat) in chapter 4).

9. That human agency and actions are interpreted to be driven by or reflections of the will of a deity has certainly been commonplace in the religions and cultures of the world, particularly when religion meets politics, up to the present day.

10. I have elsewhere (Haskell 2012:231) written on this same discrepancy in a more theoretically precise discussion of the logic of encompassment.

11. The past is of course the basis or root of the present, and thus as a source of the present hierarchically superior in relation to it; see Carlsen and Prechtel (1991), McKinnon (1991), and Sahlins (1981, 1985).

Tarascan Historicity in Its Mesoamerican Context

Myth, History, Historicity, and Understanding the Prehispanic Past

As revealed in the discussion of the analysis of the Priest's Speech presented in chapters 1 and 4, the syntagmatic relationships of paradigmatic elements and specifically the way the second half of the narrative folds back upon and mirrors the first half are key to the process of producing the centrality of Taríacuri. As discussed in chapter 3, the syntagmatic axis of narrative works with the paradigmatic axis to produce meaning, and the specific meanings thus produced will at least potentially be unique according to which axis dominates. In the Priest's Speech, the syntagmatic axis is roughly balanced and made intelligible by the paradigmatic similarities within and between the two halves of the narrative. The effect of the narrative "pivoting" (see chapters 1 and 4) through the syntagmatic relationships, however, creates the third paradigm, that of "Taríacuri," a wholly novel category in terms of the singular power and will of a personage who can create and indeed embody the kingdom. In order to discuss whether and in what ways this structure, the relationship between paradigm and syntagm, and attendant meaning thereby created are unique in Mesoamerica, it is necessary to examine and comment upon the overall need for a greater attention to the syntagmatic axis of narrative as well as discuss those analyses in which such an examination is present. Without such research and analyses, a truly valid comparison between Mesoamerican narratives is impossible. What follows are thoughts and notes for comparison along formal, paradigmatic, and syntagmatic analytic lines of inquiry.

DOI: 10.5876/9781607327493.c006

COMPARISON WITH WIDER MESOAMERICAN NARRATIVES
OF MIGRATION AND POLITICAL HISTORY

In applying the insight of historicity as a theoretical concept that concretizing the past is a powerful means of making sense of the present and advocating for a future, it is necessary to recognize the specific sociohistorical context in which the priest's narrative was told but also the wider cultural influences and symbolic systems that informed it. Investigating the latter inevitably entails comparisons and contrasts with other Mesoamerican narratives concerning the cosmos and how kingship fits into that cosmos, particularly in the context of the imposition of Spanish colonialism. To some extent we must also confront that fact that this comparative analysis is the most common mode of what is termed "structuralist" analysis: the comparison of paradigmatic transformations between myth variants in order to discover underlying patterns and the attempt to resolve irresolvable contradictions through those variations (see chapter 3). As I have already stated, there are few other narratives from the Tarascan region that are concerned with the prehispanic past, but those that do exist cast serious doubt on the unique role and power of Taríacuri in the prehispanic past as he is represented in the Priest's Speech in the *Relación de Michoacán* (see chapter 1). Comparisons with other Mesoamerican narratives from other cultural traditions reveal what is shared with the rest of Mesoamerica thanks to either cultural historical processes (diffusion of symbols and the underlying ideology of those symbols and how they ought to be understood in relation to other symbols), similar conceptions of the operation of the natural world and humans within that world, or both. Indeed, it is often difficult to untangle the two processes, and anthropological theory has demonstrated that oftentimes the one process necessarily informs the other, as when a culture will incorporate outside symbols in a manner that is consistent with some of its organizational or structural apparatus, even as this adoption changes that structure.

As identified by Seler (1993), Kirchhoff (1956), López Austin (1981), Michelet (1989), and Arnauld and Michelet (1991), there are clear parallels in the Priest's Speech of the *Relación de Michoacán* with other Mesoamerican narratives in terms of the motifs, characters, and actions, foremost among them being the intertwinement of two categories of people: "Chichimecs" and "Islanders." I have already dealt with the construction of these categories both in a preliminary fashion in chapter 1 and in a more in-depth way in chapters 4 and 5 by explaining how the many actions of various Chichimec characters both confirm this characterization while ultimately working to transform the nature of the category into an encompassing identity. In the broad outlines of the category, the Chichimecs of the Priest's Speech are very similar to the Chichimecs who are often the heroes in the Central Mexican documents. I stress, however, that this has more to do with the necessities of using this category precisely for its contrasts with its opposite, the "Toltec" or ancient "Culhua" lineage that signifies Toltec heritage and civilized and learned conduct. Particularly in the interpretations of the Michoacán and Central Mexican sources that posit some historical connection simply because they utilize the word "Chichimec" in common, the linguistic evidence of marked divergence between the two casts serious doubt on any factual ties in the "real past." We cannot therefore rely on either a phylogenetic relationship or a common migration history akin to particularly the Central Mexican sources that post a split between the groups at Lake Pátzcuaro (e.g., Durán 1994:23) to explain any commonalities between the cultures' uses of this common theme of invading Chichimecs appropriating autochthonous power and, more important, cultured legitimacy. I also regard it as at least worthwhile to consider the possibility that the word "Chichimecs" is used in both the Priest's Speech and Central Mexican sources due to the fact that Nahuatl was quickly becoming a lingua franca in the contact situations developing across Mesoamerica involving the Spaniards following the surrender of the Mexica—Stone (2004:27–28) notes a "double filter" of Castilian and Nahuatl in the translation and production process of the document. The Priest's Speech records the event of the Uacúsecha claiming a shared heritage with the Islanders (of Xaráquaro and Pacandan in particular), and so some reconstructions have supposed that the people of the islands of Lake Pátzcuaro too must have been Nahuatl speakers. As discussed in chapter 2, this is mostly unsubstantiated by archaeological evidence. It possibly contradicts what evidence does exist of long-lived material traditions in central Michoacán and slightly further afield that are unique and fairly well bounded spatially (Pollard 1997, 2000; Begun 2008), as well as linguistic data from the *Relaciones Geográficas* and ethnographic analyses of the prominence of various language of Central Michoacán in which Purhépecha is dominant. Recent, more fine-grained archaeological studies have indicated that some transitions in stylistic grammar (Pollard and Washburn n.d.) of ceramic decorations in the Lake Pátzcuaro Basin and changes in the microtechnologies of ceramic production in the Zacapu Basin (Jadot 2016), both during the Postclassic period, could shed light on the complexities of ethnicity and population shifts in central Michoacán, but more studies of these kinds are needed. The archaeological and linguistic evidence is not completely conclusive, but it does cast substantial doubt on hypotheses of widespread movements of Nahuatl speakers into the area. I do not intend to cast doubt on the presence of any Nahuatl speakers in central Michoacán; Roskamp (2010, 2012; see also Monzón, Roskamp, and Warren 2009) in particular has expanded our knowledge concerning the extent of the presence of Nahua speakers in Tzintzuntzan and central Michoacán, building on the early work of Warren (1963, 1977). I consider the most plausible and parsimonious explanation to the common presence of Chichimecs in the Priest's

Speech and Central Mexican narratives to be using the known but tangled reality and memory of movements of peoples from the north as the symbolic raw material from which to fashion a new invented tradition that was shared widely and became part of the common Mesoamerican Postclassic way of legitimizing a new form of political ideology (as in the interpretations of Gillespie 1989, 2007b; Kowalski and Kristan-Graham 2007; and López Austin and López Luján 2000).

Within this broad commonality of the contrastive but complementary identities and interactions of foreign Chichimecs and (variously named and constructed) autochthonous groups, however, it must be recognized that there is a significant departure from the Central Mexican representations. One possible "fall" to match the supposed tragedies that befall Ce Acatl Topiltzin and/or the "Toltec" people in the Central Mexican sources could be found in the tale of the priests and priestesses of Xarátanga while at Tzintzuntzan (Mechuacan in the document), who appropriate the vestments of the goddess. The priests and priestesses of Xarátanga are structurally equivalent to the Xaráquaros (the link of the "Islander" Zurumban becoming Xarátanga's priest while her cult is centered in Tariaran confirms this). Much like many of the Ce Acatl Topiltzin and "Toltec" stories, the tale of the priests and priestesses of Xarátanga does contain drunkenness as a precursor or cause of the "fall." They also depart their town, but importantly they go to the South, as far as ethnohistorians have been able to determine where Tariaran is, as opposed to the east. If it is possible to say, then, that if this tale is equivalent to the "fall" of the "Toltecs," then the Priest's Speech is essentially a telescoped version of the fall and the redemption, as the fall occurs at the *exact same place* as the eventual capital, Tzintzuntzan, particularly following Tangáxoan's dream and restoration of Xarátanga's worship there in the Priest's Speech, and the ascendance of Tzitzispandáquare at Tzintzuntzan in the historical tradition of the Nahuas of Tzintzuntzan (Monzón, Roskamp, and Warren 2009; Haskell 2013). This is different from the many various locations and manifestations of "Tollan" in the Central Mexican sources, in which the original island at Aztlán, Tollan, Coatepec, and Culhuacan are in various places in the many sources called upon to fill this symbolic and paradigmatic role of an original place of power that then the eventual capital of Tenochtitlan mimics (Gillespie 1989; Graulich 1997). In this way the Priest's Speech achieves the effect of nullifying the temporal depth that is present in the Central Mexican sources, even if that depth is due more to a mode in which history and its events and places are symbolic and paradigmatically repetitive or redundant in the Central Mexican sources, by seemingly implying due to the lack of other "Tollans" that the capital of Tzintzuntzan is merely a symbol of itself.[1] It is the only member of the paradigmatic set of "glorious capitals" that the priest drew on in the formulation of his narrative. He could have done so to emphasize its uniqueness and therefore the fact that it should remain the capital of colonial Michoacán. He could have also constructed the lack of other comparable places and narrative depth due to the fact that, as far as archaeologists are aware, Michoacán does not have a history of local or regional places that fit the description of a "Tollan" and therefore Tzintzuntzan's role as the only "Tollan" is the same as an admittance that it was and is the first "Tollan." These positions are not mutually exclusive.

There is another possible equivalence for the "Toltec" category in the Priest's Speech, but yet again this example also demonstrates how different the Priest's Speech is once again from the Central Mexican sources and their variations on the Toltec story. I have pointed out in chapter 4 the ways in which the people of Xaráquaro function as equivalent to the Toltecs given the translations of their collective name, the "Hurendetiecha," revolving around being "first" and being "skillful." However, the Xaráquaro people of the Priest's Speech lack so many of the classic elements of the "Toltec" and later Culhua peoples of the Central Mexican narratives. First, their settlement does not appear to be worthy of status as a Tollan in any way. Second, the Uacúsecha rise to power is certainly put in motion with Taríacuri's birth thanks to the marriage to the Xaráquaro fisherman's daughter, but there is nothing comparable in the tale of the Xaráquaros and interactions the Chichimecs have with them to the "fall" and "exile" of Ce Acatl Topiltzin Quetzalcoatl or the Toltecs as a group so common to the narratives and traditions from Central Mexico. The nearest equivalent to such a fall would, I suggest, be having to beg Taríacuri to return to Pátzcuaro when they are engaged in a battle over Pátzcuaro with the Corínguaros, people of Pacandan, and people of Tariaran. Taríacuri advises them that he will come to their aid and reoccupy Pátzcuaro himself if they sell themselves into slavery. While the text states that they do this, nowhere after this in the narrative does it appear that Xaráquaro has been depopulated nor lacking in lords. In this case it does not seem to be the case that Xarátanga's abode as represented in the Priest's Speech drew to any great extent on the Tollan archetype. I suggest that there is no marked end to a period of Xaráquaro hegemony as in the Central Mexican sources, because there was no period of Xaráquaro preeminence and greatness to begin with. The most that can be said in terms of a comparison between the Priest's Speech is that perhaps Xaráquaro serves as an equivalent stand-in or descendent population that carries forth some semblance of "Toltec" (I use the term loosely) heritage such as the people of Culhuacan in the Central Mexican sources who constitute both ancestors and are constructed as the proximate inheritors of the Toltec legacy by which the Mexica gain legitimacy (Gillespie 1989). In such a scenario it is possible that a previous golden age and the creation of rulership and all civilized things were discussed in the first part of the *Relación de Michoacán* that covered religion; unfortunately we will never know.[2] It is instructive that elsewhere in the text of the *Relación de Michoacán* there are mentions of points that are discussed in the first part; no such mentions of a glorious past are evident anywhere in the document as a whole.

On this note it is also interesting that the document *does* contain a story that strongly resembles some elements and/or some versions of the Ce Acatl Topiltzin narrative genre; this is the story related in the third section of the *Relación de Michoacán* as an indigenous explanation of the Spaniards' horses. That narrative of a man who loses a ball game and his son who recovers his father's is so similar to, for instance, the Mexica story of Totepeuh in the *Relación de la Genealogía* (1941) that Graulich, for example, treats them as essentially the same myth. The theme of recovering a dead father's remains, of course, a prominent if not the dominant theme in the *Popol Vuh* and the story of the Hero Twins' victory over the death lords and resurrection of 1 Hunahpu. While the story of Totepeuh in the *Relación de la Genealogía* is explicitly about the recovery of a father's remains *as* the means of succession to the kingship, in the *Popol Vuh* the Hero Twins' saga is connected to power and authority in more ambiguous ways. The document as a whole is concerned with the issue of hierarchy and kinship, and if the many commenters on the symbolism of the *Popol Vuh* and its relation to Maya (especially Classic period) kingship and the link between kings and the maize god are correct, then the resurrection of 1 Hunahpu as maize by the Hero Twins is also the story of the kingship, though symbolically and not explicitly.[3] What is evident in the *Relación de Michoacán*, then, is the presence of a story or mythic cycle that is known in various forms throughout Mesoamerica and in its most famous manifestation is brought to inform the growing dialogue between the Mexica and Spaniards concerning the nature and historical depth of indigenous kingship that nonetheless is told in a context that has no relationship whatsoever to the indigenous Tarascan kingship.

To go beyond a comparison with Central Mexican documents, some have discussed that the categories of "Chichimecs" and "Islanders" also have certain similarities to generalized "foreigner" and "authochthon" categories that are also evident in Maya narratives, particularly the *Popol Vuh* (Arnauld and Michelet 1991; Graulich 1997; Martínez González 2010; Olivier and Martínez González 2015). In Martínez González's (2010) interpretation, this distinction derives from a sociological construct perceived from a localized but also economic point of view in which persons exploiting or commanding various sectors of the economy must exist in a harmony that nonetheless rests on a hierarchical cultural logic. In another work, he also outlines how the Priest's narrative, phrased as the Uacúsecha peregrination, mimics other Mesoamerican narratives in ways that approach the centrality of the "day metaphor" of Michel Graulich's analyses. In these approaches, "autochthons" become merged with night/death lords, and "foreigners" are said to be structurally equivalent with the sun and the forces of the day that conquer night. This theme is noted in the link to the Death Lords in the *Popol Vuh*, who reside in the underworld and thus the time-space of night, who are then bested by the Hero Twins—themselves apotheosized as the Sun and the Morning Star. Graulich (1997) sees this general theme of the emergence of the sun from the earth and thus its "victory" over the forces of night in every myth and narrative that he analyzes, essentially finding recurring patterns of sky deities, earth deities, and others waging battle over who shall "reign," when, and under what conditions. Cyclicity is noted both internally in the narratives (the sun and moon / forces of night are always in motion and alternation, extending beyond the simple day metaphor to also include the alternation between the rainy season and the dry season) and externally between narratives insofar as different narratives that ostensibly related different "historical" periods are purported to tell basically the same story. It is in these analyses that, due to their inherently and exclusively paradigmatic focus, "nothing ever changes" and each narrative tells the same story, simply with different surface signs.

I do not subscribe to this analytic program in which every story is essentially the same, because to do so obscures what are potentially incredibly salient differences for understanding both particular cultures and sociohistorical moments, and I hope the present study makes a strong case for the importance of analyzing particular narratives and demonstrates the utility of a method for doing so. On the other hand, while I emphasize the importance of difference and believe that not every elementary category is a simple transformation of "autochthon" or "foreigner," I will point out that there appear to be certain features in the Priest's Speech and particularly Central Mexican narratives that have a common origin in a fundamental organizing principle, namely, the movements of celestial bodies and the sun in particular. In the Priest's Speech, Uacúsecha members move in a counterclockwise direction around Lake Pátzcuaro in two prominent sequences of action. The first follows the omen of Xarátanga's priests and priestesses turning into snakes, in which Pauacume and Uapeani travel from their settlement in Uayameo to the north and then follow the western rim of the lake basin, meet the fisherman from Xaráquaro and marry Xaráquaro women, and ultimately end up in Pátzcuaro in the south of the basin. Similarly, Hiripan and Tangáxoan follow a counterclockwise path from Asajo and its northerly environs down the west side of the lake to Erongarícuaro, Urichu, Pareo, and ultimately Pátzcuaro. Having meet with their uncle in Pátzcuaro they then settle north of that town in or around Ihuatzio, to the north. This counterclockwise movement draws on the perception of the movement of the sun on a counterclockwise cyclical (thus repetitive) path in the east to its zenith position to its setting in the west to its nadir position in the underworld, to the east to being the cycle anew. It is tempting to state that this process is continued with the move of Hiripan and Tangáxoan to Ihuatzio and ultimately the transfer of power from Pátzcuaro to Ihuatzio to Tzintzuntzan along a northerly path in the eastern part of the basin as mimicking the rising sun, but this purely ideological framework seems to conflict with what we know of the apparently historically attested transfer of power from (presumably) Ihuatzio to Tzintzuntzan in the time of Tzitzispandáquare (Monzón, Roskamp, and Warren 2009; see also Haskell 2013). At any rate the sequence of actions and movements oriented in a counterclockwise fashion is par alleled in the Central Mexican narratives concerning the Mexicas' peregrination and arrival in the Basin of Mexico. Upon their departure from Coatepec "in the Land of Tula" (Durán 1994:25), the Mexica occupy first Xaltocan in the north of the basin, and then proceed down the western part of the basin into Tepanec terri tory. They settle at Chapultepec, which was at the time part of the dominion of the Tepanec city-state Azcatpotzalco. From here the Mexica were expelled and settled in Tizaapan south of Chapultepec but still in the west, then they became allied and lived with the Culhua in Culhuacan in approximately the center of the basin (their proximate means of attaining female ennobling femininity and ancient "Toltec legitimacy). Ultimately the Mexica were displaced from there and settled on the island of Tenochtitlan, which is north of Culhuacan and in the "center" of the lake due to its nature as an island (Durán 1994:25–45). The processes are not exactly the same, and I do not propose a strict similarity between individual places in the Priest's Speech and Central Mexican narratives as some have, but the prominence of a counterclockwise migration pattern that mimics solar movements is likely due to the desire to legitimize royal houses as having origins that possess metaphorical relationships with the sun's movements as opposed to the contingencies of actual historical events and processes.

These comparisons and commonalities have largely been pointed out by other scholars who have analyzed the Priest's Speech, as noted in the citations. Pointing out these paradigmatically related motifs, as well as where and how more common motifs are borrowed yet transformed, lends itself to the realization of an important point. That point is that many of these commonalities are incorporated precisely because of their symbolic impact and not because they are what actually happened in the real past. While clearly there is a relationship between social action, ideology, and historicity (e.g., Ohnuki-Tierney 1990b; Ortner 1990; Peel 1984; Sahlins 1981, 1985, 2004; Tambiah 1985; Turner 1988a, b; Valeri 1990) and thus people do indeed act in real time according to certain schema that themselves exist thanks to ideological work, including the work of historicity (Ortner 1990; Tambiah 1985; Valeri 1990), it would be remarkable and strain credulity to imagine that every single shared motif in these narratives that span centuries in time and hundreds of miles owe their nature to past people acting in real time in accordance to these ideological frameworks—and unceasingly so. The point of ritual, in the example of ritual circumambulations that mirror the movements of the sun in its daily round in a counterclockwise fashion, is at least partially that it *is ritual* and is different from everyday or mundane/profane time and space. Drawing comparisons with cultures outside Mesoamerica, Gillespie (1989:216–222) has recognized similarities between the Aztec/Mexica narratives concerning legitimate rulership and Kuba (Bantu) narratives concerning kingship as analyzed by Luc de Heusch (1982). This constitutes an even stronger case against historical veracity and even against a shared tradition in which motifs and symbols crossed cultural boundaries to be incorporated in narratives. There is no reasonable way in which such similarities are due to historical accuracy in terms of representing a "real" past. Returning focus to Mesoamerica as a culture area, and one in which such interactions and the spread of motifs and ideological precepts definitively occurred, the lesson to be learned is once again that real historical actions cannot plausibly explain such commonalities but also that while symbolic motifs and ideological precepts did spread across cultural boundaries, this does not mean that they were deployed in narrative in uniform ways. Paradigmatic analyses of such commonalities and contrasts, in addition to shining light on variants and the logical reasons and contradictions raised by substitutions, can to some extent help us see and understand the specific manner in terms of internal deployment by examining the commonalities between exemplars of a paradigm within single narratives. By ignoring the syntagmatic or sequential aspect of narrative, however, we cannot fully achieve a comparative analytic framework for understanding why specific actors in particular sociohistorical contexts chose to compose and structure their narratives, including the use and/or possible subversion of narrational genres (Bakhtin 1981; Turner 1988a, b; Valeri 1990; White 1973, 1980; see chapter 3).

THE POETIC AND COMPOSITIONAL ASPECTS OF THE PRIEST'S SPEECH IN A COMPARATIVE FRAMEWORK

While a comparison of the individual elements and symbolic motifs and movements is productive, a comparison of the means by which the Priest's Speech was composed is also instructive of the narrative's novelty as well as how I suggest it should be understood within the "myth" versus "history" dichotomy. At a basic level of linguistic structure, one aspect of many forms of Mesoamerican narrative and poetry that is apparently absent in the Priest's Speech is the common practice of constructing couplets, referred to as diphrastic metaphor (*difrasismo* in Spanish, see, e.g., Bright 1990; Garibay Kintana 1953; Kartunnen and Lockhart 1980; Edmonson 1985 translates this construction into English as "couplet kenning"). This is most apparent in the Nahuatl practice of describing phenomena through paired word names, or terms, such as the phrase *in atl in tepetl* ("the water, the mountain") and their combination as *altepetl* ("the water mountain," meaning the city/political domain) (Bright 1990:440). The paired terms or phrases are metaphors for one another as well as the described phenomena; by approaching the phenomena in this way the sense is constructed that meaning cannot be approached directly but rather through a roundabout sense akin to approximation. However, by combining two simultaneously similar but contrastive terms, complex meanings can be understood by examining the nature of the combination and the metacategory (Lakoff and Johnson 1980) that is constructed by their juxtaposition with one another. This process of examining relationships and metacategories is why such diphrastic constructions work and why synecdoche can from a certain perspective be seen as the "master trope"—two terms that are not necessarily members of the same category are used in a way to produce a new category, a new totality of which they are now parts (e.g., Lakoff and Johnson 1980; Jakobson (in Turner); Maffie 2013:140–143, 168–169; Ohnuki-Tierney 1991 (in beyond metaphor); Turner 1991). In the Mesoamerican deployment of diphrastic metaphor, it is both the process of producing the new metacategory and the content of the metacategory that are the true meaning of the construction. The medium (diphrastic metaphor) is the message in the sense of establishing the importance of the *production* of potentially novel meanings, while simultaneously and by implication demonstrating the inadequacy of either term alone to encompass the full meaning of the referent. The use of such diphrastic metaphor is evident in some of the Nahuatl representations of the past, for example, Don Hernando Alvarado Tezozomoc's *Crónica Mexicana* (Tezozomoc [1878] 1975). The fullest expression of such an approach to meaning within narrative is the *Popol Vuh*. Edmonson (1971:xi) and de Ridder (1987:240; 1989:247) observed that the parallel couplets of the *Popol Vuh* work through the sequential juxtapositioning of common but not identical elements to actively produce meaning as the multiple potential meanings of roots and to instigate a recognition of novel commonalities between the two phrases, just as in the above discussion of Nahuatl diphrastic metaphor.

While syntagmatic relations are on the most basic level required to juxtapose related but contrastive terms within these diphrastic constructions, particularly in their use in Nahua speech, syntagmatic relationships involved in the production of meaning between such diphrastic constructions—that is, from one to another—have not been emphasized analytically. Obviously this completely contrasts with the Priest's Speech in the *Relación de Michoacán*. While it cannot be stated definitively that the priest did not use diphrastic constructions due to the fact that the only version of the narrative we have available to us is already a translation into

Spanish, I find very little evidence for their use in the narrative. Therefore while these simple and almost purely paradigmatic/metaphorical relationships are absent in the Priest's Speech, larger-order syntagmatic constructions are of course present in the Priest's Speech and in fact are constitutive of its most powerful meanings and implications, as demonstrated in chapter 4 and discussed in chapter 5.

Parallel couplets are so prominent in the *Popol Vuh* that Munro Edmonson (1971) translated the entire document by arranging it into parallel couplets. This move was criticized by Tedlock (1983:230), who pointed out that such an approach ignored other forms of poetic construction. Christensen's more recent translation discusses examples of other poetic constructions that are evident in the narrative. One such construction is the use of chiasmus, or reverse parallelism, in which a series of events or things are named and then those events or things are named in the reverse order. Christensen (2007:46–47) pulls out various instances of chiasmus from the text as examples. These examples range from the small scale of only four lines (thus only two terms that are stated once and then repeated again in reverse order) to much larger constructions spanning lines 97–274 concerning the various stages of creation of the cosmos including the creation of the earth and the division of the waters, the latter being the central element that is the last novel thing created and thus the first to be repeated. The use of chiasmus is obviously relevant to the analysis of the Priest's Speech in the *Relación de Michoacán*, as that speech is composed entirely as one big chiasmus that pivots around Taríacuri's own paradigmatic pivoting. Christensen (2007:46) states that chiasmus draws attention to the central element, as in the case of the division of waters at the midpoint in listing the stages of creation, and the Priest's Speech definitively draws attention to Taríacuri's act of pivoting both in paradigmatic and syntagmatic terms. Aside from this function of focusing attention, Christensen (2007:52) writes that the various forms of parallelism evident in the *Popol Vuh* also function as a form of mnemonic device. "This is particularly true of the chiastic type of parallelism, which may give order to large sections of a story." I argue that chiasmus within the Priest's Speech provided a framework, and possibly a well-known or widely practiced framework within indigenous oratory if it is found in both K'iche' and Tarascan narratives, for the narrative. If this is the case, then the priest likely had worked with exactly this kind of framework and been adept at using it to help him organize his thoughts and the sequential arrangement of the narrative as he did. It is evident, however, that the use of chiasmus in the Priest's Speech is not simply a matter of using it because of its function as a mnemonic device, but rather that the role of chiasmus in creating emphasis and constructing meaning was the foremost concern.

It is important to recognize, however, that the Priest's Speech cannot be characterized as a simple form of chiasmus like that evident in the *Popol Vuh*. This is because while the Priest's Speech does indeed contain a reverse order repetition of paradigmatic elements, the paradigms of the second half do not, strictly speaking mirror or repeat the paradigms of the first half. The episodes of the second half contain similar but inverted paradigms, but paradigms that are deployed in episodes and sequences of action that are novel. This must be the case for, as I discuss in chapters 1 and 4, the narrative simultaneously folds back on itself and repeats in chiastic fashion the paradigms and their syntagmatic arrangement while also carrying the story forward to its conclusion. This is a more complex form of chiasmus and one that provided a framework to the narrative but also required that the plan for the arrangement of these syntagmatically arranged episodes must have preceded in at least some form the actual narration of the story and then required their continual coordination and execution as the narrative is being told. Christensen (2007:52) notes that the poetic forms, rich symbolism, and complex storytelling of the *Popol Vuh* "can be appreciated as the eloquent creation of a master poet with a sophisticated literary heritage"; this applies, perhaps a fortiori, to the priest who narrated the story of the Uacúsecha in the *Relación de Michoacán*.

NUMBER, PARADIGM, AND SYNTAGMATIC RELATIONS AND PROCESS AT THE LEVEL OF ENTIRE NARRATIVES

Expansions by multiplication of binary contrasts are nonetheless prominent in the *Popol Vuh* and Central Mexican narratives concerning the origins of the cosmos and humanity. The *Popol Vuh* contains four attempts at creating beings who can remember and worship their creators (animals, "Mud Man," Woodmen and Reed Women and finally true humans made from maize). This process of creation and the importance of the number 4 is also present in the *Relación de* Michoacán. The narrative tells of four marriages as constitutive of the process of creating a dually composed and autopoietic Uacúsecha. Similarly, following Taríacuri's pivoting, there are four stages of creating a dually composed Uacúsecha that can reproduce itself: first Taríacuri by himself; then Taríacuri plus Hiripan and Tangáxoan; then Hiripan Tangáxoan, and Zapiuatame and his people; and finally Hiripan, Tangáxoan, and Hiquíngaxe. Commonly this cycle of creation and destruction has been interpreted in paradigmatic terms (e.g., Sandoval 1988; see critique by Gillespie n.d.), merely as repetitions of cycles of creation and destruction (excepting the final creation which of course was successful). Tarn and Prechtel (1981, 1983) note the presence of incremental progress as syntagmatic process in the *Popol Vuh* and its successive creations, but nonetheless view the narrative as telling "different versions of the *same* creation" (Tarn and Prechtel 1981:106–107; this is critiqued in Gillespie n.d.). The effect then is to view the paradigmatic aspect as the dominant mode of discussing he past, as the analysts believe that each cycle of creation is equivalent and differs only in what the analysts deem ultimately insignificant ways. Tedlock (1996) has strenuously critiqued such an imputed purely cyclical and thus paradigmatic conception of time and process among the Maya. Gillespie's (n.d.) analysis of the *Popol Vuh* from its beginning to the death of Zipacna and Cabracan reveals significant and heretofore unrecognized syntagmatic linkages and operations in the narrative. Together these indicate that the view of the *Popol Vuh* as a mostly paradigmatically repetitive narrative is a product not of the nature of the narrative itself but rather analyses of it and dominant ways of thinking about it and Mesoamerican narratives writ large, which it often stands for in a synecdochic relation (Gillespie n.d.). This is the same point, to a great extent, concerning the shortcomings of a purely paradigmatic and Levi Straussian–inspired narrative analysis as it has been practiced in Mesoamerica and in anthropology in general in which the syntagmatic axis is almost completely ignored, and thus static paradigmatic relations are by analytic process all that remain to be compared.

Graulich (1997) takes an approach to this difference between Mexica and non-Mexica representations of the "suns" (or "ages") in Central Mexican sources that is grounded in an appreciation for syntagmatic relations and specifically the opposed processes of conservation and transformation through time.[4] He notes (Graulich 1997:63–91) that, much like the four creations of the *Popol Vuh*, there is a notion of incremental progress in non-Mexica Central Mexican representations of the stories of the four suns that they contain. These four suns are divided into two sets of two in various ways, including according to contrastive ways within the same account (i.e., two suns might be linked paradigmatically to one another through one sign relation but contrasted with each other and linked to the other suns according to another sign relation). This is therefore similar to the marriages in the Priest's Speech, which can also be divided into two sets of two (two marriages to overly similar and northern/male/celestial/ex-Chichimec groups, in contrast to two marriages to categorically "Islander" groups). Interestingly, in the Mexica-influenced representations, according to Graulich, the division of four is not into two sets of two, but rather into two sets in which the first set contains the first four suns whereas the fifth sun, the age of Mexica supremacy, stands alone as an entirely new age. The production of an age of Mexica hegemony thus appears revolutionary and stands out against the backdrop of previous and apparently unchanging suns. In this way one of the effects of this novelty is to herald a new cosmological era *as* a new political era and vice versa; the two ideas become fused into one. In the Priest's Speech in the *Relación de Michoacán*, Taríacuri is also produced as a revolution in many ways—a novel agent that fundamentally remakes the world. Note how syntagmatically speaking, however, the Priest's Speech and the Mexica representations of five suns achieve this in two very different ways. The Priest's Speech does build incrementally toward the construction of a Taríacuri in a trial-and-error fashion (the marriage of the Uacúsecha to the Naranjans precedes the marriage to the Xaráquaros that produces Taríacuri; Taríacuri's failed marriage to the Corínguaros precedes the final marriage to Zurumban's daughters) and *then*, once Taríacuri is constituted as a properly dual and autopoietic character ,the story pivots as motivated by Taríacuri's personal pivoting and folds back upon itself to ultimately fundamentally reorder the political balkanization that existed at the outset of the narrative. As noted above this process involves another set of four instantiations of production. The Mexica narratives, in contrast, present a series of four suns as temporally manifested stasis (nothing new happens) until the fifth when the nature of humanity itself, and rulership along with it, is fully formed and ruled by the Mexica. If Graulich is right that the Mexica influenced narratives represent reworking available or existing cosmological frameworks for political reasons (whatever the particular motivation was), then both the Priest's Speech and the Mexica representations constitute novel formulations themselves—these concretizations are unique departures that seek to render certain political actors and/or factions as themselves unique, and it is interesting that they do so through a similar process (reworking syntagmatic relationships) but different specific methods within that process—a fundamental reworking of syntagmatically organized "events" in the case of the Priest's Speech as opposed to a predominantly paradigmatic structure that was easily manipulated because of the primacy of its paradigmatic structure/cyclical similarity in the Mexica representations.

This discussion indicates that more recognition of the syntagmatic axis of narrative must influence future scholarship and comparison among Mesoamerican narratives and the study of Mesoamerican historicity. The results of the study of the Priest's Speech fundamentally rely on this recognition of the syntagmatic axis of that narrative and the manner in which the ordering of the episodes is key to understanding the full meaning of the narrative and thus Taríacuri. The work of Graulich concerning the Mexica representations of the past that finds interesting departures from other Central Mexican sources yields another window into the complexities of how various modes of concretization and their preexisting orientations toward the primacy of either paradigm or syntagm can be reworked in ways that can be easily overlooked if one takes an overly broad view of the similarities of the accounts and thereby discounts the differences. Finally, Gillespie's (n.d.) theoretically informed analysis of the first several episodes of the *Popol Vuh* indicate that within each concretization there is a complex process of literally producing the past as an intersubjective experience in which the narrator, the audience, and the characters and actions of the story are mutually intertwined. This production at least potentially, I add, reproduces this sense of production and concretization. By this I mean that these narratives, while occupying a kind of middle ground between myth and history (e.g., "sacred history") were composed within and in their telling themselves constituted a sacred (ritual) "time-space" (see especially Tedlock 2010) in which it was potentially *expected* that the past would be produced and brought into being through the mode of poiesis and well-ordered and ordering speech that made the connection of the past to the present intelligible, as opposed to chaotic, and thus constructed its own sacredness.

Mesoamerican historicity viewed broadly, as perhaps is common in many cultures, relies not only on the physicality of the sacred books and codices but also at least in part on the perceived legitimacy within culturally constructed parameters of any particular narrational event. Those cultural parameters include the poetic and poietic function of continual production in which those poetic and poietic functions help to construct the ritual/sacred time-space of the telling and thus the sacredness of each new potentially different narrational event and the truth of the content of the narrative. This is how, I suggest, the overall sacredness and the truth claims of the narrative are brought into being, in spite of, or even because of, the possibility for what to our modern Western eyes might seem to be a radical departure from previous concretizations. We lose sight of the power of that production and the thing thus produced—a new and potentially incorporative sense of past and self—if we take a strictly paradigmatic view of narratives and ignore the syntagmatic aspect, the enabling of relativization, in the poetics and poiesis of the narrative form. As discussed in chapter 3 in the present book, the syntagmatic axis of narrative has the ability to incorporate and orient variability precisely because it exists and takes shape in a temporal flow. It can thus serve as a model and microcosm of cultural survival and syncretism in which a sense of the story and thus of the cultural self can be preserved even as it allows for change. In some cases this ability to incorporate is reflected within the story itself, as new events or characters can be brought into the fold of the story; such is the case with narratives such as the K'iche' Maya *Título de Totonicapán* and *Título* of C'oyoi as analyzed by Quiroa (2011), which include Christian themes and biblical characters. This is also the case with some of the more locally oriented documents in Michoacán, for example, the reference to Valladolid in one of the *Títulos primordiales* from Jarácuaro discussed below. Alternatively historical change can be reflected obliquely by changing, and adding to what is apparently a stable paradigmatic schema, as in the Mexica-influenced representations of five suns as opposed to four. In the case of the Priest's Speech in the *Relación de Michoacán*, the relationship between the events of the present and the past can be reworked to influence the open and contingent nature of the present by fabricating and fixing in time the events of the past while barely explicitly admitting a relationship between the two. In this manner, historical events in the

flow of time definitively impacted but are only implicitly present in the comple
fabrication and weaving together of some mix of real and fictive events that onl
take on their meaning as part of the whole in relation to their placement within th
narrative. This is the syntagmatic production and fixing of a powerful paradigm a
a certain point in time in the past for the benefit of a certain known person in th
present. This is production that thus not only appears coherent and organized, an
importantly self-organizing (autopoietic), but also, because it need not explicitl
reference the present (i.e., the context of its narration), can appear unbiased an
apolitical, in actuality heightening the impact of its biased and political effect.

CYCLICITY IN AND SURROUNDING THE TARASCAN-
SPANISH COLONIAL ENCOUNTER

The Priest's Speech concretizes a cyclical view of the flow of time that is simulta
neously similar to and different from other Mesoamerican native and developing
Mestizo indigenous traditions. The syntagmatic relations of the Priest's Speec
as discussed in chapter 4 are linear and forward moving but at the midpoint o
the narrative, a simultaneous folding-back form of chiasmus is added to and inte
grated within that forward-moving syntagmatic process. The total effect is to pro
duce internal to the narrative a Taríacuri that is all agency and order, as a mean
to producing a historical cyclicity that exists outside of the narrative and in ref
erence to Don Francisco Taríacuri. Cyclicity is apparent in other traditions from
Mesoamerica, but in different forms. As revealed in Gillespie's (1989) analysis
Moteuczoma is constructed in the numerous representations of Central Mexican
sources as a boundary figure. The repetition of the name Moteuczoma among the
royal dynasty of Tenochtitlan is no mere accident of history, or even the culturally
instituted practice of handing down specific names within a lineage. Rather, the
previous or prehispanic Moteuczoma (Moteuczoma Ilhuicamina) had an ambigu
ous relationship with this name—he has another name, Ilhuicamina, which is in
some documents given more prominence than the name Moteuczoma. He is the
only Tenochca ruler with two names. Gillespie shows that this is due to his posi
tion as a boundary figure within the royal family, just as the Moteuczoma who
met Cortés became a historical boundary figure between his people and Cortés
and, more significantly, between a prehispanic era and a colonial one. Gillespie's
analysis indicates that Moteuczoma Ilhuicamina became Moteuczoma only *after*
the Spanish Conquest because it was only then that Moteuczoma II (Moteuczoma
Xocoyotzin) became that boundary figure at the end of the prehispanic era and the
Colonial era (Gillespie 1989:167–169). Understanding Moteuczoma Xocoyotzin's
boundary position as heralding an end and a beginning (as all boundary figures do)

Ilhuicamina became Moteuczoma Ilhuicamina in order to preside over and ensure a transition between one cycle of Tenochca kings and the next, renewed, cycle of Tenochca kings. Moteuczoma's identity as a boundary figure extends further back in time in the Aztec concretizations of the past, as there is a Moteuczoma present at the beginnings of Mexica history at Aztlán (Gillespie 1989:164–165, citing Chimalpahin Cuauhtlehuanitzin's [1958:16–17] *Memorial breve* and the *Crónica mexicayotl* [Tezozomoc 1975:15–16]). Because Mesoamerican peoples' views of time and therefore history are cyclical in some sense, in representations of the past these paired or repeated names are reworked to make the names fit this idea of cyclicty—to make history repeat itself. Gillespie furthermore traces the concretization of Moteuczoma as a boundary figure who will initiate a new cycle of indigenous rule in the future not, interestingly enough, in Central Mexican representations but rather in Maya sources.[5]

A quite similar pattern of cyclicity is evidently being concretized in the Priest's Speech in the *Relación de Michoacán*. Don Francisco Taríacuri's presence in the present as the best hope for some kind of negotiation and possible reconstitution of an indigenous kingdom makes him the touch point around which a past Taríacuri is constructed. Just as important, the advocacy of this present Taríacuri necessitates the concretization of this past Taríacuri as not simply a great leader but as the dually composed agentic force that produces the kingdom both symbolically through a microcosmic embodiment and indexically through his concrete, real-world," actions. There is not enough evidence to suggest that Don Francisco Taríacuri was named after a past Taríacuri—that is, that a notion of a past Taríacuri was present at the time of the conquest to draw on when naming Don Francisco Taríacuri. I am also not suggesting that the idea of a Taríacuri was a completely novel idea. The symbolic content of Taríacuri as a centering figure and a dually composed character, judging by the rich symbolism of the name (see chapter 4), is likely to be a prehispanic concept in some form. The association with a certain bird that is said to mark the transition to the rainy season, and the association to the wind both by his name and this bird's perceived behavior, as well as other forms of evidence such as the name of the mountain that borders Tzintzuntzan and which exists in the center of the Lake Pátzcuaro Basin, are all highly significant symbolic constructs implying a centering and mediating function between opposed but complementary terms. This is precisely what is drawn upon, I suggest, in constructing his centrality as the mediator and term that encompasses, and then reproduces the combination of, the Chichimec and Islander categories. It is also worth noting in these symbolic associations that in contrast to what I say above concerning the lack of symbolic fit between the Toltecs and Culhua people of the Central Mexican corpus in certain regards, here Taríacuri himself seems to be assuming some of the symbolic associations often attributed to Topiltzin/Quetzalcoatl. I refer specifically to Quetzalcoatl's role as a boundary figure par excellence as analyzed by Gillespie (1989; see also López Austin and López Luján 2000), but also his avatar Ehécatl, a god associated with wind. Returning to the specifics of the priest's narrative in the *Relación de Michoacán* and Michoacán historicity in general, I consider "Taríacuri" as an idea or a bundle of symbolic relations constitutive of kingship or of some cosmic import in Tarascan culture to have a prehispanic origin. The fact that Taríacuri's various locations and markedly different importance in other representations of the prehispanic past, however, indicates that "Taríacuri" as a category or concept occupied no fixed point and no fixed importance within remembrances and concretizations of the past (see chapter 1). The narrative and the context of its production imply that it is the past Taríacuri who is the symbolic projection of the present Taríacuri (Don Francisco). What I mean by this is not that there was no prehispanic set of beliefs about a "Taríacuri," only that they had as yet not settled on a singular personage the way that they clearly do in the Priest's Speech. The past Taríacuri as a cultural broker, encompassing term, and embodiment of the kingdom, came into being as these attributes were needed to confer onto Don Francisco Taríacuri by implication. At the very least, drawing on established and temporally persistent ideas about kingship in Mesoamerica as composed of dual figures or entities, there was in Michoacán this idea of kings as dual figures who were microcosms of cosmic powers writ large, that such figures were powerful because they could negotiate various "social worlds," and that in the context of the colonial encounter the fact that such a dual figure is not only necessary but sitting right there worked in tandem to produce in essence both Taríacuris, past and present. In other words a Taríacuri in the past that likely was a broadly held cosmological ideal of what Mesoamerican kings were supposed to be was adapted and pinned down in the past and pinned to a figure who shared Don Francisco Taríacuri's name at precisely the time that Don Francisco himself was emerging as a potential and potentially powerful player in the ongoing development of the colonial encounter / power struggle. The priest manages to mythologize—to construct as a powerful exemplar of a larger paradigm (itself being constructed and in the process pinned down)—Don Francisco in the present not directly but by mythologizing a past Taríacuri. This is a different thing from saying that there was in prehispanic Tarascan "sacred history" an already preconstituted Taríacuri (with all of these attributes, including importantly that particular name) that through his narrative the priest simply projects onto Don Francisco. In order to make Don Francisco into the leader the priest wanted him to be, the priest took it upon himself to make this past Taríacuri he wanted *him* to be.

This cyclical notion of time thus becomes in the Priest's Speech and the colonial encounter more generally not a straightjacket of prescribed action but rather more of a resource, an ideological framework to draw upon as historicity is practiced. This is akin to Sahlins's (1999:408) useful phrase "the inventiveness of tradition" and focuses the analytic project on actions in real time that attempt to make sense of the past, present, and future as one thread of time and temporal process. At least partially constitutive of this effort is the concretization of that flow in concordance with larger cosmological precepts in order to constitute the most powerful and persuasive argument possible, even as those cosmological precepts are themselves reworked slightly in the process (following Sahlins 1981, 1985). Taríacuri in the Priest's Speech becomes a boundary figure in not exactly the same way as the two Moteuczomas in the Central Mexican representations (which was due to a large extent to their temporal/syntagmatic positioning). Rather, Taríacuri becomes a boundary figure because he is a dually composed figure who is necessary to integrate opposed social worlds and thus actively assemble and thereby embody the novel synthesis that is a new political formation. Existing at the boundary between two groups, Taríacuri stands in the middle of them and embodies their combination and encompassment.[6]

Another form of cyclicity involves the two Taríacuris. I do not at this point have an elegant model of the ideological/structural framework for these examples of repeated names akin to Gillespie's model of cyclicity in representations of Tenochca kings. While the same kind of cyclicity as representations of the Tenochca pattern of succession is not evident in the *Relación de Michoacán*, the following details of the concretizations at hand are suggestive. The past Taríacuri is the last lord of Pátzcuaro. His nephews Hiripan and Tangáxoan, along with Taríacuri's second son, Hiquíngaxe, institute the wars of conquest that establish the kingdom, and upon the initial successes of those wars the capital is moved to Ihuatzio. That place becomes the seat of Curicaueri and the location of the wealth objects and spoils of war that fund his cult. Hiquíngaxe, who assumes the leadership in Pátzcuaro, has an ambiguous status as a lord. He joins his cousins as a "sacrificer," not necessarily as a lord. Elsewhere in the *Relación de Michoacán*, only Hiripan and Tangáxoan are concretized as having invented local-level offices in a stereotypical speech that was supposedly recited at the investiture ceremonies of subordinate lords (Alcalá 2000:604). The implication is that only Hiripan and Tangáxoan—because they are the Chichimec elements of this trio of young lords—have the transformative capacity to both institute local offices and raise others to those offices. Hiquíngaxe, as an Islander, is not lordly enough in the new sense of the term to be included in that representation. What defines "lordly" has now been constructed as an encompassing and transformative capacity which is now, thanks to the Priest's Speech, grounded in a Chichimec identity. Hiquíngaxe's "Islander" status (as opposed to Chichimec identity) within the Uacúsecha and his role as sacrificer indicate that

Taríacuri is thus constructed as the last paradigmatically or categorically Chichimec Uacúsecha lord in Pátzcuaro. Don Francisco Taríacuri would, then, *resume* the presence of the Chichimec Uacúsecha lordship in Pátzcuaro. Don Pedro Cuinierángari, the indigenous governor in Pátzcuaro for most of the 1530s up to the production of the *Relación de Michoacán* itself, was not a Uacúsecha member and as such was not properly a lord; certainly this would have been the perspective of Uacúsecha loyalists and the priesthood (as discussed by Afanador-Pujol 2015).

It is also noteworthy that a similar phenomenon surrounds the representation of the two Tangáxoans. Don Francisco Taríacuri's father, Tzintzicha Tangáxoan, also exhibits the repetition of a name. In this case, there are a few curious points that suggest that this name is being "recycled," to borrow Gillespie's (1989) term for the name Moteuczoma and other repeated names of Mexica and "Toltec" kings as boundary figures. The first Tangáxoan is the member of the Uacúsecha who brings the deity Xarátanga back to Tzintzuntzan and settles there, thereby initiating the Uacúsecha lordship in Tzintzuntzan. The initiation of Uacúsecha rule at Tzintzuntzan under the auspices of a Tangáxoan is paradigmatically inverted by the end of Uacúsecha rule (or at least autonomous rule) caused by the arrival of the Spaniards and Tzintzicha Tangáxoan's capitulation to them. The named figure Tangáxoan therefore exists as a "boundary" figure marking the beginning and end of Uacúsecha rule at Tzintzuntzan, much in the same way that the Moteuczomas' places within the Tenochca dynasty marked boundary points of cycles in Gillespie's (1989) analysis of Aztec kings discussed above. There is another commonality between the two cases—the possibility that the matching of names was an ideological construction concretized in Early Colonial practices and representations of the past in order to make history conform to cyclical ideas of how the past should have been shaped and the implication of its shape for the present and future. In Gillespie's research, it is the past Moteuczoma (Ilhuicamina) whose name is altered. In the Tarascan case, it seems to be the second Tangáxoan, the one who encountered the Spaniards, who has two names applied to him. Tzintzicha Tangáxoan possibly had the name Tzintzicha before the name Tangáxoan was applied to him. In one reported speech by Zuangua (and outside of the Priest's Speech), he refers to his sons as potential heirs and names "Zincicha, who is the eldest" (Alcalá 2000:647), thereby omitting the name Tangáxoan. Twice on the same folio (Alcalá 2000:541), this last king is referred to as Tangáxoan followed immediately by an indication that he also had the name Tzintzicha. As in Gillespie's (1989:167) analysis of the Aztec kings and the addition of the name Motecuhzoma to Ilhuicamina, Tzintzicha Tangáxoan is the only Tarascan king said to have two names. Table 1.1 lists the names of Uacúsecha lords in various representations, and I have previously drawn attention to the fact that Taríacuri does not have the same prominence in any of these other representations. It is also noteworthy in this context that when Tzintzicha Tangáxoan is named in these other representations, in some cases both names are used but in the other cases when only one name is used it is always Tzintzicha. While this evidence is not conclusive, it at least suggests the possibility that with the realization that Tzintzicha Tangáxoan would be the last king in Tzintzuntzan, an effort was made to cast this event as the proper end of a cycle by marking Tzintzicha as a new Tangáxoan, thus closing the cycle of kingship in Tzintzuntzan with the same name that had initiated it. With this cycle closed, a new cycle had to be initiated.

This pattern of establishing cyclicity and repetition is not unique to the Priest's Speech, nor the *Relación de Michoacán* that contains it, but can be found in other concretizations of the past in the ethnohistoric record of Michoacán. In a discussion of two primordial titles from the island of Jarácuaro (Xaráquaro of the Priest's Speech) that were supposedly produced in 1596, Roskamp (2010b:44) notes that one document contains an origin in which Zuangua begins the migration and comes from Valladolid (prehispanic Guayangareo and modern Morelia), which became the capital of Michoacán and the seat of the diocese in 1580.[7] In this document Valladolid/Guayangareo exists as an important font of Jarácuaro's authority and lordly lineage, even as it was the locus of regional authority in the implicit end of the temporal sequence at play—the context of the production of the document and all of the circumstances of uncertain land boundaries and settlement integrity to which the document was produced as a response. The migration of the noble family of the town passes through Tzintzuntzan and ultimately ends in Jarácuaro with the founding of the town and delimitation of its territory. The title of Cherán Hatzicurin, which was used in a legal case from 1715 to 1760, opens with a date of 1509 and includes a king with an indigenous name who was the son of a king named Guzmán. This would place a Guzmán in the prehispanic era that was prominently associated with the origins of the town, likely mirroring the importance of Nuño Beltrán de Guzmán, president of the first Audiencia, leader of the first expedition into the northwest that relied upon indigenous allies including Tarascans, and overseer of Tzintzicha Tangáxoan's execution (see chapter 1), in the imposition of the colonial order. Finally, in the corpus of documents relating to Carapan, and particularly in the *Codex Plancarte*, there is a repetitive cyclicity of multiple founding events of the town, each initiated by a Uacúsecha king or warrior-representative of some Uacúsecha king. The documents themselves contain discussions of two separate confirmations of their own existence as well as of the information they contain concerning the town's origins and its territorial limits as presented therein. First there is the visitation and confirmation by Don Antonio Huitziméngari in 1545 (which would have been his first year as governor) and then a narration of the election of Don Pablo Cuiru as governor and his visit to the town in 1589 as well as his confirmation of the document in 1597 (Códice Plancarte 1959; Roskamp 2010b:45–46). There is therefore a congruence between this cyclical content of the document in the form of its repeated foundational events and taking possession of the land by marking its extent and the repeated confirmation of the document itself in the Early Colonial period in which confirming the document serves as a symbolic proxy for (re)founding the town and reasserting its territorial extent.

These other examples of constructing and concretizing cyclical events, founding episodes, and names bridging both the prehispanic and the Colonial era indicate that the cyclicity concretized by the Priest's Speech is by no means unique. I suggest it is necessary to stop seeing the Priest's Speech as the "official history" of the Uacúsecha. At the very least, while the chief priest may have endeavored that his concretization of the prehispanic past might *become* the "official state" history, I emphasize that he was an actor engaged in producing his narrative in relation to the sociohistorical context just as much or likely more so than those indigenes that produced the primordial titles just discussed. Those primordial titles reveal a concern with linking their content to preexisting places and people associated with power, and who or what exactly manifested power at the time of the documents' production of course was a product of that sociohistorical context. This is why one representation contains a reference to Valladolid, as the move of the diocese and capital to that new city was likely to have been either just completed or well cemented in the colonial order at the point in time in which that particular concretization was completed. As I have noted, however, in the Priest's Speech there is no preexisting and singular manifestation of cosmic-cum-social power. This is partly due to the fact that the Uacúsecha claimed an unmatched position—they were the ultimate sovereigns, and so they could not establish their right to rule through reference to another power, as the lords of Carapan did in claiming to be "another Tzintzuntzan" (Códice Plancarte 1959; Roskamp 2003:328; 2010b:46). Moreover, in the prehispanic era of Michoacán there does not appear to have been a "Tollan" in terms of a city at which authority, proper food, legality and morality, and crafting and the arts originated (as in analyses of Graulich 1997; Gillespie 1989; and López Austin and López Luján 2000). Teotihuacán is known to have influenced prehispanic Michoacán (Filini 2004; Piña Chan and Oí 1982; Pollard 2005), and so the lack of a reflection of the idea of such a Tollan in the Priest's Speech is a question that merits further research. What is apparent is that the priest felt the need to establish anew or for the first time a combination of elementary categories just such a manifestation of complementary and thus complete sociocosmic forces. In the process of doing this, he also took great care to construct that personification of sociocosmic totality in a way that would also aid Don Francisco Taríacuri the most in his bid for power in the colonial system. What is evident in the Priest's Speech is not cyclicity per se; while there are structural similarities between certain episodes in terms of the categories and their interaction and transformation, there are no series of episodes that completely or very closely mirror previous series of episodes as in some other Mesoamerican concretizations. Rather, through predominantly syntagmatic means and the establishment of Taríacuri as the personification of a sociocosmic totality and therefore legitimate authority, the Priest's Speech produces a cyclical vision of time and human history within cosmic cyclical time only in reference to the world outside of itself. In this way the Priest's Speech offers us a window into how a mix of social memory and cultural innovation works at a particular moment in time to produce a mode of conceptualizing time in which a temporal flow of events with two Taríacuris is manipulated such that cyclicity is produced through noncyclical means (with respect to the internal structure of the narrative). It stands to reason that a similar process took place elsewhere in Mesoamerica and that the first "Tollan" was produced in a similar manner, by reworking and fabricating a known or mostly known temporal sequence to demonstrate paradigmatic qualities that were evident through that sequence but which then took on a paradigmatic and symbolic life of its own as it continued to then be deployed in social action.

THE PRIEST'S SPEECH, THE RESULTS OF ANALYSIS, AND THE NECESSARY ROLE OF SYNTAGMATIC RELATIONS IN A MESOAMERICAN ANALYTIC FRAMEWORK

The preceding discussion of the manner in which the Priest's Speech diverges from and is similar to other Mesoamerican concretizations of the past, brief and preliminary though it may be, should be read as an indication of what can be done with a fully syntagmatic method of narrative analysis as employed in this book. Studies of Mesoamerican mythology, narrative, religion, ritual, and culture have made great strides through the application of paradigmatically oriented methods. Such studies have given us much knowledge of the "big picture" when it comes to this culture area and even in certain cases the specific cultures that comprised it. Where there have been enough sources and evidence, most notably in Nahua Central Mexico and the Maya area, we have a detailed knowledge of the nature of indigenous philosophy, religion, and the narratives that they informed. We know the basic tenets of belief, the pantheon that this term applies to when used to describe Mesoamerican religious systems, the meanings of terms and metaphors (including diphrastic constructions) and substitutions thereof, and how in practice the metaphysical realm was believed to influence and constitute the human world in these more well-known areas of Mesoamerica. However, when it comes to lesser-known cultures and polities, those well-known areas loom large and dominate the analysis and dis-cussion, making independent investigation of those lesser-known cultures nearly impossible. One example is the perception among some Mesoamerican scholars that the *Popol Vuh* is the "key" to all Mesoamerican problems of iconography, that is, there exists a problematic "Popol Vuh syndrome" in which that narrative is claimed to exist in a synecdochic relationship to all Mesoamerican narratives, encapsulat-ing and exemplifying Mesoamerican indigenous thought (Gillespie n.d.; de Ridder 1989; Robiscek and Hales 1981). The effect of such a mode of analysis is not only to push these lesser-known cultures to the periphery of analytic attention, but to render analytic inquiry of those cultures problematic from the start. If we take the Priest's Speech and use Nahua or Maya sources to "fill in the gaps," so to speak, or Tarascan/Purhépecha words and deities are from the beginning understood in part thanks to analogies to Nahua sources, then we as analysts have already changed the subjects of our investigation. Thankfully this is changing in investigations into Michoacán history, prehistory, and the cultures of the area with the dedication and work of talented historians, archaeologists, and linguists. The present work is guilty to some extent of the analytically problematic process of bringing in Nahua and Maya comparisons in helping to understand the symbolic relations of some of the characters and terms that the priest employed. This has helped to demonstrate, I hope, the richness of the narrative, the manner in which it evokes larger concepts, and the likely ways in which religion and philosophy of humans and the natural world are reflected in the narrative. It is worth pointing out, however, that the underlying analysis—the coordinated transformations of the categories, the syntag-matic operations of reversal and pivoting, the construction of episodic and paradig-matic hierarchies, the identification of a principle of a conservative but autopoietic Chichimec paradigm—was conducted without outside influence or consideration of the wider Mesoamerican literature. The delimitation of analytic boundaries is an ever-present problem, and tacking back and forth between isolating and comparing is a fruitful mode of inquiry—provided that the subject of study is in fact isolated. It must also be noted that unless each culture of Mesoamerica is studied on its own merits, this process of focusing and isolation of the subject, then "comparison" of the richness of the cultures and historicities of the Mesoamerican culture area, is impossible, since some areas will be compromised by material from other cultures with which they are supposedly being compared.

In addition, if Mesoamerican ethnohistory is to continue to take part in the larger rapprochement between history and anthropology, culture and history, I suggest that the method of analysis used here, bringing in the syntagmatic axis of narrative, be given a prominent place in the analytic toolkit of Mesoamerican schol-ars. This method is key to rigorous analysis of individual narratives (both "histories" and "myths") and is therefore indispensable to the movement to historicize the culture concept and bring both larger-scale cultural patterns and smaller-scale individual practice into focus (Ohnuki-Tierney 1990a, 1990b, 2001, 2005; Ortner 1990; Sahlins 1985, 2004). Here again this work is already underway in Mesoamerica in the form of increasingly detailed examinations of individual ethnohistoric documents and the application of new scientific techniques to evaluate the material, composition, deconstruction, artistic production, and so on, of those (e.g., Cummins et al. 2014). Close readings of documents, reading "intertextually" (Hanks 2000), the relations of visual/pictographic and textual information in single documents, the identifications of artistic "hands," and the like, bring us closer to understanding how individuals took part in cultural production and the choices that they made as part of that constructive process (e.g., Afanador-Pujol 2010, 2015; Asselbergs 2006; Douglas 2010; Diel 2008; Hanks 2010; Leibsohn 2009; Wood 2003). With Turner's method that includes the syntagmatic axis of narrative, we can now analyze both the selective (paradigmatic) and combinatory (syntagmatic) aspects of indigenous and mestizo narratives in order to examine the logics of why a particular sign, name, character, or other thing was placed when and where it was in a narrative sequence as a particular concretization at a particular moment in time, and from a particular place in the social structure and developing colonial encounter. It might be possible to examine why, for example, the same authors concretized different versions of the past at different times. We can escape a purely paradigmatic and predominantly atemporal structuralism in which similar themes and episodes within and between concretizations are seen as equivalent transformations of one another not necessarily because that is what they are, but rather because that is all that the method is equipped with—like the hammer that can only see a whole world populated with nothing but nails, purely paradigmatic structuralism has a myopic view and lack of analytic imagination, produced by a context-free lack of rigor that is a consequence of discarding the syntagmatic aspect of narrative. Following those authors who have discussed the continual flux in which Mesoamerican peoples worked and reworked their sources and the contents thereof (see chapter 2), I suggest moreover that we not see the indigenous production of concretizations and the practice of historicity as qualitatively different in the Colonial era than in the prehispanic era. The claim that the Mexica ruler Itzcoatl burned the existing books following his and their rise to power (Sahagún 1950–1982:10:189–197) is frequently cited as evidence of just this sort of historicity work. This is but one of the most dramatic examples of the same kinds of processes that we can very readily document for the Colonial era as the "structure of the conjuncture" (Sahlins 1981, 1985) of Spanish colonialism took shape that were likely occurring frequently in Mesoamerica before the arrival of the Spaniards. Particularly in the demographically, politically, and religiously volatile

Postclassic period, we should expect that the role of history as symbol, history as sacred charter, and history as prophecy mean that history was subject to at times dramatic but many other times subtle reworkings in which the skill of the narrator enabled him[8] to exhibit mastery over the form, manipulating previous works to make certain arguments, while that very mastery also allowed him to also disappear behind his creation as merely an agent of tradition and have it seem as though that creation is the most self-evident understanding of the significance of the past and how it relates to the present.

NOTES

1. I have in mind here Roy Wagner's (1986) work *Symbols That Stand for Themselves*.

2. It is important to note here that in the Central Mexican sources, certain events such as the discovery of maize are told in more cosmological terms, and these narratives share many structural traits with the stories of Ce Acatl Topiltzin Quetzalcoatl, but the stories concerning the latter are nonetheless told in a frame of reference that gives the appearance of historical time (see Graulich 1997). In other words, the absence of a grand "Tollan" in the Priest's Speech does still stand out in comparison with the Central Mexican sources.

3. Tales of the recovery of one's father's remains (or other older male relatives, including uncles) is a prominent theme throughout the Americas and is present in cultures in which kingship was absent—and therefore the theme does not necessarily have to be related to kingship and sociopolitical hierarchy. For example, Lévi-Strauss (1978:370–371) analyzes an Oglala myth in which a hero who is conceived when his mother swallows a stone, thus giving him "supernatural powers," sets out and is ultimately successful in finding and reviving his uncles (his mother's "brothers"), aided by those supernatural powers.

4. Graulich (1997:75) states that several documents are Mexica influenced and states that specifically the *Leyenda de los soles* (published as part of the volume *History and Mythology of the Aztecs: Codex Chimalpopoca*, Bierhorst 1992) and the *Historia de los mexicanos por sus pinturas* (1888–1892) "seem to contain the 'official version' of the Mexica." Graulich includes in his analysis of both Mexica-influenced and non-Mexica sources the *Codex Telleriano-Remensis, Codex Vaticanus A, Codex Azcatitlan, Codex Aubin, Anales de Tlatelolco, Historia Tolteca-Chichimeca* (also known as the *Anales de Cuauhtinchan*), *Codex Chimalpopoca* (itself containing the *Anales de Cuauhtitlan* and *Leyenda de los Soles*), *Crónica Mexicayotl, Origen de los mexicanos, Relación de la genealogía y linaje de los señores que han señoreado esta tierra de la Nueva España, Historia de los mexicanos por sus pinturas, Histoyre du Méxique,* Fray Toribio de Benavente's (also known as Motolinía) *Memoriales* and *Historia de los indios de Nueva España, Historia de las indias de Nueva España e islas de tierra firme, Crónia Mexicana, Codex Ramírez, Historia natural y moral de las indias, Monarquía Indiana,* various *relaciones* and a *Historia Chichimeca* by Fernando de Alva Ixtlilxochitl, and the works of Fray

Bernardino de Sahagún including his *Primeros memorials*, the *Manuscrito de Tlatelolco*, and the *Florentine Codex* (the *Historia general de las cosas de nueva España*).

5. The expected return of kings, whether boundary figures in the case examined here by Gillespie, or other "misunderstood" and "populist" kings (and the two phenomena—existence at the boundary and fond remembrance—are not mutually exclusive, and indeed appear to be partially constitutive of one another) is taken up most recently by Graeber and Sahlins (2017).

6. It is also worth pointing out that Gillespie's (1989) analysis demonstrates the importance of women, what she calls the "Woman of Discord," as linking various eras and enabling a new cycle to be initiated. Relevant to this discussion, a royal woman is essential to constituting the transition to a new cycle of Tenochca kings that Moteuczoma Ilhuicamina marks. In the Priest's Speech, any similar construction is either absent or only present in a very transformed way. Taríacuri obviously owes his Islander nature to the fact that his mother is an Islander, and he also gains legitimacy through his marriage to the daughters of Zurumban. Neither episode involves discord or war in the same manner as in the Central Mexican sources, however. In fact, if any discord involving a woman is present, it is that involving Taríacuri's first wife, the Corínguaro princess.

7. Roskamp (2010b:44) states that this origin in Valladolid is clear evidence that the document probably was produced in the course of the seventeenth or eighteenth century.

8. While there were apparently female priests ("priestesses") as in the episode of Xaratanga's priests and priestesses appropriating the goddess's vestments, all indications are that male priests would have been the ones to recite speeches similar in function if not content to the speech contained in the Relacion de Michoacan and analyzed here.

Epilogue

In the end, the priest's vision of the future did come to fruition, at least nominally, but not with the success that the priest likely envisioned. Don Francisco Taríacuri became governor in 1543, following the death of Don Pedro Cuinierángari. He occupied that office for only two years, until his own death in 1545. He was succeeded by his younger brother, Don Antonio Huitziméngari, who was governor until his death in 1562. Don Antonio's family line enjoyed a high degree of status and influence in colonial Mexico for generations, and other families hailing from the prehispanic upper class were able to maintain or gain significant grips on economic and social power. Of course indigenous elites and their governing institutions never regained their previous autonomy, as the indigenous priest who narrated a history of the Uacúsecha likely envisioned.

DOI: 10.5876/9781607327493.c007

References

Afanador-Pujol, Angélica. 2010. "The Tree of Jesse and the *Relación de Michoacán*: Mimicry in Colonial Mexico." *Art Bulletin* 92 (4): 293–307. https://doi.org/10.1080/00043079.2010.10786115.

Afanador-Pujol, Angélica. 2014. "Let the Waters and the Pigments Flow on these Pages: Making and Emending Landscape in the *Relación de Michoacán* (1539–1541)." In *Manuscript Cultures of Colonial Mexico and Peru: New Questions and Approaches*, ed. Thomas B. F. Cummins, Emily A. Engel, Barbara Anderson, and Juan M. Ossio A., 141–159. Los Angeles: Getty Research Institute.

Afanador-Pujol, Angélica. 2015. *The Relación de Michoacán (1539–1541) and the Politics of Representation in Colonial Mexico*. Austin: University of Texas Press.

Albiez-Zwieck, Sarah. 2013. Contactos Exteriores del Estado Tarasco: Influencias desde dentro y fuera de Mesoamerica. 2 vols. Zamora, Michoacan, Mexico: El Colegio de Michoacan.

Alcalá, Fray Jerónimo de. 1956. *Relación de las ceremonias y ritos y población y gobierno de los indios de la provincia de Michoacán*. Reproducción facsimilar del Ms IV de El Escorial, Madrid. Transcription, prologue, introduction, and notes by José Tudela. Madrid: Aguilar Publicistas.

Alcalá. Fray Jerónimo de. 2000. *Relación de Michoacán*. Moisés Franco Mendoza, coord., with paleography by Clotilde Martínez Ibáñez y Carmen Molina Ruiz. Zamora, Mexico: El Colegio de Michoacán and Gobierno del Estado de Michoacán.

DOI: 10.5876/9781607327493.c008

Anawalt, Patricia Rieff. 1992. "Ancient Cultural Contacts between Ecuador, West Mexico, and the American Southwest: Clothing Similarities." *Latin American Antiquity* 3(2): 114–129.

Armillas, Pedro. 1969. "The Arid Frontier of Mexican Civilization." *Transactions of the New York Academy of Sciences, Series 2* 31 (6 Series II): 697–704. https://doi.org/10.1111/j.2164-0947.1969.tb01993.x.

Arnauld, Marie Charlotte, and Dominique Michelet. 1991. "Les migrations postclassiques au Michoacán et au Guatemala: problèmes et perspectives." In *Vingt études sur le Mexique et le Guatemala réunies à la mémoire de Nicole Percheron*, ed. Alain Breton, Jean-Pierre Berthe, and Sylvie Lecoin, 67–92. Toulouse: Presses Universitaires du Mirail.

Appadurai, Arjun. 1981. "The Past as a Scarce Resource." *Man* 16 (2): 201–219. https://doi.org/10.2307/2801395.

Asselbergs, Florine G. L. 2006. *Conquered Conquistadors: The Lienzo de Quauhquechollan, a Nahua Vision of the Conquest of Guatemala*. Leiden, the Netherlands: University of Leiden Press.

Bakhtin, Mikhail. 1981. *The Dialogic Imagination*. Ed. Caryl Emerson. Trans. Michael Holquist. Austin: University of Texas Press.

Barba, Luis, Agustín Ortíz, Karl F. Link, Leonardo López Luján, and Luz Lazos. 1996. "Chemical Analysis of Residues in Floors and the Reconstruction of Ritual Activities at Templo Mayor." In *Archaeological Chemistry: Organic, Inorganic and Biochemical Analysis*, ed. Mary Virginia Orna, 139–156. Washington, DC: American Chemical Society. https://doi.org/10.1021/bk-1996-0625.ch012.

Barth, Fredrik, ed. 1969. *Ethnic Groups and Boundaries: The Social Organization of Cultural Differences*. Boston: Little, Brown.

Basso, Keith. 1996. *Wisdom Sits in Places: Landscape and Language Among the Western Apache*. Albuquerque: University of New Mexico Press.

Bauer, Brian S. 2004. *Ancient Cuzco: Heartland of the Inca*. Austin: University of Texas Press.

Bauer, Brian S., and Alan R. Covey. 2002. "Processes of State Formation in the Inca Heartland (Cuzco, Peru)." *American Anthropologist* 104 (3): 846–864. https://doi.org/10.1525/aa.2002.104.3.846.

Bauer, Brian S., and Douglas K. Smit. 2015. "Separating the Wheat from the Chaff: Inka Myths, Inka Legends, and the Archaeological Evidence for State Development." In *The Inka Empire: A Multidisciplinary Approach*, ed. Izumi Shimada, 67–80. Austin: University of Texas Press.

Beaumont, Fray Pablo de Purísima Concepción. 1932. *Crónica de Michoacán* (ca. 1778–1780). Mexico City: Publicaciones del Archivo General de la Nación.

Beekman, Christopher, and Alexander F. Christensen. 2003. "Controlling for Doubt and Uncertainty through Multiple Lines of Evidence: A New Look at the Mesoamerican Nahua Migrations." *Journal of Archaeological Method and Theory* 10 (2): 111–164. https://doi.org/10.1023/A:1024519712257.

egun, Erica. 2008. "The Many Faces of Figurines: Figurines as Markers of Ethnicity in Michoacán." *Ancient Mesoamerica* 19 (2): 311–318. doi:10.1017/s0956536108000412.

eltrán, Ulises. 1982. "Tarascan State and Society in Prehispanic Times: An Ethnohistorical Inquiry." PhD diss., University of Chicago.

erdan, Frances F., and Patricia R. Anawalt. 1992. *The Essential Codex Mendoza.* Berkeley: University of California Press.

ierhorst, John. 1992. *History and Mythology of the Aztecs: Codex Chimalpopoca.* Tucson: University of Arizona Press.

loch, Maurice. 1977. "The Past and the Present in the Present." *Man* 12 (2): 278–292. https://doi.org/10.2307/2800799.

oone, Elizabeth Hill. 2000. *Stories in Red and Black: Pictorial Histories of the Aztecs and Mixtecs.* Austin: University of Texas Press.

oone, Elizabeth Hill. 2007. *Cycles of Time and Meaning in the Mexican Books of Fate.* Austin: University of Texas Press.

oone, Elizabeth Hill, and Walter Mignolo, eds. 1994. *Writing without Words: Alternative Literacies in Mesoamerica and the Andes.* Durham, NC: Duke University Press.

ourdieu, Pierre. 1977. *Outline of a Theory of Practice.* Cambridge: Cambridge University Press. https://doi.org/10.1017/CBO9780511812507.

rand, Donald. 1943. "An Historical Sketch of Geography and Anthropology in the Tarascan Region." *New Mexico Anthropologist* 6–7 (2): 37–108. https://doi.org/10.1086 /newmexianthr.6_7.2.4291263.

rand, Donald. 1951. *Quiroga: A Mexican Municipio.* Smithsonian Institution, Institute of Social Anthropology Publication 11. Washington, DC: United States Printing Office.

rand, Donald. 1971. "Ethnohistoric Synthesis of Western Mexico." In *Archaeology of Northern Mesoamerica, Part 2,* ed. Gordon Ekholm and Ignacio Bernal, 632–656. *The Handbook of Middle American Indians,* Vol. 11, Robert Wauchope, general editor. Austin: University of Texas Press.

raswell, Geoffrey E. 2003. "Obsidian Exchange Spheres." In *The Postclassic Mesoamerican World,* ed. Michael E. Smith and Frances F. Berdan, 131–158. Salt Lake City: University of Utah Press.

ravo Ugarte, José. 1962a. *Historia sucinta de Michoacán.* Vol. 1, *Michoacán: El estado tarasco.* Mexico City: Editorial Jús, S. A.

ravo Ugarte, José. 1962b. "La *Relación de Michoacán.*" *Historia Mexicana* 12 (45): 13–25.

ricker, Victoria Reiffler. 1981. *The Indian Christ, the Indian King: The Historical Substrate of Maya Myth and Ritual.* Austin: University of Texas Press.

right, William. 1990. "'With One Lip, with Two Lips': Parallelism in Nahuatl." *Language* 66 (3): 437–452. https://doi.org/10.2307/414607.

Broda, Johanna. 1976. "Los Estamentos en el Ceremonial Mexica." In *Estratificación Social en la Mesoamérica Prehispánica*, ed. Pedro Carrasco and Johanna Broda, 37–66. Mexico City: INAH.

Broda, Johanna. 1982. "Astronomy, *Cosmovisión*, and Ideology in Pre-Hispanic Meso-america." In *Archaeoastronomy in the American Tropics*, ed. Anthony F. Aveni and Gary Urton. Annals of the New York Academy of Sciences 385: 81–110.

Burke, Peter. 1990. "Historians, Anthropologists, and Symbols." In *Culture through Time: Anthropological Approaches*, ed. Emiko Ohnuki-Tierney, 268–283. Stanford, CA: Stanford University Press.

Burkhart, Louise M. 2001. *Before Guadalupe: The Virgin Mary in Early Colonial Nahuatl Literature. Institute for Mesoamerican Studies Monograph 13*. Albany: State University of New York at Albany.

Byland, Bruce E., and John M. D. Pohl. 1994. *In the Realm of 8 Deer: The Archaeology of the Mixtec Codices*. Norman: University of Oklahoma Press.

Carlsen, Robert S., and Martin Prechtel. 1991. "The Flowering of the Dead: An Interpretation of Highland Maya Culture." *Man* (n.s.) 26 (1): 23–42.

Carlson, John B. 1980. "On Classic Maya Monumental Recorded History." In *Third Palenque Round Table, part 2*, ed. Merle Greene Robertson, 199–203. Austin: University of Texas Press.

Carot, Particia. 2005. "Reacomodos demográficos del clásico al posclásico en Michoacán: El retorno de los que se fueron." In *Reacomodos demográficos del clásico al posclásico en el Centro de México*, ed. Linda Manzanilla, 103–122. Mexico City: UNAM.

Carot, Patricia, and Marie-Areti Hers. 2006. "La gesta de los Toltecas-Chichimecas y de los Purépechas en las tierras de los antiguos pueblos ancestrales." In *Las vías del noroeste I: Una macroregión indígena americana*, ed. Carlo Bonfiglioli, Arturo Gutiérrez, and María Eugenia Olavarría, 47–82. Mexico City: UNAM.

Carr, David. 1986. *Time, Narrative, and History*. Bloomington: Indiana University Press.

Carr, David. 1998. "Narrative and the Real World: An Argument for Continuity." In *History and Theory: Contemporary Readings*, ed. Brian Fay, Philip Pomper, and Richard T. Vann, 137–152. Malden, MA: Blackwell.

Carrasco, Pedro. 1969. "Nuevos datos sobre los Nonoalca de habla mexicana en el Reino Tarasco." *Estudios de Cultura Nahuatl* 8:215–221.

Carrasco, Pedro. 1986. "Economía política en el Reino Tarasco." In *La sociedad indígena en el Centro Occidente de Mexico*, ed. Pedro Carrasco, 62–102. Zamora, Mexico: El Colegio de Michoacán.

Carrasco, Davíd. 1980. "Quetzalcoatl's Revenge: Primordium and Application in Aztec Religion." *History of Religions* 19 (4): 296–320. https://doi.org/10.1086/462854.

Caso, Alfonso. 1943. "The Calendar of the Tarascans." *American Antiquity* 9 (1): 11–28. https://doi.org/10.2307/275448.

Castro Gutiérrez, Felipe. 2015. "Identity and Ethnicity in Colonial Michoacán: Corporatism, Social Contract, and Individualism among the Tarascans." In *From Tribute to Communal Sovereignty: The Tarascan and Caxcan Territories in Transition*, ed. Andrew Roth-Seneff, Robert V. Kemper, and Julie Adkins, 133–144. Tucson: University of Arizona Press.

Castro Gutiérrez, Felipe, and Cristina Monzón García. 2008. "El lenguaje del poder: Conceptos tarascos en torno a la autoridad." In *Símbolos de poder en Mesoamerica*, coord. Guilhelm Olivier, 32–46. Mexico City: Universidad Nacional Autónoma de México.

Chimalpahin Cuauhtlehuanitzin, Domingo Francisco de San Antón Muñón. 1958. *Das "Memorial breve acerca de la fundación de la ciudad de Culhuacán."* Trans. and ed. Walter Lehmann and Gerdt Kutscher, Quellenwerke zur Alten Geschichte Amerikas aufgezeichnet in den Sprachen der Eingeborenen, vol. 7. Stuttgart, Germany.

Christensen, Allen J. 2007. *Popol Vuh: The Sacred Book of the Maya. Translated from the K'iche' and with notes by Allen J. Christensen.* Norman: University of Oklahoma Press.

Códice Plancarte. 1959. Notes by José Corona Núñez. Morelia: Universidad de Michoacán.

Coggins, Clemency C. 1980. "The Shape of Time: Some Political Implications of a Four-Part Figure." *American Antiquity* 45 (04): 727–739. https://doi.org/10.2307/280144.

Comaroff, John L. 1982. "Dialectical Systems, History and Anthropology: Units of Study and Questions of Theory." *Journal of Southern African Studies* 8 (2): 143–172. https://doi.org/10.1080/03057078208708040.

Comaroff, Jean, and John Comaroff. 1991–1997. *Of Revelation and Revolution.* 2 vols. Chicago: University of Chicago Press. https://doi.org/10.7208/chicago/9780226114477.001.0001.

Corona Núñez, José. 1957. *Mitología tarasca.* Mexico City: Fondo de Cultura y Económica.

Cummins, Thomas B. F., Emily A. Engel, Barbara Anderson, and Juan M. Ossio A. 2014. *Manuscript Cultures of Colonial Mexico and Peru: New Questions and Approaches.* Los Angeles: Getty Research Institute.

Da Matta, Roberto. 1970. "Mito e Antimito entre os Timbira." In *Mito e Linguagem Social*, ed. Claude Levi-Strauss, Roberto Cardoso de Oliveira, Julio Cezar Melatti, Roberto Da Matta, and Roque de Barros Laraia, 77–106. Rio de Janeiro: Tempo Brasileiro.

Darras, Véronique. 1998. "La Obsidiana en la Relación de Michoacán y en la realidad arqueológica: del simbolo al uso o del uso del simbolo." In *Génesis, Culturas, y Espacios en Michoacán*, ed. Véronique Darras, 61–88. Mexico City: CEMCA.

Davies, Nigel. 1973. *The Aztecs: A History.* New York: Putnam.

Davies, Nigel. 1980. *The Toltec Heritage from the Fall of Tula to the Rise of Tenochtitlan.* Norman: University of Oklahoma Press.

Davies, Nigel. 1987. *The Aztec Empire: The Toltec Resurgence.* Norman: University of Oklahoma Press.

Dean, Carolyn, and Dana Leibsohn. 2003. "Hybridity and Its Discontents: Considering Visual Culture in Colonial Spanish America." *Colonial Latin American Review* 12 (1): 5–35. https://doi.org/10.1080/10609160302341.

de Heusch, Luc. 1982. *The Drunken King, or, The Origin of the State*. Trans. Roy Willis. Bloomington: University of Indiana Press.

de Ridder, Rob. 1989. *The Poetic Popol Vuh: An Anthropological Study*. Holland: Rijksuniversitat Utrecht.

de Saussure, Ferdinand. 1959. *Course in General Linguistics*. New York: Philosophical Library.

Descola, Philippe. 2005. *Par-delà nature et culture*. Paris: Gallimard.

Descola, Philippe. 2016. "Transformation Transformed." *HAU* 6 (3): 33–44. https://doi.org/10.14318/hau6.3.005.

Dibble, Charles E. 1971. "Writing in Central Mexico." In *Handbook of Middle American Indians*, vol. 10, *Archaeology of Northern Mesoamerica*, Part 1, ed. Gordon F. Eckholm and Ignacio Bernal, 322–331. Austin: University of Texas Press.

Diccionario grande de la lengua de Michoacán por autor o autores desconocidos. 1991. Transcription and editing by J. Benedict Warren. Fuentes de la Lengua Tarasca o Purépecha, 4–5; 2 vols. Morelia: Fímax Publicistas.

Diel, Lori Bournazian. 2008. *The Tira de Tepechpan: Negotiating Place under Aztec and Spanish Rule*. Austin: University of Texas Press.

Dillon, Mary, and Thomas Abercrombie. 1988. "The Destroying Christ: An Aymara Myth of Conquest." In *Rethinking History and Myth: Indigenous South American Perspectives on the Past*, ed. Jonathan D. Hill, 50–77. Urbana: University of Illinois Press.

Douglas, Eduardo. 2010. *In the Palace of Nezahaulcoyotl: Painting Manuscripts, Writing the Pre-Hispanic Past in Early Colonial Period Tetzcoco, Mexico*. Austin: University of Texas Press.

Dumézil, Georges. 1949. *L'heritage Indo-Européens à Rome*. 4th ed. Paris: Gallimard.

Dumont, Louis. 1980. *Homo Hierarchicus: The Caste System and its Implications*. Chicago: University of Chicago Press.

Durán, Fray Diego. 1994. *The History of the Indies of New Spain. Translated, annotated, and with an introduction by Doris Heyden*. Norman: University of Oklahoma Press.

Edmonson, Munro S. 1971. *The Book of Counsel: The Popol Vuh of the Quiche Maya of Guatemala*. Middle American Research Institute Publication 35. New Orleans: Tulane University.

Edmonson, Munro S. 1985. "Quiché Literature." In *Supplement to the Handbook of Middle American Indians, Vol. 3: Literature*, ed. Munro S. Edmonson, 107–132. Austin: University of Texas Press.

Edmonson, Munro S. 1986. *Heaven Born Merida and Its Destiny: The Chilam Balam of Chumayel*. Austin: University of Texas Press.

.ngard, Ronald K. 1988. "Myth and Political Economy in Bafut (Cameroon): The Structural History of an African Kingdom." *Paideuma* 34:49–89.

.rrington, Shelly. 1979. "Some Comments on Style in the Meanings of the Past." *Journal of Asian Studies* 38 (2): 231–244. https://doi.org/10.2307/2053416.

.spejel Carbajal, Claudia. 2000. "Guía arqueológica y geográfica para la Relación de Michoacán." In *Relación de Michoacán*, by Jerónimo de Alcalá and coord. by Moisés Franco Mendoza, 301–312. Morelia, Mexico: El Colegio de Michoacán, and Gobierno del Estado de Michoacán.

.spejel Carbajal, Claudia. 2008. *La justicia y el fuego: Dos claves para leer la Relación de Michoacán*. 2 vols. Zamora, Mexico: El Colegio de Michoacán.

.spejel Carbajal, Claudia. 2016. "Diversidad cultural en el Reino Tarasco: Ensayo comparativo a partir de las relaciones geográficas del Siglo XIV." In *Unidad y variación cultural en Michoacán*, ed. Roberto Martínez, Claudia Espejel, and Frida Villavivencio, 89–116. Zamora, Michoacán, Mexico: El Colegio de Michoacán and the Instituto de Investigaciones Históricas of the Universidad Autónoma de México.

.augère, Brigitte. 1998. "Venados y hogares sagrados en la Relación de Michoacán: Revendicación nórdica y construcción del estado en los Pueblos Tarascos." In *Genesis, culturas y espacios en Michoacán*, ed. Veronique Darras, 89–99. Mexico City: Centro de Estudios Mexicanos y Centroamericanos. https://doi.org/10.4000/books.cemca.3398.

.augère, Brigitte. 2008. "Le Cerf Chez les Anciens P'urhépecha du Michoacán (Mexique): Guerre, Chasse et Sacrifice." *Journal de la Société des Américanistes* 94 (2): 109–142. https://doi.org/10.4000/jsa.10583.

.austo, Carlos, and Michael Heckenberger. 2007. "Introduction: Indigenous History and the History of the 'Indians.'" In *Time and Memory in Indigenous Amazonia: Anthropological Perspectives*, ed. Carlos Fausto and Michael Heckenberger, 1–43. Gainesville: University Press of Florida.

Feeley-Harnik, Gillian. 1978. "Divine Kingship and the Meaning of History among the Sakalava of Madagascar." *Man* 13 (3): 402–417. https://doi.org/10.2307/2801937.

Feld, Stephen, and Keith H. Basso, eds. 1996. *Sense of Place*. Santa Fe: SAR Press.

Fernández, Rodolfo. 2011. *Retórica y antropología del mundo tarasco: Textos sobre la Relación de Michoacán*. Mexico City: INAH.

Filini, Agapi. 2004. *The Presence of Teotihuacan in the Cuitzeo Basin, Michoacan, Mexico: A World-System Perspective*. BAR International Series S1279. Oxford: Archaeopress.

Fischer, Edward F. 1999. "Cultural Logic and Maya Identity: Rethinking Constructivism and Essentialism." *Current Anthropology* 40:473–499.

Fisher, Christopher T., and Stephen J. Leisz. 2013. "New Perspectives on Purépecha Urbanism through the Use of LiDAR at the Site of Angamuco, Mexico." In *Mapping*

Archaeological Landscapes from Space, ed. Douglas Comer and Michael Harrower, 199–210. New York: Springer. https://doi.org/10.1007/978-1-4614-6074-9_16.

Florescano, Enrique. 1994. *Memory, Myth, and Time in Mexico: From the Aztecs to Independence*. Trans. Albert G. Bork. Austin: University of Texas Press.

Florescano, Enrique. 2002. "El canon memorioso forjado por los títulos primordiales." *Colonial Latin American Review* 11 (2): 183–230. https://doi.org/10.1080/10609160022000023350.

Fogelson, Raymond D. 1974. "On the Varieties of Indian History: Sequoyah and Traveller Bird." *Journal of Ethnic Studies* 2:105–112.

Fogelson, Raymond D. 1989. "The Ethnohistory of Events and Nonevents." *Ethnohistory (Columbus, Ohio)* 36 (2): 133–147. https://doi.org/10.2307/482275.

Franco Mendoza, Moisés. 2000. "El discurso del *Petámuti* en la estructura de la lengua p'urhépecha." In Jerónimo de Alcalá, *Relación de Michoacán*, coord. Moisés Franco Mendoza, 265–284. Zamora and Morelia: El Colegio de Michoacán and Gobierno del Estado de Michoacán.

Freidel, David. 1992. "The Trees of Life: *Ahau* as Idea and Artefact in Classic Lowland Maya Civilization." In *Ideology and Pre-Columbian Civilizations*, ed. Arthur A. Demarest and Geoffrey W. Conrad, 115–133. Santa Fe: School of American Research.

Freidel, David A., Linda Schele, and Joy Parker. 2001. *Maya Cosmos: Three Thousand Years on the Shaman's Path*. New York: Perennial.

Furst, Jill. 1978. "The Year 1 Reed, Day 1 Alligator: A Mixtec Metaphor." *Journal of Latin American Lore* 4 (1) :93–128.

García Alcaraz, Agustín. 1976. "Estratificación social entre los tarascos prehispánicos." In *Estratificación social en la Mesoamérica prehispánica*, ed. Pedro Carrasco and Johanna Broda, et al., 221–244. Mexico City: CIESAS and INAH.

Garibay Kintana, Ángel María. 1953. *Historia de la literatura náhuatl, primera parte*. Mexico City: Porrúa.

Geertz, Clifford. 1973. "Person, Time, and Conduct in Bali." In *The Interpretation of Cultures: Selected Essays*, 360–411. New York: Basic Books.

Gell, Alfred. 1992. *The Anthropology of Time: Cultural Constructions of Temporal Maps and Images*. Oxford: Berg.

Gibson, Charles. 1964. *The Aztecs under Spanish Rule: A History of the Indians of the Valley of Mexico 1519–1810*. Stanford, CA: Stanford University Press.

Gibson, Charles. 1975. "Prose Sources in the Native Historical Tradition." In *Handbook of Middle American Indians*, Vol. 15, *Guide to Ethnohistorical Sources*, part 4, ed. Howard F. Cline, 311–321. Austin: University of Texas Press.

Giddens, Anthony. 1984. *The Constitution of Society: Outline of the Theory of Structuration*. Cambridge: Polity Press.

Gillespie, Susan D. 1989. *The Aztec Kings: The Construction of Rulership in Mexica History.* Tucson: University of Arizona Press.

Gillespie, Susan D. 1998. "The Aztec Triple Alliance: A Postconquest Tradition." In *Native Traditions in the Postconquest World,* ed. Elizabeth Hill Boone and Tom Cummins, 233–263. Washington, DC: Dumbarton Oaks.

Gillespie, Susan D. 2000a. "Maya 'Nested Houses': The Ritual Construction of Place." In *Beyond Kinship: Social and Material Reproduction in House Societies,* ed. Rosemary A. Joyce and Susan D. Gillespie, 135–160. Philadelphia: University of Pennsylvania Press.

Gillespie, Susan D. 2000b. "Rethinking Ancient Maya Social Organization: Replacing 'Lineage' with 'House.'" *American Anthropologist* 102 (3): 467–484.

Gillespie, Susan D. 2007a. "Different Ways of Seeing: Modes of Social Consciousness in Mesoamerican Two-Dimensional Artworks." *Baesller-Archiv* 55:103–142.

Gillespie, Susan D. 2007b. "Toltecs, Tula, and Chichen Itza: The Development of an Archaeological Myth." In *Twin Tollans: Chichen Itza, Tula, and the Epiclassic to Early Postclassic Mesoamerican World,* ed. Jeff K. Kowalski and Cynthia Kristan-Graham, 85–127. Washington, DC: Dumbarton Oaks.

Gillespie, Susan D. 2008. "Blaming Moteuczoma: Anthropomorphizing the Aztec Conquest." In *Invasion and Transformation,* ed. R. P. Brienen and M. Jackson, 25–55. Niwot: University Press of Colorado.

Gillespie, Susan D. 2015. "Journey's End (?): The Travels of La Venta Offering 4." In *Things in Motion: Object Itineraries in Anthropological Practice,* ed. Rosemary A. Joyce and Susan D. Gillespie, 39–61. Santa Fe, NM: School of Advanced Research Press.

Gillespie, Susan D. n.d. "Historias or Historia: The Popol Vuh as a Narrative of Colonial Guatemala." Paper presented at the 2009 Annual Meeting of the American Society for Ethnohistory, New Orleans, LA, Oct. 2.

Gorenstein, Shirley, ed. 1985. *Acambaro: Frontier Settlement on the Aztec-Tarascan Border. Vanderbilt University Publications in Anthropology, 32.* Nashville, TN: Vanderbilt University.

Gorenstein, Shirley, and Helen P. Pollard. 1983. *The Tarascan Civilization: A Late Prehispanic Cultural System. Vanderbilt University Publications in Anthropology, 28.* Nashville, TN: Vanderbilt University.

Gossen, Gary. 1974. *Chamulas in the World of the Sun: Time and Space in a Maya Oral Tradition.* Cambridge, MA: Harvard University Press.

Gossen, Gary. 1977. "Translating Cuscat's War: Understanding Maya Oral History." *Journal of Latin American Lore* 3:249–278.

Gow, Peter. 2001. *An Amazonian Myth and Its History.* Oxford: Oxford University Press.

Graeber, David, and Marshall Sahlins. 2017. *On Kings.* Chicago: Hau Books.

Graulich, Michel. 1997. *Myths of Ancient Mexico.* Trans. Bernard R. Ortiz de Montellano and Thelma Ortiz de Montellano. Norman: University of Oklahoma Press.

Hanks, William F. 1987. "Discourse Genres in a Theory of Practice." *American Ethnologist* 14 (4): 668–692. https://doi.org/10.1525/ae.1987.14.4.02a00050.

Hanks, William F. 2000. *Intertexts: Writings on Language, Utterance, and Context*. Lanham, MD: Rowman and Littlefield.

Hanks, William F. 2010. *Converting Words: Maya in the Age of the Cross*. Berkeley: University of California Press. https://doi.org/10.1525/california/9780520257702.001.0001.

Harkin, Michael. 1988. "History, Narrative, and Temporality: Examples from the Northwest Coast." *Ethnohistory (Columbus, Ohio)* 35 (2): 99–130. https://doi.org/10.2307/482699.

Haskell, David L. 2003. "History and the Construction of Hierarchy and Ethnicity in the Prehispanic Tarascan State: a Syntagmatic Analysis of the Relación de Michoacán." MA thesis, University of Florida, Gainesville.

Haskell, David L. 2008a. "The Cultural Logic of Hierarchy in the Tarascan State: History as Ideology in the *Relación de Michoacán*." *Ancient Mesoamerica* 19 (2): 231–241. https://doi.org/10.1017/S0956536108000357.

Haskell, David L. 2008b. "Tarascan Kingship: The Production of Hierarchy in the Prehispanic Patzcuaro Basin, Mexico." PhD diss., University of Florida.

Haskell, David L. 2012. "The Encompassment of Subordinate Lords in the Tarascan Kingdom: Materiality, Identity, and Power." In *Power and Identity in Archaeological Theory and Practice: Case Studies from Ancient Mesoamerica*, ed. Eleanor Harrison-Buck, 90–102. Salt Lake City: University of Utah Press.

Haskell, David L. 2013. "The Impact of *La Memoria de don Melchor Caltzin* (1543) on Tarascan Historiography and Ethnohistoric Modeling of Pre-Hispanic Tarascan State Formation." *Ethnohistory (Columbus, Ohio)* 60 (4): 637–662. https://doi.org/10.1215/00141801-2313858.

Haskell, David L. 2015. "Places to Go and Social Worlds to Constitute: The Fractal Itinerary of Tarascan Obsidian Idols in Prehispanic Mexico." In *Things in Motion: Object Itineraries in Anthropological Practice*, ed. Rosemary A. Joyce and Susan D. Gillespie, 63–80. Santa Fe: SAR Press.

Haskell, David L., and Christopher J. Stawski. 2016. "Re-envisioning Tarascan Temporalities and Landscapes: Historical Being, Archaeological Representation, and Futurity in Past Social Processes." *Journal of Archaeological Method and Theory*. https://doi.org/10.1007/S10816-016-9279-x.

Haskell, David L. n.d. "Legendary History in the Relación de Michoacán: Mexico's Pachacuti and the Quetzalcoatl that Wasn't." Paper presented at the American Society of Ethnohistory Annual Meeting, New Orleans, LA, October 2, 2009.

Haskett, Robert S. 1991. *Indigenous Rulers: An Ethnohistory of Town Government in Colonial Cuernavaca*. Albuquerque: University of New Mexico Press.

Haskett, Robert S. 1996. "Paper Shields: The Ideology of Coats of Arms in Colonial Mexican Primordial Titles." *Ethnohistory (Columbus, Ohio)* 43 (1): 99–126. https://doi.org/10.2307/483345.

Hassig, Ross. 1988. *Aztec Warfare: Imperial Expansion and Political Control.* Norman: University of Oklahoma Press.

Hassig, Ross. 2001. *Time, History, and Belief in Aztec and Colonial Mexico.* Austin: University of Texas Press.

Hawkes, Terence. 1977. *Structuralism and Semiotics.* London: Routledge. https://doi.org/10.4324/9780203443934.

Healan, Dan. 1997. "Pre-Hispanic Quarrying in the Ucareo-Zinapecuaro Obsidian Source Area." *Ancient Mesoamerica* 8 (1): 77–100. https://doi.org/10.1017/S0956536100001590.

Healan, Dan. 2011. "Viejos problemas y nuevas ideas sobre el urbanismo y la formación del estado en la Tula del Posclásico." In *Mesoamérica: Debates y perspectivas,* ed. Eduardo Williams, Magdalena García Sánchez, Phil C. Weigand, and Manuel Gándara, 155–182. Michoacán, Zamora, Mexico: El Colegio de Michoacán.

Herrnstein Smith, Barbara. 1980. "Narrative Versions, Narrative Theories." *Critical Inquiry* 7 (1): 213–236. https://doi.org/10.1086/448097.

Hers, Marie-Areti. 2005. "Imágenes norteñas de los guerreros tolteca-chichimecas." In *Reacomodos Demográficos del Clásico al Posclásico en el centro de México,* ed. Linda Manzanilla, 11–44. Mexico City: UNAM.

Hers, Marie-Areti. 2008. "Los chichimecas: ¿nómadas o sedentarios?" In *Continuidad y fragmentación de la Gran Chichimeca,* coord., Andrés Fábregas Puig, Mario Alberto Nájera Espinoza, and Claudio Esteva Fabregat, 33–59. Guadalajara: Seminario Permanente de Estudios sobre la Gran Chichimeca, Universidad de Guadalajara.

Herrejón Peredo, Carlos. 1978. "La pugna entre mexicas y tarascos." *Cuadernos de Historia (Santiago, Chile)* 1:9–47.

Hexter, J. 1971. *Doing History.* Bloomington: University of Indiana Press.

Hill, Jonathan D. 1988. "Introduction: Myth and History." In *Rethinking History and Myth: Indigenous South American Perspectives on the Past,* ed. Jonathan D. Hill, 1–17. Urbana: University of Illinois Press.

Hill, Robert M., II. 1991. "The Social Uses of Writing among the Colonial Cakchiquel Maya: Nativism, Resistance, and Innovation." In *Columbian Consequences,* vol. 3, ed. David Hurst Thomas, 283–299. Washington, DC: Smithsonian Institution Press.

Hirsch, Eric. 2006. "Landscape, Myth, and Time." *Journal of Material Culture* 11 (1–2): 151–165.

Hirsch, Eric. 2007. "Valleys of Historicity and Ways of Power among the Fuyuge." *Oceania* 77 (2): 158–171. https://doi.org/10.1002/j.1834-4461.2007.tb00010.x.

Hirsch, Eric, and Charles Stewart. 2005. "Introduction: Ethnographies of Historicity." *History and Anthropology* 16 (3): 261–274. https://doi.org/10.1080/02757200500219289.

Hosler, Dorothy. 1994. *The Sounds and Color of Power: The Sacred Metallurgical Technology of Ancient West Mexico*. Cambridge, MA: MIT Press.

Hosler, Dorothy. 2009. "West Mexican Metallurgy: Revisited and Revised." *Journal of World Prehistory* 22 (3): 185–212. doi:10.1007/s10963-009-9021-7.

Hugh-Jones, Stephen. 1989. "Waribi and the White Men: History and Myth in Northwest Amazonia." In *History and Ethnicity*, ed. Elizabeth Tonkin, Maryon McDonald, and Malcolm Chapman, 53–70. London: Routledge.

Hunt, Eva. 1977. *The Transformation of the Hummingbird: Cultural Roots of a Zinacantecan Mythical Poem*. Ithaca, NY: Cornell University Press.

Hymes, Dell. 1981. *"In Vain I Tried to Tell You": Essays in Native American Ethnopoetics*. Philadelphia: University of Pennsylvania Press. https://doi.org/10.9783/97815128 02917.

Ingarden, Roman. 1973. *The Literary Work of Art: An Investigation on the Borderlines of Ontology, Logic, and Theory of Literature*. George G. Grabowicz, trans. Evanston, IL: Northwestern University Press.

Jacopin, Pierre-Yves. 1988. "On the Syntactic Structure of Myth, or the Yukuna Invention of Speech." *Cultural Anthropology* 3 (2): 131–159. https://doi.org/10.1525/can.1988 .3.2.02a00020.

Jadot, Elsa. 2016. "Production céramiques et mobilités dans la région tarasque de Zacapu (Michoacán, Mexique): Continuités et ruptures techniques entre 850 et 1450 apr. J.-C." PhD diss., Université Paris I (la Sorbonne).

Jakobson, Roman. 1960. "Concluding Statement: Linguistics and Poetics." In *Style in Language*, ed. T. A. Sebeok, 350–377. Cambridge, MA: MIT Press.

Jiménez, Nora. 2002. "'Principe' indígena y latino: Una compra de libros de Antonio Huitziméngari." *Relaciones (Zamora)* 23 (91): 133–162.

Jiménez Moreno, Wigberto. 1948. "Historia antigua de la zona tarasca." In *El occidente de México: Cuarta Reunión de la mesa redonda*, 146–157. Mexico City: Sociedad Mexicana de Antropología.

Joyce, Rosemary A., and Susan D. Gillespie, eds. 2000. *Beyond Kinship: Social and Material Reproduction in House Societies*. Philadelphia: University of Pennsylvania Press.

Karadimas, Dimitri. 2012. *Animism and Perspectivism: Still Anthropomorphism?* 25–51. Indiana: On the Problem of Perception in the Construction of Amerindian Ontologies.

Kartunnen, Frances, and James Lockhart. 1980. "La estructura de la poesía náhuatl vista por sus variantes." *Estudios de Cultura Náhuatl* 14:15–64.

Kirchhoff, Paul. 1956. "Estudio preliminar: La Relación de Michoacán como fuente para la historia de la sociedad y cultura tarasca." In *Relación de las ceremonias y ritos y población y gobierno de los indios de la provincia de Michoacán*. Reproducción facsimilar del Ms IV de El Escorial, Madrid. Transcription, prologue, introduction, and notes by José Tudela, xix–xxxii. Madrid: Aguilar Publicistas.

Knapp, A. Bernard. 1992. *Archaeology, Annales, and Ethnohistory*. Cambridge: Cambridge University Press. https://doi.org/10.1017/CBO9780511759949.

Kowalski, Jeff K., and Cynthia Kristan-Graham, eds. 2007. *Twin Tollans: Chichén Itzá, Tula, and the Epi-Classic to Early Postclassic Mesoamerican World*. Washington, DC: Dumbarton Oaks.

Krech, Shepard, III. 1991. "The State of Ethnohistory." *Annual Review of Anthropology* 20 (1): 345–375. https://doi.org/10.1146/annurev.an.20.100191.002021.

Krech, Shepard. 2006. "Bringing Linear Time Back In." *Ethnohistory* 53 (3): 567–593. https://doi.org/10.1215/00141801-2006-005.

Krippner-Martinez, James. 2001. *Rereading the Conquest: Power, Politics, and the History of Early Colonial Michoacán, Mexico, 1521–1565*. University Park: Pennsylvania State University Press.

Kuthy, Maria de Lourdes. 1996. "Strategies of Survival, Accommodation and Innovation: The Tarascan Indigenous Elite in Sixteenth Century Michoacán." PhD diss., Michigan State University, East Lansing.

Kuthy, Maria de Lourdes. 2003. "El Control de los puestos políticos: La élite tarasca en el Siglo XVI." In *Autoridad y gobierno indígena en Michoacán*, coord. Carlos Paredes Martínez and Marta Terán, 153–172. Zamora, Mexico: El Colegio de Michoacán, CIESAS, INAH, Universidad de Michoacán.

Lakoff, George, and Mark Johnson. 1980. *Metaphors We Live By*. Chicago: University of Chicago Press.

Lambek, Michael. 2002. *The Weight of the Past: Living with History in Mahajanga, Madagascar*. New York: Palgrave MacMillan. https://doi.org/10.1007/978-1-349-73080-3.

Leach, Edmund. 1965. *Political Systems of Highland Burma*. Cambridge, MA: Harvard University Press.

Leach, Edmund. 1976. *Culture and Communication: The Logic by Which Symbols Are Connected*. Cambridge: Cambridge University Press. https://doi.org/10.1017/CBO9780511607684.

Leach, Edmund. 1990. "Aryan Invasions Over Four Millennia." In *Culture Through Time: Anthropological Approaches*, ed. Emiko Ohnuki-Tierney, 227–245. Stanford, CA: Stanford University Press.

Lederman, Rena. 1986. "Changing Times in Mendi: Notes Towards Writing Highland New Guinea History." *Ethnohistory (Columbus, Ohio)* 33 (1): 1–30. https://doi.org/10.2307/482507.

Leibsohn, Dana. 2009. *Script and Glyph: Pre-Hispanic History, Colonial Book Making, and the Historia Tolteca-Chichimeca*. Washington, DC: Dumbarton Oaks.

León, Nicolás. 1903. *Los tarascos: Notas históricas, étnicas y antropológicas*. Mexico City: Editorial Innovación.

León, Nicolás. 1906. *Los Tarascos*. Part 3: Etnografia post-cortesiana y actual: notas históricas, étnicas y anthropológicas, comprendiendo desde los tiempos precolombinos hasta los actuales, colegidas de escritores antiguos y modernos, documentos inéditos y observaciones personales. Mexico City: Imprenta del Museo Nacional.

León, Nicolás. [1903] 1984. *Don Vasco de Quiroga: Grandeza de su persona y de su obra*. Morelia: Universidad de Michoacán.

León-Portilla, Miguel. 1988. *Time and Reality in the Thought of the Maya*. 2nd ed. Trans. Charles L. Boilès Fernando Horcasitas, and Miguel León-Portilla. Norman: University of Oklahoma Press.

Lévi-Strauss, Claude. 1955. "The Structural Study of Myth." *Journal of American Folklore* 68 (270): 428–444. https://doi.org/10.2307/536768.

Lévi-Strauss, Claude. 1963. *Structural Anthropology*. Trans. Claire Jacobson and Brooke Grundfest Schoepf. New York: Basic Books.

Lévi-Strauss, Claude. 1966. *The Savage Mind*. Chicago: University of Chicago Press.

Lévi-Strauss, Claude. 1967a. *The Scope of Anthropology*. Trans. Sherry Ortner Paul and Robert A. Paul. London: Jonathan Cape.

Lévi-Strauss, Claude. 1967b. "The Story of Asdiwal." In *The Structural Study of Myth and Totemism*, ed. Edmund Leach, 1–47. London: Tavistock.

Lévi-Strauss, Claude. 1969. *The Raw and the Cooked. Introduction to a Science of Mythology: I*. Trans. John and Doreen Weightman. New York: Harper and Row.

Lévi-Strauss, Claude. 1973. *From Honey to Ashes. Introduction to a Science of Mythology: II*. Trans. John and Doreen Weightman. New York: Harper and Row.

Lévi-Strauss, Claude. 1978. *The Origin of Table Manners. Introduction to a Science of Mythology: III*. Trans. John and Doreen Weightman. New York: Harper and Row.

Lévi-Strauss, Claude. 1988. *The Jealous Potter*. Trans. Bénédicte Chorier. Chicago: University of Chicago Press.

Lockhart, James. 1992. *The Nahuas after the Conquest: A Social and Cultural History of the Indians of Central Mexico, Sixteenth through Eighteenth Centuries*. Stanford, CA: Stanford University Press.

Lockhart, James. 1993. *We People Here: Nahuatl Accounts of the Conquest of Mexico*. Berkeley: University of California Press.

Loewen, James W. 2009. *Teaching What Really Happened: How to Avoid the Tyranny of Textbooks and Get Students Excited about Doing History*. New York: Teachers College Press.

López Austin, Alfredo. 1973. *Hombre-Dios: Religión y política en el Mundo Náhuatl*. Mexico City: Universidad Autónoma de México and Instituto de Investigaciones Históricas.

López Austin, Alfredo. 1981. *Tarascos y Mexicas*. Fondo de Cultura y Económica, Mexico City.

López Austin, Alfredo. 1988. *The Human Body and Ideology: Concepts of the Ancient Nahuas*. Trans. Thelma Ortiz de Montellano and Bernard Ortiz de Montellano. Salt Lake City: University of Utah Press.

López Austin, Alfredo. 1993. *The Myths of the Opossum: Pathways of Mesoamerican Mythology*. Trans. Bernard Ortiz de Montellano and Thelma Ortiz de Montellano. Albuquerque: University of New Mexico Press.

López Austin, Alfredo, and Leonardo López Luján. 2000. "The Myth and Reality of Zuyuá: The Feathered Serpent and Mesoamerican Transformations from the Classic to the Postclassic." In *Mesoamerica's Classic Heritage: Teotihuacán to the Aztecs*, ed. Davíd Carrasco, Lindsey Jones, and Scott Sessions, 21–84. Boulder: University Press of Colorado.

López Sarrelangue, Delfina E. 1965. *La nobleza indígena de Pátzcuaro en la época virreinal*. Mexico City: Instituto de Investigaciones Históricas, UMAM.

Macías Goytia, Angelina. 1989. "Los entierros de un centro ceremonial tarasco." In *Estudios de Antropología biológica, serie antropológica*, vol. 100: 531–559. Mexico City: UNAM.

Macías Goytia, Angelina. 1990. *Huandacareo, lugar de juicios, tribunal*. Colección Científica, 222, Serie Arqueología. Mexico City: INAH.

Maffie, James. 2013. *Aztec Philosophy: Understanding a World in Motion*. Boulder: University Press of Colorado.

Maldonado, Blanca E. 2008. "A Tentative Model of the Organization of Copper Production in the Tarascan State." *Ancient Mesoamerica* 19 (2): 283–297.

Maldonado, Blanca. 2012. "Mesoamerican Metallurgical Technology and Production." *Oxford Handbooks Online*. doi:10.1093/oxfordhb/9780195390933.013.0045.

Maldonado, Blanca, Curt-Engelhorn-Zentrum Archäometrie Mannheim, and El Colegio de Michoacan. 2009. "Metal for the Commoners: Tarascan Metallurgical Production in Domestic Contexts." *Archeological Papers of the American Anthropological Association* 19 (1): 225–238. doi:10.1111/j.1551-8248.2009.01022.x.

Mali, Joseph. 2003. *Mythistory: The Making of a Modern Historiography*. Chicago: University of Chicago Press.

Marcus, Joyce. 1992. *Mesoamerican Writing Systems: Propaganda, Myth, and History in Four Ancient Civilizations*. Princeton, NJ: Princeton University Press.

Márquez Joaquín, Pedro. 2000. "El Significado de las Palabras P'urhépecha en la Relación de Michoacán: Glosario de voces P'urhepecha." In Alcalá, *Relación de Michoacán*, coord., Moisés Franco Mendoza, with paleography by Clotilde Martínez Ibáñez and Carmen Molina Ruiz, 693–726. Zamora, Mexico: El Colegio de Michoacán and Gobierno del Estado de Michoacán.

Márquez Joaquín, Pedro, ed. 2007. *¿Tarascos o purépecha? Voces sobre antiguas y nuevas discusiones en torno al gentilicio michoacano*. Morelia, Mexico: UMSNH, Instituto de Investigaciones Históricas.

Martínez Baracs, Rodrigo. 1989. "La conquista; los inicios de la colonización; reorientaciones." In *Historia General de Michoacán*, vol. 2, ed. Enrique Florescano, 5–122. Morelia: Gobierno del Estado.

Martínez Baracs, Rodrigo. 1997. "El vocabulario en lengua de Michoacán (1559) de Maturino Gilberti como un fuente de información histórica." In *Lengua y etnohistoria purépecha: Homenaje a Benedict Warren*, coord. Carlos Paredes Martínez, 67–162. Morelia, Mexico: Universidad Michoacana and CIESAS.

Martínez Baracs, Rodrigo. 2003. "Etimologías políticas michoacanas." In *Autoridad y gobierno en Michoacán*, coord. Carlos Paredes Martínez and Marta Terán, 61–90. Zamora, Mexico: El Colegio de Michoacán, CIESAS, INAH, and Universidad Michoacana.

Martínez Baracs, Rodrigo. 2005. *Convivencia y Utopía: El gobierno indio y español de la "ciudad de Mechuacan", 1521–1580*. Mexico City: INAH and FCE.

Martínez González, Roberto. 2010. "La dimensión mítica de la peregrinación tarasca." *Journal de la Société des Américanistes* 96 (1): 39–73. https://doi.org/10.4000/jsa.11250.

Martínez González, Roberto. 2011. "Alianza religiosa y realeza sagrada en el Antiguo Michoacán." *Revista Española de Antropología Americana* 41 (1): 75–96. https://doi.org/10.5209/rev_REAA.2011.v41.n1.4.

Matthew, Laura E., and Michael R. Oudijk, eds. 2007. *Indian Conquistadors: Indigenous Allies in the Conquest of Mesoamerica*. Norman: University of Oklahoma Press.

McCall, John C. 2000. *Dancing Histories: Heuristic Ethnography with the Ohafia Igbo*. Ann Arbor: University of Michigan Press. https://doi.org/10.3998/mpub.15520.

McKinnon, Susan. 1991. *From a Shattered Sun: Hierarchy, Gender, and Alliance in the Tanimbar Islands*. Madison: University of Wisconsin Press.

Michelet, Dominique. 1989. "Histoire, mythe et apologue: Notes de lecture sur la seconde partie de la Relación ... de Michoacán." In *Enquêtes sur l'Amérique Moyenne: Mélanges offerts à Guy Stresser-Péan*, ed. Dominique Michelet, 105–133. Mexico City: INAH, Consejo Nacional para la Cultura y las Artes, and CEMCA.

Michelet, Dominique, ed. 1992. *El proyecto michoacán 1983–1987: Medio ambiente e introducción a los trabajos arqueológicos. Collection Etudes Mésoaméricains II- 12, Cuadernos de Estudios Michoacanos 4*. Mexico City: CEMCA.

Michelet, Dominique. 1995. "La zona occidental en el Posclásico." In *Historia antigua de México*, vol. 3, ed. Linda Manzanilla and Leonardo López Luján, 153–188. Mexico City: Grupo Editorial Miguel Angel Porrúa, INAH, UNAM.

Michelet, Dominique. 1996. "El origen del reino tarasco protohistórico." *Arqueología Mexicana* 19:24–27.

Michelet, Dominique, Grégory Pereira, and Gérald Migeon. 2005. "La llegada de los uacúsechas a la Región de Zacapu, Michoacán: Datos arqueológicos y discusión." In *Reacomodos demográficos del clásico al posclásico en el Centro de México*, ed. Linda Manzanilla, 137–153. Mexico City: INAH and UNAM.

Migeon, Gerald. 1998. "El poblamiento del Malpaís de Zacapu y de sus alrededores, del Clásico al Posclásico." In *Génesis, culturas, y espacios en Michoacán*, ed. Veronique Darras 35–45. Mexico City: CEMCA. https://doi.org/10.4000/books.cemca.3395.

Mills, Barbara J., and William H. Walker, eds. 2008. *Memory Work: Archaeologies of Material Practices*. Santa Fe: SAR Press.

Monzón, Cristina. 1996. "Términos de parentesco p'urhépecha en tres documentos del siglo XVI: Resultados iniciales." *Amerindia* 21:101–110.

Monzón, Cristina. 2004. "Los principales dioses tarascos: un ensayo de análisis etimológico en la cosmología tarasca." *Relaciones (Zamora)* 104 (Autumn): 136–168.

Monzón, Cristina, Hans Roskamp, and J. Benedict Warren. 2009. "*La Memoria de Don Melchor Caltzin* (1543): Historia y legitimación en Tzintzuntzan, Michoacán." *Estudios de Historia Novohispana* 40 (40): 21–55.

Monzón, Cristina, and Andrew Roth-Seneff. 1999. "Referentes religiosos en el siglo XVI: Acuñaciones y expresiones en lengua tarasca." In *The Language of Christianisation in Latin America: Catechisation and Instruction in Amerindian Languages*, ed. Sabine Dedenbach-Salazar Sáenz and Lindsey Crickmay, 169–181. Bonn: Verlad Antón Sauerwein.

Monzón, Cristina, and Andrew Roth-Seneff. 2016. "Parentela como principio de estado: El concepto cultural 'Quahta' en las fuentes tarascas del siglo XVI." In *Nuevas contribuciones al estudio del antiguo reino tarasco*, ed. Sarah Albiez-Zwieck and Hans Roskamp, 95–120. Michoacán, Zamora, Mexico: El Colegio de Michoacán.

Moreno, Juan Joseph. 1989. *Vida de Vasco Quiroga, ordenanzas, testimonio*. Morelia, Mexico: Balsal Editores.

Munn, Nancy. 1992. "The Cultural Anthropology of Time: A Critical Essay." *Annual Review of Anthropology* 21 (1): 93–123. https://doi.org/10.1146/annurev.an.21.100192.000521.

Murillo, Dana Velasco, Mark Lentz, and Margarita R. Ochoa, eds. 2012. *City Indians in Spain's American Empire: Urban Indigenous Society in Colonial Mesoamerica and Andean South America, 1530–1810*. Portland, OR: Sussex Academic Press.

Nabokov, Peter. 2002. *A Forest of Time: American Indian Ways of History*. Cambridge: Cambridge University Press.

Nicholson, Henry B. 1957. "Topiltzin Quetzalcoatl of Tollan: A Problem in Mesoamerican Ethnohistory." PhD diss., Harvard University, Cambridge, MA.

Nicholson, Henry B. 1975 "Middle American Ethnohistory: An Overview." In *Handbook of Middle American Indians, vol. 15, Guide to Ethnohistorical Sources*, pt. 4, ed. Howard F. Cline, 487–505. Austin: University of Texas Press.

Oakdale, Suzanne. 2001. "History and Forgetting in an Indigenous Amazonian Community." *Ethnohistory (Columbus, Ohio)* 48 (3): 381–401. https://doi.org/10.1215/001 41801-48-3-381.

Ohnuki-Tierney, Emiko, ed. 1990a. *Culture through Time: Anthropological Approaches*. Stanford, CA: Stanford University Press.

Ohnuki-Tierney, Emiko. 1990b. "Introduction." In *Culture through Time: Anthropological Approaches*, ed. Emiko Ohnuki-Tierney, 1–25. Stanford, CA: Stanford University Press.

Ohnuki-Tierney, Emiko. 1991. "Embedding and Transforming Polytrope: The Monkey as Self in Japanese Culture." In *Beyond Metaphor: The Theory of Tropes in Anthropology*, ed. James W. Fernandez, 159–189. Stanford, CA: Stanford University Press.

Ohnuki-Tierney, Emiko. 2001. "Historicization of the Culture Concept." *History and Anthropology* 12 (3): 213–254. https://doi.org/10.1080/02757206.2001.9960934.

Ohnuki-Tierney, Emiko. 2005. "Always Discontinuous/Continuous, 'Hybrid' by Its Very Nature: The Culture Concept Historicized." *Ethnohistory (Columbus, Ohio)* 52 (1): 179–195. https://doi.org/10.1215/00141801-52-1-179.

Olivier, Guilhem, and Roberto Martínez González. 2015. "Translating Gods: Tohil and Curicaueri in Mesoamerican Polytheisim in the Popol Vuh and the Relación de Michoacán." *Ancient Mesoamerica* 26 (2): 347–369.

Ortner, Sherry B. 1990. "Patterns of History: Cultural Schemas in the Foundings of Sherpa Religious Institutions." In *Culture through Time: Anthropological Approaches*, ed. Emiko Ohnuki-Tierney, 57–93. Stanford, CA: Stanford University Press.

Oudijk, Michel, and María de los Angeles Romero Frizzi. 2003. "Los títulos primordiales: Un género de tradición mesoamericana del mundo prehispánico al Siglo XXI." *Relaciones: Estudios de Historia y Sociedad* 24 (Summer): 19–48.

Paredes Martínez, Carlos, coord. 1997. *Lengua y etnohistoria purépecha: Homenaje a Benedict Warren*. Morelia: Universidad Michoacana de San Nicolás de Hidalgo.

Parmentier, Richard J. 1987. *The Sacred Remains: Myth, History, and Polity in Belau*. Chicago: University of Chicago Press.

Peacock, James L. 1969. "Society as Narrative." In *Forms of Symbolic Action*, ed. Robert F. Spencer, 167–177. Proceedings of the 1969 Annual Spring Meeting of the American Ethnological Society. Seattle: University of Washington Press.

Peel, John D. Y. 1984. "Making History: The Past in the Ijesha Present." *Man* 19 (1): 111–132. https://doi.org/10.2307/2803227.

Pereira, Gregory. n.d. "El destino post mortem del género y la emergencia del Estado Tarasco." Paper presented at the Annual Meeting of the Society for American Archaeology, San Juan, Puerto Rico, April 29, 2006.

Pereira, Gregory, Dominique Michelet, and Gerald Migeon. 2013. "La migración de los purépechas hacia el norte de los y su regreso a los lagos." *Arqueología Mexicana*, no. 123 (September–October): 55–60.

Piaget, Jean. 1971. *Structuralism*. Ed. and trans. Chaninah Maschler. London: Routledge.

Piña Chan, Román, and Kuniaki Oí. 1982. *Exploraciones arqueológicas en Tingambato, Michoacán*. Mexico City: INAH.

Pollard, Helen P. 1980. "Central Places and Cities: a Consideration of the Protohistoric Tarascan State." *American Antiquity* 45 (4): 677–696. https://doi.org/10.2307/280141.

Pollard, Helen P. 1982. "Ecological Variation and Economic Exchange in the Tarascan State." *American Ethnologist* 9 (2): 250–268. https://doi.org/10.1525/ae.1982.9.2.02a00030.

Pollard, Helen P. 1987. "The Political Economy of Prehispanic Tarascan Metallurgy." *American Antiquity* 52(4): 741–752. doi:10.2307/281382.

Pollard, Helen P. 1991. "The Construction of Ideology in the Emergence of the Prehispanic Tarascan State." *Ancient Mesoamerica* 2 (02): 167–179. https://doi.org/10.1017/S095653 6100000493.

Pollard, Helen P. 1993a. "Merchant Colonies, Semi-Mesoamericans, and the Study of Cultural Contact: A Comment on Anawalt (1992)." *Latin American Antiquity* 4(4):383–385.

Pollard, Helen P. 1993b. *Taríacuri's Legacy: The Prehispanic Tarascan State.* Norman: University of Oklahoma Press.

Pollard, Helen P. 1994. "Ethnicity and Political Control in a Complex Society: The Tarascan State of Prehispanic Mexico." In *Factional Competition and Political Development in the New World,* ed. Elizabeth M. Brumfiel and John W. Fox, 79–88. Cambridge: University of Cambridge Press. https://doi.org/10.1017/CBO9780511598401.008.

Pollard, Helen P. 1997. "Recent Research in West Mexican Archaeology." *Journal of Archaeological Research* 5 (4): 345–384.

Pollard, Helen P. 2000. "Tarascans and Their Ancestors: Prehistory of Michoacán." In *Greater Mesoamerica: The Archaeology of West and Northwest Mexico,* ed. Michael S. Foster and Shirley Gorenstein, 59–70. Salt Lake City: University of Utah Press.

Pollard, Helen P. 2003a. "El gobierno del estado tarasco prehispánico." In *Autoridad y gobierno indígena en Michoacán,* coord. Carlos Paredes Martínez and Marta Terán, 49–60. Zamora, Mexico: El Colegio de Michoacán, CIESAS, INAH, Universidad Michoacana.

Pollard, Helen P. 2003b. "Development of a Tarascan Core: The Lake Pátzcuaro Basin." In *The Postclassic Mesoamerican World,* ed. Michael E. Smith and Frances F. Berdan, 227–237. Salt Lake City: University of Utah Press.

Pollard, Helen P. 2005. "Michoacán en el mundo mesoamericano prehispaánico: Erongarícuaro, Michoacán y los estados teotihuacano y tarasco." In *El antiguo occidente de México. Nuevas perspectivas sobre el pasado prehispánico,* edited by Eduardo Williams, Phil C. Weigand, Lorenza López Mestas, and David Grove, 283–303. Guadalajara, Mexico: El Colegio de Michoacán, Instituto Nacional de Antropología e Historia.

Pollard, Helen P. 2008. "A Model of the Emergence of the Tarascan State." *Ancient Mesoamerica* 19 (2): 217–230. https://doi.org/10.1017/S0956536108000369.

Pollard, Helen P. 2015. "The Prehispanic Heritage of the Tarascans (Purépecha)." In *From Tribute to Communal Sovereignty: The Tarascan and Caxcan Territories in Transition,* ed. Andrew Roth-Seneff, Robert V. Kemper, and Julie Adkins, 92–110. Tucson: University of Arizona Press.

Pollard, Helen P. 2016a. "Ceramics, Social Status, and the Tarascan State Economy." In *Cultural Dynamics and Production Activities in Ancient West Mexico,* ed. Eduardo Williams and Blanca Maldonado, 163–178. Oxford, UK: Archaeopress.

Pollard, Helen P. 2016b. "Ruling 'Purépecha Chichimeca' in a Tarascan World." In *Political Strategies in Pre-Columbian Mesoamerica*, ed. Joanne Baron and Sarah Kurnick, 217–240. Boulder: University of Colorado Press. doi:10.5876/9781607324164.c008.

Pollard, Helen P., and Laura Cahue. 1999. "Mortuary Patterns of Regional Elites in the Lake Pátzcuaro Basin of Western Mexico." *Latin American Antiquity* 10 (3): 259–280. https://doi.org/10.2307/972030.

Pollard, Helen P., and Shirley Gorenstein. 1980. "Agrarian Potential, Population, and the Tarascan State." *Science* 209 (4453): 274–277. https://doi.org/10.1126/science.209.4453.274.

Pollard, Helen P., and Thomas Vogel. 1994. "Late Postclassic Imperial Expansion and Economic Exchange within the Tarascan Domain." In *Economics and Polities in the Aztec Realm*, ed. Michael E. Smith and Mary Hodge, 447–470. Austin: University of Texas Press.

Pollard, Helen P., and Dorothy K. Washburn. n.d. "Burial Goods in the Lake Pátzcuaro Basin as Evidence of Social Change." Paper presented at the Primero Coloquio de la Arqueología en Michoacán: Costumbres Funerarias en Michoacán y sus Áreas Vecinas, November 2–4, 2016, Morelia, Michoacán.

Pulido Méndez, Salvador. 2006. *Los tarascos y los tarascos-uacúsecha: Diferencias sociales y arqueológicas en un grupo*. Mexico City: INAH.

Punzo Díaz, José Luis. 2016. "Revisando la cronología en la frontera norte de Mesoamérica Estado de Durango, México." *Arqueología Iberoamericana* 29:38–43.

Quiñones Keber, Eloise 1995. *Codex Telleriano-Remensis: Ritual, Divination, and History in a Pictorial Aztec Manuscript*. Austin: University of Texas Press.

Quiroa, Nestor. 2011. "Revisiting the Highland Guatemala Títulos: How the Maya-K'iche' Lived and Outlived the Colonial Experience." *Ethnohistory (Columbus, Ohio)* 58 (2): 293–321. https://doi.org/10.1215/00141801-1163046.

Radin, Paul. 1920. "The Sources and Authenticity of the History of the Ancient Mexicans." *University of California Publications in American Archaeology and Ethnology* 17 (1): 1–150.

Ramírez, Francisco. [1585] 1959. "Relación sobre la residencia de Michoacán (Pátzcuaro)." In *Monumenta mexicana*, vol. 2, ed. Félix Zubillaga, 474–538. Rome: Apud Monumenta Historica Societatis Iesu.

Rappaport, Joanne. 1998. *The Politics of Memory: Native Historical Interpretation in the Colombian Andes*. Durham, NC: Duke University Press.

Rea, Alonso de la. 1996. *Cronica de la Orden N. serafico P. S. Francisco, Provincia de S. Pedro y S. Pablo de Mechoacan en la Nueva Espana*. Edited by Patricia Escandón. Zamora, Mexico: El Colegio de Michoacán.

Rebnegger, Karin J. 2010. "Obsidian Production and Changing Consumption in the Lake Pátzcuaro Basin, Michoacán, Mexico." *Ancient Mesoamerica* 21 (1): 79–89. doi:10.1017/s0956536110000167.

Relación de la Genealogía. 1941. *Relación de la genealogía y linaje de los señores . . . á ruego é intercesión de Juan Canó, español, marido de Doña Isabel, hija de Montezuma.* In *Nueva Colección de Documentos para la Historia de México,* ed. Joaquín García Icazbalceta, vol. 3: 240–256. Mexico City: Editorial Chavez Hayhoe.

Relaciones geográficas de la Diocesis de Michoacán. 1958. Notes by José Corona Núñez. 2 vols. Guadalajara, Mexico: Colección Siglo XVI, 1–2.

Restall, Matthew. 1997. "Heirs to the Hieroglyphs: Indigenous Writing in Colonial Mesoamerica." *Americas* 54 (02): 239–267. https://doi.org/10.2307/1007743.

Restall, Matthew. 2004. *Seven Myths of the Spanish Conquest.* Oxford: Oxford University Press.

Richards, Aubrey. 1960. "Social Mechanisms for the Transfer of Political Rights in Some African Tribes." *Journal of the Royal Anthropological Institute of Great Britain and Ireland* 90 (2): 175–190. https://doi.org/10.2307/2844342.

Ricouer, Paul. 1985. *Time and Narrative.* Vol. 2. Trans. Kathleen McLaughlin and David Pellauer. Chicago: University of Chicago Press.

Ridder, Rob de. 1987. "Anthropology and the Art of Parallelism: The Popol Vuh as Poetry." In *The Leiden Tradition in Structural Anthropology: Essays in Honor of P. E. de Josselin de Jong,* ed. Rob de Ridder and J. A. J. Karremans, 236–250. Leiden: Brill.

Ridder, Rob de. 1989. *The Poetic Popol Vuh: An Anthropological Study.* Holland: Rijksuniversiteit Utrecht.

Ringle, William M., Tomás Gallareta Negrón, and George L. Bey, III. 1998. "The Return of Quetzalcoatl: Evidence for the Spread of a World Religion During the Epi-Classic." *Ancient Mesoamerica* 9 (2): 183–232. https://doi.org/10.1017/S0956536100001954.

Robiscek, Francis, and Donald M. Hales. 1981. *The Maya Book of the Dead: The Ceramic Codex.* Charlottesville, VA: University of Virginia Art Museum.

Rosaldo, Renato. 1980a. *Ilongot Headhunting 1883–1974: A Study in Society and History.* Stanford, CA: Stanford University Press.

Rosaldo, Renato. 1980b. "Doing Oral History." *Social Analysis: The International Journal of Social and Cultural Practice* 4 (November): 89–99.

Roskamp, Hans. 1997. "Pablo Beaumont and the Codex of Tzintzuntzan: A Pictorial Document from Michoacán, West Mexico." In *Cuadernos de Historia Latino-Americana* 5, ed. Maarten Jansen and Luis Reyes García, 193–245. Ridderkerk, Netherlands: Asociación de Historiadores Latinoamericanistas Europeos.

Roskamp, Hans. 1998. *La historiografía indígena de Michoacán: El Lienzo de Jucutacato y los Títulos de Carapan.* Leiden: CNWS Publications, 72.

Roskamp, Hans. 2001. "Warriors of the Sun: The Eagle Lords of Curicaueri and a 16th Century Coat of Arms from Tzintzuntzan, Michoacán." *Mexicon* 23 (1): 14–17.

Roskamp, Hans. 2002. "La heráldica novohispana del siglo XVI: Un escudo de armas de Tzintzuntzan, Michoacán." In *Esplendor y ocaso de la cultura simbólica,* ed.

Herón Paredes Martínez and Barbara Skinfill Nogal, 227–268. Zamora, Mexico: El Colegio de Michoacán and CONACYT.

Roskamp, Hans. 2003. "Los títulos primordiales de Carapan: Legitimación e historiografía en una comunidad indígena de Michoacán." In *Autoridad y gobierno indígena en Michoacán*, coord. Carlos Paredes Martínez and Marta Terán, 305–359. Zamora, Mexico: El Colegio de Michoacán, CIESAS, INAH, and Universidad Michoacana.

Roskamp, Hans. 2004. "El Lienzo de Nahuatzen: Origen and territorio de una comunidad de la Sierra Tarasca, Michoacán." *Relaciones: Estudios de Historia y Sociedad* 100 (Autumn): 278–311.

Roskamp, Hans. 2010a. "Los nahuas de Tzintzuntzan-Huitzitzilan, Michoacán: Historia, mito y legitimación de un señorío prehispánico." *Journal de la Société des Américanistes* 96 (1): 75–106. https://doi.org/10.4000/jsa.11264.

Roskamp, Hans. 2010b. "Memoria, identidad y legitimación en los 'Títulos Primordiales' de la Región Tarasca." In *Caras y máscaras del México étnico: La participación indígena en las formaciones del Estado Mexicano*, ed. Andrew Roth Seneff, 39–53. Zamora, Mexico: El Colegio de Michoacán.

Roskamp, Hans. 2011. "Las intrigas del gobernador tarasca Don Pedro Cuiniharangari." *Arqueología Mexicana* 19 (112): 42–47.

Roskamp, Hans. 2012. "Memories of a Kingdom: The Nahua and Tarascan Foundation of Pre-Hispanic Tzintzuntzan, West Mexico." In *Mesoamerican Memory: Enduring Systems of Remembrance*, ed. Amos Megged and Stephanie Wood, 113–128. Norman: University of Oklahoma Press.

Roskamp, Hans. 2015. "Visions of the Past: The Tarascan kingdom and the Late Colonial Primordial Titles from Michoacán." In *From Tribute to Communal Sovereignty: The Tarascan and Caxcan Territories in Transition*, ed. Andrew Roth-Seneff, Robert V. Kemper, and Julie Adkins, 113–132. Tucson: University of Arizona Press.

Roskamp, Hans, and Guadalupe César-Villa. 2003. "Iconografía de un pleito: El Lienzo de Aranza y la conflictividad política en la Sierra Tarasca, Siglo XVII." In *Autoridad y gobierno indígena en Michoacán*, coord. Carlos Paredes Martínez and Marta Terán, 217–239. Zamora, Mexico: El Colegio de Michoacán, CIESAS, INAH, and Universidad Michoacana.

Rüsen, Jörn. 2005. *History: Narration, Interpretation, Orientation*. New York: Bergahn Books. https://doi.org/10.2307/j.ctt1x76fc2.

Sahagún, Fray Bernardino de. 1950–1982. *Florentine Codex: General History of the Things of New Spain*. 12 vols. Ed. and trans. Charles E. Dibble and Arthur J. O. Anderson. Santa Fe: School of American Research and the University of Utah.

Sahlins, Marshall. 1981. *Historical Metaphors and Mythical Realities: Structure in the Early History of the Sandwich Islands Kingdom*. Ann Arbor: University of Michigan Press. https://doi.org/10.3998/mpub.6773.

Sahlins, Marshall. 1985. *Islands of History*. Chicago: University of Chicago Press.

ahlins, Marshall. 1999. "Two or Three Things That I Know about Culture." *Journal of the Royal Anthropological Institute* 5 (3): 399–421. https://doi.org/10.2307/2661275.

ahlins, Marshall. 2004. *Apologies to Thucydides: Understanding History as Culture and Vice Versa*. Chicago: University of Chicago Press.

alomon, Frank. 1982. "Chronicles of the Impossible: Notes on Three Peruvian Indigenous Historians." In *From Oral to Written Expression: Native Andean Chronicles of the Early Colonial Period*, ed. Rolena Adorno, 9–39. Latin American Series 4. Syracuse, NY: Maxwell School of Citizenship and Public Affairs, Syracuse University.

alomon, Frank. 1999. "Testimonies: The Making and Reading of Native South American Historical Sources." In *South America*. Vol. 3 of *The Cambridge History of the Native Peoples of the Americas, Part 1* (of 2): 19–95. Cambridge: Cambridge University Press. https://doi.org/10.1017/CHOL9780521630757.003.

andoval, Franco. 1988. *La Cosmovision Maya Quiche en el Popol Vuh*. Guatemala City: Serviprensa Cenroamericana.

ansi-Roca, Roger. 2005. "The Hidden Life of Stones: Historicity, Materiality, and the Value of Candomble Objects in Bahia." *Journal of Material Culture* 10 (2): 139–156. https://doi.org/10.1177/1359183505053072.

aturno, William A. 2009. "Centering the Kingdom, Centering the King: Maya Creation and Legitimization at San Bartolo." In *The Art of Urbanism: How Mesoamerican Kingdoms Represented Themselves in Architecture and Imagery*, ed. William L. Fash and Leonardo López Luján, 111–134. Washington, DC: Dumbarton Oaks.

aturno, William A., Karl A. Taube, David Stuart, and Heather Hurst. 2005. *The Murals of San Bartolo, El Petén, Guatemala: Part I: The North Wall*. Barnardsville, NC: Center for Ancient American Studies.

chama, Simon. 1995. *Landscape and Memory*. New York: HarperCollins.

chele, Linda, and Peter Mathews. 1998. *The Code of Kings: The Language of Seven Sacred Maya Temples and Tombs*. New York: Scribner.

chele, Linda, and Mary Ellen Miller. 1986. *The Blood of Kings: Dynasty and Ritual in Maya Art*. Fort Worth, TX: Kimbell Art Museum.

chele, Linda, and David Freidel. 1990. *A Forest of Kings: The Untold Story of the Ancient Maya*. New York: Morrow.

chieffelin, Edward, and Deborah Gewertz. 1985. "Introduction." In *History and Ethnohistory in Papua New Guinea*, ed. Deborah Gewertz and Edward Schieffelin, 1–6. Oceania Monograph No. 28. Sydney: University of Sydney.

choles, France V., and Eleanor B. Adams. 1952. *Proceso contra Tzintzicha Tangáxoan, el caltzontzin*. Mexico City: Porrúa y Obregón.

chroeder, Susan, ed. 1998. *Native Resistance and the Pax Colonial in New Spain*. Lincoln: University of Nebraska Press.

Schroeder, Susan, ed. 2010. *The Conquest All Over Again: Nahuas and Zapotecs Thinking, Writing, and Painting Spanish Colonialism.* Portland, OR: Sussex Academic Press.

Searle, John R. 1969. *Speech Acts: An Essay in the Philosophy of Language.* Cambridge: Cambridge University Press. https://doi.org/10.1017/CBO9781139173438.

Seler, Eduard. [1905] 1993. "The Ancient Inhabitants of the Michuacan Region." In *Collected Works in Mesoamerican Linguistics and Archaeology*, 2nd ed., vol. 4., ed. J. Eric S. Thompson and Frances B. Richardson, 3–66. Culver City, NV: Labyrinthos.

Sewell, William H., Jr. 2005. *Logics of History: Social Theory and Social Transformations.* Chicago: University of Chicago Press. https://doi.org/10.7208/chicago/97802 26749198.001.0001.

Shore, Bradd. 1996. *Culture in Mind: Cognition, Culture, and the Problem of Meaning.* New York: Oxford University Press.

Silverstein, Jay. 2000. "A Study of the Late Postclassic Aztec–Tarascan Frontier in Northern Guerrero, Mexico: The Oztuma–Cutzamala Project." PhD dissertation, Pennsylvania State University, University Park.

Smith, Michael E. 1984. "The Aztlan Migrations of the Nahua Chronicles: Myth or History?" *Ethnohistory* 31 (3): 153–186. https://doi.org/10.2307/482619.

Smith, Michael E., and Frances F. Berdan, eds. 2003. *The Postclassic Mesoamerican World.* Salt Lake City: University of Utah Press.

Smith, Michael E., Jennifer B. Wharton, and Jan Marie Olson. 2003. "Aztec Feasts, Rituals, and Markets: Political Uses of Ceramic Vessels in a Commercial Economy." In *The Archaeology and Politics of Food and Feasting in Early States and Empires*, ed. Tamara Bray, 235–268. New York: Kluwer Academic Publishers.

Stanislawski, Dan. 1947. "Tarascan Political Geography." *American Anthropologist* 49 (1): 46–55. https://doi.org/10.1525/aa.1947.49.1.02a00040.

Stone, Cynthia. 1994. "Rewriting Indigenous Traditions: The Burial Ceremony of the Cazonci." *Colonial Latin American Review* 3 (1–2): 87–114. https://doi.org/10.1080 /10609169408569824.

Stone, Cynthia. 2004. *In Place of Gods and Kings: Authorship and Identity in the Relación de Michoacán.* Norman: University of Oklahoma Press.

Stuart, David. n.d. "The Face of the Calendar Stone: A New Interpretation." June 13, 2016. Accessed March 14, 2017. https://decipherment.wordpress.com/2016/06/13/the -face-of-the-calendar-stone-a-new-interpretation/.

Sturtevant, William C. 1966. "Anthropology, History, and Ethnohistory." *Ethnohistory* 13 (Winter–Spring): 1–51.

Tambiah, Stanley J. 1985. *Culture, Thought, and Social Action: An Anthropological Perspective.* Cambridge, MA: Harvard University Press.

Tarn, Nathaniel, and Martin Prechtel. 1981. "Metaphors of Relative Elevation, Position and Ranking in Popol Vuh." *Estudios de Cultura Maya* 13:105–123.

Tarn, Nathaniel, and Martin Prechtel. 1983. "Metáforas de elevación relativa, posición y rango en el Popol Vuh." In *Nuevas Perspectivas sobre el Popol Vuh*, ed. Robert M Carmack and Francisco Morales Santos, 163–179. Guatemala City: Editorial Piedra Santa.

Tedlock, Dennis. 1983. "On the Translation of Style in Oral Narrative." In *Smoothing the Ground: Essays on Native American Oral Literature*, ed. Brian Swann, 57–77. Berkeley: University of California Press. https://doi.org/10.9783/9780812205305.31.

Tedlock, Dennis. 1996. *Popol Vuh: The Mayan Book of the Dawn of Life*. Rev. ed. New York: Simon & Schuster.

Tedlock, Dennis. 2010. *2,000 Years of Mayan Literature*. Berkeley: University of California Press.

Terán Elizondo, María Isabel. 2000. "Elementos Míticos-Simbólicos." In *Relación de Michoacán, by Fray Jerónimo de Alcalá*, coordinated by Moisés Franco Mendoza, 285–300. Morelia, Zamora: El Colegio de Michoacán and Gobierno del Estado de Michoacán.

Tezozomoc, Hernando Alvarado. [1878] 1975. *Crónica Mexicayotl*. Trans. Adrián León. Mexico City: UNAM.

Todorov, Tzvetan. 1984. *The Conquest of Mexico: The Question of the Other*. Trans. Richard Howard. New York: Harper and Row.

Tonkin, Elizabeth. 1992. *Narrating Our Pasts: The Social Construction of Oral History*. Cambridge: Cambridge University Press. https://doi.org/10.1017/CBO9780511621888.

Tonkin, Elizabeth, Maryon McDonald, and Malcolm Chapman, eds. 1989. *History and Ethnicity*. New York: Routledge.

Toren, Christina. 1999. *Mind, Materiality and History: Explorations in Fijian Ethnography*. London: Routledge.

Townsend, Camilla. 2012. "Reading Symbolic and Historical Representations in Early Mesoamerica." *Latin American Research Review* 47 (1): 177–186. https://doi.org/10.1353/lar.2012.0012.

Troulliot, Michel-Rolph. 1995. *Silencing the Past: Power and the Production of History*. Boston: Beacon Press.

Turner, Terence S. 1969. "Oedipus: Time and Structure in Narrative Form." In *Forms of Symbolic Action*, ed. Robert F. Spencer, 26–68. Proceedings of the 1969 Annual Spring Meeting of the American Ethnological Society. Seattle: University of Washington Press.

Turner, Terence S. 1973. "Piaget's Structuralism." *American Anthropologist* 75:351–373. https://doi.org/10.1525/aa.1973.75.2.02a00010.

Turner, Terence S. 1977. "Narrative Structure and Mythopoesis: A Critique and Reformulation of Structuralist Conceptions of Myth, Narrative and Poetics." *Arethusa* 10:103–163.

Turner, Terence S. 1984. "Dual Opposition, Hierarchy, and Value: Moiety Structure and Symbolic Polarity in Brazil and Elsewhere." In *Différences, valeurs, hiérarchie: Textes offerts à Louis Dumont*, ed. Jean-Claude Galey, 335–370. Paris: Editions de l'Ecole de Hautes Etudes en Sciences Sociales.

Turner, Terence S. 1985. "Animal Symbolism, Totemism, and the Structure of Myth." In *Animal Myths and Metaphors in South America*, ed. Gary Urton, 49–106. Salt Lake City: University of Utah Press.

Turner, Terence S. 1988a. "History, Myth, and Social Consciousness among the Kayapó of Central Brazil." In *Rethinking History and Myth: Indigenous South American Perspective on the Past*, ed. Jonathan D. Hill, 195–213. Urbana: University of Illinois Press.

Turner, Terence S. 1988b. "Ethno-Ethnohistory: Myth and History in Native South American Representations of Contact with Western Society." In *Rethinking History and Myth: Indigenous South American Perspectives on the Past*, ed. Jonathan D. Hill, 235–281. Urbana: University of Illinois Press.

Turner, Terence S. 1991. "'We Are Parrots,' 'Twins Are Birds': Play of Tropes as Operational Structure." In *Beyond Metaphor: The Theory of Tropes in Anthropology*, ed. James Fernandez, 121–158. Stanford, CA: Stanford University Press.

Turner, Terence S. 2017. *The Fire of the Jaguar*. Edited by Jane Fajans. With a foreword by David Graeber. Chicago: Hau Books.

Umberger, Emily. 1982. "The Structure of Aztec History." *Archaeoastronomy* 4 (4): 10–17.

Umberger, Emily. 1988. "A Reconsideration of Some Hieroglyphs on the Mexica Calendar Stone." In *Smoke and Mist: Mesoamerican Studies in Memory of Thelma D. Sullivan*, I:345–388. Oxford: British Archaeological Reports.

Urton, Gary. 1990. *The History of a Myth: Pacariqtambo and the Origin of the Inkas*. Austin University of Texas Press.

Urton, Gary. 2003. *Signs of the Inka Khipu: Binary Coding in the Andean Knotted-String Records*. Austin: University of Texas Press.

Valeri, Valerio. 1990. "Constitutive History: Genealogy and Narrative in the Legitimation of Hawaiian Kingship." In *Culture through Time: Anthropological Approaches*, ed. Emiko Ohnuki-Tierney, 154–192. Stanford, CA: Stanford University Press.

Van Zantwijk, Rudolf. 1985. *The Aztec Arrangement: The Social History of Pre-Spanish Mexico*. Norman: University of Oklahoma Press.

Verástique, Bernardino. 2000. *Michoacán and Eden: Vasco de Quiroga and the Evangelization of Western Mexico*. Austin: University of Texas Press.

Viveiros de Castro, Eduardo. 2012. *Cosmological Perspectivism in Amazonia and Elsewhere: Four Lectures Given in the Department of Social Anthropology, Cambridge University, February–March 1998*. Introduction by Roy Wagner. Hau Masterclass Series, Vol. 1. Chicago: Hau Books and University of Chicago Press.

Wagner, Roy. 1986. *Symbols That Stand for Themselves*. Chicago: University of Chicago Press.

Wagner, Roy. 2001. "Condensed Mapping: Myth and the Folding of Space/Space and the Folding of Myth." In *Emplaced Myth: Space, Narrative, and Knowledge in Aboriginal Australia and Papua New Guinea*, ed. Alan Rumsey and James F. Weiner, 71–78. Honolulu: University of Hawaii Press.

Walz, Jonathan. 2015. "Healing Space-Time." In *Things in Motion: Object Itineraries in Anthropological Practice*, ed. Rosemary A. Joyce and Susan D. Gillespie, 161–178. Santa Fe: SAR Press.

Warren, J. Benedict. 1963. *Vasco de Quiroga and His Pueblo-Hospitals of Santa Fe*. Washington, DC: Academy of American Franciscan History.

Warren, J. Benedict. 1971. "Fray Jerónimo de Alcalá: Author of the Relación de Michoacán?" *Americas* 27 (3): 306–327.

Warren, J. Benedict. 1977. *La Conquista de Michoacan 1521–1530*. Morelia, Mexico: Fimax Publicistas.

Warren, J. Benedict. 1985. *The Conquest of Michoacán: The Spanish Domination of the Tarascan Kingdom in Western Mexico, 1521–1530*. Norman: University of Oklahoma Press.

Warren, J. Benedict, and Cristina Monzón. 2004. "Carta de los principales de Patzcuaro al Obispo Vasco de Quiroga. 10 de Marzo de 1549." *Relaciones: Estudios de Historia y Sociedad* 99 (summer): 177–211.

Weigand, Phillip C. 2015a. "Territory and Resistance in West-Central Mexico, Part 1: Introduction and Archaeological Background." In *From Tribute to Comunal Sovereignty: The Tarascan and Caxcan Territories in Transition*, Andrew Roth-Seneff, Robert V. Kemper, and Julie Adkins, eds., 43–70. Tucson: University of Arizona Press.

Weigand, Phillip C. 2015b. "Territory and Resistance in West-Central Mexico, Part 2: The Rebelión de Nueva Galicia and its Late Postclassic Prelude." In *From Tribute to Communal Sovereignty: The Tarascan and Caxcan Territories in Transition*, ed. Andrew Roth-Seneff, Robert V. Kemper, and Julie Adkins, 71–91. Tucson: University of Arizona Press.

Weiner, Annette. 1992. *Inalienable Possessions: The Paradox of Keeping-While-Giving*. Berkeley: University of California Press. https://doi.org/10.1525/california/97805200 76037.001.0001.

White, Hayden V. 1973. *Metahistory: The Historical Imagination in Nineteenth-Century Europe*. Baltimore: Johns Hopkins University Press.

White, Hayden V. 1980. "The Value of Narrativity in the Representation of Reality." *Critical Inquiry* 7 (1): 5–27. https://doi.org/10.1086/448086.

White, Hayden V. 1987. *The Content of the Form: Narrative Discourse and Historical Representation*. Baltimore: Johns Hopkins University Press.

Whitehead, Neil L. 2003. "Introduction." In *Histories and Historicities in Amazonia*, ed. Neil L. Whitehead, vii–xx. Lincoln: University of Nebraska Press.

Williams, Robert Lloyd. 2009. *Lord 8 Wind of Suchixtlan and the Heroes of Ancient Oaxaca: Reading History in the Codex Zouche-Nuttall*. Austin: University of Texas Press.

Willis, Roy. 1982. "Foreword." In *The Drunken King: or, the Origin of the State*, by Luc de Heusch. trans. Roy Willis, vii–xiv. Bloomington: Indiana University Press.

Wood, Stephanie. 2003. *Transcending Conquest: Nahua Views of Spanish Colonial Mexico*. Norman: University of Oklahoma Press.

Yannakakis, Yanna. 2008. *The Art of Being In-Between: Native Intermediaries, Indian Identity, and Local Rule in Colonial Oaxaca.* Durham, NC: Duke University Press. https://doi.org/10.1215/9780822388982.

Yannakakis, Yanna. 2011. "Allies or Servants? The Journey of Indian Conquistadors in the Lienzo of Analco." *Ethnohistory* 58(4): 653–682. doi:10.1215/00141801-1333697.

Zuidema, R. Tom. 1964. *The Ceque System of Cuzco: The Social Organization of the Capital of the Inca.* Leiden: E.J. Brill.

Zuidema, R. Tom. 1990. *Inca Civilization in Cuzco.* Austin: University of Texas Press.

About the Author

DAVID HASKELL has been studying Michoacán archaeology and ethnohistory since 2001, when as a graduate student he worked with Helen Pollard at Erongarícuaro. Upon becoming interested in pursuing research in the region, he decided to undertake a reappraisal of the *Relación de Michoacán* and particularly the Priest's Speech. That decision began an engagement with the document spanning more than a decade and a half, the culmination of which is this book. Dr. Haskell wrote his master's thesis on the Priest's Speech, and his doctoral dissertation, supervised by Susan Gillespie and Helen Pollard, was an effort at theorizing, integrating, and operationalizing the insights of hierarchy and encompassment that resulted from the analysis of the Priest's Speech along with the excavation and analysis of archaeological materials from Erongarícuaro in comparison with materials from Tzintzuntzan and Urichu. Haskell's research at the site indicated that subordinate lords at Erongarícuaro were encompassed by the kings in Tzintzuntzan, but that the relationship was much more complicated and possibly tenuous than is represented in the *Relación de Michoacán*. Since obtaining his doctorate, Dr. Haskell has gone on to publish several articles and chapters in edited volumes, both solo and with colleagues, all pertaining to ethnohistoric and archaeological approaches to Tarascan state formation and Tarascan culture. Currently he is an adjunct professor who teaches archaeology and anthropology courses, with professional affiliations at the Ohio State University and Ohio University. Dr. Haskell resides in Columbus, Ohio, with his wife and son.

Index